MANCHESTER MEDIEVAL LITERATURE AND CULTURE

A LANDSCAPE OF WORDS

Series editors: Anke Bernau, David Matthews and James Paz

Series founded by: J. J. Anderson and Gail Ashton

Advisory board: Ruth Evans, Patricia C. Ingham, Andrew James Johnston, Chris Jones, Catherine Karkov, Nicola McDonald, Sarah Salih, Larry Scanlon and Stephanie Trigg and Stephanie Trigg

Manchester Medieval Literature and Culture publishes monographs and essay collections comprising new research informed by current critical methodologies on the literary cultures of the Middle Ages. We are interested in all periods, from the early Middle Ages through to the late, and we include post-medieval engagements with and representations of the medieval period (or 'medievalism'). 'Literature' is taken in a broad sense, to include the many different medieval genres: imaginative, historical, political, scientific, religious. While we welcome contributions on the diverse cultures of medieval Britain and are happy to receive submissions on Anglo-Norman, Anglo-Latin and Celtic writings, we are also open to work on the Middle Ages in Europe more widely, and beyond.

Titles available in the series

12. *Annotated Chaucer bibliography: 1997–2010*
    Mark Allen and Stephanie Amsel
13. *Roadworks: Medieval Britain, medieval roads*
    Valerie Allen and Ruth Evans (eds)
14. *Love, history and emotion in Chaucer and Shakespeare:* Troilus and Criseyde *and* Troilus and Cressida
    Andrew James Johnston, Russell West-Pavlov and Elisabeth Kempf (eds)
15. *The Scottish Legendary: Towards a poetics of hagiographic narration*
    Eva von Contzen
16. *Nonhuman voices in Anglo-Saxon literature and material culture*
    James Paz
17. *The church as sacred space in Middle English literature and culture*
    Laura Varnam
18. *Aspects of knowledge: Preserving and reinventing traditions of learning in the Middle Ages*
    Marilina Cesario and Hugh Magennis (eds)
19. *Visions and ruins: Cultural memory and the untimely Middle Ages*
    Joshua Davies
20. *Participatory reading in late-medieval England*
    Heather Blatt
21. *Affective medievalism: Love, abjection and discontent*
    Thomas A. Prendergast and Stephanie Trigg
22. *Performing women: Gender, self, and representation in late-medieval Metz*
    Susannah Crowder
23. *The politics of Middle English parables: Fiction, theology, and social practice*
    Mary Raschko
24. *Contemporary Chaucer across the centuries*
    Helen M. Hickey, Anne McKendry and Melissa Raine (eds)
25. *Borrowed objects and the art of poetry: Spolia in Old English verse*
    Denis Ferhatović
26. *Rebel angels: Space and sovereignty in Anglo-Saxon England*
    Jill Fitzgerald
27. *A landscape of words: Ireland, Britain and the poetics of space, 700–1250*
    Amy Mulligan

A landscape of words
Ireland, Britain and the poetics of space, 700–1250

AMY C. MULLIGAN

Manchester University Press

Copyright © Amy C. Mulligan 2019

The right of Amy C. Mulligan to be identified as the author of this work has been asserted by her in accordance with the Copyright, Designs and Patents Act 1988.

Published by Manchester University Press
Oxford Road, Manchester M13 9PL
www.manchesteruniversitypress.co.uk

British Library Cataloguing-in-Publication Data is available

ISBN 978 1 5261 4110 1 hardback
ISBN 978 1 5261 6075 1 paperback

First published by Manchester University Press in hardback 2019

This edition published 2021

The publisher has no responsibility for the persistence or accuracy of URLs for any external or third-party internet websites referred to in this book, and does not guarantee that any content on such websites is, or will remain, accurate or appropriate.

Typeset by Deanta Global Publishing Services

To Chris and Henry, with all of my love.

Contents

List of figures	page viii
Acknowledgements	ix
List of abbreviations	xii
Introduction	1
1 Holy islands: transformative landscapes and the origins of an Irish spatial poetics	24
2 Place-making heroes and the storying of Ireland's vernacular landscape	65
3 A versified Ireland: the *Dindshenchas Érenn* and a national poetics of space	108
4 National pilgrims: traveling a sanctified landscape with Saint Patrick	141
5 English topographies of Ireland's conquest and conversion	175
Conclusion	215
Bibliography	227
Index	241

Figures

1 Map of Europe attributed to Gerald of Wales, ca. 1200. Dublin, National Library of Ireland (N.L.I.), MS. 700, fol. 48r. Courtesy of the National Library of Ireland. *page* 176
2 Plan of the Church of the Holy Sepulchre, from Adomnán's *De locis sanctis*. Vienna, Österreichisches Nationalbibliothek MS 458, fol. 4v (ninth century). Courtesy of the Österreichisches Nationalbibliothek. 218
3 Three ogam schemes. Book of Ballymote (fourteenth century), Royal Irish Academy MS 23 P12. By permission of the Royal Irish Academy © RIA. 220
4 Twelfth-century English depiction of the cosmos showing the earth ringed by celestial circles. Walters Art Museum, Baltimore, MS W.73, fol. 2v. Courtesy of the Walters Art Museum. 221

Acknowledgements

This book would not have been possible without the support and wise input from myriad people and institutions. I am lucky to have excellent, intellectually generous colleagues in Notre Dame's Keough-Naughton Institute for Irish Studies and the Medieval Institute, many of whom helped me to harness developments in other fields to think bigger and more ambitiously about medieval Ireland and what a more broadly informed scholarship can achieve. In particular I would like to thank Sarah McKibben, Kathryn Kerby-Fulton, Tim Machan, John Van Engen, Christopher Fox, Ian Kuijt and also Lindy Brady, who has been one of Notre Dame's most stellar Medieval Institute Mellon Fellows. Substantial investment, financial and intellectual, was provided many times over by Notre Dame. Funding from the Institute for Scholarship in the Liberal Arts (ISLA) allowed for essential travel to visit and think through the many sites explored in this book. ISLA also generously underwrote costs for editing—thank you Jeremy Lowe—the book. A large Initiation Grant from the Office of the Vice President for Research provided financial support to develop the project's scope and prepared me to write competitive grant applications to complete the project. These chapters are significantly better because of the input of my writing groups, which provided buoying support throughout the writing process—thank you. I am grateful to the National Library of Ireland, Österreichisches Nationalbibliothek, the Royal Irish Academy and the Walters Art Museum for their assistance and kind permission to use the images found in this book.

Major fellowships from the National Endowment for the Humanities (NEH), and a US-UK Fulbright Fellowship, combined to give me a year, 2016–17, entirely focused on book-writing. The generous funding and collegiality I enjoyed that year as a Fulbright Fellow at the University of Nottingham were critical, and I thank my sponsors and mentors at Nottingham, Judith Jesch, Christina Lee and most especially the wise and exceedingly congenial Thomas O'Loughlin, for their support, camaraderie and insightful conversations on the diasporic cultures of the medieval Irish Sea region. My experiences as a UK Fulbright Fellow and intellectual ambassador were much richer than I could have anticipated. One early highlight of my work as a Fulbright public humanities scholar was explicating the iconography of the medieval Irish saints in the House of Lords on our Fulbright visit just after the Brexit vote, which provided me with unsuspected revelations regarding how a medievalist's scholarship can drive contemporary discussions of pluralistic national identity. I thank the US-UK Fulbright association for financial support, but also the training in how to reframe our research for much wider audiences, for the world is indeed interested. In a time when resources for research in the humanities are shrinking, I am exceedingly grateful to have received such support and mentoring from these international institutions and funding bodies that value the work we do, and motivate and enable us to do it at as high a level as possible.

I would also like to thank the many colleagues in the field of medieval studies and Irish studies who have supported my work. I'm grateful to Paul Russell and Máire Ní Mhaonaigh at the University of Cambridge, which early on hosted me as a Visiting Fellow and later invited me back to talk about this book as an Anglo-Saxon, Norse and Celtic (ASNC) guest speaker. Joseph Falaky Nagy of Harvard has served as a sounding board and advocate for this project, and has provided generous support in negotiating the often fraught field of Celtic Studies. My consideration of geospatial writing began when I was working on the European Centre and Periphery Project at the Centre for Medieval Studies (CMS) in Bergen, where we often went up into the mountains and out onto the fjords to do our scholarly thinking. I am grateful to Else Mundal, Sverre Bagge, Ingvil Brugger Budal, Åslaug Ommundsen and my CMS colleagues for their camaraderie. One of my greatest debts is to Thomas Charles-Edwards, whose brilliance and friendship have been instrumental to my work as a medievalist over the years. Some of my earliest memories of this material involved chocolate-fueled road trips with Thomas to different sites and stones. As a Chicagoan for whom the medieval world had until then been textual, these excursions were epiphanic: they initiated my understanding of how Celtic literature and history is even today highly spatial, and best practiced when one can,

Acknowledgements

as part of a community, fuse stories and sources to actual physical landscapes.

My parents, Martha and Stephen Mulligan, have always provided the warmest support. My mother's involvement has been especially important. When we climbed to the top of Knocknarea in Sligo (with my sister Jill) as part of our Queen Medb pilgrimage, and walked up Croagh Patrick years later, her participation in this project on Ireland's storied landscapes had begun, and it is fitting that my mother has been saying a novena to help me get this book finished! Finally, the most heartfelt thank you goes to my brilliant partner, Chris Abram, who read this book in its entirety and spent inordinate amounts of time talking through its ideas, and whose good humor and genius saved me from despair when the going got tough. Chris also traveled with me and our son Henry to most of the locations discussed in this book over multiple summers. From fishing Henry out of the freezing cold waters surrounding Iona, to rolling down mounds at the hill of Tara and circling pilgrimage sites at Columba's birthplace in Donegal, Chris and Henry were an integral part of the re-storying of Irish place, and have modeled how landscapes become imbued with memories: I treasure every minute of that process. This book, and all of my love, is for them.

Abbreviations

Acallam	*Acallamh na Senórach*, ed. Whitley Stokes.
Compert	*Compert Con Culainn*, ed. A. G. van Hamel.
DIAS	Dublin Institute for Advanced Studies.
DLS	Adomnán, *De locis sanctis*, ed./tr. Denis Meehan.
eDIL	*Electronic Dictionary of the Irish Language*.
Expugnatio	Gerald of Wales, *Expugnatio Hibernica*, ed./tr. A. B. Scott and F. X. Martin.
IMD	*Immram Curaig Maíle Dúin*, in *The Voyage of Máel Dúin*, ed./tr. H. P. A. Oskamp.
LL	Book of Leinster.
LU	Lebor na hUidre.
MD	*The Metrical Dindshenchas*, ed. Edward Gwynn.
MU	*Mesca Ulad*, ed. J. Carmichael Watson.
NSB	*Navigatio Sancti Brendani Abbatis*, ed. Carl Selmer.
Tales	*Tales of the Elders of Ireland*, ed./tr. Ann Dooley and Harry Roe.
TE	*Tochmarc Emire*, in *Compert Con Culainn*, ed. A. G. van Hamel.
Topographia	Gerald of Wales, *Topographia Hibernica*, ed. James Dimock.
Tractatus	*Tractatus de Purgatorio Sancti Patricii*, ed. Robert Easting.
Voyage	*The Voyage of Saint Brendan*, ed./tr. John O'Meara.
VSC	Adomnán, *Vita sancti Columbae*, ed./tr. Alan Orr Anderson and Marjorie Ogilvie Anderson.

Introduction

'All we Irish, inhabitants of the world's edge, are disciples of Saints Peter and Paul' (*sanctorum Petri et Pauli ... discipuli sumus, toti Iberi, ultimi habitatores mundi*).[1] These words, written in 612 or 613 to Pope Boniface IV by the missionary Columbanus, show an Irishman's development of the spatial imperative found in Luke 24:47 and Acts 1:8 and 13:47, that the gospel extend to all nations, reaching *ad ultimum terrae*, to the farthest reaches of the earth, and to those peoples—the Irish—located there. This is the same biblical concept that earlier convinced the evangelizing Briton Patrick to leave his own homeland and bring Christianity to Ireland, that island at the earth's uttermost margins.[2] In 632–33 the Irish bishop Cummian bitingly developed this spatial rhetoric of Irish peripherality to describe those dissenting minorities, largely Irish, who disputed the Roman dating of Easter as blemishes or irritations at the world's edges: they are located 'almost at the end of the earth, and if I may say so, but pimples on the face of the earth' (*pene extremi et, ut ita dicam, mentagrae orbis terrarum*).[3] In a description composed a century later that influenced discourses about Ireland throughout the Middle Ages,[4] the Northumbrian monk Bede more idealistically highlighted the sanctity that remoteness confers. An island limning civilization and the unknown watery regions beyond, Bede's Ireland is an otherworldly North Atlantic Promised Land, sustaining its inhabitants year round, rich in milk and honey and inimical to poisonous creatures:

> Hibernia autem et latitudine sui status et salubritate ac serenitate aerum multum Brittaniae praestat, ita ut raro ibi nix plus quam triduana remaneat; nemo propter hiemem aut faena secet aestate aut stabula fabricet iumentis; nullum ibi reptile uideri soleat, nullus uiuere serpens ualeat. Nam saepe illo de Brittania adlati serpentes, mot ut proximante terries nauigio odore aeris illius adtacti fuerint,

intereunt; quin potius omnia pene quae de eadem insula / sunt contra uenenum ualent ... Diues lactis et mellis insula nec uinearum expers, piscium uolocrumque.

(Ireland is broader than Britain, is healthier and has a much milder climate, so that snow rarely lasts there for more than three days. Hay is never cut in summer for winter use nor are stables built for their beasts. No reptile is found there nor could a serpent survive; for although serpents have often been brought from Britain, as soon as the ship approaches land they are affected by the scent of the air and quickly perish. In fact almost everything that the island produces is efficacious against poison ... The island abounds in milk and honey, nor does it lack vines, fish, and birds.)[5]

Bede's influential description evokes a biblical, Edenic vision. Five hundred years later, the twelfth-century historian Gerald of Wales, a staunch apologist for England's invasion of Ireland, wrote to desanctify Bede's Ireland. In his *Topographia Hiberniae* (ca. 1188), Gerald famously argued that

Sicut enim orientales plagæ propriis quibusdam et sibi innatis preæminent et præcellunt ostentis, sic et occidentales circumferentiæ suis naturae miraculis illustrantur. Quoties quippe, tanquam seriis et veris fatigata negotiis, paululum secedit et excedit, remotis in partibus, quasi verecundis et occultis natura ludit excessibus.[6]

(Just as the countries of the East are remarkable and distinguished by certain prodigies peculiar and native to themselves, so the boundaries of the West also are made remarkable by their own wonders of nature. For sometimes tired, as it were, of the true and the serious, she [Natura] draws aside and goes away, and in these remote parts indulges herself in these secret and distant freaks.)[7]

Throughout his text, Gerald shocks the reader with descriptions of the Irish, the 'secret and distant freaks', per O'Meara's translation, of this remote land that teeters on the edge of the known world. Gerald (and others following him, including Ranulph Higden and his Middle English translators) developed Ireland's remoteness and the consequent barbarity of its people in quite sinister and rhetorically enduring ways.[8]

Discourses on Ireland all worked in different ways to point, for better or for worse, to Ireland's peripherality and geographic outsider status, and the implications of placement at the extreme borders of the world were severe. Medieval *mappae mundi* show how far Ireland was perceived as being from the traditional center

Introduction

of the world, Jerusalem, or from an alternate focal point, Rome, the capital of Christian religious, intellectual and cultural civilization.[9] The early medieval authority Isidore of Seville, much loved by the Irish, defined all peoples in terms of the places they inhabited, and asserted that their 'faces and coloring, the size of their bodies, and their various temperaments correspond to various climates'[10] (*diversitatem enim caeli et facies hominum et colores et corporum quantitates et animorum diversitates existunt*),[11] presenting easy-going Greeks, changeable Africans and fierce, acerbically witted Gauls. The superiority, inferiority, sanctity, depravity and even monstrosity of peoples and places were based, in large part, on their relative proximity to the world's center. Location was an important determinant of whether one belonged to or was excluded from medieval socio-cultural and intellectual elites, and Ireland and its people were assigned critical roles in constructing the medieval Western world's conceptions of self and otherness.

But what responses did this belief system elicit from the Irish themselves, who saw themselves as legitimate members of European intellectual and socio-cultural communities, linked to Rome and Jerusalem through shared investment in the Church, as Columbanus explained to Boniface? What was it like to be condemned to the periphery of one's own *oikumene*, to the limits of the inhabited, civilized world? How could the Irish remap the world and its margins to establish a more vital position for themselves? This book shows how the Irish developed a literature that gave them, and the landscapes they occupied and wrote about, a central place in the medieval European imagination.

Living on an island at the very edge of the known world, the medieval Irish were in a unique position to examine the spaces of the North Sea region and contemplate how location shapes a people; consequently, we can say that Irish narratives of place form one of the richest and most complex bodies of medieval topographical writing. Experiencing this geography in many ways—as monastic *peregrini*, as penitent pilgrims, as heroic adventurers pursuing their varied quests, but also as ambitious early dynasts and later subjects of English conquest—the Irish translated the physical world around them into narratives about their identity and their transnational, even globally significant, place in the world. The Irish wrote extensively about their island and the places that surrounded them, and an immense body of poetry and prose in Latin and Irish, written from ca. 700–1250, verbally maps out Ireland, the North Atlantic archipelago and the world beyond. The Irish understood themselves in terms of the lands they came from, voyaged towards, settled, named and converted into narrative. These topographical texts and traditions all address important aspects of culture and identity (Christian, heroic, intellectual, political) and contemplate what being a medieval Irish person meant in Ireland, Britain and Europe. The same issues were approached from the opposite direction by writers in England, who also used topographic devices and tropes to help them attempt to impose an identity on the Irish that cohered with, in several instances, a colonial perspective on Ireland and its people. It is no surprise that these two topographical traditions, in many ways so closely intertwined, produced significantly different accounts of the nature of Ireland and its place in the wider world.

In *A landscape of words*, I show that the texts produced by and about the medieval Irish contain perhaps the highest concentration of literary topographies in the wider medieval European milieu: only in Ireland was a distinct genre of placelore formalized and popularized. One need not turn to lesser-known writings to prove this; medieval Ireland's canonical literary texts also establish that place-writing is globally important across literature produced by and about the Irish. Our knowledge of the Irish places named in the sources is fairly robust because of extensive study by scholars of Ireland from across the disciplines. In most cases, we know geographic coordinates and sometimes possess detailed maps and archeological reports to help us visualize the physical contours. We can often track references to the mythic and historical personages and founding figures that the sources tell us first settled them; the kings, queens and political leaders who ruled from them; and the kin-groups who occupied them, altered their contours and fought to maintain control over them. Legal texts, annals and hagiographic writings tell us about the communities who assembled together in these places for judgments, fairs and religious rituals; the slain who were buried there; the saints, holy men and women, who sanctified the landscapes with their presence. In short, much work on important Irish sites has been done, and done well, as recourse to the scholarship cited in this book will attest. Nonetheless, medieval Irish spatial *discourse*—and the artistic techniques, vocabularies, representational strategies and narrative logics developed by poets and composers in crafting those accounts—have themselves received little explicit attention. To fill that gap, rather than scrutinizing the places themselves I consider the enrichment of these places through verbal deposits, the metaphors and meanings

Introduction

gathered into them and the role of words in enculturating them, in creating 'landscapes of the mind' that maintain an abiding power even as they become detached from the soil or physical site itself.[12] My contention is that, across several centuries and textual traditions, the diverse literary representations of Irish spaces share much, such that we can begin to recognize the contours of what I call the Irish poetics of space.

A landscape of words traces the generation, dissemination across genre and time, and deployment of this well-developed medieval poetics of Ireland and the North Atlantic region more broadly. The book considers the 'greatest hits' of (and about) medieval Ireland: *Navigatio Sancti Brendani, Immram Curaig Maíle Dúin* and vernacular voyage tales, *Táin Bó Cúalnge, Acallam na Senórach*, Gerald of Wales's *Topographia* and *Expugnatio Hibernica*, and accounts of Saint Patrick's Purgatory, with representative examples from a range of genres analyzed to track the consistent foregrounding of topographical discourses. The medieval Irish did not only innovate significantly in developing a geospatial literature. In simultaneously theorizing the process and its implications, medieval Irish thinkers also enacted a medieval 'spatial turn', a focused and sustained literary consideration of what it means to be in a powerfully transformative landscape. Irish placelore also profoundly influenced other literatures of the North Atlantic region, especially through the export (and later translation) of early texts like Adomnán's *De locis sanctis*, accounts of Saint Brendan's voyage and the movement of textualized Irish places such as Saint Patrick's Purgatory throughout medieval Europe and its vernacular literatures.

Visiting Rome in Ireland and traveling the River Boyne to paradise

Topographic writing generates a literary space in which to explore, define and concretize identity, and in some subtle yet brilliant ways Irish spatial narratives show that movement away from the center of the mapped world also provided opportunities for personal and communal improvement—even a sense of superiority over more centrally placed peoples. Perhaps because of Ireland's extreme location, Irish scholars were particularly driven to devise ways of overcoming the limits imposed by physical peripherality, and to develop new means of occupying important yet inaccessible spaces.

The *Auraicept na n-Éces* ('Primer of the Poets'), an Old Irish treatise (ca. 750) on *bérla Féne*, the 'language of the Féni', or Irish people, tells that following the fall of Nimrod's Tower at Babel, Fénius Farsaid took the best and most beautiful parts of every language and from those fragments forged Irish: this remarkable pedigree ancestrally links Irish to every spoken tongue.[13] In this story, the shattered linguistic relics of the fallen peoples and places of the Old Testament are unified and restored to virtually divine status as the Irish language, with the narrative tracing movement from the cursed site of Babel to an Edenic Ireland sanctified by its use of this restored holy speech. Irish authors took great pains to show how the best and brightest decided to make Ireland their homeland, and, working within the worldview that positioned them as marginal, they revalorized their own positions by remapping the world, geographically expanding core Judeo-Christian narratives to give Ireland and its vernacular a central place. Peripherality, in myths of language, place and movement, was reworked as a marker of sanctity and accomplishment.

Like language, water, the traversable conduit for seafaring peoples, was another trope used to join the eastern and western halves of the world and prevent Ireland from being disconnected. The poem *Boand* details one of Ireland's most extensive and important waterways, the River Boyne, and confidently promotes a worldview where water links Ireland to Eden. When the waters that are absorbed into Adam's paradise next reappear in the spring of Segais, peripherality is cleverly reformulated to become proximity, and *Boand I* maps the connective vectors uniting Ireland and Eden. The poem opens in the otherworldly *síd* from which Boand (the Boyne) flows until the river 'reaches the paradise of Adam' (*co roshaig pardus Adaim*, 1.8) so that, as Kay Muhr puts it, 'the sea, and the holy rivers of Ireland and the world, are linked together in one circular motion'.[14]

Síd Nechtain sund forsin t-sléib, lecht mic Labrada lán-géir, assa silenn in sruth slán dianid ainm Bóand bith-lán ...	Sid Nechtain is the name that is on the mountain here, the grave of the full-keen son of Labraid, from which flows the stainless river whose name is Boand ever-full ...
... Sabrann dar tír Saxan slán, Tibir i ráith na Román, Sruth n-Iordanen iarsain sair, ocus Sruth n-Eufrait adbail.	... *Severn* she is called through the land of the sound Saxons, *Tiber* in the Romans' keep: *River Jordan* thereafter in the east and vast *River Euphrates.*

Introduction

Sruth Tigir i pardus búan,	*River Tigris* in enduring paradise,
fota sair síst fri himlúad:	long is she in the east, a time of
ó phardus darís ille	wandering
co srothaib na síde-se. S.	from paradise back again hither
	to the streams of this Sid.[15]

Boand, 'ever full' (*bith-lán*), is known by fifteen different names (*cóic anmand déc*, 1.5), the poet tells us, nine of which denote Irish rivers and six of which refer to international waters, including Rome's Tiber, the East's Jordan and Euphrates, and finally the River Tigris 'in everlasting paradise' (*i pardus búan*). The poet's declaration of each river's name moves us across Europe and into the Holy Land through this versified landscape. Where brightly colored rivers draw our eye around the world in the *mappae mundi*, *Boand I* enacts this movement verbally.[16] Furthermore, by referencing Adam's 'enduring paradise' (*pardus Adaim; pardus búan*, lines 9, 33), the poem shows the temporal elision characteristic of the *mappae mundi*, in which sites and scenes from the past—paradise before expulsion—are depicted as outside of time. Ireland lacks the great *mappae mundi*, but its poets map the same scheme in words: Irish landscapes are verbal rather than visual.

Boand wanders or moves about (*himlúad*) the Holy Land for a period (*síst*): personified as a pilgrim, this river makes her way from Ireland to the Holy Land, until she enters paradise and bubbles back up in the *síd*. This looping, spatial circuit about or around (*im*) is emphasized by the form and structure of the poem, and provides an example of how Irish composers developed a poetics of space and used formal devices to address and emphasize issues of movement both thematically and structurally. Specifically, the last word of the nine-stanza description of Boand's world circuit employs *dúnad* ('closing' or 'shutting'), a poetic technique of concluding a poem by meaningfully repeating its first word: as Boand makes a connective watery circuit around the world, so too the poem winds back to its opening word, the otherworldly landscape term *síd*.[17] The verses make an Irish holy site—the well of Segais at the *síd* where the Boand bubbles up after flowing into paradise—both the terminus and origin point of this fluvial circuit linking Ireland and Eden. This is an important valorization of the Irish otherworld: water can flow directly from Adam's paradise to the Síd of Nechtan, situated under a mountain and posited as an inaccessible but marked holy site, much like the Garden of Eden. Though the poem is not entirely clear, it seems to conceive of an earthly sphere in which these sites are linked, through underground waterways, the two termini, an otherworldly Irish mound and Adam's paradise, both contiguous with and terrestrially distant from each other. A stanza from another poem (*Boand II*) tells us that Christ explicitly blesses the Boyne and presents it as Ireland's Jordan, privileging another kind of contiguity with the Holy Land:

Bóand, bendacht forsin sruth	Boand—a blessing on the stream
roordaig Críst co cóem-chruth,	did Christ fair of form ordain;
conid hí ó glenn do glenn	so she from glen to glen
sruth Eorthanan na Hérenn.	is the river Jordan of Erin.[18]

Boand I and *II* make the argument that these holy geographies can be accessed locally in Ireland.

A brief Old Irish poem also suggests unexpected ways in which faraway landscapes, including the stage on which Judeo-Christian history unfolded, might be as accessible in Ireland as elsewhere:

Teicht do Róim:	Going to Rome,
mór saído, becc torbai;	Great trouble, little benefit;
in rí chon-daigi hi foss,	the king which you seek there,
mani-mbera latt, ní fogbai.[19]	if you do not carry him with you,
	you will not find him.

This poem registers disenchantment with pilgrimage, and questions the spiritual benefits of a costly journey that could be filled with threats and worldly distractions from spiritual development. Simultaneously, the poem can also be seen as an endorsement of virtual travel and imaginative spatial practice. Through text, through poetry, through the Word, the poem encourages its readers to contemplate Rome and its sought-after king, God, so that he is found in every landscape. As its author wittily remarks, God is not located in the distant, famed site of Rome itself—rather, God resides within a person, wherever he or she may be.

An interesting physically spatial analogue to this Irish skill of moving the Holy Land west is the curious fact that the placename *Róm* ('Rome') also becomes applied to Irish religious sites. As the *Dictionary of the Irish Language* (*eDIL*) records, in Irish religious literature *róm* was used to describe 'a saint's settlement in which he was buried', and a burial-ground more generally, with later poetry expanding *róm* to denote important secular sites as well, such as a king's residence.[20] The Irish Christian landscape houses several local *róma*, or little Romes, and readers of this poem might envision themselves finding God at nearby sites of piety, where prayer and liturgical practice make Rome and the saints part of local geography. Hagiographical writing also bears witness to this localization of Rome in Ireland, as Lisa Bitel demonstrates in her important study of early medieval Irish sacred landscapes. For instance, Bitel shows how Cogitosus, in his *vita* of Brigit, uses ekphrastic descriptions featuring the terms, images and spatial logics of an urban, romanized Christian landscape, to legitimize the rural Irish site of Kildare as a powerful *civitas* and depict its saintly founder, Brigit, as presiding over a New Jerusalem in Ireland. With his verbal description of Brigit's church and tomb, Cogitosus 'intended his text to parallel and evoke a work of architecture rather than illuminating its physical reality', and he thus filled his account with details and 'practical visual cues for those ignorant of Rome but desirous of it, and who sought it in Brigit's city'.[21] Cogitosus, Bitel demonstrates, fashions architectural spaces from words so his audience can experience a pilgrimage through Brigit's *vita*: words persuasively recoded rural Irish spaces as sacred Christian landscapes evocative of Rome and *romanitas*.[22] Irish language and landscape show us that Rome and what it represents can be experienced at home in Ireland. Discipleship of Peter and Paul, as Columbanus pointed out, brings Rome to Ireland, but language and ekphrastic description further concretize those links. In Ireland's physical environment, words are overlain onto local spaces in powerfully appropriative ways: this is one important element of an Irish poetics and practice of space.

As the composer of *Techt do Róim* asks, why travel to the Holy Land when, in many ways, the Holy Land and 'what you seek' is right here in Ireland? The Boyne is already linked to paradise; the Irish language is a restoration of pre-Babel tongues; 'Rome' and God can be found in any Irish churchyard; and, as we will see in Chapter 1, the holy sites can be inhabited through narrative topographies like those written by the Irish abbot of Iona, Adomnán (ca. 624–704). The sources make the argument that God and the wondrous world could be made available to all, no matter one's location, resources or physical limitations. Places and experiences central to Judeo-Christian identity are available in the Irish Sea region, overlain onto a real landscape, but also materialized in literary form.

Writing and the Irish landscape

> All around me greenwood trees
> I hear blackbird verse on high
> quavering lines on vellum leaves
> birdsong pours down from the sky.[23]

Words and landscape interlace in transformative ways, thereby becoming more than the sum of their parts, as suggested by Ciaran Carson's artful rendering of this Old Irish stanza, which was written around 800–50. The full text (with Ruth Lehmann's more literal translation) records that

Dom-farcai fidbaide fál
fom-chain loíd luin–lúad nád cél;
h-úas mo lebrán, ind línech,
fom-chain tríech inna n-én.
	A hedge of a wood-thicket looks
	  down on me;
	A blackbird's song sings to me (a
	  message not concealed)
	Above my little book, the lined one,
	the twittering of birds sings to me.

Fomm-chain coí menn, medair
  mass,
hi m-brot glas de dindgnaib doss.
Débráth! nom Choimdiu coíma:
caín-scríbaimm fo roída ross.
	The clear-voiced cuckoo calls to
	  me, a lovely speech
	in a gray mantle from bushy
	  dwellings.
	God's Judgment! The Lord
	  befriends me!
	I write fair under the great wood of
	  the forest.[24]

This poem is often cited to evidence a specifically Irish celebration of nature, with figures like the ninth-century Irish philosopher John Scotus Eriugena formulating a parallel understanding of nature as a medium for connection with God in his discussions of theophany and creation, as Alfred Siewers has argued.[25] Irish embrace of the natural world has provided a much-discussed contrast with early English distancing from nature, and the belief, articulated by Jennifer Neville, that 'For the Old English poet, the representation of the natural world helps to create the context of helplessness and alienation that motivates the seeking of God. For the Irish poet the representation of the natural world creates the context of wonder and joy that surrounds the seeking of God.'[26]

Introduction

To claim, however, that the Irish were more in touch or positively engaged with nature than their other North Atlantic neighbors would be to misrepresent the complexity of their project and its products. Wonder and joy characterize many of the aesthetically delightful landscapes created by Irish poets, yet these texts require more than marveling at creation—these landscapes of words accomplish important spiritual, intellectual, cultural and political aims. Irish place-writing is often so skillfully done that we overlook its intricacy, but a sustained examination highlights a persistent and conscientiously deployed methodology of spatial writing and practice: there is far more than environmental awe here, and verbalized Irish landscapes are rarely decorative backdrops.

The poem cited above demonstrates a deep appreciation for nature, but perhaps more valuably it provides a window on how writing and reading become intertwined with experiencing nature and the landscape. As Daniel Melia has observed, the text makes consistent use of all sorts of devices—poetic, linguistic, syntactical, thematic—to show the scribe surrounded by and infused with the landscape in his literary practice. The lines of the manuscript page trail off into lines of birdsong to envelop the speaker; and, as text and environment become fused, so too do its practitioners: the warbling, gray-cloaked cuckoo is also the figure of the cowled monk writing his joyful lyrics. Melia shows the myriad ways that the poem formally embodies the interlacing of text and environment to both structurally and thematically convince us of the benefits of conceptualizing landscape and literature together: the poem's metrical structure, with incessantly interlacing alliteration and rhyme, wraps around both monk and speaking birds; its linguistic devices, prepositions, verb forms and infixed pronouns continuously place the poet in their middle; environmental descriptions show the speaker peacefully enfolded simultaneously by forest and poetry. As Melia writes, 'this, I think, is the point, the preferred subject of the poem, that the embrace of words, of trees, of music, of language, and of nature is ultimately the embrace of the Lord himself, just as every element in the poem is representation of His embrace'.[27]

Moving to the inscription of this poem in the manuscript's margins, on another level we understand that the poet, through words, through imagining himself writing well in a forest, brings that treed space into a scriptorium. Scribes and readers gaze on a page, yet find themselves hearing birds trill, seeing a manuscript's leaves give way to green-leafed trees. These links provide a vernacular parallel to Latin puns involving *liber*, both 'book' and 'tree-bark'.[28] Though it is not verbally framed as such, we might read this poem as a riddle whose solution is any of the several Irish words that refer to both arboreal and codicological leaves: Irish *duille, duillend* or *duilleóg*, or perhaps *bileóc*, related to *bile*, a large tree, but also an especially venerated, sacred tree.[29] Yet this much-admired Old Irish poem moves beyond clever schoolroom punning as it leads us through a thoughtful meditation within its forest of words. The verses of this poem are generated in a linguistic and cultural context which can imagine books as trees, leaves as pages, and singing, writing and reading as the creation of a green-branched grove in which we can take shelter and dwell. An Irish literary poetics is, in important ways, also a poetics of place.

Terminology: a poetics of Irish space

When the foundational spatial theorist Gaston Bachelard calls for an appreciation of poetic utterance in contemplating spatiality, and states that 'We must listen to poets',[30] I am inclined to agree, for Ireland's poets have much to say, and their works reveal rigorous consideration of how to write space. The author of the Old Irish *Auraicept na nÉces*, or 'Primer of the Poets', tells us that reading a text—in this case an ogam inscription—is like climbing a tree. Each hand reaches up to grab onto another letter or word, meaning literally grasped as the body pulls itself along the letters of the text:

> Is amlaid im-drengar ogum amal im-drengar crann .i. saltrad fora frém in chroinn ar tús 7 do lám dess remut 7 do lám clé fo deoid. Is íar-sin leis 7 is fris 7 is trít 7 is immi.

> (Ogam is climbed like a tree, that is, treading on the root of the tree first with your right hand before you and your left hand finally. It is after that it is along and towards it, through it and around it.)[31]

The *Acallam*'s Saint Patrick similarly remarks, generating the proverb (*in tseinbriathar*), that '*gablánach in rét an scéluighecht*' ('storytelling is a branching business!').[32] Patrick's point is that narrative is a complicated affair, with *gablánach* denoting a branching structure that also figuratively connotes complexity, yet the proverb still asks us to consider story and landscape, texts and trees, together. Like the *Fidbaide* poet who imagines his literary process as the production of birdsong from within a treed sanctuary, the *Auraicept* directs Ireland's readers to climb up, to hoist ourselves onto the branches and to see what the world looks like from there. As shown throughout this study, audiences are encouraged and expected to move into these virtualized worlds in different ways: to journey along the pilgrimage routes; to join the voyagers in their currach; to learn and then traverse heroic Ireland's map with Cú Chulainn; to climb the famed heights with the *dindshenchas* poets; to circle Ireland with Patrick and Caílte; to walk Saint Patrick's Purgatory with the Knight, armed only with faith.

These texts exemplify a spatial poetics; each audience member must also become a spatial practitioner to use these narratives properly and productively, and the texts contain subtle instructions and examples of how to make it happen. We climb these trees, grab onto their various branches and, through reading, perch within the space the text builds for us. Through descriptive phrasing, dialogue and direct speech, identification with the main characters and transmission of the embodied experiences of these spaces, the literature is structured to provide geographic and temporal portals into verbalized landscapes. Manuscript pages are presented to us as cultivated landscapes that we weave through as our eye travels down a page's ruled lines. This is one aspect of what is meant by the term 'spatial practice'—imaginative movement into the verbalized landscapes actualized by the texts. The book's discussions of spatial practice also, however, encompass the motions, often exemplary, of characters within the text, and on occasion describe the movements of historical people through physical landscapes, such as the paths traced through Ireland by traveling poets, journeying pilgrims and everyday people as they walked a landscape that had been long imbued with story—spatial practice can be physical or imaginative, or both simultaneously.

In this book, I use the phrase 'poetics of Irish space' to include a number of elements, though I strive to ensure that context makes these meanings clear. Briefly, however, a poetics of Irish space denotes writing about Ireland and Irish landscapes by both Irish and non-Irish composers, using Latin or the vernaculars. 'Irish poetics of space' encompasses the ways that Irish authors write non-Irish spaces (such as Adomnán's narrativization of the Holy Land). I've employed the term 'poetics' because I want to evoke the power of verbal artistry as a way to explore, postulate and refine ideas about the relationships between landscape and literary form. When the composers I discuss reflect on the spatial textual forms they pursued and produced, they express their findings through their craft with an attentive eye to aesthetics.[33] I think in several cases these medieval authors would argue that the most persuasive way to teach a poetics of Irish space is to do it well, to create a text that will be circulated, imitated, recopied and, hopefully, enshrined in tradition because it delights and is valued: a poetics of Irish space expressed and theorized as exemplum. One of the strengths of a persuasively conceived poetics is that it shows us rather than simply tells us; it grabs our imagination and pulls us into its world before we even realize we have internalized it and have come to know something new from the inside.

The phrase 'poetics of space' is suggestively open, and invites innovation and creative inflection. Never institutionalized or prescriptive, as the use of alternative terminology like 'theory' or 'grammar' of space might imply, the virtue of a poetics is its dynamic nature: it artfully takes new forms under the shaping guidance of each storyteller, poet, translator, scribe or even reader. This is not to deny, however, several consistencies in structure and form, and I aim throughout to identify characteristics, logics and devices that are shared across texts and traditions; but 'poetics' has a malleability that admits, even expects, ongoing reworkings. I therefore use 'poetics of space' to cover a number of things: environmental imagery and metaphor; descriptions of landscape creation and change; the fixing of story and history onto geographies through placenames, as well as subtler ways of planting and furrowing narrative into geographic contours; the virtual inhabitation of verbalized landscapes; and the clever ways in which geographic rhetoric, language and logics are used to define Ireland and the Irish people. A poetics of Irish space, then, encompasses a great many modes, devices, characteristics and styles, but all are unified in the production of landscapes of words, places that become powerfully accessible and inviting, enduring through their verbalization and textual inscription.

Ecocriticism and ecopoetics have informed my readings of Irish literature and place-writing, and there is scope and appetite for more extensive explorations in this area.[34] However, the sources I consider are first and foremost (though not exclusively) concerned with how humans make places, record their stories in the environment and appropriate landscapes for their own diverse purposes. Irish spatial discourses are primarily anthropocentric, and very rarely ecocentric. A poetics of Irish space celebrates the environment; however, the human voices and hands that materialize the landscape in speech and manuscript are of greater interest. We are left with the impression that, for the medieval Irish, one of the best

Introduction

ways to experience the environment is through words. And overreliance on the tools and terminology of a theoretical literature originating in times, places and environmental concerns not necessarily shared with Ireland's spatial poets, or an overly enthusiastic translation of medieval Ireland's processes and techniques into contemporary frameworks, can obscure the logics of the medieval sources, and those must be the initial focus. I have therefore only sparingly used an ecocritical vocabulary in this study.

For the same reasons, I have also avoided reading these sources explicitly through the lens and vocabulary of spatial theory, another rich multi-disciplinary scholarship that has long convinced us of the ways in which space and place are cultural constructs. My engagement with the Irish sources is heavily informed by various strands of spatial theory, and I do appropriate some of its terminology, most notably the idea of 'spatial practice' in discussing how a medieval Irish spatial poetics creates meaning though explicit attention to space and the vectors that shape it. Contemporary thinkers thus find their way into the discussion where their insights can clarify the primary sources. Nonetheless, I have also tried to limit theoretical jargon to allow the composers of the sources, and their characters, to articulate spatial literary concepts using the logics and imagery of medieval Ireland. Again, I hope that this will avoid a reductive approach, highlight some unexpected models for spatial thinking and practice and help us to appreciate the ways that medieval people probed, developed and theorized the links between space, place and language.

Structure of the book

The book largely adheres to a chronological organization to show how Ireland's spatial poetics developed over 600 years. Chapters 1 and 5 treat Latin texts that circulated extensively in Britain and Europe, written by Irish, English and Anglo-Welsh authors. Also widely translated into several vernaculars, these texts fired medieval Europe's imagination regarding the lands and peoples inhabiting the most remote spaces of the Western world, and provided the enduring foundations for Europe's views of Ireland and the Irish. Chapters 2–4 attend to Irish vernacular literary texts that show a development and refinement of a poetics of space and place. Aside from *Táin Bó Cúalnge*, these sources remain little-known outside of Celtic Studies, but they demonstrate how a poetics of space and place became a kind of national cultural project in

Ireland, and their highly nuanced products point to the successes of medieval Ireland's early spatial turn. Taken together, the Latin and vernacular sources show a long, continuously developed poetics of space and place that had extensive impact throughout the medieval period (and beyond—contemporary Irish writers are still celebrated for their particular genius in place-writing).

Chapter 1 identifies geography's central role in the earliest texts produced by and about the Irish ca. 700–900. I begin with one of the first Holy Land pilgrimage accounts composed in Britain, the widely circulated *De locis sanctis*, written by the Irishman Adomnán, and reproduced by an admiring Bede in the *Historia Ecclesiastica*. After identifying how *De locis sanctis* models successful spatial writing, I consider how Adomnán applied his methodologies of Jerusalem place-writing to North Atlantic holy sites in *Vita Sancti Columbae*. I then show how foundational accounts of Holy Land pilgrimage produced in Britain inform Irish texts about voyages in the holy waters surrounding Ireland and Britain, popularly conceived of as a Western *herimum in ociano*. The islands of the North Atlantic (including Ireland) are often envisioned as otherworldly lands of milk and honey, whose nature is largely determined by their position limning civilization and the unknown watery regions beyond. With the ocean conceived as a transformative frontier between the mortal world and the heavenly, the seascapes outside Ireland allow travelers and *peregrini*, historical and fictional, access to otherworldly, often revelatory spaces. A desire to investigate these places and be changed by them motivates the monastic Irish voyagers whose stories are told in the eighth-century Latin *Navigatio Sancti Brendani*, which circulated widely throughout Europe; the lay protagonists of the closely related vernacular Irish voyage texts (*immrama*) undergo parallel experiences as they move through these same geographies. These Irish spatial narratives provided an early and influential model for composers in Ireland, Britain and Europe to write texts inviting imaginative travel to holy places from the Dead Sea to the Irish Sea.

Shifting onto the plains, hills and forests of the Irish landmass and into the Irish language, the spatial poetics exemplified by earlier texts remain prominent, and ideas of Irish heroism are expressed through topographic narratives and spatially oriented language. Chapter 2 traces the development of the poetics of space in Ireland's heroic literature (ca. 900–1160) through a primary focus on medieval Irish literature's most celebrated figure, the warrior Cú Chulainn. I situate narratives from *Táin Bó Cúalnge*

Introduction

alongside other texts from the Ulster Cycle to track how a spatial hero is constructed. Cú Chulainn is initially named Sétanta—one might translate this as 'path-finder' or 'journeyer'—and tales of his birth and boyhood deeds place surprising emphasis on his ability to navigate new environments and internalize storied maps of the territory. The *Táin*, which features Cú Chulainn as its hero, is framed by a cosmogonic tale in which two otherworldly bulls, paralleling the narrative's place-making warriors, tear through all of Ireland in their fight to the death: anger, battle-frenzy and looping circuits give Ireland its geographic contours and placenames. An eloquent Cú Chulainn's increasing mastery of placelore and the erotics of place are examined in *Tochmarc Emire* ('Wooing of Emer'). A brief look at *Mesca Ulad* ('Drunkenness of the Ulstermen') queries how Ulster's spatially savvy hero is not ultimately immune to displacement: Cú Chulainn loses himself and the men of Ulster in hostile territories, and their frenzied ride transforms the landscape—their journey levels hills, clears trees and drains rivers—and generates a (mis)reading of the drunken, careening heroes as environmental features rather than humans, which also problematizes violence and heroic excess. Though often overlooked as mere background, the Irish landscape is one of the most fully developed characters in Ireland's heroic literature. The chapter concludes with Saint Patrick conjuring the long-dead Cú Chulainn from the earth to tell his story in *Siaburcharpat Con Culaind* ('Phantom-chariot of Cú Chulainn'): the discussion thus ends by highlighting issues regarding spatial narrative, textuality and the redemptive function of storytelling.

In the twelfth century, a period of significant Church reform and political upheaval, Irish geopoetical literature nonetheless flourished. Chapter 3 considers the *Dindshenchas Érenn* ('Placelore of Ireland'), a collection of around 200 poems and 200 prose pieces about named places comprising medieval Ireland's most explicitly topographical narratives, which was formally brought together as a cohesive corpus and first attested in the Book of Leinster manuscript. Despite its size and clear popularity (it is preserved in over twenty manuscripts), scholars, including Edward Gwynn, the editor of the five-volume *Dindshenchas*, have dismissed this collection as 'tiresome catalogues of names', 'parasitic' in its integration of multiple historical, mythological and literary traditions.[35] That the composers were doing something powerful becomes apparent, however, if we recognize the *dindshenchas* as an imaginative and well-executed construction of a virtual Ireland. This chapter considers the narrative topographies of the *Dindshenchas Érenn*, looks at the role of the *dindshenchas* place-making poets as medieval Ireland's geographers and tracks ideas about the use of verse as the appropriate literary form in which to write and formalize Ireland's landscape. The poets suggest that the verbalized territories of the *dindshenchas* poems, simultaneously real and imagined, were to be contemplatively accessed, virtually inhabited and moved through in an appropriative act. This, furthermore, was an act of collective national imagining. The island-wide bardic curriculum demanded that by the eighth year of training poets were able to recite the entire topographic corpus on demand, and multiple *dindshenchas* texts advertise the poets' ability to conjure lost sites and spaces with their words and visionary abilities. The *Dindshenchas Érenn* thus becomes a national landscape, a virtual Ireland created, performed and preserved by the poets and scribes of Ireland.

Chapter 4 looks at the late twelfth- or early thirteenth-century *Acallam na Senórach* ('Conversation of the Elders'), medieval Ireland's longest piece of literature at 8,000 prosimetric lines. Set in the fifth-century past, the *Acallam* resurrects both Saint Patrick and the pagan hero Caílte to lead a pilgrimage through a reimagined Irish topography, merging sacred and secular to posit a revalorized, sanctified Ireland for a post-conquest audience. The *Acallam* advocates walking and physical movement through an Ireland composed of green, wild, watery, outdoor spaces as knowledge-creating, while also promoting the benefits of imaginative engagement with a storied environment. The *Acallam* furthermore deploys a geospatial poetics to 'naturalize' Saint Patrick: as in the Irish legends of kingship and sovereignty, Patrick is endorsed by the land. His actions show an increasingly harmonious relationship with Ireland's environment, and culminate in his composition and delivery of Irish-language topographical poems. Patrick becomes a saintly practitioner of the Irish poetics of place, and the British-born foreigner is by the end of the text embraced as Ireland's patron saint. By modeling Irish spatial practices through a range of characters transformed over the course of the narrative, the *Acallam* shows the diverse members of Irish (and English) society how to engage with Ireland as a richly storied, sanctified national space. Written in Ireland after the English invasion and conquest, the *Acallam* illustrates a productive relationship between Ireland and Britain forged through travel: an Irish warrior and British saint walk and talk Irish place together. As explored in Chapter 5, the apologist Gerald of Wales, writing a few decades earlier, used topographic rhetorics to silence Irish voices; the *Acallam* might thus be seen as a response to a disenfranchising colonialist poetics of Irish space.

Chapter 5 addresses how Church reformers and participants in the English invasion of Ireland also developed and consumed a poetics of Irish place to argue for their own entitlement to Ireland via texts first created and disseminated in the 1180s. I turn first to the works of Gerald of Wales, whose *Topographia* and *Expugnatio Hibernica* show Ireland physically rejecting the 'unworthy' Irish from the landscape and embracing more environmentally savvy English and Welsh settlers, exhorting them to plant themselves in Irish soil. I examine the process by which the identities of Ireland's invaders are mapped onto the territory, and show how a changed Ireland is generated through textual culture, particularly important when in historical reality Ireland resisted full conquest. Gerald's oration of the *Topographia* in Oxford in 1188 furthermore accomplished the importation of his imagined Ireland back to England. I argue that these oral performances created a virtual Ireland, traveled, conquered and, to some extent, inhabited, by all who read or heard Giraldus's account. Such writings about Ireland emerge afresh not just as records of conquest but as actual textual conquests of land. To show how an exported textual Ireland provided a spiritual and contemplative testing ground for a different kind of international reader, the chapter then turns to the pilgrimage site of Saint Patrick's Purgatory in the north of Ireland. Accounts of this Irish purgatory were first composed in the 1180s (*Tractatus de Purgatorio Sancti Patricii*), but were repeatedly copied, circulated and translated over the next 500 years: 150 manuscripts of the Latin text survive, and another 150 manuscripts confirm its translation into virtually every European vernacular. Transformative journeys to purgatory and the earthly paradise within Irish space are a terrestrial development of the voyage narratives that open the book, but also the manifestation of an English poetics of Irish place. While Saint Patrick's Purgatory is a site of pilgrimage, its rhetoric nonetheless suggests a heroic, crusading conquest of Ireland's dangerous spaces in which English reformers also became textual heroes. As in Gerald's own spatial poetics, the *Tractatus* narrative's Irish purgatorial landscape ultimately, I suggest, writes the Irish out so as to privilege other perspectives and agent positions. In conclusion, I examine how both Gerald's works and the *Tractatus* accomplished the export of an English poetics of Irish space which became highly influential throughout Europe.

Between 700 and 1250, Ireland's textual geographies attained high levels of sophistication, pointing to a conscious deployment of discursive Irish landscapes. Rooted in the physical geography of Ireland, these geospatial narratives ultimately moved beyond the land itself and became powerful, portable worlds that could be accessed and occupied by readers and listeners anywhere and at any time. The broad diachronic scope of this book, covering some six centuries of writing, demonstrates the ongoing centrality of spatial discourses to the development of identities of the Irish and their North Atlantic neighbors, as well as the ways in which place-writers responded to changing historical and political circumstances. Through focused studies of important texts, *A landscape of words* places the poetics of Irish space into the bigger picture of how, and why, medieval people wrote space, place, landscape and environment. The literatures of Irish place comprise an extensive and highly developed corpus from which medievalists and scholars of place can learn much. The Venerable Bede even claimed that Irish writing might offer a potent lifesaving elixir:

> Denique uidimus, quibusdam a serpente percussis, rasa folia codicum qui de Hibernia fuerant, et ipsam rasuram aquae inmissam ac potui datam talibus protinus totam uim ueneni grassantis, totum inflati corporis absumsisse ac sedasse tumorem.
>
> (We have seen how, in the case of people suffering from snake-bite, the leaves of manuscripts from Ireland were scraped, and the scrapings put in water and given to the sufferer to drink. These scrapings at once absorbed the whole violence of the spreading poison and assuaged the swelling.)[36]

Though his meaning is literal here, we might consider Bede's sentiments about Irish texts on another level as well. As Máire Ní Mhaonaigh has written, 'Literary exchanges undoubtedly formed part of the intense contact between Ireland and England in Bede's own time and later and it may be that their eastern neighbours learned much from the confident control the Irish had of their own written tongue.'[37] The multivalent products of a sanctified geography, Irish letters exceed the sum of their parts. Words that emanate from this Western island of milk and honey have power, a belief that we will see developed across the texts produced by and about the Irish. Irish manuscripts might save us, Bede suggests, and it is worth drinking deeply from them.[38]

Introduction

Notes

1. *Columbanus, Epistolae*, v. 3 in *Sancti Columbani Opera*, ed./trans. G. S. M. Walker (Dublin: DIAS, 1957), pp. 38–9.
2. See references in to Patrick's *Confessio usque ad ultimum terrae* and *extremis terrae* in Ludwig Bieler (ed.), *Libri Epistolarum Sancti Patricii Episcopi* (Dublin: Royal Irish Academy, 1993), 1, 38, pp. 57, 78. See also Thomas O'Loughlin, 'Patrick on the Margins of Space and Time', in K. McGroarty (ed.), *Eklogai: Studies in Honour of Thomas Finan and Gerard Watson* (Maynooth: National University of Ireland, Maynooth, 2001), pp. 44–58.
3. *Cummian's Letter De Controversia Paschali*, ed./trans. Moira Walsh and Dáibhí Ó Cróinín (Toronto: Pontifical Institute for Mediaeval Studies, 1988), pp. 72–5.
4. Available widely in Latin, by the late ninth or tenth century Bede's account had even been translated into Irish. Próinséas Ní Chatháin, 'Bede's Ecclesiastical History in Irish', *Peritia* 3 (1984), 115–30.
5. Bede, *Historia ecclesiastica* [hereafter *Historia*], I.1, in *Bede's Ecclesiastical History of the English People*, ed./trans. Bertram Colgrave and R. A. B. Mynors (Oxford: Clarendon Press, 1969), pp. 18–20.
6. Gerald of Wales, *Giraldi Cambrensis Opera*, Rolls Series, vol. 5, ed. James. F. Dimock (London: Longman, 1867), *Præfatio Secunda*, pp. 20–1.
7. Gerald of Wales, *The History and Topography of Ireland*, ed./trans. John O'Meara (New York: Penguin, 1982), p. 31.
8. See Elizabeth Rambo, *Colonial Ireland in Medieval English Literature* (Selingrove, PA: Susquehanna University Press, 1994), pp. 35–40 and Kathy Lavezzo, *Angels on the Edge of the World* (Ithaca, NY: Cornell University Press, 2006), pp. 54–8.
9. Though these discourses circulated in Ireland, maps themselves are rare, and there there appears to be no native Irish term for map. Rolf Baumgarten, 'Geographical Orientation of Ireland in Isidore and Orosius', *Peritia* 3 (1984), 91.
10. Isidore of Seville, *The Etymologies*, trans. Stephen Barney *et al.* (Cambridge: Cambridge University Press, 2006), p. 198.
11. Isidore of Seville, *Etymologiae*, ed. W. M. Lindsay (Oxford: Clarendon Press, 1911), IX.ii.105.
12. The phrasing adapts that of Seamus Heaney, 'The Sense of Place', in *Preoccupations* (London: Faber & Faber, 1980), p. 132. Fully quoted below in Chapter 3, note 72.
13. Anders Ahlqvist (ed.), *The Early Irish Linguist: An Edition of the Canonical Part of the Auraicept na nÉces* (Helsinki: Societas Scientiarum Fennica, 1983), pp. 47–8.
14. Kay Muhr, 'Water Imagery in Early Irish', *Celtica* 23 (1999), 200.

15 Edward Gwynn (ed./trans.), *The Metrical Dindshenchas*, 5 vols (Dublin: Royal Irish Academy, 1903–35), III, pp. 26–9. Henceforth *MD*. The texts and translations cited here are Gwynn's, though I have occasionally edited the translations for clarity. Roman numerals refer to volume numbers, with the following Arabic numerals denoting page numbers.
16 An overview of *mappae mundi* and their rivers is David Woodward, 'Medieval Mappaemundi', in J. B. Harley and David Woodward (eds.), *The History of Cartography, Volume 1: Cartography in Prehistoric, Ancient, and Medieval Europe and the Mediterranean* (Chicago, IL: University of Chicago Press, 1987), pp. 286–368, with rivers table at p. 327.
17 *Dúnad* with *side* also occurs at the end of stanzas 19, 20 and 23.
18 *MD* III, pp. 34–5.
19 The text, preserved in the margins of a Greek New Testament glossed in Latin, probably by an Irish monk at Saint Gall, is edited in Rudolf Thurneysen, *Old Irish Reader* (Dublin: DIAS, 1981), p. 41. Translation is my own.
20 See *eDIL* s.v. róm.
21 Lisa Bitel, *Landscape with Two Saints: How Genovefa of Paris and Brigit of Kildare Built Christianity in Barbarian Europe* (Oxford: Oxford University Press, 2009), p. 139.
22 Bitel, *Landscape*, pp. 145–58.
23 Translated by Ciaran Carson, 'The Scribe in the Woods', in Maurice Riordan (ed.), *The Finest Music: Early Irish Lyrics* (London: Faber & Faber, 2014), p. 4.
24 Ruth Lehmann (ed./trans.), *Early Irish Verse* (Austin, TX: University of Texas Press, 1982), p. 25.
25 See Alfred Siewers, *Strange Beauty: Ecocritical Approaches to Early Medieval Landscape* (New York: Palgrave Macmillan, 2009), and 'The *Periphyseon*, the Irish "Otherworld", and Early Medieval Nature', in Willemien Otten and Michael Allen (eds.), *Eriugena and Creation* (Turnhout: Brepols, 2014), pp. 321–47.
26 Jennifer Neville, *Representations of the Natural World in Old English Poetry* (Cambridge: Cambridge University Press, 1999), p. 37.
27 Daniel Melia, 'A Poetic Klein Bottle', in A. T. E. Matonis and Daniel Melia (eds.), *Celtic Language, Celtic Culture: A Festschrift for Eric P. Hamp* (Van Nuys, CA: Ford and Bailie, 1990), p. 194.
28 See Mary Carruthers, *The Craft of Thought: Meditation, Rhetoric, and the Making of Images, 400–1200* (New York: Cambridge University Press, 1998), pp. 160–1.
29 *eDIL* s.v. duille; s.v. duillend; s.v. duilleóg; s.v. 1 bileóc.
30 Gaston Bachelard, *The Poetics of Space*, trans. Maria Jolas (Boston, MA: Beacon Press, 1994), p. 89.
31 *Auraicept*, §6.5–6, p. 51.

32 Whitley Stokes (ed.), *Acallamh na Senórach* in *Irische Texte*, vol. IV (Leipzig: S. Hirzel, 1900), lines 3669–70. This translation is given by Ann Dooley, *Playing the Hero: Reading the Irish Saga Táin Bó Cúalnge* (Toronto: Toronto University Press, 2006), p. 40.

33 Several Irish tracts on poetry and its practitioners are extant—see for instance the eighth-century law tract *Uraicecht na Ríar: The Poetic Grades of Early Irish Law*, ed./trans. Liam Breatnach (Dublin: DIAS, 1987). As tracts on poetic composition such as the Old Irish 'Cauldron of Poesy' show, even prescriptive treatises are simultaneously metaphor-laden creative compositions: see Amy Mulligan, '"The Satire of the Poet Is a Pregnancy": Pregnant Poets, Body Metaphors and Cultural Production in Medieval Ireland', *Journal of English and Germanic Philology* 108.4 (October 2009), 481–505.

34 Though widely criticized, two such studies are Francesco Benozzo, *Landscape Perception in Early Celtic Literature* (Aberystwyth: Celtic Studies Publications, 2004), and Siewers, *Strange Beauty*. For a survey of Celtic environmental literature and its scholarship, see A. Joseph McMullen and Kristen Carella, 'Locating Place and Landscape in Early Insular Literature', *Journal of Literary Onomastics* 6 (2017), 1–10.

35 *MD* I, p. 75; *MD* V, p. 95.

36 Bede, *Historia*, I.1, pp. 20–1.

37 Máire Ní Mhaonaigh, 'Of Bede's "Five Languages and Four Nations": The Earliest Writing from Ireland, Scotland and Wales', in Clare Lees (ed.), *The Cambridge History of Early Medieval English Literature* (Cambridge: Cambridge Universtity Press, 2012), pp. 99–119, at 119.

38 See Chapter 3 on the Western Apache belief that wisdom sits in places and we must drink from them.

1
Holy islands: transformative landscapes and the origins of an Irish spatial poetics

Bede writes that 'in the remotest angle of the world' (*in extremo mundi angulo*) a good, wise man (*bonus et sapiens*), equipped with the highest knowledge of the scriptures, 'wrote a book on the holy places which is useful to many readers and especially to those who live very far from the places where the patriarchs and apostles dwelt, and only know about them what they have learned from books'.[1] Through the writings of the Irish monk Adomnán, abbot of Iona, the places of the Holy Land come to the British Isles. Adomnán's *De locis sanctis* (*DLS*), most likely written between 679 and 688,[2] is the earliest extant account of travel to Jerusalem written in Britain. In it Adomnán, one of Europe's most learned scholars, tells the story of a Gaulish bishop's journey to the Holy Land, after which a storm delivers him to Adomnán, who uses the bishop's reports, other sources and his own literary innovations to develop a verbalized Jerusalem. Having rendered this holy landscape into words and onto manuscript pages, Adomnán then bestows the valuable gift on the scholarly Anglo-Saxon King Aldfrith (referred to as Flann Fína in Irish sources), who, more than any other Anglo-Saxon king before or after him, was poised to appreciate and advance an Irish literature of the holy places. Likely raised in Ireland and trained by Irish scholars,[3] 'more culturally Irish than he was Anglo-Saxon and more fluent in Gaelic than he was in Old English',[4] Aldfrith uses his position to promote this Irish-authored text. Bede tells us that King Aldfrith actively disseminated *DLS* throughout his kingdom: 'through his kindness (*largitionem*), it was circulated for lesser folk to read'.[5] Aldfrith was Adomnán's ideal reader and patron, and he had a keen eye for a potential bestseller.

Bede carries forward Aldfrith's mission of propagating Adomnán's text among an Anglo-Saxon readership by featuring a precis of *DLS* in his *Historia*.[6] Adomnán's *DLS* thus becomes a regally endorsed Irish rendering into words of the Christian world's most important landscape; its ambitious goal is to allow the wider population of the British Isles, who live far from the Holy Land (though perhaps not as far as Adomnán himself), to nonetheless know and travel it through this book. This Irish poetics of holy space was propelled into extensive European circulation, so that 800 years later pilgrims and writers of travel literature were still relying on what became one of the most widely read accounts of the Holy Land: DLS is preserved in more than thirty-nine manuscripts and quoted throughout the Middle Ages.[7]

An Irishman writing space in the North Atlantic, Adomnán and his composition of a travel narrative fusing geography and biblical exegesis was catalyzed by an appeal Augustine made in the fourth century when Christian interest in sacred topography was growing, and when 'movement in a geographical space was presented as one way of appropriating, understanding and recalling the Christ'.[8] As Thomas O'Loughlin has shown in his excellent study of DLS as scriptural exegesis, Augustine argued 'that among the skills or tools needed by the Christian scholar to resolve the "knots" [*aenigmata*] in the Scriptures was a book/books on the geography of Palestine', and Adomnán fulfilled this need with DLS.[9] Interest in the Holy Land and the uses to which a detailed engagement of its places were put ultimately widened the geography of the East, however. As O'Loughlin explains, for Christians in the West, temporally and geographically distant biblical events nonetheless 'directly affected every moment of their lives', and they expected prophesied scriptural events to similarly involve and 'overtake them wherever they actually lived. As such, the DLS is as much a blueprint for a sacramental Holy Land on Iona or in Northumbria as it is a piece of geography.'[10] Adomnán produced a transformative and richly exegetical geographic text focused on Holy Land sites; however, his complex scripting of Jerusalem's topography also provided a model for writing the North Atlantic world. The accounts of voyaging monks seeking a local *herimum in ociano* in Adomnán's own *Vita Sancti Columbae* (*VSC*) and the anonymously authored voyage tales (*Navigatio Sancti Brendani* and vernacular Irish *immrama*), which place the Promised Land of the Saints in the watery spaces beyond Britain and Ireland, show how by the late eighth century an Irish poetics of space combined the geographies of the East and the West. The present chapter traces this development and its expansion from religious writing about the Holy Land into wider forms of literature of and about the North Atlantic.

Arculf and Adomnán: creating a spatial narrative

Any successful spatial narrative needs a path, and a pathfinder—eyes through which we gaze on the text's remarkable places, feet to carry us along the road, hands with which we reach out and feel that cool stone or the holy water running over our fingers. Through this figure, the audience or readership gains a persuasive sense of having been there and experienced contact with the wondrous things described. Adomnán provides such a guide in Arculf, and instills our trust in him as a careful observer and authoritative reader of the holy places of Jerusalem. Arculf is referred to by name eighty-six times in *DLS*,[11] which is in striking contrast to Bede's reworking of the text, in which Arculf is not mentioned even once after his initial introduction, with Bede providing a catalogue of sites rather than an embodied journey through them. A holy bishop from Gaul knowledgeable of distant places, Arculf is described by Adomnán as 'a truthful and quite reliable witness' (*uerax index et satis idoneus*) who spent nine months in Jerusalem's environs 'traversing the holy places in daily visitations' (*loca sancta cotidianis uisitationibus peregrans*).[12] As Adomnán presents it, in response to the Irish monk's careful questioning Arculf describes the holy sites, with Adomnán subsequently structuring his *DLS* narrative to impart an immediate experience of these places via Arculf's body and impressions. Throughout the text, this traveler is referred to reverentially as 'holy Arculf' (*sanctus Arculfus*),[13] with friendly familiarity as 'our Arculf' (*Arculfus noster*)[14] or, in phrasing that emphasizes community, 'our brother Arculf' (*noster sanctus frater Arculfus*).[15] In several cases Adomnán also quotes Arculf's speech, giving another level of immediacy and veracity, and transporting us to the performed present of the Holy Land stage itself.[16]

Through the character Arculf, Adomnán animates the Holy Land and helps us to be imaginatively present on the pilgrimage.[17] *DLS* transmits an embodied, sense-based engagement with the Holy Land, as illustrated by multiple examples. For instance, Arculf is described viewing various relics, emphasized by the formula 'with his own eyes' (*qui illud propriis conspexit obtutibus*).[18] His physical touch is also consistently noted. When Arculf sees the chalice from which Christ drank while on the cross and after his resurrection, through an opening in the reliquary's lid 'he touched it with his own hand which he had kissed' (*manu tetigit propria osculatus*),[19] an act that can be understood as bringing Christ's lips to his own. Arculf engages physically with relics and sites, his bodily contact both verifying and channeling the concrete reality of the divine, and Adomnán's prose helps us experience these miracles. At the very hour of the anniversary of Christ's Ascension, Arculf is present on site and feels the intense blast of wind so strong that 'all lie stretched face downward on the ground until the terrible tempest passes' (*omnes tamdiu in terra prostratis uultibus superstrati iacent donec illa terribilis procella pertranseat*).²⁰ In Bethlehem, the water originally poured from a vessel to bathe the newborn Christ miraculously continues to flow from a rock: 'Our friend Arculf saw it with his own eyes and washed his face in it' (*Quam noster Arculfus propriis obtutibus inspexit et in ea faciem lauit*).²¹ At the River Jordan, where John baptized Jesus, Arculf relates that he 'swam to and fro across the stream' (*transnatuauit fluuium*), and reports that at the holy site a tall cross is planted in the river bed. Here the water rises up to 'the neck of a very tall man standing' (*ad collum lingissimi uenit stantis uiri*), or during dry months, 'to his breast' (*ad mamellas*).²²

Adomnán includes details that encourage the audience to similarly envelop themselves in the holy sites, and, as in the previous paragraph, we imagine the feeling of being immersed in that water to the neck or breast depending on where we are in the seasonal calendar. At the Dead Sea, which Arculf 'used to frequent' (*frequentauit*), the salt was tested by his 'three senses' (*tribus sensibus*), those of 'sight and taste and touch' (*uisu et tactu atque gustu*).²³ Adomnán then gives the Dead Sea's measurements, which demonstrates how Adomnán situates sense-based experiences within well-attested Holy Land cartographies. Measurements are also provided when Arculf drinks from the well, twenty oriai or forty cubits deep, where Jesus requested water from a Samaritan woman (John 4). When Adomnán explains that 'an oria or cubit is the measure formed by both arms extended on either side' (*oria ergo siue cubitus utriusque manus a latere extensio utroque*),²⁴ we are inclined to extend our own arms to understand the well's depth, and thus comprehend Holy Land spaces using our own bodies, but from a significant geographic remove. Adomnán provides bodily cues and access points in his travelogue to help the audience become involved: to understand how it might look, feel—even taste—to be present in these distant holy places.

In other cases, Adomnán uses the present tense and skillful dramatic narration so the audience too can witness a miracle involving a famed relic. In his wonderful account of the linen cloth or napkin that remained in the sepulcher once Christ had risen (John 20:1–9), the 'King of the Saracens, Mavias' (Muawiyah I, or Caliph

Mu'āwiyah ibn Abī Ṣufyān, r. 661–80 CE) is called on to judge whether the 'infidel Jews' or the 'Christian Jews' should gain custodianship of the object. When placed in a fire, the cloth takes on a life of its own, and, rising intact from the flaming pyre, it begins to

> surgens quasi auis expansis alis coepit in sublimae uolare et utrasque desidentes contra se populi partes et quasi in procinctu belli consertas sedentes acies de summis prospiciens.
>
> (flutter on high like a bird with outstretched wings gazing down from above on the two factions of the people thus at variance with one another, two armies set as it were in battle array.)[25]

After swooping about for a few minutes, the miraculous cloth then floats down and swerves towards the party of Christians who have been exhorting Christ all the while, and alights among them.

Adomnán captures our attention with the spectacle of the animated cloth transformed into a divinely sent bird that soars above crowds marshaled like two armies, a battlefield image familiar from North Atlantic heroic literature; he uses dramatic stories and arresting, resonant imagery to enliven technical descriptions of the faraway Holy Land and its treasures. Adomnán also suggests how an audience remotely situated might celebrate this miracle:

> qui Deo gratias leuatis ad caelum manibus agentes cum ingenti laetatione ingeniculantes sudarium Domini magna cum honorificentia suscipiunt ad se de caelo uenerabile emisum donum ymnificasque laudes Christo eius donatori ...
>
> (Lifting their hands to heaven they give thanks to God with great rejoicing, and falling on their knees they receive with great honor this venerable gift sent down to them from heaven. They render hymns of praise to Christ its donor ...)[26]

By occupying the performative present of this scene, the readership or listening congregation can physically participate with the original witnesses, lifting hands, thanking God, falling on knees and singing hymns. Adomnán's prose elides differences in time and space and allows his audience to revere the miraculous relics present in Jerusalem's Holy Places, even while situated in Britain and Ireland. Adomnán constructs a landscape of words that the reader or listener is invited to imaginatively inhabit and experience—the cues and details he gives us, mediated via Arculf's body, make this experience real.

Practicing, writing and reading a Holy Land

By emphasizing Arculf's input and movements through the Holy Land, we become familiar with him as an observant, attentive wayfarer, but Arculf's mode of spatial practice in *DLS* also privileges repetition. Arculf routinely visits important places multiple times: 'Arculf, who used often to visit (*frequentabat*) the sepulcher of the Lord ... told me this definitely'[27]; 'A sedulous frequenter (*sedulus frequentator*) of the holy places, the holy Arculf used to visit the church of the holy Mary'[28]; 'Arculf, a frequenter of the above-mentioned holy places (*frequentator locorum*), visited a field in Bethany',[29] and so on.[30] On the one hand, a goal of these formulae is to build Arculf's authority as someone who has observed these sites carefully—not just once or twice, but many times over. The larger point, however, is that Adomnán's *DLS* also endorses our own slow engagement and repeated visitation of these places. While Arculf models physical practice, audiences can undertake this imaginatively, and, as we have seen, Adomnán's text is carefully constructed for a distant body of readers and listeners, and not just Jerusalem tourists. Indeed, even for travelers to the Holy Land, pilgrimages were driven, framed and later reanimated by textual models. We know that in later periods an important element of pilgrimage was writing one's own account, and later returning to it and other authors' descriptions, to meditatively relive the experience and gain ongoing devotional benefits.[31] Actual pilgrimage was only one part of the encounter, and thus Holy Land texts were of prime importance for both virtual and actual pilgrims.

The frequency with which the Iona community (and other participants in the Divine Office more generally) would have thought, heard and read about these places in other contexts, is important for understanding Adomnán's expectations of how *DLS* might be used. Adomnán starts our virtual journey in *DLS* with a verbal map of Jerusalem, numbering the towers (eighty-four) and gates (six) linked by the city's walls. Adomnán then provides an itinerary that follows a clockwise route, the traditionally auspicious direction for an Irish journey: 'That is the order then when you make the circuit from the above-mentioned gate of David, northwards and then eastwards, through the spaces between the various gates and towers' (*Hic itaque ordo per earundem portarum et turrium intercapidines a porta Dauid supra memorata per circuitum septemtrionem uersus et exinde ad orientem dirigitur*).[32] It is no surprise that we begin at the gates, and are not given directions for traveling to the Holy Land from the British Isles. Few readers would physically undertake the actual pilgrimage; many, however, would mentally contemplate Jerusalem at a significant geographic remove. O'Loughlin explains that 'Regarding the walls and towers, Psalm 47:12–14 tells its hearer—and the community of Iona would have heard it at least once a week in the Office—to walk around Jerusalem and narrate the number of her towers (*narrate in turribus eius*) and to study her walls so that the next generation may be told of God's care. Adomnán has now made this information available.'[33]

The scene that immediately follows in *DLS* is a description of Jerusalem's cleansing and new beginning every September; it also suggests the cyclical liturgical calendar and the annual celebration of important moments in Judeo-Christian history.[34] Adomnán describes Jerusalem's situation atop a hill, where every year, on September 12, people from many nations arrive to do business, their goods carried by livestock that fill the city with a stench and cover the roads with excrement. However, God has arranged Jerusalem on an incline so that on the very night the throngs depart, heavy rains fall and purifying torrents rush through to cleanse the city and its environs of 'abominable filth' (*sordes abhominabiles*), and 'after such a baptism of Jerusalem straightaway the copious flood ceases' (*et post talem Hierusolimitanam baptizationem continuatim eadem pluuialis exuberatio cessat*).[35] Through God's spatial planning, Jerusalem becomes a routinely purified holy place, annually cleansed by rains that remove the detritus of secular peoples and worldly transactions. While the mercantile throngs are not punished, the event echoes the biblical Flood and typologically linked Christian baptism, and *DLS* gives the impression that Jerusalem, through God, seeks to erase all marks of the contemporary peoples who use it.

Adomnán thus writes of a Jerusalem cleared of local, contemporary inhabitants at the point of our virtual entry into this verbal landscape. This also works to facilitate an identification of the sacred places as the text's main characters, a principle that underlies the idea of pilgrimage itself and exemplifies the belief that Jerusalem's spaces are the most important, sanctity-exuding relics. Additionally, although this land is holy for multiple religions, Adomnán's language choices make it clear that Jerusalem is baptized, an act that appropriates it for a Christian readership. Adomnán's aims are spiritual, with his travelogue devoid of the overt political and colonial intent of later pilgrimage narratives produced during the Crusades. Nonetheless, as we will see, rewriting revered places as emptied of their contemporary inhabitants to entice the audience's own inhabitation and settlement is a strategy developed across the spatial literatures of Ireland, from the *dindshenchas* poems to Norman-authored texts like Gerald of Wales's *Topographia* and H. of Saltrey's *Tractatus de Purgatorio Sancti Patricii*. Finally, this scene highlights some particularly Irish interests and devices in writing a holy poetics of space. The significance given to cleansing waters, baptismal immersion and purification, both in the opening of *DLS* and throughout the text, also drives the Hiberno-Latin and Irish vernacular accounts of religious travelers and voyaging pilgrims, who are transformed in Western holy spaces, those purifying, even baptismal, waters beyond Iona in the 'remotest angle of the world' from which Adomnán wrote, as explored later in this chapter.[36]

My focus has been on Adomnán's verbal mappings, yet many manuscripts of *DLS* also feature his drawings of the most significant holy structures (see Figure 2 in the Conclusion).[37] Their creation is described by Adomnán within the text itself, who explains that his plans are based on 'the model which (as already stated) the holy Arculf sketched for me on a wax surface' (*exemplar quod mihi, ut superius dictum est, sanctus Arculfus in paginola figurauit cerata depinximus*).[38] These diagrams are provided to facilitate mental comprehension, yet they additionally serve as templates for Western holy places and demonstrate how iconic Jerusalem structures might become conceptually fused with church buildings in Britain and Ireland. The image of the Temple of Jerusalem in the Book of Kells Temptation Scene (likely produced on Iona), for instance, appears to have been modeled on Iona's principal church, and attests to the ways in which sacred landscape features bring East and West together.[39] Adomnán's manuscript renderings of Holy Land spaces, verbal and visual, were appropriated and materialized in several ways by North Atlantic communities to be practiced locally. The reader can mimic Arculf, visiting these sites time and again, through liturgical practice and ritual, individual contemplation and possibly even prayer at material sites with architectural links to Jerusalem.

Repeated contemplation of important sites is key, and a text, as a re-readable narrative, makes that possible. *DLS* opens with the statement that Adomnán interviewed Arculf and accurately recorded his experiences, but the process continues: 'I first wrote it down on tablets: it will now be written succinctly on parchment' (*et primo in tabulis describenti ... quae nunc in membranis breui textu scribuntur*).⁴⁰ Adomnán makes us conscious witnesses to the process of writing: the conversion of Arculf's oral testimony into notes made on a wax tablet, which is then reworked into the polished textual account preserved in manuscript form. While other books contain information about Jerusalem (as Adomnán attests), Adomnán himself creates a text that allows for embodied reading by conveying what Arculf saw, felt and experienced on his circuit (*circuitum*) of Jerusalem.⁴¹ Arculf and other sources provide the material, but Adomnán crafts the verbal landscape, and ongoing attention to the writing process reminds us that *DLS* represents Adomnán's narrative design. The narrative reworking is more crucial than the source—in fact, it has even been suggested that Arculf is himself a fiction: the shipwrecked bishop who washes ashore to Adomanán is—surprisingly for a high-ranking churchman—unattested by any other sources.⁴² Irrespective of Arculf's historical status, the point is that Adomnán develops these materials into a form that, as Bede commends, allows those in distant places to know the Holy Land though his words. Adomnán asks those who read *DLS* to pray for Arculf, but Adomnán's own role in setting out these experiences, also warrants an appreciative audience's prayers:

> Horum ergo lectorem ammoneo experimentorum ut pro me missello peccatore eorundem craxatore Christum iudicem saeculorum exorare non neglegat.
>
> (Thus I admonish the reader of these experiences that he neglect not to pray Christ the judge of generations on behalf of me, the writer, a wretched sinner.)⁴³

As shall be seen throughout this book, the act of writing or textualizing places for later consumption is continually emphasized; and though his authorship is often overlooked, Adomnán's *DLS* is a foundational model for what it is to write space, to create inhabitable landscapes from words.

From Holy Land wayfaring to wavefaring: Adomnán's *Vita Sancti Columbae*

I argue that *VSC*, completed 697–704,⁴⁴ is a development of the Hiberno-Latin spatial poetics we see exemplified in *DLS*; in *VSC*, Adomnán looks west and maps out North Atlantic holy places.

Adomnán's biography of 'the saint's life in pilgrimage' (*VSC* II.10) traces Columba's own spatial practice: both his literal journeys through the island of Iona as well as his participation in monastic voyaging into unknown waters. Columba is constructed according to the model of Christ: Jesus's acts and movements sanctify Jerusalem, and Adomnán's Columba does the same for Iona and its environs by enacting Christ-like miracles. Indeed, a final act before he dies is to climb a hill to gaze over and bless Iona's monastic island landscape, with monks and pilgrims later retracing these routes in their own processions, occasionally carrying Columba's healing relics with them.

As Jennifer O'Reilly points out, while Columba was famed as a highly learned scholar, and Adomnán could have cited his learned exegesis on events in Christ's life, in *VSC* Adomnán instead presents him as a living embodiment of Jesus and other biblical figures.[45] In arguing that 'Adomnán's two works are more complementary in objective and technique than has generally been recognized', O'Reilly notes that the miraculous stream which bathed the newborn Christ (*DLS* II.3, discussed previously), is reproduced in *VSC* (II.10) when Columba generates water from a rock to baptize a local child, thus fusing a Holy Land miracle to the North Atlantic coast and generating a holy spring that, Adomnán assures us, one can still visit on Iona.[46] It is worth recalling O'Loughlin's analysis of how scriptural moments in Jesus's life detailed in Adomnán's writings were routinely meditated on as part of the Divine Office. Combined with Christ-like miracles performed by Columba in Iona's landscape, this shows Adomnán's efforts and skill in allowing Holy Land miraculous events and places to be reenacted, performed and experienced on the site at Iona (or at any of the locations where *DLS* and *VSC* were read). Early readerships and audiences could thus overlay Holy Land places, events and spatial practices onto their own North Atlantic locales. As in *DLS*, Adomnán also uses language, literary devices and formal structures to invite the audience into the experience of these holy spaces and their saintly practitioners, and some of his most impressive scenes move us from land and into water. Writing on an island from which several voyages took place, perhaps as part of a possible North Atlantic exploratory program at Iona,[47] and attuned to the very real dangers of sailing unpredictable waters, Adomnán shifts from a spatial poetics of terrestrial wayfaring to wavefaring.

The appropriation of biblical figures and narratives for North Atlantic seascapes begins immediately in *VSC*. Adomnán introduces Columba by explaining that he shares a name with the prophet Jonah[48]; though the name sounds different in each language, the Hebrew *iona*, Greek *peristera* and Latin *columba* have identical meaning, and the association by name of the two prophets is also meaningful, as Adomnán tells us: 'So good and great a name is believed not to have been put upon the man of God without divine dispensation' (*Tale tantumque vocabulum homini dei non sine divina inditum providentia creditur*).[49] Adomnán figures Columba as the latter-day Irish embodiment of a biblical prophet who has undergone a penitential voyage in a sea-beast's belly (perhaps referencing Columba's self-imposed exile from Ireland), and who, the wiser and holier for it, possesses insights into both the deep and its creatures.[50] Several of Columba's miracles involve prophecies regarding sea-beasts and voyages, and he often intervenes to calm seas or subdue water monsters with prayer so that others may return safely to firm land. Adomnán shapes a vision of voyaging and travel as important but dangerous—this links the two texts. In *DLS* the main character, Arculf, only narrowly escapes death at sea and, shipwrecked, washes ashore, where he delivers his story to Adomnán, who creates a narrative Jerusalem so that others might gain the benefits yet be spared the journey. Adomnán's *VSC* similarly conveys the idea that voyages are perhaps best undertaken in manuscript boats on seascapes of words rather than within the frequently threatening environment of the North Atlantic.

In one episode, Columba foresees a 'prodigious monster' in the waters beyond Iona and advises the monk Berach to avoid the route. When Berach ignores Columba's words, it is no surprise that an enormous sea monster (*cetus*) 'rose up like a mountain, and opened gaping jaws, with many teeth' (*se instar montis eregens, ora aperit patula nimis dentosa supernatans*),[51] giving us (and the monks) a terrifying view into this beast's maw. Berach and his companions only narrowly survive and stay afloat in the wake generated by the creature's movement. A counter-example modeling obedience to and the power of calling on God is provided when the saint informs another monk, Baithéne (successor to Columba as abbot of Iona), of that same sea-beast. Baithéne responds that both he and the beast are under God's power: '"Go in peace", said the saint; "your faith in Christ will protect you from this danger"' (*Sanctus 'Vade' ait, 'in pace. Fides tua in Christo té ab hoc defendet periculo'*).[52] Baithéne and his monks encounter the whale; yet, while all the others are frightened, Baithéne fearlessly raises his hands to bless both the sea and the sea monster, which then dives under the waves and disappears to plague them no more. *VSC* is populated with such examples,[53] and Adomnán's writing style, his use of dialogue and dramatic scene-setting, help the audience access the experience of drifting in the wake of a marvelous beast, protected by invoking God, as well, of course, by the distance the manuscript page provides.

In several cases, Columba foretells or speaks of events elsewhere as they unfold, which typically involves quoting Columba's speech directly. Multiple scenes elaborate the three voyages of Cormac as a 'soldier of Christ' (*Christi miles*) seeking 'a desert place in the ocean' (*herimum in ociano*).[54] The account of Cormac's third voyage most clearly models virtual travel, with Columba, situated on the island of Iona, participating in the voyage mentally from a physical remove. Cormac and his companions nearly lose their lives after fourteen days and nights of fierce winds drive them to the northernmost regions so that 'such a voyage appeared to be beyond the range of human exploration, and one from which there could be no return' (*ejusmodi navigatio ultra humani excursus modum et inremeabilis videbatur*).[55] On the tenth hour of that ominous fourteenth day, they are surrounded and almost overwhelmed by dreadful creatures—very small, but extremely dangerous and covering the ocean's surface:

> quae horribili impetu carinam et latera pupimque et proram ita forti feriebant percusura, ut pellicium tectum navis penetrales putarentur penetrare posse.
>
> (and these struck with terrible impact the bottom and sides, the stern and prow, with so strong a thrust that they were thought able to pierce and penetrate the skin-covering of the ship.)[56]

Terrified and weeping in alarm, Cormac and his voyagers pray to God, who helps those in times of need. We are shown the risks of moving beyond the known human world in a hide boat; Adomnán's prose expresses the urgency of the situation as well as the voyagers' fear and immediate vulnerability.[57] The passage calls us to transport ourselves to the scene and participate in quelling these frightening waters. We learn that, though distant in body, Columba is nonetheless 'in spirit present with Cormac in the ship' (*spiritu tamen praesens in navi cum Cormaco*); and, ringing the bell to summon the monks to the oratory, he prophetically declares,

Fratres, tota intentione pro Cormaco orate, qui nunc humanae discursionis limitem inmoderate navigando excessit. Nunc quasdam monstruosas ante non visas et pene indicibiles patitur horrificas perturbationes. Itaque nostrís commembribus in periculo intollerabili constitutís mente conpati debemus fratribus, et dominum exorare cum eís. Ecce enim nunc Cormacus cum suís nautís faciem lacrimís ubertim inrigans Christum intentius precatur, et nos ipsum orando adjuvemus, ut austrum flantem ventum usque hodie per xiiii. dies nostri miseratus in aquilonem convertat. Qui videlicet aquiloneus ventus navem Cormaci de periculís retrahat.

(Brothers, pray with your whole might for Cormac, who now in his voyage has far exceeded the bounds of human travel. Now he endures the terrors of certain horrible and monstrous things never before seen, and almost indescribable. In our minds, therefore, we must share the sufferings of our brothers, our fellow-members, who are placed in unendurable danger; and we must pray to the Lord with them. For now behold Cormac, copiously watering his face with tears, prays earnestly with his sailors to Christ, and let us help him in praying, that Christ may take pity upon us, and may turn into a north wind the south wind that has blown for fourteen days, until today; so that this northerly wind may bring Cormac's ship out of its dangers.)[58]

Geographic expanses are collapsed when Columba miraculously hears the call of his monks; so too for the audience of *VSC*, spatial and temporal distances disappear, and we are transported into the narrative's world. Columba verbally conjures up Cormac and his voyagers, the sea's swell and the suffering it causes; then, using direct address, he commands his monks in Iona, and the readership or audience too, to participate: 'we must share the sufferings'; 'we must pray to the Lord'; 'now behold Cormac ... and let us help him in praying'. These interventions are successful, and Columba, praying before the altar, rises, thanks God and wipes his own tears, saying they must all congratulate the friends they have prayed for, because God will change the winds to deliver the monks back to Iona. And 'simultaneously, with his words' (*et continuo cum ejus voce*), the winds are reversed.[59] Cormac's boat returns safely, and Adomnán in conclusion highlights the greatness and wisdom of this blessed saint who can command the winds and ocean by invoking Christ's name.[60] These passages model virtual engagement with distant locations and events, and, through Columba's actions and Adomnán's writing, the audience travels dangerous yet instructive places in safety.

Though testifying to the marvels of the ocean and the power of uttering Christ's name, the journeys depicted by Adomnán hardly serve as advertisements for the benefits of actual voyaging: most characters narrowly avoid death on their perilous travels. Often, these voyagers, like Cormac and another monk, Baitán, fail to find a 'desert place in the sea', and their stories warn against such travel, with the texts structured so that the audience experiences great relief when the voyagers avoid shipwreck and return to familiar land. Westley Follet observes that, when considering Cormac's and Baitán's unsuccessful attempts to locate desert spaces in the ocean, 'we are led to wonder if the author of *Vita Columbae* did not entirely approve of such activities and is quietly trying to make a point ... when read allegorically, his tales of Cormac and Baitán may have given the most stout-hearted monk second thoughts about seeking his *herimum, in ociano* or elsewhere'.[61] In short, Adomnán, like many other writers (including Cassian, and perhaps also Pope Gregory I and Gildas, Follett surmises), seems to suggest that the life of an isolated hermit who voyages to find the desert spaces of the Atlantic, whether for exposure to wondrous and miraculous things or to practice a disciplined, eremitic life, cannot really be advocated. Life as part of a community is the preferred alternative. While a desire for actual travel is understandable, more can perhaps be accomplished by reading or imaginatively undergoing these voyages, while continuing life as part of a terrestrial community. Adomnán provides a solution. I argue that, with his writing, Adomnán enables verbalized engagement with these remote and dangerous places so that both monastic communities and other audiences might have access to the transformations catalyzed by imaginative spatial movement through the marvelous seascapes of the North Atlantic.

A pearl of God ('*margarita Dei*') from the North Atlantic: *Navigatio Sancti Brendani*

Saints Columba (521–97) and Brendan of Clonfert (486–575) have been linked for a long time. Adomnán, the first writer to record Brendan's existence, describes in *VSC* their meeting on an island near Iona where Brendan, having sailed from Ireland, witnessed Columba's sanctity in the form of a bright ball of fire shining upward like a column of light above Columba's head as he performed the consecration at the altar.[62] The French scholar Paul Tuffrau even argues that Columba himself was the *Navigatio*'s composer,[63] with Brendan telling his story to Iona's holy abbot, similar to how the shipwrecked Arculf was deposited on the shore in front of another Iona abbot, Adomnán, to deliver his travel account. While this delightful scenario is a fiction, the impression that the Columban *familia* was involved in the production of what became one of medieval Europe's most popular narratives is understandable. *Navigatio Sancti Brendani Abbatis* (*NSB*) ('Voyage of Saint Brendan the Abbot') is a Latin account of this Irish monk's journey to the North Atlantic's holy places.[64] Like Adomnán's own compositions, *NSB* is a rich spatial narrative structured to invite virtual habitation of its verbalized landscapes and seascapes. It emphasizes the value (and difficulty) of properly reading a landscape, of comprehending its features and powers. It models repeated spatial practice, or wayfaring movement, through landscapes narratively endowed with transformative properties, which, when appropriately engaged, can make the traveler, virtual or actual, wiser, holier, more heroic. Finally, anticipating both later Irish vernacular texts and some recent ecocriticism, it insinuates a belief that the environment is not so much a textual backdrop as a central character whose story warrants deep contemplation.

The *NSB* was written by an Irish monk, and, per current scholarly consensus, was most likely composed in Ireland some time between the second half of the eighth and the beginning of the ninth century[65]; though, as James Carney has argued, *NSB* represents a culmination of the development of materials about Brendan circulating from the early seventh century.[66] Part allegory, part monastic devotional text, part gripping travel tale, *NSB* became very popular and widespread in its Latin form, as its preservation in 120 extant manuscripts—a number that must originally have been much higher—attests.[67] This Irish engagement with North Atlantic spaces was furthermore appropriated throughout medieval Europe, demonstrated by *NSB*'s extensive translation into almost every medieval European vernacular (Old Norse, Middle English, French, German, Dutch, etc.), with the interesting exception of Irish.[68] The *Navigatio* shaped perspectives on (and maps of) North Atlantic island spaces and seascapes west of Ireland for centuries. While some have been moved to replicate the journey, most famously Timothy Severin,[69] by far the greatest impact has been on text and imagination. For many audiences, *NSB* has modeled, through the brilliant tale of a trip around an astounding Irish archipelagic space, how to encounter, understand and be improved by remarkable physical environments.

Holy islands

The voyage's leader is Brendan, proclaimed as a 'pearl of God' (*margarita Dei*) by a man who materializes on a remote island with sustenance for the famished voyagers on Holy Saturday.[70] A pearl is a seed of sand, embraced by the bi-valve oyster, which, over lengthy time in the waters, matures into a lustrous, precious jewel. The text subtly implies that, like the pearl in its oyster, saintly Brendan, encased in the currach that is his shell, is nourished, developed and transformed by his seven-year journey through God's waters. Seafaring makes Brendan into a pearl of God, and an attentive audience can also be improved by imaginatively voyaging with Brendan at the helm: every reader and listener, *NSB* suggests, can claim a seat in Brendan's vessel.

Ox-hide currachs and story-filled boats as books

NSB opens with a story within a story, bringing the themes of narrative and verbalization of spatial experience to the fore. When the monk Barinthus visits Brendan on his return from traveling to the Land of Promise of the Saints, Barinthus weeps deeply at his removal from that holy place, and throws himself to the ground. As Barinthus mourns for this paradise lost, Brendan kindly kisses him, lifts him up and asks Barinthus instead to generate joy (*laetitia*) by telling his story: 'Show us the word of God and nourish our souls with the varied wonders that you saw in the ocean' (*Indica nobis uerbum Dei atque refice animas nostras de diuersis miraculis, que uidisti in oceano*).[71] As Brendan directs in this opening paragraph, what is desirable is a story, a narrative of seascape wonders, one that has the power to delight listening spirits.

The importance of talking about places and valuing discourses of space also features in Barinthus's brief narrative of his voyage to the Land of Promise of the Saints. This Edenic island can be reached via a cloud-enveloped journey and is situated a few hours beyond the monastic Island of Delights, itself three days' sail west of Ireland. Barinthus and his companions come to a river dividing the island, when a glowing figure appears and tells the sorrowful monks that, though the Lord has shown them this place, the land beyond the river is for his saints, and they may not cross. When their response is to ask the man his name and origin, he explains that the place they occupy now, this holy island, is the real subject worth pursuing: 'Why do you not ask me about the island?' (*Quare me non interrogas de ista insula?*)[72] he admonishes, and proceeds to detail the island's properties and how they transform human experience. The travelers have been there for a year, he explains, without feeling the need for food, drink, clothing or sleep, for Jesus is the light of the island and it is thus always day, the island having been such a paradise from the beginning of time. This man's account of the Promised Land of the Saints, and their gazing on it, is meant to be enough, for physical access is not part of God's plan for them. A pastoral metaphor delivered by the community members left behind at the monastic settlement off Ireland's coast reinforces this: 'Why, fathers, have you left your sheep wandering in the wood without a shepherd?' (*Cur, patres, dimisistis uestras oues sine pastore in ista silua errantes?*)[73] A message that monks belong with their communities, and that verbalized knowledge—the holy man's report as well as Barinthus's own to Brendan and his monks—perhaps should be enough, is implied throughout Barinthus's emotional performance.

Nonetheless, at the beginning of the story, Brendan seems to hear only part of the message, and is ignited by desire to visit this place himself. The next morning, Brendan seeks advice from the monks, his spiritual co-warriors (*conbellatores*):

> quia cor meum et omnes cogitaciones mee conglutinate sunt in una uoluntate. Tantum si uoluntas Dei est, terram de qua locutus est pater Barinthus, repromissionis sanctorum in corde meo proposui quaerere.
>
> (for my heart and all my thoughts are fixed on one determination. I have resolved in my heart if it is God's will—and only if it is—to go in search of the Promised Land of the Saints of which father Barinthus spoke.)[74]

When Brendan asks the monks, 'What advice would you give?' (*quod consilium mihi uultis dare?*),[75] his direct address invokes a response from the audience as well, perhaps suggesting that we must also decide whether narrative engagement is enough. Given Brendan's confession that the exploratory desire overwhelms all others, and the holy man's explicit directive to Barinthus that they are not to enter the land God maintains for his saints, one suspects that Brendan's response is to be read as rash and not altogether appropriate for a monastic leader. His obedient monks, however, say nothing, except that, having left their families and sacrificed their earthly inheritance, they will accept all consequences in following their leader.

As it turns out, compared to Barinthus's voyage of three days to the Land of Promise, Brendan's seven-year voyage, filled with challenges, terrors and wonders, problematizes the wisdom of actual travel. Brendan's monks, in their admission that they will sacrifice all to accompany him, proleptically comprehend this. As already discussed in this chapter, Adomnán's accounts of Arculf's shipwreck and the Columban monks' narrow escapes encode warnings about actual voyaging. Anticipating the problem of how to gain the benefits without risking the journey, Adomnán provides contemplative landscapes built of words. The *NSB* author does the same. By the time we are empathetically inflamed with Brendan's curiosity to explore the waters beyond Ireland in *NSB*, we find that we have already embarked on a safer version of the journey and proverbially entered the boat. We were reminded of this excellent possibility by Brendan's opening request for a story, a spirit-lifting account of the wonders Barinthus saw on his voyage.

Because Brendan was not sated by Barinthus's brief narrative, he potentially seeks to improve on it. Thus, Brendan and his monks set out for a distant region where, atop a mountain reaching out into the sea, Brendan pitches a tent in a place now known as 'Brendan's seat', where there is just enough space for one boat. The landscape that provides the starting point for their voyage fits perfectly—the beach just accommodates their currach—and the impression that they move through ordained spaces in the appropriate vehicle is developed elsewhere in the text.[76] Their boat is purpose-built onsite:

> Sanctus Brendanus et qui cum eo errant, acceptis ferramentis, fecerunt nauiculam leuissimam, costatam et columnatam ex silua, sicut mos est in illis partibus, et cooperuerunt illam coriis bouinis [atque rubrucatis] in roborina cortice. Et linierunt foris omnes iuncturas pellium ex butyro...
>
> (Saint Brendan and those with him got iron tools and constructed a light boat ribbed with wood and with a wooden frame, as is usual in those parts. They covered it with ox-hides tanned with the bark of oak and smeared all the joints of the hides on the outside with fat.)[77]

While it is a boat that is explicitly being made here, the description also suggests manuscript production: the use of the *lunellum* and other iron tools to scrape and clean the hide, which is then stretched and fixed with weights onto a wooden frame; the ox-hide eventually covered, not with fat, but with ink and illumination.

The lines separating in our minds the hides that form the boats from the hides that make the story, folded over to create manuscript pages, are collapsed. By engaging with the text, the audience gains a place within the currach, the space of encounter, and is thus permitted and encouraged to undertake the literary voyage.[78]

While the voyage tales feature a main character whose name gives the text its title ('Voyage of Saint Brendan' or 'Voyage of the Currach of Máel Dúin'), there are typically several anonymous people on board, and the readership or audience for the texts might imagine themselves as these largely nameless voyagers. As we will see, the *NSB* narrator sets scenes up from the perspective of the voyagers and skillfully manipulates the flow of information about places and events so that the audience experiences horror, revulsion and the need for flight simultaneously with the voyagers. This is a persuasive way of facilitating imaginative involvement, of helping the audience to participate, getting into the boat by getting into the book.

By highlighting what I call the 'boat as book' motif and its imagery, I argue that for many audiences, especially medieval readers, the ox-hide coracles could signify something beyond boats, and offer an increased scope of references to also suggest material literary production. Like *DLS* and *VSC*, *NSB* is highly concerned to model and describe literary spatial practice, to explore these seascapes through words and to allow the voyage to be undertaken by all readers and audience members. What does the *Navigatio* propose about how to read a landscape text, about how to move through topographical Irish writing? Here, and in the vernacular voyage tales as well, I maintain that we see a sophisticated conceptualization of the idea that we are to literally voyage, or 'row-about' these narratives; that the book or manuscript is our vessel of cognitive transport and contemplation.

Like Adomnán's spatial narratives, *NSB* includes details about emotive, corporeal and universal human experience—we hunger and thirst with the monks; are terrified when storms, monsters and demons attack; and celebrate when land is finally sighted. The narratively adept author is keen to convey the difficulties of the watery trials: for instance, the monks are blown for three months all around the ocean, and 'they could see nothing but sky and sea' (*Nihil poterant uidere nisi celum et mare*).[79] We too are relieved when they finally come to an island, but in a dramatic heightening of our shared anxiety they are repeatedly blown back over four days so that the desperate, weeping monks (*cum fletu*) beg God to help them, for they are utterly exhausted. Finally, after three days of prayer and fasting, they reach land.[80] The monks and Brendan frequently have tears in their eyes,[81] and these emotional cues model an affective pious practice that can move the audience as well, suggesting how we might not just imagine but also feel it for ourselves. *NSB*, like Adomnán's *DLS* and *VSC*, provides a script for our embodied experience of the text—it is not just a catalogue of holy sites in the waters beyond Ireland but also a set of guidelines showing how we might react and learn from time we spend in the boat. Significant detail is included in *NSB* to provide a convincing virtual encounter and trigger the transformative physical effects of moving through a sacred environment: these are key elements of an Irish poetics of holy space.

What do we gain by inhabiting the textual world of *NSB*? In several instances the narrative moves the audience through an unknown environment from the perspective of the naïve crew of monks rather than the wise visionary, Brendan. In passages that parallel the riddling watchman device used to great dramatic effect in vernacular Irish and Welsh texts, we also are called on to 'solve' and contemplate the nature of land, water and animals, through varied defamiliarizing techniques, which cause routine elements to be seen afresh in newly meaningful, often artistically enriched ways.[82] In one case, Brendan thinks he spies a man's shape perched on a rock, whereas the monks say it is a bird or ship; the shape is eventually discovered to be Judas Iscariot, a figure with rich symbolic resonances whose presence shows that the monks travel in a seascape that is far more than a naturalized North Atlantic space.

Another scene has us share the monks' confusion when we land on an 'island' whose nature is only later revealed in discussion with a knowing Brendan, who himself declines the experience of dwelling in this unusual space. Brendan and his monks are given food and sent to an island in the distance where they will pray from Holy Saturday until Easter morning and then celebrate the Resurrection. They row, but when the boat comes to a standstill, on Brendan's advice the monks jump out to pull it ashore. 'The island was stony and without grass. There were a few pieces of driftwood on it, but no sand on its shore' (*Erat autem illa insula petrosa sine ulla herba. Silua rara erat ibi, et in litore illius nihil de arena fuit*), and there the monks spend the night praying; but Brendan stays in the boat, 'For he knew the kind of island it was, but he did not want to tell them, lest they be terrified' (*Sciebat enim qualis erat illa insula, sed tamen noluit eis indicare, ne perterrerentur*).[83] Like the monks, we lack Brendan's knowledge, and so the suspense (and our own anxieties) are raised by his mysterious refusal to come ashore, and the knowledge that the others should be terrified. The *NSB* composer expertly builds the tension and spins out the scene, providing the easily visualized, familiar details of masses being said and fish and joints of meat being seasoned, and a fire being lit under their pot. 'When, however, they were plying the fire with wood and the pot began to boil, the island began to be in motion like a wave' (*Cum autem ministrarent lignis ignem et feruere cepisset cacabus, cepit illa insula se mouere sicut unda*),[84] and they call out for Brendan to save them. He pulls each one into the boat, and, abandoning everything else on the island, they sail away and the island drifts out to sea, their burning fire visible two miles away. Brendan then asks, 'Brothers, are you surprised at what this island has done?' (*Fratres, admiramini quod fecit hec insula?*),[85] and the audience is poised to answer with the confused monks that yes, it terrifies them deeply. Brendan tells them not to fear, that overnight God revealed to him that the *insula* is actually the greatest of all creatures in the ocean, named Jasconius; and we realize that the island's bareness, with only a few trees dotting its surface, is the enigmatic, riddling imagery of a water-beast's barnacled skin.

A year later they row again to the 'island', where they find last year's cooking pot, and Brendan articulates this marvelous space's lesson, telling the monks to watch and pray: 'Reflect on how God has subjected the savage beast under us without any inconvenience to us' (*Considerate quomodo subiugat Deus inmanissimam bestiam subtus nos sine ullo impedimento*),[86] after which they settle themselves on the 'island' to keep the Easter Vigil as before. The unlikely physical proof of the cooking pot that remains a year later implies that the sea-beast has not returned to the depths and flung the pot off in his movements, but has remained afloat, waiting to host the Easter Vigil for the voyagers God sends. Part of the message is that the world, the environment, is neither solid nor inhabitable until God makes it so.

Passages like these, which play on our capacity for misrecognition—such as the continued use of the term *insula* even when this creature has swum off—destabilize our reading of the landscape as a static, straightforward background against which events unfold. Here, the island is given a name, Jasconius, a form of Irish *iasc* ('fish'), though a variant in one manuscript of the *Vita Brendani* is the name 'Casconius,' with the Irish word for Easter, *Cásc*, making it in this one case an Easter beast.[87] Given a name and a

Holy islands

distinct identity, this 'island' moves of its own accord; and, even once its nature is known, the voyagers land and rest overnight on it for six successive years—in the miraculous sea, a massive beast is an island. This much-discussed sea-beast is known in other contemporary sources from Ireland and the British Isles. In the *Physiologus*, unsuspecting sailors land on the creature and similarly build fires, at which point it dives to the bottom of the sea, dragging the sailors and their ship down with it, and is allegorized as the wily devil that tempts sinners, their deeds binding them to the Devil who drags them into hellish fires.[88] In the vernacular of another North Atlantic tradition, the Old English Exeter Book includes a poem on a devilish sea monster that similarly outwits sailors before dragging them down to their deaths, as demons lure sinners into damnation.[89] Jacqueline Borsje provides an exhaustive survey of potential sources and resonances for related sea-beasts in Irish and Hiberno-Latin texts, and shows how diffuse the tradition of watery sea-beasts was in the early Irish and Hiberno-Latin sources. Isidore in the *Etymologiae* (XII.vi.8) equates the whale that swallowed Jonah with the Devil, based on Jonah's utterance that on leaving the whale's belly he emerges from the mouth of hell; this seems to underlie the further attribution of devilish nature to the island-beast.[90] Clearly a popular story that circulated widely in the North Atlantic, several *NSB* audience members would have recognized in Jasconius a beguiling, devilish monster, perhaps even a hell-mouth figure.

The scene in *NSB* is perhaps all the more remarkable in leading us to ultimately understand Brendan's 'island' in a completely different way: while all other sources include moralizing details regarding the beast's devilish nature, the Irish account shows a positive engagement where prayer is key. In the Irish-authored North Atlantic space of *NSB*, Jasconius is successfully rewritten to demonstrate the harmony achieved between Brendan's voyagers and the terrifying monsters of the ocean, now transformed into temporarily inhabitable landscapes. The Easter Vigil over Christ's body is reenacted in the North Atlantic, and, while the allusions are inexplicit and complicated, the voyagers' masses and vigils on the monster's back gesture, via Isidore's account of Jonah and *NSB*'s explicit paschal timing, towards Christ's Harrowing of Hell. The prayerful monks survive what could have been a final trip to the ocean's bottom, and a hellish 'landscape' becomes divine testimony. The voyagers, too, become more lustrous and pearl-like by participating in biblical events staged in and localized to the North Atlantic.

Another highly instructive oceanic marvel is encountered on Easter Sunday, when the boat comes to an extremely tall, wide tree so thickly covered with white birds that barely a branch or leaf can be seen. Brendan ardently desires to understand the symbolism of the tree and, weeping, throws himself to the ground and makes an impassioned plea to God to reveal the secret he sees before him.[91] Later, sitting in the boat, Brendan is approached by one of the birds, whose beating wings ring like a bell; when the bird gazes at Brendan, Brendan realizes God has answered his prayer. The bird explains that they are fallen angels and outlines their ongoing spatial practice, which, I argue, intentionally parallels the rowing about of Brendan and his crew: 'We wander through various regions of the air and the firmament and the earth, just like the other spirits that travel on their missions' (*Vagamur per diuersas partes aeris et firmamenti et terrarum, sicut alii spiritus qui mittuntur*), though they take the form of birds on Sundays and holy days to sing God's praise.[92] The bird informs Brendan that he and his monks have completed the first year of their seven-year journey, will return to this tree every Easter and, finally, will find the Land of Promise of the Saints. At vespers, beating their wings melodically, the birds sing, 'A hymn is due to thee, O God, in Zion, and a vow shall be paid to you in Jerusalem' (*Te decet hymnus, Deus, in Syon, et tibi reddetur uotum in Jerusalem*).[93] At the various canonical hours, the birds continue their praise. In some cases, the words they sing performatively parallel the changing landscape around them: 'When the dawn rose they chanted: "May the radiance of the Lord, our God, be upon us!"' (*Cum aurora refulsisset, ceperunt cantare: 'Et sit splendor Domini Dei nostri super nos'*).[94] Finally, the bird returns to give Brendan an itinerary for the next year (providing, as in the preface to *DLS*, a convenient index of sites for the audience as well). The monks set sail as the birds appropriately chant the very spatial Psalm 64: 'Hear us, God, our savior, our hope throughout all the boundaries of the earth and in the distant sea' (*Exaudi nos, Deus, salutaris noster, spes omnium finium terre et in mari longe*).[95] A medieval northwestern European audience who knew the psalms by heart could mentally move through the psalm's verses (which include details about God stilling the waves and watering the earth so it yields up fruits) and reflect on the psalm's relevance to Brendan's voyage, as well as on their own experiences at the western ends of the earth.

While this magnificent flock of birds constitutes a miraculous spectacle, the birds themselves are also representative of the celebrants of the liturgy familiar in churches throughout Christendom. As Martin McNamara writes, in *NSB*, 'with its account of the chanting of the divine office, the prolonged fasts and such like, the institutions and practices of monastic life in an Irish environment are faithfully reproduced',[96] making the text a *speculum monachorum*, as Elva Johnston phrases it.[97] This scene, like so much of the exotic, wonder-filled voyage, is also familiar, local and routinely practiced. What the monks experience at those distant ends of the earth is analogous to what any Christian might experience daily as part of liturgical devotions. The fallen angels in their white plumage are similar to mortal Christians who hope for redemption and respite through prayer and psalm singing. We might see *NSB* as a topographically grounded exegesis of these psalms—biblical lessons appropriated and re-dressed in the familiar environmental setting of the North Atlantic.

Furthermore, in other ways *NSB* shifts the Christian East into the geography of the West. On one island west of Ireland, the Devil appears as an Ethiopian boy, a localizing appropriation of an episode based on Athanasius' *Life of Anthony*.[98] Another island is filled with a fragrance like that of pomegranates (*malis punicis*),[99] the scent of the 'Phoenician apple' (*punicum malūm*) here perfuming the islands of the West. Paul the Hermit's island features a spring gushing out from a rock whose excess flow is then neatly re-absorbed.[100] This multi-layered North Atlantic rendition of Moses's water-producing miracle is reminiscent of the holy spring at Christ's nativity described in *DLS* and Iona's miraculous spring as it is presented in *VSC* (see previous discussion). These examples, along with the citation of Psalm 64's verses about the ends of the earth, illustrate how *NSB* maps the features and practices rooted in the Bible's Jerusalem onto the North Atlantic.

Brendan and his voyagers finally, after a seven-year circuit, reach their destination—the holy island whose description by Barinthus catalyzed their oceanic pilgrimage. Coming through a heavy darkness, a bright light shines around them, and they find their boat has reached the shore of a paradise covered in fruit trees and richly provided with springs. The island is so large that forty days' trekking does not bring them to its edges; and, when they reach the river described by Barinthus, a man approaches and explains this is the Land of Promise of the Saints they began searching for seven years earlier—their journey has been extended by God, who wanted first to reveal to them the diversity of his mysteries or wonders in the great ocean (*secreta in oceano magno*).[101] They return home with precious stones (serving as both relics and testimony of their voyage) and a prophecy made to Brendan that soon will be the 'final day of your pilgrimage' (*dies peregrinacionis tue*).[102]

Much is illuminated in this conclusion. God does not deliver them to this land until they have witnessed, experienced and learned from the ocean's mysteries. One must study, contemplate and be transformed by the seascape before gaining a view and knowledge of (if not complete spatial access to) the Land of Promise. Returning to the importance of narrative, the *Navigatio* concludes their return home with a narrative delivery of a seascape of words and insular wonders: Brendan tells (*narrauit*) all he recalls of the voyage and the wonders God revealed to him.[103] Finally, by using *peregrinatio* to refer to Brendan's life, *NSB* explicitly links the water-bound pilgrimage we have just participated in to the metaphorical life-journey we all undertake. *NSB* shows that the voyage is always already a part of daily life and practice: each wavefaring voyager, gazing out from a boat or a book, can be enriched by those 'wonders in the deep' God provides for exegetical benefit.

Immrama: rowing about in vernacular Irish boats

While concerned with monastic life, the manuscript history of the highly readable *NSB* shows that its audiences extended beyond a clerical readership. Representatives of one of the earliest vernacular Irish narrative genres, the *immrama* (sg. *immram*, literally 'rowing about'), which record the adventures experienced by a currach-borne group of voyagers led by an eponymous figure (as in *NSB*), and which explicitly fuse the heroic and Christian worlds of the early North Atlantic, similarly engaged multiple audiences.[104] The *immrama* are texts about spatial movement as transformation—traveling is slow, thoughtful, revelatory; and, like Brendan, the successful participant can be made into a kind of pearl by the end of the watery voyage. These spatial practices and textual geographies were not only for God's saints, but for all Irish people. Though the Church consistently plays an important role, some *immrama* feature lay protagonists rather than saintly clerics whose redemption is beyond doubt.[105] Drifting through a largely non-navigable ocean, the voyagers land on terrifying and wondrous islands whose topographies and inhabitants are marvelous and monstrous and, I suggest, in the Augustinian and Isadorean

Holy islands

senses, are meant to *monstrare*, 'show', and *monere*, 'warn'.[106] Implicit in several scenes is the understanding that geography can alter character and behavior, with exceptional figures completing revelatory journeys through these spaces. The landscapes of the *immrama* are not neutral backdrops—as Johnston writes, 'the islands were states of mind and cultural statements'[107]—but, in addition to altering the nature of individuals, the Western islands and their inhabitants also operate as reflections of the voyagers and embody important object lessons, as in the Hiberno-Latin poetics of space. Indeed, the vernacular voyage tales, of which four are extant, share many of the same motifs, plot devices and even islands with Hiberno-Latin *vitae* and related tales like *NSB*. Discussion here is confined to selected scenes from the longest and richest voyage tale, the prose *Immram Curaig Maíle Dúin* (*IMD*) ('Voyage of the Currach of Máel Dúin').[108] The manuscripts are later than the eighth- or ninth-century composition of the text: the fragmentary text in Lebor na hUidre (LU) dates to ca. 1100, and the more complete Yellow Book of Lecan text belongs to the fourteenth century.[109]

IMD probes issues of identity, moral development and locating an appropriate home, themes mediated through the beings and landscapes encountered, as a brief summary of the tale demonstrates. Taunted by an envious peer, Máel Dúin discovers his parents are not the king and queen of Munster, and though the queen proclaims him as a true son, raised at the same breast, cradle and lap as the king's sons, Máel Dúin rejects this, and so the queen takes him to his biological mother, a nun. This unnamed nun explains that, just as she proceeded to strike the church bell at midnight years earlier, she was raped by Ailill Ochir Ága ('Ailill of the Edge of Battle'), a raider killed by marauders at some point after he had attacked and impregnated her.[110] Máel Dúin is thus identified as a tense bodily hybrid of two diametrically opposed lifestyles (violent warrior and woman of the church). Continuing what might be characterized as a search for origins, genealogical and spatial, Máel Dúin travels to his father's kindred and is welcomed; yet on hearing that his murdered father remains unavenged, Máel Dúin plans revenge. Told that he can reach the territory of Ailill's slayer only by sea, to ensure his mission's success he follows a druid's directions to build a boat three hides thick, and fixes the departure date and crew number; his three foster-brothers, however, in a common motif, jump in at the last minute as supernumeraries.

The voyage begins, and at midnight (*medón aidchi*), a temporally liminal point particularly suitable for transformation and redemption, they prepare to land and kill his father's slayer.

Just as one voyager utters words thanking God for revealing their quarry so quickly, a great wind (*gáeth mór*) blows them out to open sea and thwarts the blood-feud. Familiar from the Hiberno-Latin travel accounts, nature, here exemplified by winds and weather, shows agency and dictates movement. Máel Dúin instructs his crew to ship the oars and cease rowing, for 'wherever it will please God to bring it, He will bring [it]' (*an leth bus ail do Dia a brith beraigh*), their currach moving across the sea and into the 'great, limitless ocean' (*ocian mór nemforcendach*).[111] The voyage metamorphoses from a revenge raid into a penitential, redemptive journey, these two voyage types—the secular raid by boat and the spiritual *peregrinatio*—both well attested as repeated historical and textual events. After encountering numerous islands, and successfully navigating and learning from their challenges, the voyagers come full circle, and one year and four (variantly seven) months later they find themselves back at the scene of the potential crime that needs to be avenged. The voyage has been transformative, and on his return Máel Dúin accepts welcome from the leader of his father's killers, forgives the murderer and puts on the new clothes that mark his re-admission into society as well as the successful negotiation of his violently conflicted origins. Endowed with powerful narrative agency, at the close of the tale Máel Dúin articulates his story, to the joy and enlightenment of the people of Ireland. A vernacular poetics of Irish space is developed, and a lay audience is invited to benefit by participating in the text as virtual voyagers on Máel Dúin's currach.

IMD opens with a Latin precis of the narrative: 'Concerning the voyage of Máel Dúin during one year and four months and the unknown wonders which the undivided Trinity showed him in the limitless ocean' (*De nauigatione Mael Duin anno intigro 7 .iiii. mensibus 7 de mirbuilibus ighnotis quae indiuisa trinitas illi ostenndit in ociano infinito*).[112] The Latin phrasing highlights the text's association with the Hiberno-Latin voyages, as does the understanding of the ocean as the space through which voyagers contemplate God's *mirabilia*. Even more explicit references show how *IMD* was conceptualized as a conscientious vernacular development of a Hiberno-Latin poetics of Irish space. On their voyage Máel Dúin and his crew encounter the last survivor of Brendan's voyagers, and he shows them Brendan's tablet (*pollere brenaind*, from Irish *póllire*, itself from Latin *pugillāria*), which accompanied them on their pilgrimage (*ailithre*) across the ocean: they bow before the tablet, and Máel Dúin kisses it.¹¹³ This fascinating metatextual scene leads the audience to first consider the written status of *NSB*. The implicit assumption is that one can only justify bringing tablets on a voyage in a crowded boat to write, presumably to record what is seen on the ocean and collect the elements that will go into a well-crafted narrative. The drive to transform and fix what is witnessed into writing as soon as possible is attested across the texts examined in this study—the literature consistently promotes the importance of text and manuscript culture in verbally concretizing space for current and future readers and listeners. Secondly, the scene causes us to note that Máel Dúin and his companions fittingly revere Brendan's voyage-tablets as sacred relics: the *pollere brenaind* comprises the drafting materials for the voyage and the islands that also inform the tale in which they are characters. There is a sophisticated nod to *IMD*'s nuanced poetics of Irish space: the text draws attention to the mechanics of its own creation and hints at the operational belief that the voyage is both a literary and a maritime practice.

Finally, guidelines for understanding Máel Dúin's voyage and reliving it as text are reinforced at the end of the narrative as well. When they return from the 'great, limitless ocean' (*ocian mór nemforcendach*)¹¹⁴ and Máel Dúin makes peace with the enemy, 'they related all the marvels which God has revealed to them, according to the word of the prophet who says: "one day this will be pleasing to remember"' [Vergil, *Aeneid* 1.203] (*Adfiadatar iarom inna huile adhamra ro foillsighestar Dia doib iar mbrethir inn fatha asbeir: haec olim meminisse iuuabit*).¹¹⁵ Máel Dúin returns to his district, and Diurán Leccerd deposits five half-ounces of gold netting found on their journey, as well as treasure, relics and proof of their otherworldly encounters, on the altar at Armagh. One manuscript (Egerton 1782) adds that 'Now Aed Find, chief sage (*ardecnuid hErind*) of Ireland, arranged this story as it stands here; and he did [so] for delighting the mind and for the people of Ireland after him. *Finit*' (*Rochóruid im Aed Finn ardecnuid hErind in sgélsai amal ata sunt comad er ghairdechad menman dorighni 7 do doinib hErinn hé ina diaigh. Finit*).¹¹⁶ As elsewhere, the voyaging texts draw our attention to the process of writing these seascapes into circulatable text, verbalized voyages that will themselves travel to delight an extensive audience.

'Speak to the earth, and it will teach you' (Job 12:8): insular transformations

On their voyage to the islands beyond Ireland's coast, Máel Dúin and his crew encounter approximately thirty-two islands, which include Edenic oases, islands of monstrous beasts and richly decorated fortresses with well-laid tables, enchanting music and beautiful women, as well as the more modest homes of Desert-Father-esque hermits. Máel Dúin is the first to disembark and explore (*dofoichlenn*, from *do-foichell*, 'traverses, moves across, travels') an island,[117] and we subsequently watch the voyagers come to know the island places through walking them, literally establishing their boundaries, and conducting circuits of their spaces. Many of the early islands provide food and hospitality, or drive the voyagers away in terror when they comprehend the size and fierceness of the inhabitants. As in *NSB*, the uncertainty of the voyagers and their fates is emphasized largely through the familiar and universal bodily sufferings like pangs of hunger: the voyagers are often 'a long time rowing without food and in hunger until they found an island'.[118] Many of these islands are represented in other voyage tales; some are specific to *IMD* and illuminate distinctive aspects of Máel Dúin's revelatory journey.

One island features a large beast that runs as swiftly as the wind in a circuit about (*imma-cuairt*) the island before climbing to its highest point. In the first instance, the beast stands on its head and performs a feat called 'straightening of the body',[119] in which the creature's bones and flesh revolve within its unmoving skin, while at other times the skin whirs around like a mill while bones and flesh remain fixed. After this display, the creature leaps up and conducts another circuit of the island,[120] again returning to perform a bodily contortion at the island's highest and most visible point, so that the lower half of the body's skin remains still while the top half spins around like a millstone. On witnessing these contortions, all of which split the body into two unhappy parts, Máel Dúin and his companions flee as quickly as they can. Máel Dúin and the monster are further linked by the act of stone-throwing. As the voyagers bolt from the island, the beast pitches stones at the departing boat, which mirrors the earlier scene in which Máel Dúin is poised to throw a stone over church ruins, but, like the attempted slaughter of his father's killer and the beast's attack, that act is frustrated when the boat pulls away.

What is one to make of this beast? One possibility is that this relatively early encounter, occurring on the seventh of thirty-two islands, suggests Máel Dúin's own embodiment of two diametrically opposed lifestyles (he is the child of a nun, raped by a raider). One might thus read the monster as a double of Máel Dúin, with its body's warring halves and frantic circuits, which elsewhere establish authority or define home territory (as discussed in later chapters), reflective of a conflicted Máel Dúin's lack of a spatial and genealogical home. The beast's circling movements may also perhaps point to what will become the mode of their resolution, the redemptive watery circuits of Máel Dúin's voyage. Máel Dúin's difficult resolution of two pasts, his birth from a violent union and dispossession from his *patria*, a homeland that is only obtainable after the revelatory experience of wandering through an initially unknowable landscape, spatially exemplifies the process of identity negotiation. While the beast continues to circle his island, Máel Dúin escapes to continue on his own journey. Further islands are visited, and Máel Dúin shows an increasing (though not infallible) spatial wisdom: he can recognize, read and respond to the varied landscapes accurately and identify what these spaces can offer him and his voyaging companions, resulting in an increasing ability to control his own behavior within these powerful spaces. As the Book of Job records, 'speak to the earth, and it will teach you, or let the fish of the sea inform you. Which of all these does not know that the hand of the Lord has done this?' (Job 12:8–9). Máel Dúin, his voyaging companions and the *IMD* audience are presented with a voyage and a text that encourages a close reading of the landscape and its inhabitants whose messages are written in God's own hand.

The power of these islands and seascapes to transform those who move through their environments is also addressed explicitly. Máel Dúin and his crew sail to an island halved by a fence and see a huge man dividing up flocks of sheep. When he throws a white sheep over the fence to where the black sheep are, the white sheep turns black. When in turn he flings a black sheep to the area occupied by the white sheep, it turns white, an episode presumably related to Jacob's breeding of striped lambs in Genesis 30:31–43.[121] Instead of fleeing immediately, a curious Máel Dúin performs a variant experiment: he and his companions throw a white stick to the black side—it turns black, and the black stick they throw to the white side turns white. Seeing this, he declares they will not land here, for fear they will change color like the sticks, and they escape.¹²² Their statement prefigures a subsequent encounter during which some of the crew's number have their identities eroded with shocking speed.

They sail to an island occupied by a large number of people with black bodies and clothes who continuously wail and lament. When one of Máel Dúin's foster-brothers lands, right away he becomes 'of their color' (*comdath*) and proceeds to behave precisely like the inhabitants by crying and lamenting with them.¹²³ Crew members are sent to retrieve the foster-brother, but they are unable to distinguish him from the other islanders, and soon those rescuers begin to wail and are in need of rescuing themselves. Máel Dúin sends yet another group ashore, but, having observed the attributes of the island and formulated a plan for successfully moving through its environment, this time he commands them to cover their noses and mouths, not breathe in any of the air and gaze only at their own companions. They succeed in recovering all crew members except the transformed foster-brother, who must be left behind. When Máel Dúin, back in the boat, asks what they saw in the island, they respond that they do not know, but that they mimicked what they saw and acted according to the custom (*bes*) of the people among whom they were situated.¹²⁴

This island of compulsive transformation speaks to the concept, articulated visually by Macrobian zone maps, that you are where you live—that place dictates not only character but body as well. As Isidore of Seville describes it, 'In keeping with the differences in climate, the looks of men, their color, and their stature vary, and different dispositions appear.'¹²⁵ Farther north, Saxo Grammaticus applied this geographic concept to another insular periphery in asserting that Iceland contains a spring 'which by the virulence of its gaseous waters destroys the original nature of any object'.¹²⁶ In *IMD*, a foster-brother is irrevocably altered and left behind, permanently merged into the landscape of the island of wailing: this identifies a wariness of encounter, and a fear that movement in foreign and unknown spaces can be dangerous. Extremes are to be avoided, and, as in the Hiberno-Latin accounts, the transformations that the voyagers seek do not always yield positive outcomes, though the most heroic, skilled readers of signs and oceanic wonders are rewarded with success. The negative examples point to a larger concept, operative in all of these tales, that the oceanic geographies west of Ireland are imbued with powers that work on those who move through them.

Holy islands

The transformative characteristics of these island environments, and their waters in particular, can be very positive and desirable. Towards the end of the voyage, after visiting a handful of islands hosting wise and holy hermits purified by their time in the Atlantic's desert spaces, we come to a climactic scene in *IMD*'s thematic development of transformation through voyaging and watery spatial practice. In a riddling manner similar to *NSB*'s delineation of Judas Iscariot and Jasconius, the voyagers watch a cloud approaching, which they identify as a bird when they see beating wings. They initially fear the great bird will carry them out to sea, but its talons instead transport a typologically evocative tree-branch the size of a large oak, topped with fresh leaves and thick with heavy, red fruits or berries (*bolga derga*) that resemble grapes (*fínemna*),[127] reminiscent of vine decoration on insular high crosses depicting Christ's life and salvation history, as Clancy has pointed out.[128] Máel Dúin and his voyagers witness this creature's three-day transformation in a scene replete with further baptismal and resurrection imagery. At midday, two large eagles fly from the southwest, and after resting before the bird they strip its jaws, eyes and ears of vermin until the evening, at which point all three birds consume the fruits from the branch. From the following morning until midday they continue to pick lice and vermin, also plucking and removing its old feathers, scales and mange.

> Medon lai imorru lomarsat na bolga din chruib 7 nos bruiddís cona nguilbnib frisna clocho 7 foscerditís iarom isind loch co raba a uan derg fair. Luidh iar sen an t-én mor isand loch 7 bói occa nigi and co focus do díudh lái.
>
> (At midday, however, they stripped the berries from the branch and with their beaks they were breaking them against the stones and then casting them into the lake, so that its foam became red. After that the big bird went into the lake and remained washing itself therein nearly till the close of the day.)[129]

The great bird then settles again on a hill. Next morning, the eagles return to attend to its body, making its plumage sleek, until midday, when they leave, in a scene reminiscent of the preparation of Christ's own body for burial before his followers must depart to keep the Sabbath.[130] The bird remains there, preening its feathers and 'shaking its wings until the end of the third day'. Its plumage restored,

trath terte an tres lái 7 foluastar fo tri immon indsi 7 foruim biucan
airisse arin tecluim cetna 7 luid ass iar sen hi fot a lleith asa tudh-
chaidh riam. Déiniu 7 tressiu a luamuin an fecht sain andas ríam
combo follus doib uile ba hathnudhugh dó a senddataigh a n-oitigh
iar mbreithir innd atha adbeir. *Renouabitur ut Aquila iuuentus tua.*

(at the hour of tierce on the third day it soared up and flew thrice
round the island and alighted for a little rest on the same hillock ...
Swifter and stronger was his flight at that time than before, so that it
was manifest to them all that this was his renewal from old age into
youth, according to the word of the prophet who said [Psalm 102:5]:
'Youth is renewed like the eagle.')[131]

Following this display, Diurán Leccerd (*Diurán* 'Poet'), a second-
ary leader on this voyage who both accompanies the unrepent-
ant voyager onto a potentially dangerous island and obtains part
of a wondrous gold net to deposit on Armagh's altar, correctly
interprets the scene and elects to perform the bird's own ritual,
immersing himself in the waters too, like Arculf, discussed previously, and so many other pilgrims to Jerusalem who bathe in
the Jordan. Witnessing the great wonder (*moradamra*), '"Let us
go into the lake", he said, "to renew ourselves where the bird has
been renewed"' (*Tiagham ar se isan loch diar n-athnudugh baile anro
hathnuighedh an t-en*).[132] The others balk, fearing the bird has poi-
soned the waters, but Diurán does not doubt. Bathing himself and
drinking deeply from the water, as long as he lived Diurán's eyes
maintained strength, neither tooth nor hair fell from his head and
he remained free of weakness and sickness from then on. Psalm
102:5, quoted in this passage, is the source of a widespread tradition of the great bird's rejuvenation and rebirth through bathing
in the waters, with bestiary accounts allegorizing the eagle (and
phoenix) as both Christ and the cleansed sinner who casts off old
clothes and old ways to follow a new path.[133]

These readings also fit (and prefigure) the specifics of Máel
Dúin's narrative trajectory: at the end of *IMD*, after being allegorically bathed and purified by his watery voyage, he is dressed
in new clothes, contiguous with his decision to pursue a path of
forgiveness and righteous Christian living. The detail of the great
tree branch and its foamy red waters that extend new life—not only
to the bird, but to other believers who immerse themselves as does
Diurán—suggests blood, death and resurrection. It is perhaps narratively dissatisfying that it is Diurán, not our main character Máel
Dúin, who enters the restorative red waters in this scene, but it

may be significant that the poet, the literary practitioner and the figure associated with the donation of a valued relic to Armagh, has this honor of being explicitly transformed by divinely endowed waters. Voyaging also, however, enacts this. A central theme of the voyage literature is that movement over waters and long-term spatial practice are transformative, that through sailing God's limitless ocean and immersive reading of the seascape's *mirabilia* one can be cleansed and reborn.

That this lesson is to be internalized, that the bird exemplifies appropriate human behavior too, is posited in the penultimate island visited, which opens with another riddle-like scene. Along with the crew, we spy across the waves a shape that resembles a white bird, but as the boat comes closer, it is revealed that this 'bird' perched on a rock is human, a formerly thieving cook whose voyage turned into a penitential journey like Máel Dúin's. Lacking actual plumage, as a result of his long tenure in purifying waters his body has, in the image of the holy hermit, lost the need for material clothing by being covered in his own white hair. Similarly, though he first stepped onto only tiny bit of rock jutting above the waters, the rock has grown to provide him a hermit's cell, reminding us of how these Atlantic waters were deemed holy places where divine will can miraculously create land itself. In a further paradisiacal motif, his island has become perfectly temperate—he does not suffer extremes of temperature or buffeting winds. Animals provide this sinful cook turned model Atlantic desert hermit with food: initially raw salmon and a cup of whey, but finally a morsel of fish and the eucharistically suggestive bread and 'good liquor' (*daglind*).[134] The paralleling of the redeemed bird with the human hermit, and, finally, the linking of this story to Máel Dúin's own is highlighted when the hermit instructs Máel Dúin to live out what he has learned on his voyage: he declares they will reach their country and that Máel Dúin will find his father's slayer there in a fortress. 'And slay him not, but forgive him, for God has saved you from many perils, and you, too, are men deserving of death' (*7 níro marbaigh, acht tabruidh dilghudh dó, fo bithin robar saersi Dia di morguasachtaib imdaib 7 basa fir bidhbuidh báis do chena*).[135] Clancy rightly links the account of the Hermit of Tory to Máel Dúin: 'to attain his goal, or to get his boat to go where he wants, he must first sever himself from his past, sinful life. When the boat crew first sees the hermit, he is covered only in his white hair, and here we should anticipate the new clothes given to Máel Dúin and his companions when they reach the bandits' island.' As Clancy explains, the voyage of Máel Dúin operates as a second baptism rich with the influential 'meaning of water in salvation history'.[136]

As in the Hiberno-Latin voyage tales, *IMD* encourages the audience to contemplate the meaning of the voyage not just from the belly of the hide-covered curragh but also from the pages of the vellum manuscript. The audience and readership of the *immrama* move, with Máel Dúin and his crew, through the topographically organized narrative with its string of island inhabitants, miracles and marvels. They too experience the homecoming in Ireland joyfully, as a unified community changed by the marvels they have witnessed. Máel Dúin returns to his own district, but the narration of his travels becomes celebrated throughout the land. Arranged in narrative form, the experience of this voyage will for years to come delight the minds of the people of Ireland (*doinib hErind*).[137]

With the ocean conceived as a transformative frontier between the mortal world and the heavenly, the seascapes outside Ireland allow travelers and *peregrini* access to otherworldly, often revelatory spaces. For when one speaks to the earth, listens to the fishes and learns to follow the tracks that open up, transformation and the ability to thrive in newly imagined spaces becomes possible. The texts discussed in this chapter enticed audiences in Ireland, Britain and Europe to imaginatively travel the holy places from the Dead Sea to the Irish Sea, and these overtly Christian travel tales provided some of the earliest models for an Irish poetics of space. And as we shift in Chapter 2 onto the plains, hills and forests of the Irish landmass, and into the world of vernacular heroism, we begin to see how this spatial poetics was further developed through the heroic landscapes of Ireland.

Notes

1. Bede, *Historia*, v. 15, pp. 506–7.
2. Adomnán, *De locis sanctis* [*DLS*], ed./trans. Denis Meehan (Dublin: DIAS, 1958). References are to book and chapter of *DLS*, with page numbers denoting the facing Latin text and Meehan's English translation. *DLS* was likely written once Adomnán became abbot (March 22, 679) and sometime before he visited England and Aldfrith's court in 685–86 and 687–88. See Thomas O'Loughlin, *Adomnán and the Holy Places: The Perceptions of an Insular Monk on the Locations of the Biblical Drama* (London and New York: T & T Clark, 2007), p. 6.
3. See Colin Ireland, 'Where Was King Aldfrith of Northumbria Educated? An Investigation of Seventh-Century Insular Learning',

Traditio 70 (2015), 29–73. The authoritative study of early Ireland and the figures connecting Ireland and Britain in this period is Thomas Charles-Edwards, *Early Christian Ireland* (Cambridge: Cambridge University Press, 2000).
4 Barbara Yorke, 'Adomnán at the Court of King Aldfrith', in Jonathan Wooding (ed.), *Adomnán of Iona: Theologian, Lawmaker, Peacemaker* (Dublin: Four Courts Press, 2010), pp. 44, 47.
5 Bede, *Historia*, v. 15, pp. 506–7.
6 Bede fully credits Adomnán, yet subsequent readers mistake the text and literary enterprise as Bede's own and forget Adomnán. Even the Middle Irish translation of *DLS* draws on Bede's precis and attributes authorship to him without mentioning Adomnán. See O'Loughlin, *Holy Places*, pp. 91–2; and Vernam Hull, 'The Middle Irish Version of Bede's *De Locis Sanctis*', *Zeitschrift für celtische Philologie* 17 (1928), 225–40.
7 O'Loughlin, *Holy Places*, pp. 181–2, 187–203, 251–2.
8 O'Loughlin, *Holy Places*, p. 16.
9 O'Loughlin, *Holy Places*, p. 7.
10 O'Loughlin, *Holy Places*, pp. 175–6.
11 O'Loughlin, *Holy Places*, p. 52.
12 *DLS, Preface*, pp. 36–7.
13 *DLS* I.1. pp. 40–1 and II.19, pp. 90–1. The formula 'As the holy Arculf relates' appears at I.21, pp. 64–5 and *DLS* I.23, pp. 66–7.
14 *DLS* II.19, pp. 88–9.
15 *DLS* I.12. pp. 58–9. Repeated at *DLS* II.11.
16 *DLS* II.3, II.5, II.6, II.7, II.21.
17 Valuable studies of pilgrimage and its literature include Mary Campbell, *The Witness and the Otherworld: Exotic European Travel Writing, 400–1600* (Ithaca, NY: Cornell University Press, 2001); Nicole Chareyron, *Pilgrims to Jerusalem in the Middle Ages* (New York: Columbia University Press, 2005); Victor Turner and Edith Turner, *Image and Pilgrimage in Christian Culture* (New York: Columbia University Press, 1996); John Wilkinson, *Jerusalem Pilgrims before the Crusades* (Warminster: Aris & Phillips, 2002); and Suzanne Yeager, *Jerusalem in Medieval Narrative* (New York: Cambridge University Press, 2008). For Irish practices, see Thomas Charles-Edwards, 'The Social Background of Irish *peregrinatio*', *Celtica* 11 (1976), 43–59; and Katja Ritari, *Pilgrimage to Heaven: Eschatology and Monastic Spirituality in Early Medieval Ireland* (Turnhout: Brepols, 2016).
18 *DLS* I.8, I.9, I.11.
19 *DLS* I.7, pp. 50–1.
20 *DLS* I.24, pp. 68–9.
21 *DLS* II.3, pp. 76–7.
22 *DLS* II.16, pp. 86–7.

23 *DLS* II.17, II.18, pp. 88–9.
24 *DLS* II.21, pp. 92–3.
25 See *DLS* I.9, pp. 54–5.
26 *DLS* I.9, pp. 54–5.
27 *DLS* I.2, pp. 44–5.
28 *DLS* I.12, pp. 56–7.
29 *DLS* I.25, pp. 68–9, and again at *DLS* II.1, pp. 74–5.
30 See also *DLS* I.15, pp. 60–1; I.19, pp. 62–3; I.23, pp. 66–7; III.3, pp. 108–9.
31 See Yeager, *Jerusalem in Medieval Narrative*, p. 33.
32 *DLS* I.1, pp. 40–1.
33 O'Loughlin, *Holy Places*, p. 35.
34 O'Loughlin, *Holy Places*, pp. 116–18.
35 *DLS* I.1, pp. 42–3.
36 Irish and British scholars of the seventh century knew far more of water and the ocean and its tides than their Holy Land counterparts (see Marina Smyth, 'The Word of God and Early Irish Cosmology', in Ann Dooley *et al.* [eds.], *Early Irish Cosmology* [Toronto: Pontifical Institute of Mediaeval Studies, 2014], pp. 112–43). It is not surprising that Adomnán, abbot of an island monastery, gives his own coastal audiences a watery Holy Land.
37 See Michael Gorman, 'Adomnán's *De locis sanctis*: The Diagrams and the Sources', *Revue Bénédictine* 116 (2006), 5–41.
38 *DLS* I.2, pp. 46–7.
39 Tomás Ó Carragáin, *Churches in Early Medieval Ireland: Architecture, Ritual and Memory* (New Haven, CT: Yale University Press, 2010), pp. 14–15, 78–81.
40 *DLS* Preface, pp. 36–7.
41 *DLS* I.1, pp. 40–1.
42 See O'Loughlin, *Holy Places*, pp. 61–2; David Woods, 'Adomnán, Arculf and the True Cross', *Aram* 18–19 (2006–7), 405; and François Chatillon, 'Arculfe a-t-il réellement existé?', *Revue du Moyen Âge latin* 23 (1967), 134–8.
43 *DLS* III.6, pp. 120–1.
44 Adomnán, *Vita sancti Columbae* in *Adomnán's Life of Columba*, ed./trans. Alan Orr Anderson and Marjorie Ogilvie Anderson (London: Thomas Nelson and Sons Ltd., 1961) (*VSC*). References are to the book and chapter number, with page numbers denoting the facing Latin text and the Ogilvies' English translation. Dating discussed in J. M. Picard, 'The Purpose of Adomnán's *Vita Columbae*', *Peritia* 1 (1982), 167–9.
45 Jennifer O'Reilly, 'Reading Scriptures in the Life of Columba', in Cormac Bourke (ed.), *Studies in the Cult of Saint Columba* (Dublin: Four Courts Press, 1997), p. 106.
46 O'Reilly, 'Reading Scriptures', pp. 86, 88.

47 Dan Tipp and Jonathan Wooding, 'Adomnán's Voyaging Saint: The Cult of Cormac ua Liatháin', in Wooding (ed.), *Adomnán of Iona*, p. 241.
48 Columbanus (d. 615) similarly writes: 'I am called *Jona* in Hebrew, *Peristera* in Greek, *Columba* in Latin, yet so much is my birthright in the idiom of your language that I use the ancient Hebrew name of Jonah, whose shipwreck I have almost undergone' (Letters 5.16). Quoted in Richard Sharpe, *Adomnán of Iona: Life of St Columba* (London: Penguin, 1995), pp. 242–3.
49 *VSC* Preface, pp. 180–1.
50 See discussions of Jonah and Columba in Jacqueline Borsje, *From Chaos to Enemy: Encounters with Monsters in Early Irish Texts* (Turnhout: Brepols, 1996), pp. 116–17, 120; and Varese Layzer, *Signs of Weakness: Juxtaposing Irish Tales and the Bible* (Sheffield: Sheffield Academic Press, 2001), pp. 74–103.
51 *VSC* I.19, pp. 246–7.
52 *VSC* I.19, pp. 246–7.
53 For instance, *VSC* I.4, pp. 220–1.
54 *VSC* II.42, pp. 440–1.
55 *VSC* II.42, pp. 443–5.
56 *VSC* II.42, pp. 444–5.
57 Small beasts also pierce the currach's hide in *Immram curaig Uí Chorra*, as discussed in Tipp and Wooding, 'Voyaging Saint', p. 247.
58 *VSC* II.42, pp. 444–7.
59 *VSC* II.42, pp. 446–7.
60 *VSC* II.42, pp. 446–7.
61 Westley Follett, 'Allegorical Interpretation in Adomnán's *Vita Columbae*', *Eolas* 2 (2007), 23. Baitán's voyage is at *VSC* I.20, pp. 248–51.
62 *VSC* III.17, pp. 500–1.
63 Paul Tuffrau, *Le merveilleux voyage de Saint Brandan à la recherche du Paradis* (Paris: L'artisan du livre, 1925), p. 18.
64 Carl Selmer (ed.), *Navigatio Sancti Brendani Abbatis from Early Latin Manuscripts* (Notre Dame, IN: University of Notre Dame Press, 1959). References are to the chapter and line numbers of *NSB*. The English translations are John O'Meara (trans.), *The Voyage of Saint Brendan* (Gerrards Cross: Colin Smythe, 1961) (henceforth *Voyage*). References are to page numbers.
65 As detailed by Elva Johnston, *Literacy and Identity in Early Medieval Ireland* (Woodbridge: Boydell Press, 2013), n. 137, p. 51. Carl Selmer (*NSB*, pp. xxvii–xxix) argues for composition on the continent in the tenth century, while James Carney ('Review of Selmer, Navigatio', *Medium Aevum* 32 [1963], 43) argues for composition in Ireland during the first half of the ninth century, supported by both Mario Esposito, 'L'édition de la "Nauigatio S. Brendani"', *Scriptorium* 15

(1961), 288 and Giovanni Orlandi, *Navigatio Sancti Brendani* (Milan: Istituto Editorial Cisalpino, 1968), pp. 72–3, 131–60. A convincing argument for composition in Ireland in the eighth century is made by David Dumville, 'Two Approaches to the Dating of *Navigatio Sancti Brendani*', *Studi Medievali* 29 (1988), 95–9.
66 Carney, 'Review', p. 44.
67 See discussion and list of the extant Latin manuscripts in *NSB*, pp. xxvi–xxvii, 105–16.
68 Carl Selmer, 'The Vernacular Translations of the *Navigatio Sancti Brendani*: A Bibliographical Study', *Medieval Studies* 18 (1956), 150–1. Irish-language hagiographic texts related to Brendan were available, and share much with the Latin *Navigatio*.
69 Timothy Severin, *The Brendan Voyage* (London: Abacus, 1978).
70 *NSB* 9.24.
71 *NSB* 1.11–4; *Voyage*, p. 3.
72 *NSB* 1.55–60; *Voyage*, p. 5.
73 *NSB* 1.66–7; *Voyage*, p. 5.
74 *NSB* 2.4–7; *Voyage*, p. 7.
75 *NSB* 2.7–8; *Voyage*, p. 7.
76 *NSB* 4.4–6. Later, a stream and harbor are just wide enough to admit the currach (*NSB* 11.9–10 and 26.17–18).
77 *NSB* 4.6–10; *Voyage*, p. 8.
78 On the currach as metaphor for mortal life see Jonathan Wooding, 'St Brendan's Boat: Dead Hides and the Living Sea in Columban and Related Hagiography', in John Carey et al. (eds.), *Studies in Irish Hagiography: Saints and Scholars* (Dublin: Four Courts Press, 2000), pp. 77–92.
79 *NSB* 12.2–3; *Voyage*, p. 25.
80 *NSB* 12.8.
81 *NSB* 1.9, 11.21, etc.
82 On the watchman device, see Patrick Sims-Williams, *Irish Influence on Medieval Welsh Literature* (Oxford: Oxford University Press, 2010), pp. 95–133.
83 *NSB* 10.5–8; *Voyage*, p. 18.
84 *NSB* 10.13–5; *Voyage*, p. 18.
85 *NSB* 10.20–1; *Voyage*, p. 19.
86 *NSB* 15.38–9; *Voyage*, p. 37.
87 Noted by Bieler and discussed by Borsje, *Chaos to Enemy*, p. 125.
88 F. J. Carmody (ed.), *Physiologus latinus* (Paris: E. Droz, 1939), pp. 40–6.
89 Albert Cook (ed.), *The Old English Physiologus* (New Haven, CT: Yale University Press, 1921), p. 23.
90 See Borsje, *Chaos to Enemy*, pp. 119–21, 124–9.
91 *NSB* 11.25.
92 *NSB* 11.41–2; *Voyage*, p. 21.

93 *NSB* 11.51–2; *Voyage*, p. 22.
94 *NSB* 11.66–7; *Voyage*, p. 22.
95 *NSB* 11.110–11; *Voyage*, p. 25.
96 Martin McNamara, *The Psalms in the Early Irish Church* (Sheffield: Sheffield Academic Press, 2000), p. 360.
97 Elva Johnston, 'A Sailor on the Seas of Faith: The Individual and the Church in *The Voyage of Máel Dúin*', in Judith Devlin and Howard Clarke (eds.), *European Encounters* (Dublin: University College Dublin Press, 2003), p. 240.
98 See *NSB*, note 25, p. 85.
99 *NSB* 18.16.
100 *NSB* 26, Webb 241.
101 *NSB* 28.26–7.
102 *NSB* 28.29; *Voyage*, p. 69.
103 *NSB* 29.4.
104 See overview of the genre in Jonathan Wooding (ed.), *The Otherworld Voyage in Early Irish Literature: An Anthology of Criticism* (Dublin: Four Courts Press, 2000), pp. xi–xix.
105 Thomas Clancy, 'Subversion at Sea: Structure, Style and Intent in the *Immrama*', in Wooding (ed.), *Otherworld Voyage*, p. 203. See also Johnston's discussion of *IMD*'s historical religious contexts in 'Sailor on the Seas', pp. 239–69.
106 Isidore, *Etymologiae*, XI.iii.2; and Augustine of Hippo, *De civitate dei*, ed. Bernard Dombart and Alfonso Kalb (Turnhout: Brepols, 1955), XXI.8.
107 Johnston, 'Sailor on the Seas', p. 240.
108 H. P. A. Oskamp, *The Voyage of Máel Dúin: A Study in Early Irish Voyage Literature* (Groningen: Wolters-Noordhof, 1970). References are to the sections or chapters of *IMD*, with the following page numbers denoting the facing Irish text and Oskamp's English translation.
109 Fragments are also found in the sixteenth-century Harleian MS. 5280 and Egerton MS. 1782 (ca. 1517). Early linguistic forms in the text suggest that it may first have been written in the eighth or ninth century (A. G. van Hamel (ed.), *Immrama* [Dublin: DIAS, 1941], pp. 20–4; Carney suggests the ninth century in 'Review', 49). A verse paraphrase, likely composed in the late tenth or early eleventh century, is found in the *Yellow Book of Lecan* and Harleian MS. 5280.
110 For the Irish legal context of a nun's rape see Lisi Oliver, 'Forced and Unforced Rape in Early Irish Law', *Proceedings of the Harvard Celtic Colloquium* 13 (1993), 93–106.
111 *IMD* 1, pp. 108–9.
112 *IMD* Preface, pp. 100–1.
113 *IMD* 30, pp. 160–1. Note that here the navigator saint, Brendan of Clonfert, is confused with Brendan of Birr. Regarding the derivation of Ir. *póire* from Lt. *pugilláría*, see Damian McManus, 'A

Chronology of the Latin Loan-Words in Early Irish', *Ériu* 34 (1983), 37–8.
114 *IMD* 1, pp. 106–9.
115 *IMD* 34, pp. 176–9.
116 *IMD* 34, pp. 177–9, notes 13 and 3.
117 *IMD* 3, pp. 110–11.
118 *IMD* 7, pp. 114–15.
119 This is a feat also performed by the hero Cú Chulainn in the same manuscript (LU, 73a).
120 The phrasing that the beast 'ran around' (*reitigh timchell*) the island features *timchell*, a form of the same term (*do-foichell*, 'traverses, moves across, travels') used to describe Máel Dúin's own earlier island circuit (*IMD* 3, pp. 110–11), verbally links their spatial practices.
121 The same color-changing sheep are found in the Welsh romance *Peredur vab Efrawc*. See John Carey, 'The Valley of the Changing Sheep', *Bulletin of the Board of Celtic Studies* 30 (1983), 277–80.
122 *IMD* 12, pp. 124–5.
123 *IMD* 15, pp. 128–9.
124 *IMD* 15, pp. 128–9.
125 Isidore, *Etymologiae* IX.ii.105.
126 Saxo Grammaticus, *Gesta Danorum: The History of the Danes*, vol. I, ed. Karsten Friis-Jensen and trans. Peter Fisher (Oxford: Clarendon Press, 2015), p. 15.
127 *IMD* 30, pp. 160–1.
128 Clancy, 'Subversion', p. 214.
129 *IMD* 30, pp. 162–3.
130 Matthew 27:59; Mark 15:46; Luke 23:53–56; and John 19:38–42.
131 *IMD* 30, pp. 162–3.
132 *IMD* 30, pp. 163–4.
133 Cf. the bleeding, salvation-preaching tree of *Immram Snédgusa 7 Mac Riagla* ('Voyage of Snédgus and Mac Riagla') whose blood 'was royal ointment, was wine, was communion, a holy relic', discussed in Clancy, 'Subversion', p. 214. See also Valerie Jones, 'The Phoenix and the Resurrection', in Debra Hassig (ed.), *The Mark of the Beast: the Medieval Bestiary in Art, Life, and Literature* (New York: Garland, 1999), pp. 99–115.
134 *IMD* 33, pp. 172–3.
135 *IMD* 33, pp. 172–3.
136 Clancy, 'Subversion', p. 206.
137 *IMD* 34, pp. 178–9.

2
Place-making heroes and the storying of Ireland's vernacular landscape

The popular tale *Do Foillsigud na Tána Bó Cúailnge* ('The Revealing of the *Táin Bó Cúailnge*' or 'Cattle-Raid of Cooley', hereafter *Foillsigud*) describes how the Irish poets gave the *Táin*, heroic Ireland's most important text, to a keen visiting scholar in exchange for Isidore of Seville's *Etymologiæ*.[1] According to the Book of Leinster (LL), the tale's earliest manuscript witness, the *Táin* was then taken eastwards (*sair*) out of Ireland to Europe.[2] This trade and the *Táin*'s movement to Europe (and possibly Rome itself, for another version identifies the *Táin*'s exporter as *súi rómanach*, a 'Roman scholar' specifically)[3] imagines vernacular Irish literature as valued in medieval Christendom's continental centers of knowledge and prestige. *Foillsigud* also records, however, the embarrassing consequence that by the sixth century the *Táin* had been lost to Ireland. The Irish poets, whose main task was to preserve Ireland's stories and histories, could not remember their most significant narrative. Accordingly, in the tale Ireland's chief poet, Senchán Torpéist, prepares to send his pupils to Europe in a desperate search for the *Táin*—in one variant a saint curses the poets with loss of heaven (*nem*) and earth (*talam*) if they linger two nights in one place before recovering it.[4] Losing native literature and lore is to be punished, it seems, by perennial wandering and dispossession of home and heaven.

Nonetheless, a remarkable plot twist demonstrates that there is ultimately no need for the poets to travel beyond Irish space, for narrative resides in the very contours of the landscape itself. As they begin their quest in Ireland, Muirgein, son of Senchán Torpéist, seats himself before a 'bright, wonderful stone' (*liic lúaichthech málgel*) marking the burial site of the ancient warrior Fergus mac Róich, a central character in the *Táin*.[5] When he chants an incantatory poetic verse to the stone, a great mist descends for three days and nights, and Fergus materializes to recite the *Táin*, beginning to end. The *Táin Bó Cúalnge* is saved: not by a Roman scholar or an itinerant consulting a far-flung manuscript, but by a poet who speaks to a stone and recuperates from the Irish earth a native hero to perform the epic tale.[6]

Foillsigud positions Fergus as our 'place-maker', to use anthropologist Keith Basso's formulation, a figure summoned from the earth who 'speaks as a witness on the scene' to take us back to events that transpired in these spaces long ago. To Basso, 'the place-maker's main objective is to speak the past into being, to summon it with words and give it dramatic form, to *produce* experience by forging ancestral worlds in which others can participate and readily lose themselves'[7] (emphasis in original). Fergus uses his words to bring the land into being: his fog-shrouded three-day performance generates the ancient, storied Irish landscape that then becomes a written place-world accessible to sixth-century poets and subsequent audiences. A story reclaimed from a stone embedded in the landscape constitutes a fitting origin for such a spatially oriented text as the *Táin*.

As discussed in Chapter 1, virtual pilgrimage through the holy places verbalized in Adomnán's *De locis sanctis* was understood to provide spiritual enrichment and even confer sanctity. Similarly, by participating and losing themselves in the *Táin* place-world summoned by Fergus's words, a listening audience could gain blessing and safety: a ninth-century triad (Triad 62) on the marvels of the *Táin* records that hearing the *Táin* narrated confers one year of protection (*coimge bliadna*).[8] *Tromdám Gúaire* ('Gúaire's Heavy-hosting') additionally tells us that Saint Ciarán of Clonmacnoise writes out a copy of the *Táin* on the hide of his dun cow: legend has it that whoever lay on the hide was translated directly to heaven.[9] As will be discussed in this chapter, in *Siaburcharpat Con Culaind* ('The Phantom-chariot of Cú Chulainn') Saint Patrick similarly conjures the long-dead *Táin* hero Cú Chulainn to tell his story, and rewards the warrior with a place among the saints. Story saves, and narrative can provide a path to heaven, even for Ireland's pagan warriors. Like Chapter 1's verbalized holy spaces, the *Táin* (and other stories featuring Cú Chulainn) imparts benefit and blessing to those who move through this heroic Ireland that fuses text and landscape.

This chapter traces the poetics of space in Ireland's heroic literature (ca. 900–1160) to show how Ireland's landscape becomes embedded within narrative. The hero Cú Chulainn, medieval Irish literature's most famous character and the unifying element in this discussion, is first and foremost a warrior. Additionally, he is arguably heroic Ireland's most productive and conscientious placemaker. His actions range from the expected—physically altering the landscape and endowing it with place names memorializing his deeds—to the surprising—lecturing on learned placelore and modeling the importance of fusing journey with topographic storytelling. Virtually every aspect of Cú Chulainn's biography contains a spatial dimension, and though a focus on one character necessitates moving across many distinctive texts, examining a single character's representation by multiple composers over several periods reveals the very consistency of a spatial poetics across Ireland's heroic literature.

The chapter situates narratives from the *Táin*, and more specifically, the LL *Tain*,[10] alongside other texts from the Ulster Cycle to illustrate this distinctively *spatial* hero's development and demonstrate Cú Chulainn's mastery of both physical landscapes and verbalized placelore. The discussion considers Cú Chulainn's depiction in *Táin Bó Cúalnge* and the associated tales *Compert Con Culainn* ('Conception of Cú Chulainn'), *Tochmarc Emire* ('Wooing of Emer') and *Mesca Ulad* ('Drunkenness of the Ulstermen'). Finally, the chapter returns to issues of spatial narrative, textuality and the recuperative function of storytelling by concluding with *Siaburcharpat Con Culaind*.

Plotting Cú Chulainn in an Irish book of nature

In her study of the *Táin*, textuality and hero-writing, Ann Dooley perceptively remarks that 'in a pastoral/heroic world the first proficiency of the hero/stalker is an ability to inscribe his mark, erase, manipulate and read the "book" of nature itself as the great originary residuum of natural signs'.[11] Like Chapter 1's voyaging heroes, multiple scenes establish Cú Chulainn's ability to navigate difficult environments and overcome their challenges; to effectively read situations and respond with the right performance; and finally to encode messages in the landscape that project his power. Every stage of Cú Chulainn's biography demonstrates his efforts to move from peripheral to principal positions, to literally and figuratively find his way to heroic centrality among the Ulaid. Cú Chulainn evinces expertise in heroic spatial practice and environmental remodeling, with the result that discourses about Cú Chulainn, as well as his own topographical acts, produce a distinct 'book of nature'.

Compert Con Culainn ('Conception of Cú Chulainn'), composed in the eighth or ninth century and preserved in the early twelfth-century Lebor na hUidre (LU) and later manuscripts,[12] is a mythologically rich tale linking the hero's birth to extreme environmental changes. It features a triple birth and land devastation by birds that raze the Ulster stronghold Emain Macha. After his female charioteer, Deichtine, leads the king of Ulster and his followers on a circuit around Ireland pursuing the birds and their beautiful melodies, a massive snowfall forces the Ulaid to seek shelter in a house at the ancient ritual site Brú na Bóinne (Newgrange, built ca. 3200 BCE). Overnight, the woman of the house bears a child, assisted by Deichtine (who is also Conchobar's daughter, or variantly sister). In the morning, the otherworldly house has vanished and all that remains are the newborn child, who is nursed by Deichtine but later dies, and two foals, also born overnight, which survive and become Cú Chulainn's own stallions.

The second pregnancy in the tale occurs when Deichtine takes her first drink of water after mourning the mysterious child's death, and a creature leaps from the liquid into her mouth. That night as she sleeps the god Lugh tells her she is pregnant with his son, explaining that his was the otherworldly house at Brú na Bóinne and that the child is to be named 'Sétanta'; yet this pregnancy is ended before a child is born. Finally, after she marries Súaldaim mac Róich, in the story's third pregnancy episode Deichtine gives birth to a son. LU (only) records that '[The name] Sétanta was given to him' (*doberar Sétanta fair*),[13] and the account details that he will be raised and taught by Ulster's most eminent figures, including the warrior Fergus, the poet Amairgen and the sage Sencha. These details of fosterage are significant: as we will see, Cú Chulainn collects, verbalizes and disseminates Ireland's topographic lore, and, like his wise fosterers, he becomes an eloquent place-maker.

The name Sétanta may also provide insight into the hero's nature. Osborn Bergin, arguing against various etymologies proposed for this obscure name, shows that Middle Irish scribes and composers, working within a rich tradition of etymological play, identified the first element as *sét*, meaning 'path' or 'way'. While Bergin dismisses their interpretation as linguistically bogus, medieval Irish scholars, wrongly or not, seized on the epistemic truth of this false etymology associating 'Sétanta' with path-making or way-finding.[14] Though one cannot claim with the translator Jeffrey Gantz's certainty that 'his original name, Sétantae [*sic*], means "one who has knowledge of roads and ways",[15] the name's pathfinding associations have important resonances for Sétanta. The king Conaire, whose name comes from *conar* ('path'), provides a parallel: in the account of his downfall, *Togail Bruidne Da Derga* ('Destruction of Da Derga's Hostel'), proper spatial practice is key. Conaire conducts his own circuit of Ireland—wrongly, as it turns out, for his reign and his life come to a grisly end by the close of the narrative.[16] Of further importance is Sétanta's mother. In *Compert*, Deichtine is a skilled spatial practitioner equipped with significant topographic knowledge, for 'it is she who was the charioteer' (*Is sí ba harae*)[17] who drives the king around Ireland on the circuit with which Sétanta's birth-tale commences. Crucially, though scholars have typically focused on his divine parentage, that Sétanta's mother is a charioteer provides another genealogy empowering this hero as a hereditary pathfinder.

Sétanta's spatial precocity reveals itself at the next stage of his biography, as recorded in the *Macgnímrada* ('Boyhood Deeds') section of the *Táin*.[18] Narrated by Fergus and other exiles to the men of Ireland as they prepare for combat with Ulster's hero, the *Macgnímrada* introduces Sétanta as a five-year-old boy. Drawn by the stories of Ulster, Sétanta decides to walk alone from the isolated outpost of Mag Muirthemne to join the famed boy-troop at Emain Macha, Ulster's royal center. His mother tries to dissuade him—Emain is distant and the route mountainous—but when she withholds directions the wayfaring child declares that he will thus make his own calculation (*ardmes*, 757); he sets off, making easy progress towards the destination (and destiny) he has chosen so early in his biography. Reaching Emain's playing field, Sétanta is attacked by 150 Ulster youths seeking a fight to the death when he enters their territory without permission.

He bests the Ulster boys easily. When the king Conchobar intervenes to prevent him from going too far in his counter-attack, the boy, who only names himself at this point, says he behaves so aggressively because he did not receive the honor that, as a son of the king's sister, he had expected after traveling from lands far away (*a tírib imciana*, 794). Conchobar then points out to him the dangers of traveling such distances and of entering alien territory without protection and proper ceremony, and explains that Sétanta must as an outsider secure the boy-troop's protection, which he does. However, in a display of his superior martial strength Sétanta forces the defeated boy-troop to come under his own protection, establishing his new role as defender of Ulster. The narrative not only establishes Cú Chulainn's heroic superiority in battle, it underscores the danger of traveling into new territory as an alien without security or social place. The text suggests how it could easily have gone the other way, with the boy killed because of improper movement into Ulster's stronghold. (Indeed, Cú Chulainn's son Connla will also experience such violence when he approaches Ulster's shores from abroad without naming himself and is slain by Cú Chulainn's own hand.)[19] The way one moves and crosses boundaries is critical to survival in heroic Ireland.[20] Finally, and notably, this early story is told by the exile Fergus to an audience comprising both Ulster exiles and the men of Ireland, who now approach Ulster territory as hostile raiders.

The next episode of the boyhood deeds, in which Sétanta receives the name of Cú Chulainn, also centers on the violent policing of Ulster's borders. This time it is told by Conchobar's son, whose name, Cormac Cond Longas ('Head of Exiles'), refers to his exodus from Ulster following his father's treasonous slaughter of Uisliu's sons. Cormac's story heightens the sense of anxiety by illustrating what awaits those who trespass into Ulster territory. Cormac tells them of the time when Conchobar sets off for a feast hosted by the smith, Culand. The king sees Sétanta and announces that 'fortunate is the land' (*mo chin tír*, 843) from which the boy came. Conchobar invites the child to Culand's feast, and the boy says he will come once he has finished playing. When Conchobar declares 'You do not know the way at all, little boy' (p. 161) (*Nídat eólach etir, a meic bic*, 854), Sétanta replies that 'I shall follow the trail of the company and the horses and the chariots' (p. 161) (*Gébat-sa slichtlorg in tslúaig 7 na n-ech 7 na carpat*, 855). Echoing the first bold journey that he made to Emain Macha, Sétanta is depicted as an unusually gifted pathfinder who, as his name suggests, inherently knows the way. While the other children return home to their mothers and fathers, this little boy tracks Conchobar's retinue to Culand's house.

Once there, the boundary-trespassing issue is triggered. Unbeknownst to the boy, following the arrival of the main party Culand has released Ulster's fiercest hound to patrol his lands and destroy trespassers; and the drama increases as we witness Conchobar carelessly forget his invitation to the child, who now approaches armed only with his ball and toys. The hound's terrifying baying as he sees the little boy resounds 'throughout the territory' (*fosnaib túathaib*, 878), leading the king and Ulstermen to lament what they believe will be Sétanta's inevitable death. When it is revealed that he has actually slain the hound with his ball, the group celebrates the boy's survival. At the same time, Culand is fretful at the loss of his own border guard, so the boy declares he will train a new bloodhound, and says 'I shall myself be the hound to protect Culand's flocks and cattle and land during that time' (p. 162) (*Bam cú-sa imdegla a almai 7 a indili 7 a feraind in n-ed sain*, 904–5.)

The demise of the bloodhound signifies the birth of a new hound, Ulster's defender. When it is suggested that the boy now be called Cú Chulainn ('Hound of Culand'), he emphatically says no (*nithó*), for 'I prefer my own name, Sétanta mac Sualtaim' (p. 163) (*Ferr lim mo ainm fodéin, Sétanta mac Sualtaim*, 908–9).[21] Balking at the loss of his name Sétanta, he only accepts the name Cú Chulainn when the druid Cathbad tells him it will be forever famous throughout Ireland and Scotland. This episode endows Cú Chulainn with his name and function, and to an extent it also dictates the medium through which his rage will henceforth be expressed: when the territories he guards are threatened, the proverbial Hound of Ulster will transform into a ferocious, snapping-jawed dog. As emphasized in his *ríastrad* ('distortion'), briefly discussed in the following, Cú Chulainn's violently pounding palate and gapingly distended mouth and chest copy the bloodhound's chopping jaws, while his beating heart is also likened to a hound's baying (2279–83). Cú Chulainn's canine attributes and name underscore the character's spatial development into an unparalleled boundary guard. As Conchobar earlier declared, fortunate is the land from which the boy came. Fortunate too, from an Ulster perspective, are those Ulster territories Cú Chulainn has successfully traveled through and which he now undertakes to protect. The wayfaring boy's initially transgressive yet always bold movements into dangerous spaces map out the Ulster landscape and plot its boundaries with his feats: Cú Chulainn's movements delineate the text's geography.

The name change semantically shifts him from a pathfinder to a border defender as well. Accordingly, Cú Chulainn's successes as a medieval Irish hero derive from both geographic knowledge and practical experience of the Irish landscape. This is exemplified when the seven-year-old boy takes up arms on a prophetic day to gain everlasting fame. Keen to prove himself, late in the day Cú Chulainn persistently harangues Conchobor's charioteer, Ibar mac Riangabra, until he agrees to conduct a circuit with Cú Chulainn around Emain Macha—they drive three times around Emain (*fo thrí timchull,* 981). Still unwilling to end the day, Cú Chulainn seeks further spatial knowledge. He asks,

> 'Ocus in tsligi mór sa imthéit sechond, gia leth imthéit?' ar in mac bec. 'Cid taí-siu di?' ar Ibar ... 'Maith lim, a maccáin, prímsligeda in chóicid d'iarfaigid. Cia airet imthéit?' (990–4)
>
> ('And this great road which goes past us, where does it lead?' said the little boy. 'Why do you bother about it?' said Ibar... 'I wish, fellow, to ask about the chief roads of the province. How far does it go?') (p. 165)

Ibar tells him it extends to Áth na Foraire, and when Cú Chulainn asks why it is so called, the charioteer explains that an Ulsterman always keeps watch (*foraire*) there on behalf of the province.

Cú Chulainn, born of a charioteer, understands the importance of internalizing a storied map of the province to enable his defense of it: not only the names and locations of its major arteries, but the histories of the names, the *senchas* or lore of the places, and the strategic information those names encode. When Cú Chulainn seizes the opportunity to do so, the charioteer finds this curious— of course a charioteer needs topographic knowledge to drive the chariot to the right place, but evidently geography and placelore do not typically feature in a warrior's training. Cú Chulainn is once again unusual: his taking up of arms and his official initiation into the life of a warrior spark a simultaneous desire for topographic knowledge, implying that spatial knowhow is an essential (and perhaps even unique) element of Cú Chulainn's skillset as champion and defender of the province.

Subsequent passages also suggest that, while gathering information is important, actual spatial practice is invaluable. Cú Chulainn immediately grasps the significance not only of moving through the spaces to internalize their information, but also of appropriating them and leaving his own mark. In the influential formulations of spatial theorist Michel de Certeau, space is made powerful and dynamic by movement: 'A *space* exists when one takes into consideration vectors of direction, velocities, and time variables. Thus space is composed of intersections of mobile elements. It is in a sense actuated by the ensemble of movements deployed within it ... In short, *space is a practiced place.*'[22] After Cú Chulainn has solicited information about the road, he moves through the landscape itself, experientially learning the route to the ford at the province's border. Though the charioteer worries that it is time to be safely

Place-making heroes and the storying of Ireland's vernacular landscape   73

home once they reach the ford, Cú Chulainn perseveres and asks the name of a hill and its cairn (Slíab Moduirn and Findcharn). Proceeding to the hill's summit, Cú Chulainn requests that the charioteer 'teach me (all the places of) Ulster on every side for I do not know my way at all about the territory of my leader Conchobar' (p. 167) (*tecoisc-siu dam-sa Ulaid ar cach leth dáig ním eólach-sa i crích mo phopa Conchobuir etir*, 1052–3). The charioteer then identifies by name several environmental features (hills, plains, mounds, open spaces, glens and their hidden nooks and corners), strongholds (*dúne*) and renowned places (*dindgnai*) in the province of Ulster. Turning to a great plain to the south, Mag mBreg, Cú Chulainn repeats the request for further instruction: 'Show me the buildings and renowned places of that plain' (p. 167) (*Tecoisc-siu dam-sa déntai 7 dindgnai in maige sin*, 1058), and Ibar names several of the country's mythic and ritually significant sites, including Temair, Tailtiu, Cleitech and Cnogba, and Bruig Meic in Óc and, moving the plot forward, the fortress (*dún*) of the sons of Nechta Scéne.

In this scene Cú Chulainn desires to comprehend first the province and then, moving father afield, the landmarks of the Boyne Valley, arguably Ireland's cultural capitol in which so many sites of ritual, political and legendary importance are concentrated. He orients himself and gains a totalizing overview of the land from above, an act that is followed by physically moving through the spaces he sees. When Cú Chulainn and the charioteer reach the last-mentioned fortress, Cú Chulainn reads an ogam message inscribed on a pillar-stone there challenging all warriors to combat. In response he uproots the stone and derisively tosses it into a pool, and the seven-year-old then proceeds to decapitate Nechta Scéne's three fierce sons. Keenly aware of pageantry's power, in addition to the warriors' heads Cú Chulainn also brings two wild stags and sixteen swans he has tamed to complete the impressive spectacle of the newly armed warrior, master of birds, beasts and men encountered in hostile lands, returning to Emain Macha.

In this extended episode, when Cú Chulainn asks to be taught the language of the landscape he seeks to move through, it prepares him, and reminds the audience, to read places for story and knowledge. He is not, however, content merely to hear the names. The hero's process also involves gazing on, moving physically within and dominating those places (and their inhabitants) as defender of Conchobar's territory. Cú Chulainn is a virtuoso spatial practitioner, and his tracks 'weave places together'.[23] In this initiation episode, Cú Chulainn learns the significance of the land and the meaning of its landmarks to gain fluency in the language of Ulster and a broader understanding of Irish topography but also, through spatial practice, to prepare for an inscription of his own acts and narratives on the landscape—to write himself into the Irish 'Book of Nature'. Cú Chulainn's actions are prompted by an overheard prophecy that whoever took up arms that day would live a short life, though his deeds and fame would endure forever (926–7). The landscape, placenames and topographic narratives of the *Táin* and Ulster Cycle stories provide that enduring record, as becomes even clearer in *Tochmarc Emire*.

'Righthandwise I drive around you': *Tochmarc Emire*

Tochmarc Emire (*TE*) ('Wooing of Emer') is one of the pre-tales or accounts that set up the events of the *Táin*. The generation of *TE* is complex, and contains linguistically early and late sections; the episodes discussed next are not later than the eleventh or early twelfth century, however, and thus broadly contemporaneous with the LL *Táin*.[24] *TE* tells the story of Cú Chulainn's search for a fitting wife, and one can imagine this bridal-quest narrative entertaining diverse audiences at marriage feasts or other social gatherings. The story also models a sophisticated use of spatial language, logics, images and metaphors—both Cú Chulainn and Emer, the woman he woos, are masters of the poetics of space and place.

The first conversation between Emer and Cú Chulainn models what might be called an erotics of landscape. Emer opens the exchange by situating herself as one who makes a circuit around Cú Chulainn, moving in the traditionally propitious southwards, or righthandwise, direction: '"Righthandwise I drive around you", she says; that is, May God smooth it [the road] before you' (*'Dess imríadam dúib,' ol sí, .i. Día do réidiugud dúib*, §17), the scribe supplying what he understands to be a Christian equivalent of the blessing. Both make the same point, but Emer's (pagan) greeting gives her an active role as moving agent, as chariot-driver or horse-rider, which figures this dance of courtship in terms of a spatial movement that loops a welcome suitor into a potential bride's active orbit.[25] Referring to the many forms of protection her father erects around her, Emer goes on to describe herself in topographic terms as 'a road that cannot be entered' (*conar nád forémthar do chonair caílérmaim*, §18), a line that potentially picks up on those just mentioned about God smoothing the road for Cú Chulainn in the scribe's Christian re-working, and makes the conversation even more suggestively loaded for an audience alert to bawdy double entendres. As discussed by William Sayers, throughout this exchange we find significant sexual symbolism worked out through 'the homology of the human body and the Irish landscape'.[26] Here Cú Chulainn might be seen as following Emer's lead in using a sexual, spatial vocabulary in their allusive verbal courtship.

For a territorial defender and a spatially adept hero originally named Sétanta there could be no more fitting mode of wooing than through eroticized topographic discourse. Emer's question, 'Which is the path you came on?' (*Cisí conar dolod?*, §17), leads to Cú Chulainn's riddling description of his route to the 'landscape' (Emer) he sees before him. This shift of Emer from spatial practitioner to the space itself is not altogether surprising, given the prominence of the well-worn sovereignty trope that depicts the land as a woman.[27] When he sees Emer's breasts, Cú Chulainn proclaims that 'beautiful [is] this plain, the plain beyond the yoke' (*Caín in mag sa mag alchuing*, §27) which he repeats verbatim three times (thus allowing the audience to register the riddling language). The double yoke was, quoting Cyril Fox, 'rounded and peaked to a single terret on each side of the bar', so that, as William Sayers interprets it, 'The plain is the girl's abdomen. The images of yoke and plain beyond, drawn from the cultivation of the land, recall the overall wooing journey, the road that no one enters and, more importantly, the myth of the goddess of territorial sovereignty (cf. the rounded hills called *dá chich Anann*), who assured the fertility of the land, man and beast.'[28] Emer responds three times that 'Nobody approaches this plain' (*Ní rúalae nech in mag sa*, §27) without accomplishing a range of feats, which Cú Chulainn must (and later will) successfully perform. Here, Emer furthermore uses spatial discourse to identify herself as a *dindgna*, an eminent landmark and 'high place' when she states that she is 'Tara of women ... that is, as Tara is above every hill, thus I am above every woman in purity' (*Temair ban ... .i. amal atá Temair ós cach thulaig, sic atúsa ós cach mnaí in gensa*, §18.) Spatially, she is the most famed of hills, Ireland's pre-eminent site—a fitting partner for this hero.

Cú Chulainn and Emer part following their richly toponymic dialogue, and in the very next scene Cú Chulainn delivers an extended lecture to his charioteer (as well as the tale's audience) explaining the conversation's landscape kennings, the names and origin stories of the places previously referenced. In a reversal of the *macgnímrada* scene in which Cú Chulainn asked the charioteer Ibar to teach him about the places in which he was not yet *eólach* ('knowledgeable'), a now professorial Cú Chulainn delivers a treatise on the landscape and how to speak it. The text records that Cú Chulainn discusses these places explicitly to 'shorten their path' (*do irgairdiugud a séta*, §29): in other words, to provide entertainment while they journey. Similar phrasing in the *Táin*, we recall, described how the young Sétanta 'shortened his path' (*ic athgardigud a śliged*, 760) traveling to Emain Macha (and later to Culand's house, 875) with his playthings (hurling stick, ball, javelin); by *TE* he has graduated to discussions of placelore. Using toponymic narratives to pass the time implies that, as articulated in other texts discussed in this book, storytelling about places is believed to confer entertainment, pleasure and benefit.

Spatial rhetoric and placelore are prominent in Cú Chulainn's and Emer's allusive conversation, and more so in Cú Chulainn's remarkably lengthy exegesis of it: Cú Chulainn shows his fluency in the vernacular of Irish topography.[29] For instance, when Cú Chulainn narrates three origin stories about the Ulster capital, the performance turns Cú Chulainn into both source and mouthpiece for a central piece of Ulster *dindshenchas*. Cú Chulainn is presented in *TE* as we have it as surprisingly well versed in the lore of heroic Ireland's places, which coheres with the Ulster Cycle's portrait of Cú Chulainn as a warrior who consistently pursues (and achieves) mastery of Irish geography and placelore. Indeed, across the sources Cú Chulainn is often successful as a warrior explicitly because of his knowledge of the Irish landscape and his unique relationship with its environmental features.

In a play on the names of rivers and kings, *TE*'s Cú Chulainn even suggests that he is both kin to and champion of the landscape of Ireland, its rivers specifically. When Emer enquires about his *slondad* (meaning act of naming or self-description, patronymic, lineage), in a complex series of puns Cú Chulainn refers to himself as *nia*, denoting both 'champion' and 'sister's son' of one of Ireland's rivers: 'I am nephew/champion of a man who vanishes into another in the Wood of the Bodb' (*Am nia fir dichet i n-aile i Ross Bodbae*, §27). In his detailed exegesis of the conversation with Emer, Cú Chulainn untangles this allusive statement: in the Ross ('wood') of the Bodb (another name for the war-goddess Morrígan), one river, called the Conchobar, flows into the Dofolt (glossed as *móel*, or 'hairless') to form a single stream (*óensruth*, §49).[30] As Cú Chulainn explains, he is *nia* 'of that man' (*fir*) Conchobar twice over: first as nephew, for 'I am son of Dechtire sister of Conchobar' (*am mac Deichtire sethar Conchobuir*), and secondly as champion, for 'I am Conchobar's strong-man' (*am trénfer Conchobuir*, §49). While one of his goals is to establish his status as family member and champion of Ulster's king, Cú Chulainn uses multivalent language to also figure himself as kin to Ireland's rivers. The connection is furthered in the *Táin* when the rivers assist Cú Chulainn in his defense of Ulster,³¹ and other streams participate in healing the injured warrior (discussed later in the chapter). Cú Chulainn's extended discourse also constitutes a performance of Ireland's placelore and a model for how to 'talk place'—he has become an expert on and a teacher of Irish spatial practice, both verbal and physical, fitting his larger biography as Sétanta, a pathfinding warrior with a deep knowledge of Ireland's landscape.

Many events take place before Cú Chulainn, a year later, successfully accomplishes the challenges that threaten his union with Emer, but placelore and the heroic construction of a storied landscape are as prominent in *TE*'s closing lines as in its opening passages. As Cú Chulainn and Emer escape her father Forgaill, their acts give the landscape new placenames, and the pair who first courted in toponymic language finally create *dindshenchas* together. To get to Emer, Cú Chulainn first slays more than 300 men, then makes a great leap, holding Emer and her foster-sister (plus their weight in gold and silver), over three ramparts. When one warrior, Scenmenn, catches up with them, Cú Chulainn dispatches him at the ford (*áth*), and from that deed 'it is called the Ford of Scenmenn' (*dogarar Áth Scenmenn*, §86). Cú Chulainn next kills 100 attackers. Emer remarks, 'It is great the deed you did' (*'Is mór in glond dorignis'*), to which Cú Chulainn replies, 'Glondáth ['Ford of the Deed'] shall be its name forever' (*'Bid Glondáth a ainm co bráth'*, §86). Similarly, when they reach a place formerly called Ráe Bán ('White Plain'), Cú Chulainn hews down the opposing army 'until streams of blood burst forth' (*coro maidset na srotha fola*), leading Emer to comment, using phrasing which translates human bodies into landscape features, that Cú Chulainn has made a hill (*tilach*) of earthen sods (*fót*) of bloody gore (*cró*) at that site; the placename record preserves this act 'So that it is called Crúfóit from it' (*Conid de sin dogarar Crúfóit*, §87). This toponomastically invested text further states that when his horses kick up clods of earth so that several sods (*fóit*) fly about as Cú Chulainn pursues the attackers, the ford (*áth*) is thus renamed Áth nImfúait (§87).

In *TE* Cú Chulainn privileges a spatial poetics in his own exchanges; he provides a guide to understanding complex discourses rich in toponymic references, some of which present him as kin to Ireland's natural features; and finally the hero reshapes the landscape and generates new additions to Ireland's placelore or *dindshenchas*, through his acts and Emer's commentary on them. Cú Chulainn makes stories, but he also tells us how to unlock them. Through storytelling travels with his charioteer, he models how moving through Ireland's landscape is best accomplished by simultaneously moving through its topographic lore. *TE* is a tale of courtship that also shows Cú Chulainn's increasing mastery of a poetics of Irish place and his understanding of how Ireland becomes a storied landscape that rewards attentive readers. Many of these features characterize Cú Chulainn's behavior in the *Táin* as well.

'What manner of path is this on which we go?':
Finding one's way through the *Táin*

To delve further into Cú Chulainn's deep connection with the landscape, we must turn to the *Táin*. The route of the *Táin* is mapped in verbal and visual detail immediately following prefatory material detailing the events leading up to the cattle-raid. The LL manuscript presents the placenames vertically in two columns (the following prose section fills a third) separated by red and white bars which are attenuated animal bodies: tails at the top extend into stylized heads and clawed legs at each column's base, and each line's initial *f* is filled with red or white pigment.[32] The list reads

> Sligi na Tána in so 7 tossach in tšlúagid 7 anmand na sliged dochúatar cethri ollchóiced Hérend i crích Ulad .i. i Mag Cruinn, for Tóm Móna, for Turloch Teóra Crích, for Cúl Sílinni, for Dubfid, for Badbna, for Coltain, for Sinaind, for Glúine Gabur, for Mag Trega, for Tethba túascirt, for Tethba in descirt, for Cúil, for Ochain, for Uata fothúaid, for Tiarthechta sair ... (279–85)

> (This is the route of the Táin and the beginning of the hosting together with the names of the roads on which the men of the four great provinces of Ireland travelled into the land of Ulster: to Mag Cruinn, by way of Tuaim Móna, by Turloch Teóra Crích, by Cúl Sílinne, by Dubfid, by Badbna, by Coltan, across the river Shannon, by Glúine Gabur, by Mag Trega, by northern Tethba, by southern Tethba, by Cúil, by Ochain, by Uata northwards, by Tiarthechta eastwards ...) (p. 145)

As splendid verbally as it is visually, the full litany runs to almost seventy placenames. Such lists typically operate as mnemonic devices for organizing narrative events, and we expect the

Place-making heroes and the storying of Ireland's vernacular landscape   79

placenames here, as at the opening of Adomnán's *De locis sanctis*, to provide an index of the sites and episodes described in the body of the text. But, as Ann Dooley explains, the list (and the parallel list in Recension I) fails as an index or comprehensive itinerary of the narrative, and does not accurately map its sequenced events.[33] It includes places with known geographic coordinates as well as unidentified sites. Some placenames are etymological inventions, alliterative pairs and compounds. Finally, the sheer number of names overwhelms us—other problems aside, few listeners or readers could generate a mental map of a seventy-stop journey—and the list's alliterative, rhyming character encourages us to respond to the names as sounds or aesthetically pleasant formulae that verbally engage rather than geographically direct.

One effect of an extremely long placename list is that it embodies (intentionally or not) the spatial complexities of the undertaking, and demonstrates to the audience how essential it is to be guided through unfamiliar territories by a knowledgeable and sympathetic navigator. Queen Medb's complaint as her forces are misdirected along an impossibly circuitous route might also be applied to the aforementioned placename list:

A Ḟerguis, ca rádem de?
Cinnas conaire amse?
Fordul fodess is fothúaid
berma dar cech n-ailethúaith. (371–4)

('Oh Fergus, what do we say of this? What manner of path is this on which we go? Past every tribe we wander north and south.') (p. 148)

Medb and the men of Ireland, who seek quick movement on a geographically direct route to secure a prize bull, and the audience attempting to mentally map the *Táin*'s route, are denied this guidance. Being unable to see (and follow) the right or obvious path is a recurring experience in the *Táin*, an account of a dangerous, multiply thwarted, meandering raid led by Fergus, an Ulster exile with conflicted loyalties. As such, the imprecise litany of placenames that opens the *Táin* may be precisely on point in anticipating the difficulties Medb and Ailill's forces will have in successfully moving through Ulster territory. The list heightens audience awareness of the extensive scope of Irish toponymy and the geographic detail that the cattle-raid and its literary record will cover—without a hero, it is easy to lose the path.[34] And we know that this saga hero in particular possesses the essential spatial knowledge and topographic discursive skills to be victorious: he will find the path and write his story into Ireland's landscape.

Regarding Cú Chulainn's acts of inscription, Ann Dooley has deftly shown how the 'myth' or 'the "idea of writing" functions within the text as magically effective, setting up script or the written object as potent sign of the main and sole literate hero'.[35] In one key scene, Cú Chulainn inscribes a terrifying message into the landscape that advertises the violence its author will mete out to those who breach Ulster territory, forcing Medb and Ailill's great army to take another path. Cú Chulainn performs his textual ritual by carving an ogam message into a protective amulet to replace him as border guard so that he can depart to spend the night with a lover.[36] Specifically, he cuts an oak sapling in a single stroke and 'standing on one leg and using but one hand and one eye, he twisted it into a ring and put an ogam inscription on the peg of the ring' (p. 150) (*ro sníastar ar óenchois 7 ar óenláim 7 óensúil 7 doringni id de. Ocus tuc ainm n-oguim 'na mennuc inn eda*, 457–9). He then pulls the ring from the narrowest to the widest part of the standing stone at Ard Cuillen. When the army encounters the words carved onto the oak encircling the stone pillar but cannot comprehend them, Fergus provides a dramatic reading—the message forbids passage unless that same ritual writing feat is performed; flouting this command will result in slaughter. Though they must cut down a forest to clear a new path, the army nonetheless obeys the message and leaves the area—Cú Chulainn's words have the power to determine the movements of his opponents. The environment then seems to conspire with Cú Chulainn against the men of Ireland by producing, before they set up camp, a great snowfall reaching 'to the shoulders of men, to the flanks of horses and to the shafts of chariots' (p. 151) (*co formnaib fer 7 co slessaib ech 7 co fertsib carpat*, 517), which immobilizes and greatly discomforts the army. The imagery of a space that erases the presence of the army and their tracks also reminds us that, while Cú Chulainn uses environmental features to display messages and mark his control of spaces even while absent, the opposing forces, unable to construct a text in response, are literally whitened out and subsumed. The *Táin*'s heroic landscape only accepts, preserves and broadcasts the inscriptions made by select worthy figures, it seems.

In a subsequent environmental inscription scene, Cú Chulainn goes to a wood to cut a four-pronged forked pole in a single stroke, and, after pointing and charring it, he 'put an ogam inscription on its side' (p. 153) (*dobreth ainm n-oguim 'na táeb*, 562–3). With the tip of a single hand he forcefully catapults it out of his chariot and into the earth. While he constructs this ritualized message at the ford, two enemies and their charioteers come upon him, but before they can decide who will behead Cú Chulainn, he attacks them, skewers their four heads on the four prongs and sends their horses and chariots, reddened by the decapitated corpses they still bear, back to the now-panicked men of Ireland. When they approach the forked, bloodied pole in the stream and see only a single warrior's tracks, they marvel in fear. Notably, a placelore account conveys the identity of this opponent to the gathered audience of warriors (as well as the *Táin*'s readers and listeners). Ailill asks Fergus the ford's name—Áth nGrena—and Fergus adds that because of the forked pole (*gabul*), 'Áth nGabla shall be its name forever now' (p. 154) (*bid Áth ṅGabla a ainm co bráth*, 601–2). Fergus then declaims performative verses fusing the new name to the place and into memory, with the term *áth* ('ford') providing the first and last words of a six-quatrain poem in the poetical device called *dúnad* ('closing'), which metrically serves to emphasize the nature of the ford as well:

Áth ṅGrena, claímchlaífid ainm
do gním Chon rúanaid rogairb.
Fail sund gabuil cethri ṁbend
do cheist for feraib Hérend ... (604–8)

Áth ṅGrena a ainm mad co se,
méraid ra cách a chumne.
Bid Áth ṅGabla a ainm co bráth
din gabail atchí 'sind áth. (624–7)

(Áth nGrena will change its name because of the deed performed by the strong, fierce Hound. There is here a four-pronged forked branch to bring fear on the men of Ireland ...

Áth nGrena was its name hitherto. All will remember it. Áth nGabla will be its name forever from that forked branch which you see in the ford.') (p. 154)

The speech-act models an environmental reading methodology: deeds generate placenames; forked branches must be read and their message and authorship considered.

Following his poem, Fergus explains that the message written on the pole prohibits, as with the previous sign, any to pass unless the same feat is performed. After destroying several chariots and provoking Medb to warn him about treasonous behavior, Fergus successfully withdraws the wooden pole and composes another poem, which he ends by declaring that the topographic element, the forked branch, will endure in memory:

> Nuchum thá ní rádim de
> im dála meicc Deictire,
> concechlafat fir is mná
> din gabuil sea mar atá. (681–2)

(I have no more to say concerning the son of Deichtire [Cú Chulainn], but men and women shall hear of this pole (*gabuil*) as it now stands.) (p. 156)

This pole, a tree branch repurposed to encode a textual message and rooted back in the environment, becomes famed as both subject and carrier of story. Fergus and Cú Chulainn's shared methodology is to express message and story through the landscape and to ask the audience or readership to note the forked pole itself, with its inscription. Like the generation of the *Táin* from the landscape—specifically Fergus's gravestone described in *Foillsigid*, or the numerous *Táin* episodes in which the slain leave both their bodies and their names on environmental features and places across Ireland—this scene shows us how to plant story and actively embed narrative in the Irish landmass. As discussed elsewhere in this book, other narratives set in the Christian period incorporate the materials and technologies of manuscript culture into their stories. Here the *Táin*'s composers employ environmental elements—sticks sharpened and soot-blackened like styli, and twisted wooden withes carved with ogam characters—to explore the issues of textualizing or writing landscape. The *Táin*'s heroic spatial practitioners use terms, implements and images appropriate to an imagined, pre-Christian setting. The landscape is figured as a manuscript that records the deeds of Ireland's heroes who flourished before monastic writing culture was there to preserve their feats; the pre-eminent hero Cú Chulainn excels in marking topographic materials and inscribing new paths through Ireland to record his, and its, story.

Heroic combat: violent circuits and healing movement

Martial spatial practices that not only record but also reshape environmental contours are a major element in the *Táin*, and Cú Chulainn is one of the narrative's most formidable place-makers. As if anatomically priming him for these topographic feats, his most violent landscape transformations are preceded by his bodily distortion, the *ríastrad*, which has been discussed from multiple angles,[37] though the highly topographic nature of the *ríastrad* and its significance for understanding Cú Chulainn as a distinctly spatial hero have not been previously addressed. Cú Chulainn's *ríastrad* significantly opens with the imagery of a powerful river that overwhelms anything in its path, and which also resonates with *TE* descriptions of Cú Chulainn as kin to rivers:

> Is and sin cétríastarda im Choin Culaind co nderna úathbásach n-ilrechtach n-iṅgantach n-anachnid de. Crithnaigset a chairíni imbi immar chrand re sruth nó immar bocṡimind ri sruth cach ball 7 cach n-alt 7 cach n-inn 7 cach n-áge de ó mulluch co talmain. (2262–5)

> (Then his first distortion came upon Cú Chulainn so that he became horrible, many-shaped, strange, and unrecognizable. His haunches shook about him like a tree in a current or a bulrush against a stream, every limb and every joint, every end and every member of him from head to foot.) (p. 201)

While initially held in thrall to the force torrentially flooding over him, the description goes on to reveal a body that internalizes this force to ultimately power a warrior's performance. The text employs a range of images, but environmental and zoomorphic images are particularly prominent. For instance, Cú Chulainn retracts one eye so deeply into his skull a crane could not pluck it out; his pounding heart sounds like a bloodhound's howling; his hair becomes as densely spiky as sharp hawthorn branches that might impale apples (2273–86, pp. 201–2). In his most powerful form, this warrior is figured in the terms of Ireland's landscape and the creatures that inhabit it: Cú Chulainn's *ríastrad* emphasizes his role as a distinctly topographic hero. Just as he defines, manipulates, articulates, writes on and memorializes the landscape, his hero's body is shaped, powered and written as the landscape, by the landscape, like landscape.

It has been pointed out that Cú Chulainn's bodily transformation is passively constructed with the preposition *imm* ('around, about'),[38] so that the distortion, as cited previously, moves *im Choin Culaind*, literally 'around Cú Chulainn'. Cú Chulainn's ensuing circuits reproduce the spatial logic of the *ríastrad*: he becomes the threatening element that encircles and overwhelms the object of his violence. In preparation for a first attack, Cú Chulainn drives his chariot heavily (*trom*) in a great circuit (*mórthimchell*) outside the four great provinces of Ireland (*cethri n-ollchóiced ṅHérend*), so that

> Dollotar rotha iarnaidi in c[h]arpait hi talmain corbo leór do dún 7 do daiṅgen feib dollotar rotha iarnaide in charpait i talmain, úair is cumma atraachtatar cluid 7 coirthe 7 carrge 7 táthlecca 7 murgrian in talman aird i n-aird frisna rothaib iarnaidib súas sell sechtair. Is airi focheird in circul ṁBodba sin mórthimchell chethri n-ollchóiced ṅHérend ammaig anechtair arná teichtis úad 7 arná scaíltís immi ... (2306–12)

> (The iron wheels of the chariot sank deep into the ground so that the manner in which they sank into the ground [left furrows] sufficient to provide [materials for] fort and fortress, for there arose on the outside as high as the iron wheels dikes and boulders and rocks and flagstones and gravel from the ground. The reason why he made this warlike encircling [literally, circling of the Bodb, a war-deity] of the four great provinces of Ireland was that they might not flee from him and that they might not disperse around him ...) (pp. 202–3)

Cú Chulainn replicates the spatial logic of his *ríastrad* in his own warlike circuits: as he is encircled by a powerful fury, he too stalks in circles to envelop and overwhelm the enemy. His circling motions carve Ireland into a militarized space that can provide defenses, forts and fortresses, as well as natural barricades to contain the enemy. As Cú Chulainn's body is transformed for warfare by an encircling fury, so too is Ireland's landscape remade through the spatial hero's movements.

The next lines in the passage develop the earlier carving of defensive embankments into the landscape, yet here human flesh becomes the building material. Cú Chulainn

> fálgis fálbaigi móra de chollaib a bidbad mórthimchell in tṡlóig ammaig annechtair, & dobert fóbairt bidbad fo bidbadaib forro co torcratar bond fri bond 7 méide fri méide, bas sé tiget a colla. (2314–17)

(threw up great ramparts of his enemies' corpses outside around the host. And he made the attack of a foe upon foes among them so that they fell, sole of foot to sole of foot, and headless neck to headless neck, such was the density of their corpses.) (p. 203)

Cú Chulainn's attack brutally transforms the land. While the goal is to show how many he kills, the imagery and terms of his battle victories are spatial and relate to architecturally changing the landscape.

Following the cataclysmic slaughter, Medb and Ailill determine that single combats will be less wasteful, and the text in response now generates placename stories that record Cú Chulainn's victories and the identities of the slain. For instance, the jester Tamon, killed with a stone from Cú Chulainn's sling, is commemorated at Áth Tamuin (Ford of Tamon, 2461–72, p. 207); one beheaded warrior generates the name Cennáit Ferchon (Headplace of Ferchú, 2510–31, p. 209); and the blood (*fuil*) let by swords (literally weapons of iron, *iarn*) is memorialized by the ford Fuil Iairn (2599–604, p. 211). These lead up to the single-combat that constitutes the *Táin*'s most famous episode, Cú Chulainn's dramatic battle with his beloved foster-brother, Fer Diad, which gives the placename Áth Fir Diad (Ford of Fer Diad, 2603, p. 211). Dark environmental imagery and spatial logic express the human and social drama of this three-day fight. We immediately sense that the environment, elements and otherworldly beings are on Cú Chulainn's side: when he climbs into his chariot on the first day of fighting, 'around him shrieked goblins and sprites and fiends of the glen and demons of the air' (p. 217) (*gáirsetar imme boccánaig 7 bánanaig 7 geniti glinne 7 demna aeóir*, 2845–6). This cry from the spirits of land and firmament is orchestrated by the Túatha Dé Danann, who use their otherworldly powers over nature to increase Cú Chulainn's ability to inspire terror.

Reminding us of the topographic terms and logic used in the courtship exchange with Emer, the close relationship of Fer Diad and Cú Chulainn is also expressed spatially: they are travelers beloved of each other, journeying through the world together. Cú Chulainn declares that

Dá mbámmar ac Scáthaig
a llus gascid gnáthaig,
is aróen imréidmís,
imthéigmís cach fích.

Tú mo chochne cride,
tú m'aiccme, tú m'fine. (3002–7)

(When we were with Scáthach, by dint of our usual valor we would fare forth together and traverse every land. You were my loved comrade, my kin and kindred.) (p. 220)

Cú Chulainn reminds Fer Diad that it is not right for them to fight, as formerly they went together 'into every wood and wasteland, every secret place and hidden spot' (p. 221) (*cach fid 7 cach fásach, cach dorcha 7 cach díamair*, 3068–9). He then moves to poetry to lament that

Ropar cocle cridi,
ropar cáemthe caille ...
aróen imréidmís,
imthéigmís cach fid (3072–8).

(We were loving friends, we were comrades in the forest ...
Together we would ride and range through every wood) (p. 221).

Cú Chulainn conceptualizes the bond with his beloved foster-brother as one developed spatially, by bold travel through and joint negotiation of wild landscapes. As in his dialogue with Emer, Cú Chulainn here uses the language and logic of the environment and movement through it to articulate his relationships with the people most important to him: even Cú Chulainn's human relationships are topographical.

The forest-faring comrades are well matched over the next two days of fighting. However, a climactic scene on the third day of combat highlights Cú Chulainn's greater kinship with the environment, assuring his bitter triumph. Cú Chulainn chooses to fight in the water, where he can perform the 'feat of the ford' (p. 227) (*cluchi inn átha*, 3286) which has up to now defeated all champions, but Fer Diad nonetheless begins to gain the upper hand. In response to this change in fortunes, environmental and animal-based insults are shouted by Cú Chulainn's charioteer, Láeg, to incite Cú Chulainn to overcome Fer Diad:

Rot śnigestar mar śnegair cuip a lundu. Rat melestar mar miles mulend múadbraich. Ra[t] tregdastar mar thregdas fodb omnaid. Rat nascestar mar nasces féith fidu. Ras léic fort feib ras léic séig for mintu... (3305–8)

… Place-making heroes and the storying of Ireland's vernacular landscape

(He has belabored you as flax (?) is beaten in a pond. He has ground you as a mill grinds malt. He has pierced you as a tool pierces an oak. He has bound you as a twining plant binds trees. He has attacked you as a hawk attacks little birds . . .) (pp. 227–8)

Described with parallel rhetoric in which weakness shifts to empowerment, Cú Chulainn then rises up 'as swift as the wind, as speedy as the swallow, as fierce as the dragon, as strong as the air' (p. 228) (*i llúas na gaíthi 7 i n-athlaimi na fandli 7 i ndremni in drecain 7 i nnirt inn aeóir*, 3311–12).

This combat against Fer Diad is intense and cataclysmic. Compelling alliterative prose discloses that, as they clash, again the 'sprites and goblins and spirits of the glen and demons of the air screamed' (p. 228) (*gársetar boccánaig 7 bánanaig 7 geniti glinni 7 demna aeóir*, 3327–8). Horses become frenzied, and 'women and boys and children and those unfit to fight and the mad among the men of Ireland broke out through the camp south-westwards' (p. 228) (*goro memaid de mnáib 7 maccaémaib 7 mindóenib, midlaigib 7 meraigib fer ṅHérend trisin dúnud síardess*, 3336–7). The point is to demonstrate that the violence is so fierce it overwhelms all present, not only the combatants. Significantly, the expressive mode is spatial: all non-warriors lose control of their movements and do a wild circuit southwestwards, or counter-clockwise—an inauspicious direction. Further expressing cosmic breakdown, the combat between Cú Chulainn and Fer Diad is so intense 'that they forced the river from its usual course and extent' (p. 228) (*gora lásetar in n-abaind assa curp 7 assa cumac[h]ta*, 3329–30) so that its bed becomes completely dried up. These apocalyptic scenes reveal the effects of violence on the environment and the community, and show how people and places are transformed by warfare, as Lowe has explored.[39] In this scene, furthermore, environmental mayhem is expressive of social mayhem: when Cú Chulainn kills his foster-brother, Fer Diad, in what might be read as the emotional climax of the *Táin*, demons of the glen shriek; non-combatants are maddened by the violence into making cursed loops through the landscape; and a river—life-force and medium of support for Cú Chulainn— dries up, expelled from its course as a result of the brutal combat.

Though he survives, Cú Chulainn, too, very nearly dies in this confrontation, yet he manages to perform a lament for Fer Diad. Comprising twenty-seven stanzas, Cú Chulainn's elegy concludes with the statement that Banba (Ireland) has never nurtured, 'nor has there traveled over land or sea' (*níra chind de muir ná thír*,

3594), a noble warrior of greater fame than Fer Diad. Following Cú Chulainn's moving verbal performance, which transmits a sense of combat's psychologically decimating effects, the text shifts to the survivor's healing. Cú Chulainn's own body, torn up in the combat such that 'the ford was red with the blood from the warrior's body' (p. 228) (*corb forrúammanda in t'áth do chrú a chuirp in chathmíled*, 3341), is carried

> go glassib 7 go aibnib [críchi Conaille] Murthemne do thúargain 7 do nige a chneda 7 a chréchta, a álaid 7 a ilgona i n-agthib na srotha sain 7 na n-aband. Dáig dabertis Túatha Dé Danand lubi 7 lossa ícce 7 slánsén for glassib 7 aibnib críchi Conailli Murthemne do fortacht 7 do fórithin Con Culaind comtís brecca barrúani na srotha díb. (3599–604)

> (to the streams and rivers of Conaille Muirthemne to wash and cleanse his wounds and his stabs, his cuts and many sores, against the current of those streams and rivers. For the Túatha Dé Danann used to put herbs and healing plants and charms on the streams and rivers in Conaille Muirthemne to help succour Cú Chulainn, so that the streams used to be speckled and green-surfaced from them.) (p. 235)

Like the regenerative lake in *Immram Curaig Maíle Dúin* (discussed in Chapter 1), the *Táin*'s waters are endowed with restorative powers; and they are instrumental in healing Cú Chulainn. Following this remarkable scene, the names of the twenty-one participating rivers are enumerated, in LL listed in a column and bracketed off by a decorative white bar with zoomorphic terminals: Sás, Búan, Bithlán, Findglais, Gleóir, Glenamain, Bedg, Tadg, Teleméit, Rind, Bir, Brenide, Dichaem, Muach, Miliuc, Cumuṅg, Cuilen, Gainemain, Drong, Delt, Dubglass (3605–8, p. 235).[40]

The environment, particularly its waters, rallies to the side of Cú Chulainn: the territory of Ulster defends and supports Cú Chulainn as he defends it, here and elsewhere. As suggested in Cú Chulainn's punning self-identification as *nia*, both the family member and champion of the rivers, this healing scene further attests to Cú Chulainn's kinship with Ireland's natural features and the otherworldly beings that work through them.

Final battle: *Táin* geographies remade

The importance of being able to accurately read the landscape, comprehend what it contains and determine a fitting strategy in response to its challenges—a particular skill of the pathfinding and wayfaring hero Cú Chulainn—is developed in terms of a lack of spatial savvy on the part of Medb, Ailill and their representatives. When the Ulster forces arrive to do battle, they are initially misrecognized as landscape features. The messenger Mac Roth scans the plain on behalf of Medb and Ailill and sees

> in nglascheó mór ra ercc in comás eter nem 7 talmain. Andar leiss batar indsi ás lochaib atchondaic ás fánglentaib na cíach. Andar leis batar úama ursloicthi atchonnaic and i rremthús na cíach cétna. Andar leis ba línanarta lín lángela ná bá snechta síthalta ac snigi ratafarfáit and tri urdluich na cíach cétna, ná andar leis ba éochain de ilénaib ilerda ingantacha imda, ná ba hilbrec[h]tnugud rétland roglan i n-aidchi reóid rošolais, nó ba haíble teined trichemrúaid. (4183–91)

> (a great grey mist which filled the void between heaven and earth. He seemed to see islands in lakes above the slopes of the mist. He seemed to see yawning caverns in the forefront of the mist itself. It seemed to him that pure-white linen cloths or sifted snow dropping down appeared to him through a rift in the same mist. He seemed to see a flock of varied, wonderful, numerous birds, or the shimmering of shining stars on a bright, frosty night, or the sparks of a blazing fire.) (p. 251)

Fergus takes Mac Roth's verbalized landscape portraits (extending over sixty lines), which provide an aesthetically appealing, tranquil and artful vision of an idealized environment, and with rhetorical drama moves us, like Brendan's voyagers landing on the 'island' Jasconius (discussed in Chapter 1), from an inviting space to the prospect of impending slaughter. In the answering lines to the passage excerpted previously, Fergus reveals that the great mist is formed by the breath of horses and heroes combined with the dust-clouds their movement generates: the islands floating above the lakes, with their rounded hills and mounds, are warriors' heads above their chariots; the gaping caves are equine and human nostrils deeply and swiftly breathing in the sun and wind (4200–11, p. 251). This instance of the watchman device relies on spatial riddling, and Mac Roth, acting on behalf of Medb and Ailill, is unable to accurately read the landscape laid out before him: an attacking army is mistakenly interpreted as a pleasant swathe of Irish land. When the army arrives for the final battle, this idyllic landscape gives way, through the violence of war, to an apocalyptic, violently torn-up environment.

At the final battle, in a series of linked acts, Fergus, Cú Chulainn, Medb and the bulls remake Ireland's landscape, performances that are both physical and narrative, and fuse story to geographic contours. The first blow to the environment is prompted when the king of Ulster cruelly taunts Fergus using the terms concerning homeland and exile from it. Conchobar boasts he is the

> fer rat indarb át chrích 7 át ferand 7 át forbba, fer rat chuir i n-adba oss 7 fíadmíl 7 sinnach, fer nára léic leithet da gabail badéin dit chrích ná dit ferand dait . . . (4751–3)

> (man who banished you from your land and territory and estate, one who drove you to dwell with deer and hare and fox, one who did not permit you to hold even the length of your own stride in your land and territory . . .) (p. 267)

Accepting that this tragedy has indeed befallen him, for the first time in the narrative Fergus prepares to turn his massive sword, an ancient otherworldly weapon 'as big as a rainbow in the air' (p. 268) (*métithir ra stúaig nimi i n-aeór*, 4776–7), against the Ulaid, until another exile, Conchobar's own son, convinces Fergus to enact his wrath on the landscape instead. Fergus thus shears off the 'tops of the three hills which are still there in the marshy plain as evidence. Those are the three Máela of Meath' (p. 268) (*trí cindu dina trí tulchaib, go failet 'sin ríasc bad fiadnaisi. Gorop íat na trí Máela Mide and sain*, 4778–9). This scene, in which Fergus is mocked for losing access to his homeland, ends with his defacement of the geography before him—anger, shame and longing for his own territory are converted into destruction of Meath's topography.

As Cú Chulainn hears Fergus's sword striking Conchobar's shield before the exiled warrior turns to decapitate Meath's heights, Cú Chulainn jumps from his sickbed so that the hoops (*túaga*) and bindings (*bacca*) holding his injured body together burst from his wounds, reaching as far as Mag Túaga in Connacht and Bacca in Corco M'rúad (4788–90)—Cú Chulainn's wounds are mapped onto the landscape and his body bursts open to create gory placelore. If we allow ourselves to visualize it, the ensuing description provides a grotesque spectacle: 'The dry wisps of tow which plugged his wounds soared into the uppermost air and firmament as high as larks soar on a day of fair weather when there is no wind' (p. 268) (*Lotar na suipp sesca bátar 'na áltaib i cléthib aeóir 7 firmiminti feib is sía thiagait uiss i lló áille nád bí gáeth*, 4790–1). Not permitting us to hover with the birds in the fair firmament, our gaze descends to a nightmarish landscape polluted by warfare in which, like the larks that are gore-soaked bindings, rivers are blood: 'His wounds broke out afresh and the trenches and furrows in the earth were filled with his blood and the tents from his wounds' (p. 268) (*Ra gabsat a fuli ilgremma de gorbo lána tairchlassa 7 eittrigi in talman dá fhulib 7 dá gáeib cró*, 4791–3).

Forty lines later, Medb also carves out trenches in the earth with her body fluids and creates new placenames when her *fúal fola* (literally 'urine of blood') arrives in the midst of battle: flowing from her, it cuts 'three great trenches in each of which a household can fit. Hence the place is called Fúal Medba' (p. 269) (*trí tulchlassa móra de co taille munter in cach thurchlaiss. Conid Fúal Medba atberar friss*, 4830–2). Proximity requires that these passages are considered together, and while Cú Chulainn is popularly celebrated as the hero, and Medb the misogynized villain, here the blood of both figures is shown as carving up, even destroying or polluting the land, conveying a more global meditation on the spatial ills of combat, warfare and human destruction of revered places. This is further emphasized when, a few lines later, Cú Chulainn takes his sword and, having granted safe crossing to Medb's army, channels his fury into the land; just like Fergus before him, 'he smote a blow on the three blunt-topped hills at Áth Luain, as a counterblast to the three Máela Mide, and cut off their three tops' (p. 270) (*rabert béim dona tríb Máelánaib Átha Lúain i n-agid na trí Máela Mide goro ben a trí cindu díb*, 4843–5). The territory is denuded of its noble heights, its *dindgna*, the victim of both Fergus's and Cú Chulainn's martial frustrations, and the landscape's gory new riverbeds flow with the blood of both Medb and Cú Chulainn.

The episode is closed by Fergus's statement that 'As when a mare goes before her band of foals into unknown territory, with none to lead or counsel them, so this host has perished today' (p. 270) (*Feib théit echrad láir rena serrgraig i crích n-aneóil gan chend cundraid ná comairle rempo, is amlaid testa in slúag sa indiu*, 4849–51). These lines are most famously read as the LL's sexist denunciation of Medb and the so-called inevitable failure of women leaders. This misogynistic statement, however, also conveys derision in terms of unsuccessful spatial practice and erroneous movement in alien and hostile territories: Medb, Fergus claims, has failed as a navigator and pathfinder, and Fergus's words are meant to evoke earlier scenes. For instance, Medb had ordered a wall of protective shields erected to conceal her from Cú Chulainn's missiles (p. 175, 1334–7). More memorably, at the beginning of the *Táin* we are told of a rather unlikely scenario in which Medb only travels enclosed by chariots—two on each side—so that she and her golden crown remain untouched by 'the clods of earth cast up by the horses' hooves or the foam dripping from the bridle-bits or the dust raised by the mighty army' (p. 153) (*fótbaige a crúib greg nó uanfad a glomraib srían nó dendgur mórslúaig nó mórbuiden*, 583–4). Indeed, in *Acallam na Senórach*, a text that valorizes deep engagement with the land (see Chapter 4), when Saint Patrick enquires about Medb, Caílte also rather preposterously characterizes her as a queen so squeamish of physical contact with the environment that, in an exaggeration of the *Táin* description, she requires thirty-six chariots around her so that not even a splash of mud from the path might reach her or her robes.[41] These rhetorically vivid scenes aim to produce, with Fergus's condemning words, a picture of Medb as a leader intentionally cut off from, and hence unable to strategically scrutinize, the landscape she and her troops move through.

Also implicit in the criticism of a mare's ability to lead the herd is the suggestion that a stallion would have navigated victorious passage. Medb had, of course, enlisted the assistance of Fergus mac Róich, whose patronymic can be etymologized to 'great stallion' (*ro-ech*).[42] However, uncooperative stallions with strong alliances to other herds can prove a significantly greater liability than a help and will often show a lack of concern for successfully steering a herd through alien territory. Furthermore, Ann Dooley has pointed out that mares typically lead groups of horses, as stallions are wild and unreliable, and a medieval audience well versed in animal husbandry and equine behavior would likely question Fergus's unlikely claim regarding a mare's innate inability to guide the herd.[43]

It is worth revisiting the foundational events of this *táin* or 'cattle-raid,' which also use animal imagery to rhetorically highlight Medb's failures in terms of space and territorial defense. The LL *Táin* opens to the royal couple Medb and Ailill arguing over which of them possesses greater wealth (and thus power and authority). Ailill reports he had not heard of Medb's riches, for her property was routinely plundered and carried off by neighboring enemies (8–10); this constitutes a charge of Medb's inability to defend her borders and strongholds from plundering foes. The importance of land, the maintenance of its boundaries and their defense is further developed in terms of the spatial acts of the legendary prize bull, the Findbennach, a hyper-masculine creature that arrogantly refuses to remain within the bounds a woman's pasture circumscribes around him (71–5). When the bull migrates from Medb's to Ailill's fields, this gives Ailill wealth greater than Medb's own, and the text seems calculated to portray a woman, Medb, as someone who cannot effectively maintain or police the borders of her land to protect her treasures—a prize bull can just wander off to establish himself in another field. The text provides an easy invitation to dismiss Medb simply on the grounds of gender; prove the unsuitability of women as rulers; and laugh as a mighty bull, a powerful symbol of masculinity, undermines a queen's authority and rejects her claims to power over him by simply walking away. But what is also at stake is Medb's own desire to regain territorial control of Crúachu and enforce her authority to make decisions about that space and the larger province of Connacht. This requires raids into alien territories and an attempt to move another great bull from its home into a foreign land. It is a large-scale spatial gamble that fails, Fergus wants us to believe, because she is a 'mare'. All of these details work together to portray strategic wayfaring and spatial movement as masculine activities. And while Medb has Fergus given the task of safely leading her troops through hostile lands, a conflicted Fergus seems to use his knowledge to thwart a successful and speedy raid into Ulster territory. Indeed, as the *Táin* shows by consistently highlighting Cú Chulainn as the spatial hero, rather than an excitable, unreliable great stallion or *ró-ech*, it is a bloodhound that is required, a *cú*, to maintain the boundaries and sniff out the best paths; but such a figure is not among Medb's followers.

Like the warriors before them, at the end of the epic the two prize bulls, Findbennach Aí of Crúachan and the Donn Cúailnge of Ulster, dig up the ground in their violent, earth-moving clashes. At one point, we learn that the Donn Cúailnge is spatially discombobulated, and, as we by now expect, this is an almost fatal mistake: the Findbennach savvily uses 'the confusion of the Donn Cúailnge's journeying and wandering and travelling' (p. 271) (*meirbflech a astair 7 a imthechta 7 na sliged barin Dond Cúalnge*, 4879–80) to gore the spatially overwhelmed Donn in the side. The Donn Cúailnge, however, rallies when he is taunted by Cormac Cond Longas, just as the charioteer's goading helped Cú Chulainn regain advantage over Fer Diad. Launching on an enraged and brutally violent circuit, 'the bulls traversed the whole of Ireland in that night' (p. 271) (*ra sirset na daim Hérind uili in n-aidchi sin*, 4892). The Donn Cúailnge dismembers the Findbennach and strews the white bull's body parts across the Irish landscape: a gory heap (*crúach*) of its liver lands in a place called Crúachna Áe; the ford (*áth*) where the bull's haunch or loin (*lón*) is deposited is known as Áth Luain; when more of the liver (*tromm*) is carried east to Meath it is left in Áth Troim; and when he flings the thigh (*láraic*) it lands in Port Láirge, with the rib-cage (*clíathaig*) pitched into Áth Clíath (4901–9, p. 272). The landscape is altered, and absorbs the bodily members of the slain, but it is renamed to preserve the account of this cosmic final battle and violent resolution of Ireland's great cattle-raid.

In a tragic scene that is reminiscent of Cú Chulainn's own distorted loss of control and inability to distinguish between friend and foe while in the throes of battle rage, the Donn Cúailnge, turning north, ultimately finds his way home, but he cannot halt his slaughter, and attacks the innocents of his territory: the women, boys and children who had been lamenting or keening (*ac coínud*) their beloved bull. Once the Donn Cúailnge has destroyed those whom he earlier protected (his body could shelter 100 from heat and cold, no evil spirit would approach the district in his presence and his musical lowing brought delight to all inhabitants throughout the territory, 1325–33), the creature turns away from his home landscape and perishes, in a topos of spontaneous heartbreak, from grief: 'After that he turned his back to the hill and his heart broke like a nut in his breast' (p. 272) (*Tuc a druim risin tilaig assa aithle & ro maid cnómaidm dá chride 'na chlíab*, 4916–17). Transformed by violence and displacement, neither bulls nor exiled warriors can return home.

Drunken circuits and apocalyptic spatial practice: *Mesca Ulad*

Mesca Ulad (*MU*) ('Drunkenness of the Ulstermen'), a text that shares much with the closing of the *Táin* in its apocalyptic rendering of the Irish landscape, explores a disoriented Cú Chulainn's movement into foreign and hostile territories. A now-fragmented narrative, probably originally composed ca. 1100, *MU*'s first half is preserved in LL, the same manuscript that contains Recension II of the *Táin*, with a second half, divergent in both plot and character, contained in LU.[44] The spatial issues and plot elements relevant to the present argument appear in the first half of the story, and thus it is primarily the LL text discussed here.[45]

MU's opening describes Ireland's ancient divisions: Amairgen (a son of Míl) grants the underground regions of Ireland to the Túatha Dé Danann, who go into the hills while the sons of Míl maintain control of Ireland above ground. The text moves forward

Place-making heroes and the storying of Ireland's vernacular landscape 95

in time to the province of Ulster, which has been partitioned into thirds and shared among Cú Chulainn, Conchobar and Fintan, son of Níall Níamglonnach. Cú Chulainn is summoned to Emain Macha, and travels 'by the most direct roads, by the shortest paths' (*i trémdirgi na sliged, i n-athgardi na conar,* 53–4). When Cú Chulainn arrives in Emain Macha, Conchobar requests that he give his third of Ulster to Conchobor for a year, which he does, on the condition that Conchobar improve the province during his rule. Fintan similarly grants his third to Conchobar. The province flourishes, and the expectation is that Conchobor will remain ruler of a unified Ulster. Fintan and Cú Chulainn simultaneously prepare feasts for all of Ulster, but when invitations for the concurrent celebrations arrive, violence breaks out, and it looks as if the province will be destroyed in the fighting. At Conchobar's request, his son Furbaide, beloved foster-son of Cú Chulainn, intervenes, weeping and lamenting until Cú Chulainn asks him what is wrong. The boy responds that now, when the province is flourishing and has become a 'well of plenty' (*topor tuli*), Cú Chulainn is damaging (*adgell*) and completely ruining (*admilliud*) it in exchange for a feast lasting but a single night (177–9). This child's emotional appeal about the land successfully halts the destruction, and it is determined that Fintan's feast at Dún Dá Bend will be attended for the first half of the night, and Cú Chulainn's for the second.[46]

When his charioteer, Láeg, determines midnight has arrived, travel to Cú Chulainn's feast begins, though the women and children and the weak are permitted to stay behind. Cú Chulainn starts them off at a leisurely pace, but when his horses break out into a war-frenzied gallop, literally a 'bright sudden-start of the Bodb' (*bánbidgud bodba,* 253–4) that is similar to his own violent *circul mbodba* in the *Táin*, the rest of the horses follow in this crazed circuit. Their route takes them well beyond Cú Chulainn's fortress at Mag Muirthemne—based on identification of several of the placenames cited, the spree covers a largely clockwise circuit from the north of Ireland towards the east and then southwards across all of Ireland, landing them in the hostile territory of Cú Ruí's Temair Lúachra, unidentified but perhaps, Hennesey argues, on the border of Kerry and Limerick.[47] Their furious and misdirected gallop across Ireland apocalyptically decimates the landscape as they move across it. They flatten every hill (*cach tailach*); they leave a wake of leveled hollows or valleys (*fóenglenntaib*) behind them; their iron-wheeled chariots slash the roots of very great trees (*fréma na ralach romór*) as they drive through forests of oak (*fidbad dara*) so that the land becomes a place of cleared plains (*crích machairi*); and their galloping horses disperse the water and stones from the streams (*na hessa*), fords (*na hátha*) and estuaries (*na hinbera*) so that the riverbeds are completely emptied and dried, and will remain so for a long time (269–77).

As the division of Ulster into thirds shows, what constitutes fitting stewardship of and sovereignty over the land is a core theme in *MU*, and this episode can be profitably considered as part of that nexus. The Ulaid's transformative trek across Ireland on one level participates in a network of stories that tell of converting wild, hilly and forested territories into arable land. Nonetheless, that the landscape becomes bone dry suggests something more sinister, and makes it impossible to read the Ulaid's apocalyptic, flattening passage as an agriculturally fructifying conversion of dense forests into cultivated earth. Their drunken, destructive, 'scorched-earth' spatial practice, with the warlike start of the horses and the leveling, drying effect on the landscape, is reminiscent of the environmental destruction resulting from Fer Diad and Cú Chulainn's socially cataclysmic battle in the *Táin*, as well as the *Táin*'s combatants' (both humans and bulls) final topographic assaults on the hills and the landscape more generally.

In scenes that add humorous elements of human fallibility to this tale, the Ulaid must face the fact that they have become terribly lost on their drunken journey from one feast to another. Conchobar first airs his doubts: 'We haven't met with this road between Dún Dá Bend and Dún Delga (before)' (*Ní fhuarammar in slige se etir Dún Dá Bend 7 Dún Delga*, 277–8), with the others confirming his suspicions that they are indeed not within Ulster's borders at all. Conchobor asks who will determine their whereabouts and map their position in this unknown landscape. The trouble-making Bricriu nominates Cú Chulainn, who has claimed that 'there is no district in which he has not massacred one hundred of that district' (*na rabi tricha cét na dernad argain cét cacha trichu cét*, 291–2). Cú Chulainn takes full responsibility, reconnoiters the territory with his charioteer and, gazing out from Áne Chlíach (identified as Cnóc Áine or Knockainy in County Limerick), establishes their location by identifying landmarks, including hills, mountains, a pool and the forests that surround them in a passage that orients the audience as well. Citing John O'Donovan's statement that 'I viewed these mountains from *Cnoc Aine* on the 5th August, 1840, and found this description remarkably correct', Hennessy comments that Cú Chulainn's orienting statements in the text point to the remarkable toponymic knowledge of the Irish.[48]

While Cú Chulainn ascertains their location, a great snow now falls on *MU*'s border-crossers as they dally in hostile territory, just as in the *Táin* when the forces of Medb and Ailill enter Ulster territory only to be engulfed in a blizzard. However, in contrast to the men of Ireland, who were covered by the snow, here the quick-thinking Ulster charioteers successfully construct shelters for their horses from stone columns (*columna clocc*), which, the text records, are known as *Echlasa Ech Ulad* ('Stables of the Ulaid Horses') and survive as topographic evidence of their building achievements (308–12). The Ulaid, we see, can succeed within and even permanently alter alien landscapes to preserve stories of their feats. Reporting back to Conchobar, Cú Chulainn offers to lead the Ulaid back home before their enemies sense their presence, yet this is deemed a coward's plan, and the Ulaid instead elect to remain for a day and night, leaving tracks to advertise their movements in this hostile territory. While Cú Chulainn offers pathfinding to take them home, the Ulaid collectively prefer to continue on their destructive wild ride.

They finally draw near to Temair Lúachra, where Medb and Ailill are visiting Cú Ruí. One druid put on watch by Medb suspects he sees a host approaching, while in the usual terms of the watchman device another druid insistently misreads the approaching host as a stand of great oaks (*na daire romóra*), their chariots as royal strongholds (*rígrátha*), their shields as stone columns (*na colomna cloch*) and their red-pointed spears as the 'stags and wild animals of the land with their horns and antlers above them' (*uiss 7 altai na crích cuna mbennaib 7 cona congnaib úasu*, 368–85). A collection of verses delivered by the skeptical druid extends the arboreal, avian and bestial imagery to further develop the environmental elements of the approaching Ulaid, all the while pointing out that this is not, indeed, the bucolic landscape spectacle the more naïve druid believes it to be. The poetry dramatically involves us in imagining all of the environmental possibilities before returning us to the more alarming vision of an enraged host, whose arrival is formulaically cataclysmic. Repeating their earlier warlike 'bright sudden-start of the Bodb' (*bánbidcud bodba*, 493, also at 253), the Ulaid's advance causes shields and weapons to clatter to the ground, thatching falls from the houses, teeth chatter and people faint, and it is as if the ocean (*in muir*) floods over from the world's remote corners (*cernaib in betha*) (498–9). Although the

Ulaid declare on their arrival that they have not come to fight, but arrive in the merriment of drunkenness (*medarmesci*, 842), under the guise of being feasted they are nonetheless imprisoned in an iron house around which 150 smiths kindle great fires. It looks, then, like the Ulaid's apocalyptic circuit and the environmental threat they pose will conclude in their own fiery extermination.

It is at this point that the LL version abruptly ends. It is problematic to treat the narrative picked up by the LU portion as a continuation, but it does nonetheless provide an ending to the story, in which the Ulaid escape the iron house, Cú Chulainn leads them back to his fort and a forty-day feast and Conchobar henceforth maintains a kingship without destruction (*cen coscrad*, 1062). In striking contrast to the LL portion, LU shows virtually no interest in place or placenames, environmental features or rhetoric, and though the Ulaid make their way home, this feat is depicted as one of strength rather than spatial power or navigational savvy.

MU, incomplete in all manuscripts and thus a narrative of disparate halves, does not link or address in any explicit way these issues of spatial malpractice, or the fact that the Ulaid, both king and warriors, are almost (but not quite) decimated in what would have been the Ulster Cycle's greatest tragedy. Yet descriptions of a wasted landscape signify a tragic state of affairs in other contexts. Reminiscent of the images of a ravaged Ireland concluding the *Táin*, fuller development occurs in *Togail Bruidne Da Derga* ('Destruction of Da Derga's Hostel'), which shares several narrative elements with *MU*: a mad gallop around Ireland, a burning house, a king's beloved son who attempts to intervene, a watchman's extended environmental descriptions, a landscape destroyed and entirely parched, such that the dying king cannot get a restorative drink, with verbal play on *laith* ('draught') and its lenited homonym *flaith* ('lordship, sovereignty') emphasizing the significance of Ireland's depleted water sources, and so on.[49]

Does *MU* denounce a 'scorched earth' heroic mode of hypermasculine spatial practice? It is ultimately a hostile territory that the Ulaid warriors subject to their destructive movement—the twice-mentioned frenzied, demonic circuits of the battle-deity Bodb are the ravaging spatial practices of warfare. In *MU* this is retrospectively claimed to be part of the Ulaid's articulated plan to show their bravery—they do not want to skulk home, and deem it cowardly to conceal their tracks in enemy territory. Nonetheless, that they are almost destroyed on this journey seems suggestive of a broader critique of heroic excess and arrogance. The *mesca*

Ulad, or 'intoxication' of the Ulaid, calls attention more globally to the consequences of the warrior class becoming destructively inebriated with power and violence, and literally losing their ability to safely navigate the world around them. We might recall the remarks of the king's son, Furbaide, who at the story's opening weeps and laments for the way in which a beloved landscape can be changed from a well-spring of plenty into a wasted land overnight, through the destructive bickering of warriors whose desire for heroic pre-eminence often trumps the well-being of the territory they defend. That the dangerous consequences are noted and lamented by *MU*'s characters might be expected. These messages would presumably also have resonance for audience members living in a heroic society that both celebrated the power of its warriors and registered the destructive environmental consequences of warfare. Although there is a happy ending, the narrative highlights the dangers of reckless spatial practices, with the entire male population of Ulster almost incinerated in an iron house when Cú Chulainn, the Ulster Cycle's most skilled wayfaring warrior, near catastrophically fails to lead the Ulaid from Dún Dá Bend to his own home.

Heroic landscapes and redemptive storytelling

MU ultimately shows a dislocated Cú Chulainn's recovery of an impressive topographical awareness and internalized map of even those lands most distant from Ulster: knowledge of Ireland's territories is shown, sometimes with biting irony, to be one of Cú Chulainn's particularly famed skills. Across the Ulster Cycle's narratives, Cú Chulainn is consistently depicted as a warrior uniquely appreciative of and skilled in the minutiae of Irish places, an expert Irish spatial practitioner and environmentally attuned hero embraced and enabled by the territories he defends.

A triple-birth story associates his entry into the world with an avian razing of Emain Macha that occasions an Ireland-wide circuit led by his charioteer mother, culminating in a stop at Ireland's ancient ritual site, Brú na Bóinne, where a massive snow falls. Spatial and environmental elements continually re-appear throughout the biography of Sétanta/Cú Chulainn: this pathfinder and hound defends the territory of Ulster while its environmental components also support the hero—waterways in particular, which are given an agency that other land features are not, bear out his punning claims to be river-kin and champion. His kinship with the land is not only exemplified through his movement and the ways his actions endow the land with contours and placenames: in *TE*, this placelore expert and performer of *dindshenchas* teaches the stories and founding narratives of Ireland's places to while away the time the journey takes. In the *Táin*, the rivers support and heal him, and the stones and trees operate as the textual surfaces on which this literate hero carves binding messages in the ogam alphabet. *MU* calls into question the environmental destruction of heroic excess and the dangers of navigational failure, but it also showcases Cú Chulainn's regard for his own province and its fitting, bounty-producing rule. The account of Cú Chulainn's death at the hands of the satirists provides a relevant spatial detail as well. Gravely wounded, Cú Chulainn nonetheless gathers his entrails to seek a drink from a nearby loch. He then goes to the 'pillarstone which is in the plain' (*coirthi cloiche file isinmaig*)[50] and binds himself to it with his belt or girdle so that he can die standing. The landscape's jutting stones, earlier message bearers that apotropaically defended Ulster on his behalf, in his last moments physically support him and become the backbone allowing him a heroic last stand. Cú Chulainn is a warrior uniquely engaged with the landscape, ultimately fused with it; and spatial physical and narrative practices characterize and structure his biography.

This chapter opened with a discussion of Fergus's generation from the cold earth of Ireland to tell the story of the *Táin*. In *Siaburcharpat Con Culaind* ('Phantom-chariot of Cú Chulainn'), linguistically dated to the late tenth or early eleventh century,[51] Loegaire, the skeptical king of Tara, refuses to believe in God or Patrick until Patrick conjures Cú Chulainn, dead some 450 years, so that Loegaire might see and speak to the ancient hero. This is granted, and twice Cú Chulainn appears. Significantly, he enters *Siaburcharpat* in the environmental terms of the watchman device—he appears as a landscape misrecognized by the consistently short-sighted pagan king, and it is Patrick's scribe, Benén, who reads the scene for Loegaire. Loegaire reports to Patrick that he sees a piercing, frigid wind (*gaíth n-úair*, 9240) coming over the plain. Benén explains that this is the wind from hell (*gáeth iffirnd*, 9243) as it opens to release Cú Chulainn. When Loegaire asks about the heavy fog (*tromchíaich máir*, 9244) descending upon them, Benén identifies it as the breath of the approaching men (Cú Chulainn and his charioteer) and their horses (*anala fer 7 ech*, 9246). Where Loegaire sees a natural feature—a great flock of ravens (*feóchúni mair*, 9247) reaching up to the clouds of heaven (*nélaib nime*, 9248)—Benén correctly recognizes sods of earth (*fóit*, 9249) kicked up by Cú Chulainn's horses. Cú Chulainn appears as an environmental spectacle, and it is Patrick's Christian scribe, Benén, who reads the 'landscape' correctly to identify him. The hero does not linger to converse with Loegaire, yet when Patrick declares that through God's power Cú Chulainn will return, he reappears. Cú Chulainn speaks, in verse, of his heroic exploits and hellish suffering, and his statements emphasize the entombing powers of the landscape. 'Believe in God and Saint Patrick, oh Loegaire, so that the waved surface of the earth might not come across you' (*Creit do Dia 7 do náem Patraic a Laogaire ná túadaig tond talman torut*, 9301–2), he urges. He states that every champion (*rúanaid*) is bound by the law of earth (*reacht ná talam*, 9303), alliteratively reiterating that *cach triúin talam cach naib nem*, 9303–4) or 'for every strong man, earth, for every holy one, heaven'. Through Cú Chulainn's poetic performance, and his argument in favor of God and movement to heaven over being enveloped by the earthly, material world, Loegaire is ultimately swayed. Cú Chulainn himself twice requests a place in heaven, notably in terms of a new land to inhabit. He implores Patrick at the beginning of his account 'that you would bring me with your faithful into the lands of the living' (*romucca lat chretmecho/hi tírib na mbeó*, 9299–300), and he similarly closes his poetic performance by requesting of Patrick 'that you bring me with your faithful ones into the land that you drive about' (*romfuca lat chretmecho / is tir immaréid*, 9534–5), namely, the territory of heaven. Patrick, here also an active spatial practitioner whose riding or driving about (*immaréid*) demarcates a land for believers, grants it: Cú Chulainn is given the divine blessing or seal of approval by Saint Patrick, and at the close of *Siaburcharput*, while 'earth came across Loegaire, heaven was declared for Cú Chulainn' (*dodeochaid talam tar Loegaire adfiadar nem do Choin Culaind*, 9539–40).

Patrick's act in granting Cú Chulainn heaven following the story he tells of his warrior's life recuperates Cú Chulainn as an important hero and source of Irish literary culture. Cú Chulainn warns Loegaire that champions will be covered over by the earth and bound within the landscape. However, through the interventions of Saint Patrick, the spatial hero who started life as the pathfinder Sétanta and comes back as the repentant warrior Cú Chulainn finds a route that will transport him beyond the Irish landscape and into the territory that, riding about in saintly circuits, Patrick has marked out for the faithful.

Significantly, though the characters and events are from pre-Christian Ireland, even these stories are developed so that the textual element is nonetheless part of the larger narrative complex. The presence of Patrick's scribe Benén implies that Cú Chulainn's account is recorded and ultimately preserved on manuscript pages, perhaps as the *Siaburcharpat* itself. As becomes apparent in *Acallam na Sénorach*, in which Patrick continually orders Benén to write down the ancient *fíana*'s stories of Ireland's past, Benén's role in *Siaburcharpat* suggests a scribe's involvement in converting an orally delivered narrative into an authorized text to be circulated among Ireland's elites, as Elva Johnston has posited.[52] As we will see in Chapter 3, the poets and Ireland's bardic elites clearly grasped the importance of converting the heroes, adventures and storied landscapes of the past into heightened verbal forms, preserving them through inscription onto LL's pages. Place-making figures like Cú Chulainn, who story Ireland's heroic landscape and mark the centrality of a spatial poetics in Ireland's heroic literature, chart a path that culminates in the formalization of a place-lore genre and manuscript tradition in which the landscape itself, Ireland, becomes the hero of the text.

Notes

1 See discussion of the different versions in James Carney, *Studies in Irish Literature and History* (Dublin: DIAS, 1955), pp. 165–79 and Kevin Murray, 'The Finding of the *Táin*', *Cambrian Medieval Celtic Studies* 41 (Summer 2001), 17–23. It is worth noting that the later *TBCIII* or Recension III of the *Táin* has Cú Chulainn himself slaying the *sencháid* ('chroniclers' or 'historians') of the *Táin*. As Joseph Nagy points out, this account suggests that it is not poor storytelling memory, but Cú Chulainn's 'overwhelming violence' that is to blame for the *Táin*'s loss. See Joseph Nagy, 'How the *Táin* Was Lost', *Zeitschrift für celtische Philologie* 49/50 (1997), 604.
2 Murray, 'Finding', p. 21.
3 Dublin, Royal Irish Academy, MS D.iv.2 variant, cited in Carney, *Studies*, p. 167.
4 Kuno Meyer, '*Die Wiederauffindung der Táin Bó Cúalnge* [Egerton 1782, fo. 87 b]', *Archiv für Celtische Lexikographie* 3 (1905), 2. *Tromdám Guaire* also records this curse made by the hermit-saint Marbán. Carney, *Studies*, p. 178.
5 Murray, 'Finding', p. 22. See also John Carey, 'Varia II: The Address to Fergus's Stone', *Ériu* 51 (2000), 185.

6 For issues of orality and literacy highlighted in this tale, see Joseph Nagy, *Conversing with Angels and Ancients* (Ithaca, NY: Cornell University Press, 1997), pp. 17–20, 307–17. Recent discussion of early Ireland's secondary-oral environment and how 'the oral and written were in continual interaction' in creating textual communities and identities is found in Johnston, *Literacy and Identity*, pp. 157–76 (quote at p. 157).
7 Keith Basso, *Wisdom Sits in Places* (Albuquerque, NM: University of New Mexico Press, 1996), p. 32.
8 Kuno Meyer (ed.), *Triads of Ireland* (Dublin: Hodges Figgis, 1908), p. 8.
9 Carney, *Studies*, p. 179; its miraculous nature is also discussed in Nagy, *Angels and Ancients*, p. 310.
10 The *Táin*, according to scholarly consensus, was first written down as a complete text in the ninth century, and is preserved in three distinct versions. Recension I is taken primarily from the Lebor na hUidre manuscript (ca. 1100), and its terse prose, plus earlier date, have made it the more frequent subject of scholarly analysis. In the mid-twelfth century, Recension I was worked into a more polished and unified narrative: inconsistencies and doubled episodes were removed, and *rémscela* or 'pre-tales' explaining the *Táin*'s background events, and rhetorical flourishes characteristic of the period, were added. This version, known as Recension II, is contained in the LL manuscript (ca. 1160). A third Early Modern Irish version, Recension III, is fragmentary and late, dating to the fifteenth–sixteenth century. Recension II is used here for multiple reasons. First, it frames the larger conflicts as the result of spatial movement, the migration of exiled warriors, but also that of a prized bull from a woman's herd to a man's. Secondly, *dindshenchas* or placelore texts are for the first time organized as a national *Dindshenchas Érenn* in LL (see Chapter 3). Thirdly, though Recension I is earlier, it was the mid- to late twelfth century when major ecclesiastical reforms took root and events leading to the English invasion developed, and this context for the LL manuscript, its scribes and users make it the more compelling version for this study. Nonetheless, one must not overemphasize differences, as in most cases parallel passages occur in both recensions, and therefore several points pertain also to Recension I. For further background, see Rudolf Thurneysen, *Die irische Helden- und Königsage* (Halle: M. Niemeyer, 1921), pp. 96–244; Cecile O'Rahilly (ed./trans.), *Táin Bó Cúalnge from the Book of Leinster* (Dublin: DIAS, 1967), pp. xiv–lv and *Táin Bó Cúailnge: Recension I* (Dublin: DIAS, 1976), pp. vii–xxii; William O'Sullivan, 'Notes on the Script and Make-up of the Book of Leinster', *Celtica* 7 (1966), 1–31; and Gearóid Mac Eoin, 'The Provenance of the Book of Leinster', *Zeitschrift für celtische Philologie* 57 (2009–10), 79–96.

11 Dooley, *Playing the Hero*, p. 33.
12 The story is preserved in two versions, Version I, from the now lost Cín Droma Snechta of the first half of the eighth century, and Version II, a late eighth- or ninth-century expansion of Version I. The earliest Version I witness is Lebor na hUidre, and forms the basis of the edition cited here. See *Compert Con Culainn*, ed. A. G. van Hamel, *Compert Con Culainn and Other Stories* (Dublin: DIAS, 1978), pp. 1–10 (henceforth referred to as *Compert*). References to the Irish text are to section numbers with page numbers following; English translations are my own.
13 *Compert* §6, p. 6 (note 6.9).
14 See possible etymologies for the name in Eoin Mac Neill, 'Varia. I', *Ériu* 11 (1932), 130–1. Bergin refutes many of Mac Neill's claims, but cites multiple examples demonstrating that 'Middle-Irish writers derived it from "sét", "way"'. Bergin concludes that 'these etymologies are not to be taken seriously', yet the fact that the Middle Irish audience probably accepted the link is important. Osborn Bergin, 'Varia. I', *Ériu* 12 (1938), 235.
15 Jeffrey Gantz, *Early Irish Myths and Sagas* (New York: Viking Penguin, 1981, rept. 1986), p. 131.
16 See *Togail Bruidne Da Derga*, ed. Eleanor Knott (Dublin: DIAS, 1936), lines 170–81, p. 6, for Conaire's prohibitions, which relate to appropriate movement and the presence of specific figures on the road before him. See analysis of this problematic journey in Ralph O'Connor, *The Destruction of Da Derga's Hostel* (Oxford: Oxford University Press, 2013), pp. 72–3, 104–28.
17 *Compert* §1, p. 3.
18 All citations from the *Táin* are, unless otherwise stated, from O'Rahilly (ed./trans.), *Táin Bó Cúalnge from the Book of Leinster*. References are to line numbers; page numbers refer to O'Rahilly's English translation, which I have occasionally edited for clarity.
19 See *Aided Óenfir Aífe* ('Death of Aife's One Son') in van Hamel (ed.) *Compert*, pp. 9–15; English translation in Thomas Kinsella (trans.), *The Táin* (London: Oxford University Press, 1969), pp. 39–45. See discussion in Joanne Findon, *A Woman's Words: Emer and Female Speech in the Ulster Cycle* (Toronto: University of Toronto Press, 1997), pp. 84–106.
20 See Pádraig Ó Riain, 'Boundary Association in Early Irish Society', *Studia Celtica* 7 (1972), 12–29.
21 This statement is absent from *TBCI*.
22 Michel de Certeau, *Practice of Everyday Life*, trans. Stephen F. Rendall (Berkeley and Los Angeles, CA: University of California Press, 1984), p. 117.
23 de Certeau, *Practice of Everyday Life*, p. 97.

Place-making heroes and the storying of Ireland's vernacular landscape   105

24 Version III of *TE* is contained in full in the fourteenth-century MS R.Ir.Ac.D.4.2 (Stowe), though an incomplete text including later interpolations and emendations is also found in LU (late eleventh or early twelfth century) and other later manuscripts. On this complex manuscript tradition, see van Hamel (ed.), *Compert*, pp. 16–17; and Gregory Toner, 'The Transmission of *Tochmarc Emire*', *Ériu* 49 (1998), 71–88. References are to the edition of *TE* in van Hamel (ed.), *Compert*, and citations refer to section numbers. English translations are my own.
25 In *Siaburcharpat Con Culaind* Cú Chulainn requests access to heaven, characterized as the land Patrick drives around (*tir immaréid*, 9534–5) (see Chapter 3).
26 William Sayers, 'Concepts of Eloquence in *Tochmarc Emire*', *Studia Celtica* 26–27 (1991–92), 130.
27 For an overview, see Amy Mulligan, 'The Anatomy of Power and the Miracle of Kingship: The Female Body of Sovereignty in a Medieval Irish Kingship Tale', *Speculum* 81.4 (2006), 1019–34.
28 Sayers, 'Eloquence', p. 135.
29 Cú Chulainn's 265-line explanation begins on column 2, folio 75 r and ends on column 1, folio 76 v in RIA MS D iv 2 (Stowe). See a comprehensive analysis of speech in *TE* in Sayers, 'Eloquence', pp. 126–40.
30 The hairless river denotes Cú Chulainn, frequently depicted as beardless. See Sayers, 'Eloquence', p. 136.
31 *TBCI*, 1158–64. See Joseph Nagy, 'The Rising of the River Cronn in *Táin Bó Cúailnge*', in Anders Ahlqvust (ed.), *Celtica Helsingiensa* (Helsinki: Societas Scientiarium Fennica, 1996), pp. 129–48.
32 See page 56 of LL (Trinity College Dublin MS 1339), at www.isos.dias.ie, accessed June 5, 2017.
33 Dooley, *Playing the Hero*, pp. 44–51.
34 Indeed, O'Rahilly's *TBCII* index lists over 300 distinct placenames.
35 Dooley, *Playing the Hero*, pp. 30–3.
36 The fact that many ogam characters (termed *feda*, plural of *fid*, 'wood, tree') are named after trees (oak, birch, willow, alder, hazel, ash, pine, etc.), and that ogam inscriptions (carved along the angled edge of standing stones) are widely visible features jutting out of the landscape like tree-trunks, is intriguing in terms of *Táin* depictions of a pre-Christian heroic writing system as arboreal and specific to outdoor landscapes. See Damian McManus, *A Guide to Ogam* (Maynooth: An Sagart, 1991). For interactive 3D images and maps plotting ogam stones, see https://ogham.celt.dias.ie, accessed June 5, 2017.
37 The most thorough study of Cú Chulainn is Ann Dooley, *Playing the Hero*, though also see Doris Edel, *Inside the Táin: Exploring Cú Chulainn, Fergus, Ailill, and Medb* (Berlin: Curach Bhán, 2015), and Kate Mathis, 'Review: Edel, Doris, *Inside the Táin*', *Zeitschrift für celtische Philologie* 64 (2018), 459–68. Other studies of the

ríastrad include P. L. Henry, '*Furor Heroicus*', *Zeitschrift für Celtische Philologie* 39 (1982), 235–42; Jeremy Lowe, 'Kicking over the Traces: The Instability of Cú Chulainn', *Studia Celtica* 34 (2000), 119–29; Sarah Künzler, *Flesh and Word: Reading Bodies in Old Norse-Icelandic and Early Irish Literature* (Berlin: De Gruyter, 2016); Amy Mulligan, 'Form and Function of the Grotesque Body in Medieval Irish and Norse Literature' (D.Phil diss., University of Oxford, 2003), 'Cú Chulainn, Isidore of Seville and the Erasure of a Warrior's Body: Heroic Crisis and Irish Independence', in James Buickerood (ed.), *From Enlightenment to Rebellion* (Lewisburg, PA: Bucknell University Press, 2018), pp. 33–46; Tomás Ó Cathasaigh, 'The Body in *Táin bó Cúailnge*', in Sarah Sheehan, Joanne Findon and Westley Follett (eds.), *Gablánach in Scélaigecht* (Dublin: Four Courts Press, 2013), pp. 131–42; and William Sayers, 'The Smith and the Hero: Culann and Cú Chulainn', *Mankind Quarterly* 25.3 (1985), 227–60 and '*Airdrech, Sirite* and Other Early Irish Battlefield Spirits', *Éigse* 25 (1991), 45–55.
38 See Sayers, '*Airdrech, Sirite*', p. 53, and Lowe, 'Kicking over the Traces', p. 124.
39 Jeremy Lowe, 'Contagious Violence and the Spectacle of Death', in Maria Tymoczko and Colin Ireland (eds.), *Language and Tradition in Ireland: Continuities and Displacements* . Maria Tymoczko and Colin Ireland (Amherst and Boston, MA: University of Massachusetts Press, 2003), pp. 84–100.
40 See the column on page 89 of the LL manuscript at www.isos.dias.ie, accessed June 5, 2017.
41 Whitley Stokes (ed.), *Acallamh na Senórach*, in *Irische Texte*, vol. IV (Leipzig: S. Hirzel, 1900), lines 3859–70. Cited and discussed in Ann Dooley, 'Speaking with Forked Tongues', in Sarah Sheehan and Ann Dooley (eds.), *Constructing Gender* (New York: Palgrave Macmillan), 2013, p. 183.
42 Patricia Kelly, 'The *Táin* as Literature', in J. P. Mallory (ed.), *Aspects of the Táin* (Belfast: December Publications, 1992), p. 79.
43 Dooley, *Playing the Hero*, p. 182.
44 See O'Connor, *Destruction*, pp. 163–5; Uáitéar Mac Gerailt, 'The Edinburgh text of *Mesca Ulad*', *Ériu* 37 (1986), 153–5; and Tomás Ó Concheanainn, 'The Manuscript Tradition of *Mesca Ulad*', *Celtica* 19 (1987), 13–30.
45 The edition cited is *Mesca Ulad*, ed. J. Carmichael Watson (Dublin: DIAS, 1941, rept. 1983) (*MU*). References to the Irish text are to line numbers; English translations are my own.
46 Dún Dá Bend has been identified as Mount Sandel, Co. Derry, though some argue it refers to a nearby stone fort. See Richard Warner, 'Láeg's Line: A Route for the Gods?', in Martin Huld *et al.* (ed.), *Archaeology and Language: Studies Presented to James P. Mallory* (Washington, DC: Institute for the Study of Man, 2012), pp. 55–72.

47 William M. Hennessey (ed.), *The Mesca Ulad, or, The Intoxication of the Ultonians* (Dublin: Royal Irish Academy, 1889), pp. iv, ix–x. See also the placename index in Carmichael Watson (ed.), *MU*, pp. 126–9, 131.
48 Hennessey, *Mesca Ulad*, pp. x–xi.
49 An excellent analysis of *Togail* and its constituent tropes is O'Connor, *Destruction*.
50 Whitley Stokes (ed./trans.), 'Cuchulainn's Death', *Revue Celtique* 3 (1876–8), 181–2.
51 See Thurneysen, *Irische Helden- und Königsage*, pp. 567–71 and Gerard Murphy, *Ossianic Lore and Romantic Tales of Early Ireland* (Dublin: Colm O Lochlainn, 1955), p. 21. The oldest version is that preserved in LU, and the text cited here is from the diplomatic edition of *Lebor na Huidre: Book of the Dun Cow*, ed. R. I. Best and O. Bergin (Dublin: Hodges Figgis, 1929, rept. 1972), pp. 278–87. References are to line numbers, and translations are my own. Other later versions are found in British Library Egerton 88 and British Library Additional MS 33,993.
52 Elva Johnston, 'The Salvation of the Individual and the Salvation of Society in *Siaburcharpat Con Culaind*', in Joseph Nagy (ed.), *The Individual in Celtic Literatures* (Dublin: Four Courts Press, 2001), pp. 124–5.

3
A versified Ireland: the *Dindshenchas Érenn* and a national poetics of space

Wisdom sits in places. It's like water that never dries up. You need to drink water to stay alive, don't you? Well, you also need to drink from places. You must remember everything about them. You must learn their names. You must remember what happened at them long ago. You must think about it and keep on thinking about it. Then your mind will become smoother and smoother. Then you will see danger before it happens. You will walk a long way and live a long time. You will be wise. People will respect you.[1]

The Irish would certainly agree with the Western Apache that places contain wisdom from which we can, to great benefit, drink deeply. The siting of wisdom in places, and the planting of stories and histories in the landscape, has been an important element in Irish texts from the earliest times to the present day. In the eleventh and twelfth centuries, however, Irish poets and scribes began to formalize these placelore texts as a cohesive and extensive genre covering all of Ireland, a collective *Dindshenchas Érenn*: the 'wisdom, lore or traditional knowledge' (*senchas*) of the 'high places, noteworthy, noble sites' (*dind*) of Ireland (*Érenn*). While other medieval literatures do feature spatial writing, with narratives and characters moving through richly detailed geographies, Ireland is unique in producing several manuscripts that each bring together 100 to 200 placelore texts, the *Dindshenchas Érenn*, whose unifying characteristic is the mapping of narrative and lore onto specific, named sites. In these *dindshenchas* accounts, places, rather than characters or events, are the leading elements: each composition, poetic and prose, opens with the statement of a placename, and a multi-layered meditation on its significance (mythical, historical, political, etc.) is developed in the subsequent lines.

The *Dindshenchas Érenn* is an extensive and popular Middle Irish corpus containing approximately 207 poems and 207 prose pieces, preserved in some twenty manuscripts and represented by three recensions: A (poems), B (prose) and C (combined metrical and prose entries).[2] As a collection of frequently copied and reworked texts from a long-standing placelore tradition, with some pieces attributed to specific ninth- to eleventh-century poets, it is a body of writing that defies easy dating.[3] The Book of Leinster (LL), however, which contains most of the poems discussed here, is the earliest manuscript witness of the *Dindshenchas Érenn* by about two centuries, having been compiled between 1151 and 1224—Elizabeth Duncan has recently argued that Scribe A, who was responsible for most of the *dindshenchas*, was most likely writing between 1151 and 1163.[4] It preserves 112 poems (A), varying in length from four to about fifty stanzas filling thirteen manuscript pages, as well as seventy-eight prose *dindshenchas* entries (B) occupying seven manuscript pages—lost folios may also have contained further entries.[5] LL separates the poetic and prose texts; and my analysis concentrates on the poetry to track ideas about the use of verse as an appropriate literary form in which to write and formalize Ireland's landscape. Specifically, this chapter focuses on those LL poetic texts that provide insights into the concept of placemaking poets as medieval Ireland's geographers, and our intermediaries in accessing Ireland's verbal topographies. While other countries, like medieval England, produced elaborate world maps, or *mappae mundi*, Ireland did not participate in the production of elaborate cartographies. Rather, it was the class of poets who staked out the role of Ireland's mapmakers, with medieval Irish geography becoming a verbal undertaking rather than a cartographic one. Irish *senchas*—tradition, ancient history, storied lore and knowledge and a kind of narrativized 'wisdom'—sits in Ireland's textual places, to cite Basso's words.

In the suggestive opening lines of one *dindshenchas* poem on Temair (Tara), the legendary seat of the high kings of Ireland, the medieval poet ponders the process by which Ireland's geographic sites begin to gain power as verbalized, imagined places.

Temair Breg, cid ní diatá
Indisid a ollamna!
cuin do dedail frisin mbruig?
cuin robo Temair Temair?

Temair Breg, from what is it named?
Declare, oh sages!
When did it part from the place?
When did Tara become *Tara*?[6]

As with any complex piece of literature, there are multiple ways to understand these lines. The question regarding Tara's 'parting from the place' can be read as a simple onomastic inquiry about when 'Temair Breg' became known as 'Temair'. Or, from an environmental perspective, the question of when Temair became separated from (*do dedail*) the *bruig* (land, region, border, monumental site)⁷ might refer to the creation of the mounds and other archaeological features that separate Tara's iconic earthworks from the rest of the landscape. Edward Gwynn, who undertook the gargantuan task of producing a five-volume edition of the metrical *dindshenchas* still used today, made these suggestions in 1903.⁸ These lines draw us into a poet's sophisticated contemplation of the split between actual geographies and those that take on literary dimensions: verbalized topographies are transformed into new sites as they are unmoored from the landscape and re-rooted in a place within a poem, a manuscript, or someone's memory. Might these verses indicate a theoretically nuanced understanding of the creation of verbal worlds and textual high places that are, ultimately, independent in many ways from the physical place itself? The poets who enshrined and eternalized these places with their words, the compilers who gave them manuscript form and the later readers and listeners who attuned themselves to the play and power of words, might all have pondered at what point a verbalized place takes on substance and convincing contours.

It bears repeating: when did the idea of Tara diverge from the place itself? When did Tara become 'Tara' the poem, the literary entity? These lines provide a refrain for this chapter—how do these *dindshenchas* sites depart from their material geographies, and how does one access them? Furthermore, what is the point, and impact, of developing a collective, national narrative topography? To what uses was a virtual, verbal geography put in twelfth-century Ireland and beyond? What the *dindshenchas* poems show us is that some of the most compelling medieval Irish sites are places made of words rather than stone and soil. Verbalized topographies, extensive virtual landscapes and rich, temporally layered places that exist within the verses of a poem, become a *Dindshenchas Érenn* from which a nation might drink deeply and wander through to live a long, wisdom-filled life.⁹

Place-making on the page: 'By my art you may see in memory a plain populous as the land of Tara'

Irish placelore accounts that highlight the landscape, Ireland itself, as the main character coalesce in the remarkable collection known as the *Dindshenchas Érenn*, yet individual placelore accounts feature throughout medieval Ireland's literary traditions. The voyage tales and Ulster Cycle texts of Chapters 1 and 2 feature main characters who travel the landscapes and seascapes detailed in the texts, and their actions generate the plot as they move meaningfully between the disparate sites. In *Tochmarc Emire*, the hero Cú Chulainn collects and speaks about Ireland's *dindshenchas* to pass the time in a pleasant way, and the *Táin* too might be read as an extended placelore account—shorn of its onomastic material, as Ruairí Ó hUiginn has pointed out, the *Táin* is a very thin story.[10] As is further explored in Chapter 4 with regard to the *Acallam*, individual placelore accounts are used to powerful effect in several prosimetric narratives—embedded placelore is perhaps the identifying characteristic of Irish literature. The *dindshenchas* poems, however, develop placelore in some novel and very important ways. Many of the *dindshenchas* accounts feature a poet or speaker who, often using first- and second-person forms of direct address, requires the audience's participation, and asks us to inhabit the described landscape and contemplate its features and history, but without a main character, plot or narrative to intervene or shape our responses to the textual landscape. For that reason, the goals and effects of the *dindshenchas* poems on the audience are dramatically different from other Irish spatial literature, and can allow us insight into how Irish literati envisioned the audience's direct engagement with and use of discursive landscapes. The audience's involvement is essential—the poets command us to behold, listen, look out, and gaze upon the landscapes they conjure up. They lead us to insert ourselves into the verbal worlds that unfold before us, to rub shoulders with and learn from the fates of the characters who earlier populated these places. The *dindshenchas* poems comprise a body of Irish topographical texts that are uniquely crafted to speak directly to the audience and readership—we become familiar with landscapes both geographically and temporally distant, and make these places our own through experience of the poetry. These poems enable us to grasp how Irish composers comprehended literary composition, and versification in particular, as a way of cultivating, accessing and honoring revered landscapes.

Multiple *dindshenchas* poets make reflective statements, suggesting they understood themselves to be creating landscapes and 'high places' and not just describing existing sites to us; the poets use their specialized skills and bardic vocabulary to generate transformed sites that, when versified, become multi-dimensional worlds to inhabit and travel through. The *dindshenchas* poets rightly see their words as empowered to crystallize and solidify: their verses create new places and constitute additions to the world. For instance, the *dindshenchas* poem *Bend Etair II* ('Howth Head II') draws attention to the almost divine power of the poet's art and compositional process, and shows us how he creates a bright landscape from darkness. It opens with the poet addressing us in the first person, which effectively pulls us into the poem's intimate space:

Cid dorcha dam im lepaid,	Though it is dark for me in my bed,
cid scél fromtha is fír-deccair,	though narration is testing and truly
imréil fri solad slimda	difficult,
cach romag cach rodindgna	illustrious with the success of eulogy
	is every famous plain, every great
	landmark.
Mar nobeinn fri forgla fert	When I had to do with the most
ós cech forba cen anrecht,	famous mounds
gním cech cuiri fo chuimsi	above every domain without injustice,
condat uili imṡuilsi.	the achievement of every host fittingly
	[was put],
	so that all are illuminated.[11]

Though we start out in the poet's dark room, lying, perhaps eyes closed, on a bed, we are quickly moved to a view of plains and landmarks that shine forth because of the power of the praising poetry. The poet marks the contrast between the lightless, non-topographical starting point (the dark room) and the illuminated landscape he verbally generates in a 'testing and truly difficult' act.

While the actual O'Neill-McCarthy letter, in which the famed depiction of the bardic creative process described next is preserved, has been shown to be an eighteenth-century forgery, it nonetheless resonates strongly with the images of poetic composition given in *Bend Etair*[12]:

> The Professors ... gave a Subject suitable to the Capacity of each Class, determining the number of Rhimes, and clearing what was to be chiefly observed therein as to Syllables, Quartans, Concord, Correspondence, Termination and Union, each of which were restrain'd by peculiar Rules. The said Subject ... having been given over Night, they work'd it apart each by himself upon his own Bed, the whole next day in the Dark, till at a certain Hour in the Night, Lights being brought in, they committed it to writing.[13]

A versified Ireland

Our *Bend Etair* poet, like the popularly imagined bardic students, sits in the dark and composes a poem. He generates and can see the bright poetic place, and brings it, an illuminated landmark, to the audience. It is worth remembering that one of the main terms for poet, *file*, pl. *filid*, comes from a root meaning 'to see' (cognate with Welsh *gweled*, 'see').[14] These poets were highly conscious of their power to create worlds through versified language: to generate a space, a land, out of nothing, out of a dark, isolated room. In this dramatic poetic creation we hear biblical echoes, and one is reminded not only of God's performative speech-acts generating light and landmasses at the start of Genesis, but also the recognition in John 1:1 that Creation is a performative utterance, a verbal act: *In principio erat verbum*, with God pronouncing the world into being. It would be unusual if the poets, fully steeped in biblical tradition, were not also gesturing toward this grand cosmogonic act in their own verbal land creations. The *dindshenchas* poets forge topographies from words and give us, the audience, a new world. They create and materialize new places with their artful words, and they confidently advertise their power to do so.

One poet, identified as 'F.' in LL, claims that his art (*dán*) will allow us see a populated landscape; he then goes on to construct from lines of verse the 'Ridge of Dairbre' (*Druim nDairbrech*), an otherwise unknown place memorializing a man named Dairbre, slain in battle. F. uses his poetic craft to excavate Dairbre's Ridge and its history, crystallizing it in our memory so that, as stated in the closing lines, we too can benefit from the *fír*, or truth, of this newly revealed place:

Cid diatá in druim nDairbrech?	From what is the hill of Druim Dairbrech named?
ba mór lá rathuill teglach;	For many a day the household increased;
rem dán atchí co cuimnech	by my art you may see in memory
clár buidnech mar thír Temrach.	a plain populous as the land of Tara.[15]

The versified *Druim nDairbrech* conjured by the poet allows a kind of temporal collapse, so that we move through a ridge populated with several mighty inhabitants (further detailed in the poem's subsequent lines). The term *clár*, which denotes a flat surface and is here juxtaposed with the *tír* ('land') of Tara, is appropriately rendered 'plain' in Gwynn's translation. *Clár* has a wide semantic range, however: it denotes several flat objects, including a table and gaming board, but, most significantly, writing tablets (it glosses Latin *tabula*) and part of the sounding board of the *crott*, or harp. The poet explains that by his *dán* (meaning art, profession, gift, poem and poetry)[16] we see in our minds the *clár*: here, I argue, we catch an artist's punning reference to his craft, the idea that the crowded plain is also the writing tablet covered with lines of verse, which ultimately becomes the poem's manuscript page. The *dindshenchas* poetics of Irish space knowingly blurs the lines between text and landscape, and encourages us to see landscape as literature and text as territory.

The poem's next stanza continues this interweaving of words and space:

Druim nDairbrech is dún álaind, Druim Dairbrech, it is a fair fort,
múr gainmech fo thuind   A sandy rampart by the lank-sided
  tóeb-sheing;   billow;
láid báird bas greimm ria   the lay of a bard that will be
  glé-raind   profitable in tuneful verse
fégaim din beinn aird óebind.   I see from the lovely lofty height.[17]

The poet declares that 'I behold,' or perhaps 'I spy' (*fégaim*); the verb *fégaid* is potentially related to terms for keenness, implying close attention as well as looking and scanning.[18] What does F. see? From this height (*ard*), which provides a rhyme with the bard's or poet's lay (*láid báird*) of the previous line, he locates his poem-in-becoming, the words laid out in the imagined landscape, which he then proceeds to verbalize. The poet here is performatively articulating the 'land-text': he generates this topography in his poem and simultaneously speaks from within the poem's geographic space, 'from the lovely, lofty height' (*beinn aird óebind*). In the closing stanza, we are reminded of the value of contemplating and imaginatively inhabiting this versified height.

In cnocc-sa catha in chomlaind,   This hill of the array of battle
a éicsiu datha derbaim: O swift poets, I declare,
maith dia fír in lá labraim   good for its truth is the day I speak of,
d'fáglaim cid diatá in deg-druim. for learning whence is named the
                                    noble hill.[19]

This hill and its importance are confidently proclaimed, or even 'established' (*derbaim*, from *derbaid*, certifies, proves, confirms, attests)[20] by the poet, who explains that learning the truth (*fír*) of

A versified Ireland

the ridge's legend is good and valuable. The closing lines employ *dúnad*, the spatial poetic device that provides a cyclical repetition of the poem's opening words (see further discussion below), here with some innovation and attention to the transformative power of poetry: Dairbrech's Ridge (*druim nDairbrech*) has by the conclusion of the *dindshenchas* verses become superlative, the 'best' or 'noblest' (*deg*) ridge. The audience watches as the storied ridge is built up and established by the poet's verses; by visiting this poetic site, in memory and on the manuscript page, we are enriched. The site itself has not been identified and, as in other cases, might not have been known by the original audience either—perhaps it never was traveled by anyone apart from the poet and his readers. Both explicitly and through use of multivalent terms with literary connotations and double entendre, the poet suggests that the places we visit are also the marks on the manuscript page: this is a landscape of words.

We see further poetic awareness and play with language as an act of landscape creation in a poem attributed to Cináed úa hArtacáin about Achall, a hill whose name commemorates a celebrated woman. 'Achall' serves as the first word of stanza one, and the last word of stanzas three through twenty-two, thus providing ongoing *dúnad* and an incantatory chanting of the name throughout the poetic performance. Early on we are told that Achall, daughter of Cairpre, died *do chumaid Eirc, erctha raind* ('from grief for Erc provinces were filled with it').[21] As Gwynn remarks, however, *erctha raind* could also be rendered as 'stanzas were filled', *rand* also being a common term for a stanza or quatrain of verse.[22] Territories might indeed be overrun with grief, but the poet Cináed, whose livelihood depended on payment for his compositions, is simultaneously advertising that placelore poetry can contain and transform this grief. The slippage between and fusion of poetic stanzas and provinces are resonant in the context of *dindshenchas* composition, and Cináed's word choices develop these echoing overlaps.

This poet, like F. discussed earlier, inserts himself into the versified topography he has created, and develops the concept of moving about in a verbal landscape, a literary spatial practice:

Co raib inad for nim nár do Chináed úa Artacán; rofitir rind-chert cech raind; is é ic imthecht i nAchaill. A.	That there may be a place in high heaven for Cináed úa hArtacáin: he knows the rule of rhyme for every verse; it is he that goes to and fro in Achall.[23]

The stanza suggests, in a common medieval trope, that the poet should be rewarded with a place in heaven for his virtuoso composition. The poet's 'going about' (*imthecht*) denotes actual movement, yet, given the previous line's claim that the speaker knows all metrical rules, we must also visualize the poet as one who weaves deftly through lines that alliterate and assonate back and forth, which dart about and are bound into successive stanzas through the 'rules of rhyme' he mentions—this too is a to-ing and fro-ing through '*Achall*', which is indivisibly now a place and a poem. Giving another potential literary pun based on partial homophony with *Achall* (also declined as *Achaill* throughout the poem), there is also a type of rhyme known as *aicill rhyme*. While *aicill* rhyme is not a major feature of this poem, occurring only four times in twenty-two stanzas, the poet is potentially alluding to a metrical feature in his placelore composition. The larger point, however, is that this verbalized topography, *Achall*, is both rhyme and metrical place-making. These poets, and the audiences that prized their work, understood the links, explicit and pun-based, between landscapes and words. Moreover, they recognized and proclaimed the virtues of composing such verses—the poet deserves heaven—as well as repeating, circulating, copying and preserving them.

The poet's role as place-maker, and the ways words can develop and reveal a storied landscape that differs from what could ever be observed at the real geographical site, are explored in the poem *Cend Febrat*, ascribed in LL (only) to the poet Mac Raith úá Paain. Using first-person language, and developing his presence in the text, the poet narrates a visit to Cend Febrat, a known site that is part of Slieve Reagh in County Limerick. The poet allows us a view of a world that is very different from what might have been glimpsed by actually visiting the site in medieval times:

Cend Febrat, álaind slíab sen,   Cend Febrat, it is a beautiful
adba robúan na ríg-fer,   mountain,
atchíu, is adba fír-fial hé,   enduring home of the royal men;
d'eis na ríg-fían co rogné.   I see it is a truly comely home
                                                 since the days of the royal warriors,
                                                   noble of form.

Tánac-sa lá co moch-moch   I came on a day in early morning
tar Cend Febrat na n-úar-scoth ...   over Cend Febrat of the cool flowers ...

A versified Ireland

Domrimart gáir na gáithe im chotlud co cíall-báithe, ba dál fri gáise glaine, eter láime láechraide.	The sound of the wind lulled me; to sleep with a vacant mind and there I met with pure poetic lore among the hands of warriors.
Mar rochotlas, cóem in mod, and fofúaras m'airfiteod: tarfas dam co fír i fat cach síd fail i Cind Febrat.	As I slept (pleasant the manner) therein I met with the theme of my song: there was shown me truly and in full every fairy-mound that is at Cend Febrat.[24]

This evocation of a nobler, more populated past in contrast to the deserted quietness that seems to have characterized these sites in medieval Ireland is typical of many *dindshenchas* poems. This text, however, pays special attention to the poet's role in generating the vision and apprehending what becomes a more complete verbal geography. The poet sees or discerns (*atchíu*) this place, and is able to access it and then excavate his poem from it. It is important that the poet gains the poem while sleeping, which is another way of reminding us that the material contained in the poem is not simply what can be observed in the landscape itself—the poet goes deeper, with sleep representing both imagination and a retreat into the poet's mind, as well as the space of inspiration and divinely granted gift and vision. The poet tells us that as he slept, he 'discovered' or 'found' (*fofúaras*, from *fo-gaib*)[25] his *airfiteod*, his song or performance piece, from *airfitiud*, 'act of entertaining, delighting, especially with regard to music or minstrelsy', with the additional related meaning of 'gratification, satisfaction'.[26] The poets developed their role as specialist figures who, as the poems tell us, travel to these places—we often have the poet locate himself within the landscape—but the poem we are left with, the storied account or 'truth' (*fír*) of the place, using F.'s term, is only revealed because the poet has special skill and an ability to get beneath the surface of the actual, time-bound physical site.

Indeed, in some cases, the poet explicitly shows that the landscapes are internal and contained within the poet himself. As one poet writes,

Bágaim mo dul dia labrad	I proclaim that I am going to tell of
co slúag n'álaind n-imadbal,	them
as mo threbthus fo thurad	to a host, beautiful and vast,
ria senchas ria saerbunad	bringing from my fruit-laden homestead,
	their legend, the story of their noble origin.[27]

In these lines, about the Galway plain called Mag Aidne, the poet conceives of his memory, his skill and his store of narrative and poetic utterance combined as an environmental feature, as a farm or dwelling, that can nourish those who visit it in their imagination.[28] The *dindshenchas* poets emphasize that their compositions are not mere descriptions of places, but are specialized excavations of elements which come from the fertile plains of the imagination. The *dindshenchas* sites were not just metrical descriptions of places that poets saw; they created their verbal landscapes to be inventive and richly imagined worlds and events, supplementary to rather than derivative of material or historical realities. The poets might start with a known place, but they used their craft to develop historical and mythical layers to build something new.

Formalizing a poetics of place-writing

Though placelore is central to the whole Irish literary tradition, it was during the eleventh and twelfth centuries that the *dindshenchas* really took off as a distinct genre, its formalization witnessed by such things as its inclusion in treatises on the bardic curriculum and its organization as a cohesive textual corpus in manuscripts such as LL.[29] As Murray puts it, 'The formation of the *dinnshenchas* corpus thus represents a deliberate fashioning and cohesive structuring of disparate component elements from the late Old Irish period onwards, and may be viewed in the words of Ann Dooley (2013, 66) as "a totalizing genre project", one which, "flourished in the Middle Irish period [ca. 900–1200] in particular"'.[30] Though I have thus far tried to show the ways that the *dindshenchas* poets innovated to create some surprisingly brilliant and reflective placelore compositions, it is also important to recognize that their verses exemplify the requirements of a rigidly exacting, institutionally structured poetic tradition as well.

Many of the verses examined advertise the *dindshenchas* poets as uniquely talented place-makers and visionaries. As Dagmar Schlüter observes, 'The writer or the speaker of the *dindsenchas* in verse is definitely well-aware of his role as the guardian of cultural memory, whereas in the prose, as elsewhere in the corpus of medieval Irish texts, the author is hardly ever present.'[31] To a significant degree, it is also the specialized vocabulary and the metrical forms the poets expertly manipulate for their expressive needs which further differentiate their compositions from prose explanations and give them status as authors with the capacity to lead us through their verbal worlds. One must not underestimate the extensive training and skill required to create what are often remarkable products, for the poets worked within a very conservative tradition that did not allow for much deviation from established norms and expectations.

For instance, the *dindshenchas* poems in particular, and Irish syllabic or bardic poetry in general, were composed in one artificial, standardized literary dialect that was uniform throughout medieval Ireland: a nationally relevant and intelligible *dindshenchas* was made possible by the use of a bardic vocabulary that resisted regionalization.[32] It was, however, extensive enough to allow for an expanded, highly complex number of forms and spellings (many of them otherwise unattested) to fit stringent metrical requirements. The poems are typically composed of four-line stanzas of seven syllables each and adhere to strict rules of syllabic stress, rhyme, assonance, consonance and alliteration, both within the line and between the different lines in the stanza. The commonest meter used in *dindshenchas* poetry is *deibide*, composed of seven-syllable quatrains, *a* rhyming with *b*, and *c* rhyming with *d*. While there are variations, and other meters are used as well, *deibide* exemplifies the complexity and highly ornamented nature of the *dindshenchas* poem. The end rhymes are between words of unequal syllabic length: the end-rhyming word in *b* is one syllable longer than in *a*, rhyming a stressed and an unstressed syllable—English *bit* and *rabbit* is the example Eleanor Knott gives. *Deibide* also requires alliteration between two words in each line: the final syllable of *d* has to alliterate with the preceding stressed word, and there must be at least two internal rhymes between *c* and *d*.[33]

These metrical requirements are exacting, but a successful composition, according to their numerous rules, also appears to have imparted a very desirable kind of verbal strength and weight. *Dindshenchas* poets understood these complex verse forms as powerful, stabilizing and preservative, and the appropriate kind of ornamentation for Ireland's revered places, as suggested by a poem about the hill Ceilbe. Ceilbe was the subject of a prose entry featured in most copies of the *Dindshenchas Érenn*, including LL, yet lack of a metrical *dindshenchas* legend on Ceilbe drove Muirches mac Pháidín Uí Máolchonaire (d. 1543) to compose verses to honor and preserve the place appropriately. Others agreed with the need for a poem, for Uí Máolchonaire's versified text was subsequently paired with the prose text in four manuscript copies of the *Dindshenchas Érenn*. He wrote that

Mithid dam comma Ceilbe,	It is time for me to make verse on
is airilled d' Athairne,	Ceilbe,
ré th'aithme, ní hicht mbille,	it is a service due to Athairne
ris cen aisde is inglinne.	[legendary poet];
	to commemorate you [Ceilbe]—no
	feeble deed—
	a tale without verse is insecure.

Caibdel cen chomma ar Cheilbe	A chapter without verse on Ceilbe—
dob éisledach d' Fhercheirtne:	it was remiss of Fercheirtne
tlacht ní thig cen rúad, ge raib,	[legendary poet]:
ris cen a dúar 'na dechair.	ornamental beauty comes not
	without a dye,
	nor does a tale last without poetry
	to follow it.[34]

This poet communicates the view that the elaborate verse form secures high places like Ceilbe, possibly with a reference to manuscript aesthetics in the ornamental polish, *tlacht*, and the *rúad*, reddening dye. While the poet may use the prose description or 'tale' (*ris*) as source material, it is the poetic topography built out of the intertwining, composed lines of verse, the metrically structured words (*aisde, dúar, comma*), which are special and become a site of prestige, permanence and resilience. Even when the physical place the poem refers to changes, when its original inhabitants are dispossessed or deprived of authority over it, or simply move away from the area, the versified *Ceilbe* remains unchanged and accessible through poetry and manuscript pages. The tightly wound and elaborately interwoven sequences of words, spun together by a poetic specialist, are solid entities that cannot easily be undone.

    A largely consistent structure is also adhered to in the *dindshenchas* poems' subject matter. They usually open with the placename itself, in lines that run something like, as quoted earlier, 'Tara, what does it come from?'—the question is then followed by

A versified Ireland

an explanatory account. Across the 112 poems in LL there is variation, but most of the poems typically catalogue noteworthy figures and events associated with the place, rather than environmental details or dimensions. While the *dindshenchas* poems revolve around topography, and the place itself is the leading character in each account, it is important to note that spaces lacking story attract very little interest, and nature lyrics are largely absent from the corpus. Significantly, the natural world in Irish literature generally becomes deserving of poetic form, and is manuscript-worthy only once that natural space becomes storied—that is, once the landscape has been cultivated by narrative and plot of some type: the environmental poetry of the *dindshenchas* is largely anthropocentric. A *dindshenchas* account might detail how a mound was created or a plain cleared, or how a lake formed as the result of a flood punishing a crime or taboo social act; or it might describe an exquisite structure built at a regal site or the community that a great sacred tree's branches sheltered. Very occasionally, the setting of the poem moves outside of Ireland—in one interesting case (as discussed in the Introduction) the River Boyne (*Boand*) flows across Europe and the Holy Land to finally wander into Eden—but generally the focus is on Irish places.

Furthermore, the subjects of *dindshenchas* accounts span the pre-Christian and post-Conversion periods, and often within the frame of a single poem we can observe a smooth movement between pagan mythologies and Christian theologies—Ireland's places easily accommodate both. The majority of *dindshenchas* poems take their images and versions of the landscape back to the earliest periods, thus giving ancient and mythologically rich color to these virtual landscapes. Several characters are drawn from mythological texts about the first settlements of Ireland and the gods and goddesses of the Túatha Dé Danann (*Lebor Gabála Érenn* being a major source), with references to Ulster Cycle figures like Cú Chulainn, Queen Medb and the warriors featured in the *Táin* coming next in popularity. Poems also celebrate the *fíana*, warriors associated with Finn mac Cumaill; and various kings and Christian saints garner attention. Just about all Irish myth, history, literature and lore are brought together in the *Dindshenchas Érenn*, and the full indigenous heritage of medieval Ireland makes its way into this uniquely Irish literary landscape.

It is clear, therefore, that the poets' intention was never to simply hold a mirror up to an existing place and describe its physical contours in verse. Steeped in written traditions of history and learning, the poets were concerned to present the *senchas*, the lore or wisdom of a place. While the placenames that drive the *dindshenchas* 'have the power to invoke and preserve the past', as Gregory Toner remarks, 'it is well known that many of these interpretations are entirely fanciful and it has often been remarked that a story connecting the name to an ancient mythological or supposedly historical character is frequently preferred over a sober but ultimately more factual etymology'.[35] Therefore, even when a placename is straightforward and suggests fitting topographic features, the *dindshenchas* poets would often intentionally re-interpret or complicate it to tie the placename to legendary ancestors, a favorite way of doing so being 'lexical fission'.[36] Namely, in what many recognize as the style of Isidore of Seville, medieval Ireland's favorite Church scholar, the poets would split multi-syllabic placenames into different elements and weave a story from characters or events those constituent elements resembled or evoked. A placename consisting of terms for a hill's environmental features might, for instance, be fancifully re-etymologized as the name of a people who lived and enacted their dramas on that hill. For the *dindshenchas* composers, projecting the venerability of the land's esteemed inhabitants was far more important than an account that might have been linguistically accurate or descriptive of environmental features.

Furthermore, the inclusion of older names unattested outside of the poem often provided the poet—and *dindshenchas* poets were learned figures who shared the antiquarian tendencies of other Irish literary composers—with the impetus to add mythical and legendary layers to a place, many of which may have been inventions on their part.[37] As Kevin Murray writes, '*ad hoc* literary invention of placenames to reinforce extant narratives would also seem to have played a significant role in the creation and cultivation of *dinnshennchas*'.[38] This method of composition has drawn considerable scholarly scorn as derivative, 'parasitic' and awkward, and clearly annoys those interested in a more geographically precise, linguistically responsible or historically accurate *dindshenchas*.[39]

For the literary scholar, however, it also points to extreme creativity on the part of the poets and their interest in developing virtualized textual landscapes that do far more than describe or reflect known realities—they were confidently using a range of onomastic and toponymic tools to cultivate new spaces. Through placenames—both familiar names attached to real geographies as well as those generated for narrative purposes—the Irish *dindshenchas* poets thus created new, peopled topographies in the literature.

Dindshenchas poetry turns environmental spaces into storied Irish places by verbally planting them with Ireland's myths and traditions and populating them with famed ancestors.

A main goal of the poems themselves is, therefore, to make clear that the physical environment, and oftentimes the names that attach to it, reveal little to the uninitiated. As one poem records,

'Diamair' ar cach sluág sona,	'A secret', says every fortunate host,
'senchas maige Mucroma:	'is the legend of Mag Mucrime:
ní furáil sái no ollam'	necessary is the help of sage or bard',
ar cach ái 'dia fursonnad'.	says each of them, 'to illuminate it'.[40]

Even the inhabitants of a place, familiar with its visual and environmental features, need a poet versed in the *dindshenchas* to reveal the significance of a storied site; and, for the right price, Ireland's highest-ranking poets were able to provide that service.

Finally, I want to emphasize one of the formal elements of an Irish poetics of space and place employed by these texts. The *dindshenchas* poems typically conclude with the repetition of their opening words, the device of *dúnad* (discussed above), which returns us to the poem's point of origin, often the titular placename itself. Verbally and structurally, our listening and reading practices of the poems are rendered as imaginative loops that mimic important physical movement—kings, heroes and saints conduct circuits of Ireland, and voyagers row cyclically about a sanctifying North Atlantic in physical spatial reflexes of *dúnad*. It is also significant that the term *dúnad*, when declined as an o-stem, refers to an encampment, 'entrenchment, or fort' erected by a host, which may be a temporary or permanent protective architectural feature: the poems provide cultural homes, mental fortresses in which one might find refuge.[41] Though it is difficult to determine if the kinds of Joycean punning and wordplay beloved of Ireland's Hisperic Latinists and other medieval writers were consciously practiced to the same extent by the *dindshenchas* poets, it is important to note the potential levels of architectural wordplay available in these versified topographies, which make subtle links between words, poetry and protective landscape structures. This literary device, which mirrors actual spatial practice, is another element of how the Irish cultivated and systematized a unique spatial poetics in the metrical *dindshenchas*.

These are, presumably, all elements that would have been part of the formal study of *dindshenchas*, which was, to put it in punning terms, the culmination, pinnacle or height (*dind*) of a poet's training. According to an eleventh-century Middle Irish tract on bardic training, study of *dindshenchas* was required of poets in their eighth year. In addition to the 'wisdom-tokens of the *fili*' (*fi scomarca filed*), verse-types such as the architecturally conceived 'fair palisade' (*clethchor choem*) and other bardic elements, the poets were expected to learn 'placename lore and the prime tales of Ireland besides, which are to be related to kings, princes, and noblemen' (*dínshenchus 7 primscéla Hérend olchena fria naisnéis do rígaib 7 flaithib 7 dagdhoínib*).[42] Those who completed their bardic training were expected to hold this virtual Ireland in their memories, to be able to recite and recreate Ireland's verbal topography on demand. The explicit inclusion of a distinct genre of *dindshenchas* as part of the formally recognized training for poets who reached the most advanced stages of their craft shows its extremely high status—*dindshenchas* occupied a position alongside Ireland's chief tales and was deemed to provide suitable entertainment for Ireland's political elite.

Several scholars have discussed the ways in which the *dindshenchas* mnemonically indexes Ireland's cultural history,[43] thus organizing it for those cultural guardians whose main task was to preserve Ireland's *senchas*, or history, lore and wisdom. However, it was not only the poetic class that revered and appreciated the information the *dindshenchas* encoded; so too, it appears, did the class of patrons and some of the highest-ranking figures in Ireland. As seen in Chapter 2, Cú Chulainn asks about places to gather knowledge essential to successfully guard Conchobar's territory, and we should imagine that several medieval Irish people would have seized on the educational function of *dindshenchas* as well. *Dindshenchas* became an important and, one imagines, pleasant way to learn about the country. Through the *dindshenchas* the landscape becomes a critical teaching text on the cultural curriculum for Ireland's nobles as well as its poets. The enshrinement of the professional requirement that the best poets know—and are thus able to perform—the *dindshenchas* points to a formal, institutionalized investment in Irish placelore with an impact extending far beyond the bardic schools themselves.

Several poems depict the *dindshenchas* poet as a spatially mobile figure; in some compositions the poet details himself walking to, or resting in, the landscape, which on one level reflects the itinerant nature of the profession. While it was a marker of status and privilege to be legally able to cross borders in medieval Ireland, the benefits of national movement were accompanied by substantial risks, and poets formed one of the few legal groups that maintained status and legal protection outside of their home *túatha* or familial territory (others included clerics, lawyers and master artisans).[44] Trained to work beyond strictly local concerns, poets were mobile figures who crossed into significantly more territories than the average medieval Irish person. For instance, when in the *Táin* the charioteer explicates the placename Áth na Foraire ('Ford of the Watch') for Cú Chulainn, we learn that though the border guard primarily monitors movement, meets warriors and confronts anyone who might do the province harm, he deals with another group that routinely conducts circuits of Ireland: he ensures that no poets (*áes dana*) depart the province without proper pay; and on their entry he delivers them to Emain so that their first poetic performances are before the king (994–1003). In a nod to the importance of poets, a literate class that travels safely throughout Ireland to culturally unify the nation, the *Táin* shows how warriors and watchmen ensure the itinerant poets get proper treatment and payment throughout the country. Poetic treatises and narrative literature track the national movement of the highest level of poets, and the *dindshenchas* travels with them to make even distant Irish sites accessible through the poet's words in every king's hall.

The role of the *dindshenchas* as part of the nation's education is further envisioned in stanzas (featured only in the LL version) in a very long *dindshenchas* poem rich in the terms that denote the Irish as a cohesive nation or people—forms of 'Ériu' appear eight times, and references to Ireland's saints (Patrick, Brigit, Kevin and Columba) permeate the poem.[45] Though the text encompasses much of Ireland through references to multiple assembly sites, the eponymous subject of the poem is Carmun, the site of Leinster's main *oenach*, assembly or fair, an important political and social gathering which, the poem records, received the blessing of Saint Patrick himself. The LL version of the poem lists the types of tales and texts to be performed at the fairs—it includes *togla* ('destructions'), *tána bó* ('cattle-raids') and *tochmorca* ('wooings'), like *Táin Bó Cúalnge* and *Tochmarc Emire*, for instance, but also refers to *slisnige* (tablets) and *dúle feda* ('books of lore'), or written materials.[46] Most significantly for understanding the reach of the *dindshenchas*, we learn that a visitor to Carmun would be treated to *dublaídi dindsenchais dait* ('dark lays of the Dindshenchas for you').[47] While the term *dublaídi* certainly points to the expectation that it is the poet who will provide the illuminating light of exposition for these learned and hence 'dark' or 'black' lays composed in a complex bardic linguistic register, *dub* is also the common term for ink, so that these are also written, inked lays.[48] These lines suggest that on occasions such as the fair, poems and other written texts were envisioned as moving back and forth across the oral-literate spectrum, showing us how audiences for these learned texts were both scholarly and popular, with texts fixed in writing nonetheless enjoying a dynamic life that moved them beyond a small elite in possession of the technologies of literacy and access to the manuscripts themselves. Returning to the contents of the poem, its verses then cover Ireland's other main assembly sites and describe the performance of instructive and entertaining material at the Feast of Tara and Fair of Emain, including consideration of Ireland's divisions as well as 'the knowledge of every cantred in Ireland' (*fis cech trichat in Hérind*)—these LL verses advertise the national relevance and reach of this literature.[49]

Schlüter makes the excellent point that *Carmun*'s list of genres parallels the components of LL's own, and 'the transmission of the poem is thus a strategy by the compilers who thus legitimated the contents of their manuscript'.[50] I would further argue that when LL scribes who wrote out this poem, so rich in national language and imagery, set it at Ireland's major assembly sites and included unique stanzas referencing literary performance and the use of tablets or books, they were also knowingly creating a national literary event for the manuscript page. In their verbal creation of this space and its inscription on vellum, as well as in LL's inclusion of the cited narratives themselves, they allowed their reading and listening audience to go to the fairs materialized on the manuscript page. Through *Carmun*, and especially its textually focused stanzas, the LL scribes were also legitimating a national poetics and imaginative practice of Irish space that fuses poetry, place and performance.

From local utterance to national discourse: mapping a country with poetry

The codicological arrangement of the *Dindshenchas Érenn* texts also points to sophisticated play with the relationship between verbalized topographies and Ireland-wide spatial practices. As discussed in this chapter's opening, the *Dindshenchas Érenn* differs from Ireland's other spatial narratives in that the audience or reader is the main character and pathfinder. It is through reading that we generate our itinerary and quite literally plot out a journey through place-poems that are otherwise narratively disconnected. Though we meet some of the same poetic guides at the sites, the manuscript requires that we make our own way to the next stop on the *dindshenchas* trail. At the most basic level, the larger *Dindshenchas Érenn* manuscript tradition is structured so that the reader, moving from place-poem to place-poem, conducts a virtual trek around Ireland's landscape of words.[51]

It is thus no surprise that the redactor of Recension C (containing poetry and prose), which Ó Concheanainn identifies as the earliest recension of the *Dindshenchas Érenn* from which A (the poetry in LL) and B (the prose version preserved in LL and elsewhere) are made, had a clear geographic plan in mind: one that emphasizes the importance of the spatial practice which structures so much of medieval Irish literature. There are some places that are unidentifiable, as well as some articles (many relating to Meath, positioned in the center of Ireland) added at the end that do not adhere to a geographical pattern. Yet, as Bowen puts it, 'all things considered, the redactor was reasonably successful in the attempt to impose a geographical pattern, and that pattern, of course, corresponds to the traditional circuit of Ireland, "right-handwise [clockwise] about Uisnech", which *senchas* identified as the centre of the island'. Recension C starts with Tara, after which the articles move to the provinces of Meath, Leinster, Munster, Connacht and Ulster; each province's individual placelore entries primarily follow the same, auspicious clockwise order as well. It is, of course, not a perfectly precise or fully ordered itinerary, as

> The *Dindshenchas* is made up of an accumulation of individual legends, and the places within a given province to which they are attached do not necessarily lie in a line, either straight or curved. Moreover, an intimate and exact knowledge of their locations would require a degree of topographical literacy which it would be inappropriate to demand of any single twelfth-century author (or school, for that matter). The locations of many of the places in the *Dindshenchas* are unknown to us today, and some of them may well have been unknown even to the learned writers of that time.[52]

Nonetheless, it is remarkable that Recension C achieves an overarching structure by which its readers make a clockwise circuit of Ireland through its manuscript pages. The reader becomes a virtual traveler and moves like the wise spatial practitioners (including kings, warriors and saints) who journeyed in this auspicious direction around Ireland, oftentimes to demonstrate their fitness as rulers and social leaders.

Though it lacks explicit directions on how to proceed from point to point and move forward along an itinerary, as in pilgrims' guides, the *Dindshenchas Érenn*'s organizational scheme and the details, images and information contained in the individual poems allow for the possibility of undertaking a virtual circuit of Ireland: a reader or audience member travels across the nation's rich, eminently populated narrative topography by reading through the manuscript or experiencing the oral performance of these *dublaídi dindšenchais* ('dark' or 'inky lays of the Dindshenchas'), perhaps at the provincial fairs and feasts as described in the poem *Carmun* discussed previously.[53] In several respects, the *Dindshenchas Érenn* resembles pilgrimage accounts like Adomnán's *De locis sanctis*: Jerusalem's holy places provide parallels with Ireland's own nationally sacred sites. As narratives of Holy Land pilgrimage permit readers and listeners to mentally visit identity constituting religious sites, so too the *Dindshenchas Érenn* enables its audiences to know Ireland's notable places, to meditate on them and their importance. Few people in medieval Ireland had the opportunity to traverse the entire country or visit the numerous sites featured in the *Dindshenchas*. But through hearing, reciting or reading the *Dindshenchas Érenn*, they would come to know, and sometimes venerate, Ireland's places. Furthermore, even when a particular *dindshenchas* poem describes a real, frequently visited site, one's physical experience could be greatly enhanced by imaginatively engaging, through poetry, story and lore, with that site's past and present, mythic and historic. The poets grasped this, and crafted their placelore poems to facilitate that multi-sensory experience.

While much of the *Dindshenchas Érenn* relies on geographic logic and allows for virtual travel through a coherently mapped out Irish literary landscape, there is also an occasional disconnect between the *dindshenchas* and the actual geography of Ireland. Common editorial assessments of the *dindshenchas* poems are that its locations cannot be precisely known, as in 'this place is doubtful',[54] or that it is 'impossible to say which of several places is intended', and multiple *dindshenchas* sites are simply declared unknown and unidentifiable.[55] This is deemed a fault, and editors often conclude that the placenames are bogus: incompetent scribes must have miscopied or misunderstood the texts or names, or the original poets themselves must have had no real geographic knowledge, as some of the maps verbalized in the poems, or the people who moved through them, simply cannot be laid onto the real geography of Ireland. Yet, the very characteristics that have led to this dismissive treatment of the *Dindshenchas Érenn* as a flawed and substandard geographic embarrassment help us to grasp why it is so valuable.

When we resist the understandable, even natural, urge to use the *Dindshenchas Érenn* primarily as a source for fixing the coordinates of important places to the Irish landmass or to recuperate accounts of what happened where, we can begin to let these poetic places work on us as literary inventions that have, returning to the opening quote, 'parted from the place' to become textual entities that may or may not conform to a material geographic reality. Michelle O'Riordan convincingly argues that while bardic poetry has benefited from fact-oriented studies concerned to identify battle-sites and establish their political contexts, it is also necessary to consider 'the literary contingencies which determined how the "facts" are presented in the artefact—the poem. In this, and in other ways, the composition assumes an independence from the "facts" which enhances our understanding both of the cultural and of the political context of the creation of the literary artefact'.[56] This is even more pressing in studying the *dindshenchas*. Considering the placelore poems as art forms independent, in important (and deliberate) ways, of 'the facts'—such as their actual geographic referents—frees us to focus on the myriad creative things they, and their composers, sought to accomplish. This approach is absolutely necessary in certain cases, as we know that some *dindshenchas* accounts invented entirely new places (and placenames).[57] Enough *Dindshenchas Érenn* sites are geographically identifiable, however, that the audience remains oriented in the part of the country or province being described: it is this mixture of mappable sites and unknown places, some perhaps entirely fictitious, which gives a sense of reality, of comprehensible and familiar spaces, with the unfamiliar sites slotting into place in the different regions and serving to expand the known territories and heroically peopled spaces of Ireland. We are in Ireland, but a richer, multivalent and more powerfully transformative Ireland.

What can these artful, poetic re-imaginings and narrative expansions of Irish spaces accomplish? By reinvigorating characters to restage significant events in the poem's verses, important figures begin to 'converse' with each other as they are brought to life and planted alongside each other in the Irish literary landscape. Though he does not linger on the implications or address their performative power, Gregory Toner rightly declares that 'the name *is* a link to the past—to the very instant of naming. The name pronounced in some distant era is frozen in time and creates a link between the event of naming and the present.'[58] In the *Dindshenchas Érenn*, so many of the events, figures and myths that have been significant throughout the ages in establishing a sense of Irishness are marshaled together as a cohesive community populating the literary topography of Ireland, and they are conjured through the poet's utterance of the placename. These poems furthermore provide an inviting point of entry for an audience to access wisdom or *senchas* by watching events unfold in the poem's hills and plains. Placenames are articulated, and stories, known from elsewhere (the very 'parasitic' lack of originality Gwynn disdains) are potentially shorthand references that can economically convey lessons, histories, shared pasts and community ideals and taboos.[59] The *dindshenchas* poems create multi-layered and instructive snapshots of important places in the minds of their listeners and readers.

Their potential power is illuminated by comparison with more fully documented contemporary Western Apache placenaming practices. When Western Apache community members want to provide advice and guidance, they do not speak directly but rather recite a list of placenames which, in the manner of the *dindshenchas*, have stories attached to them and lessons embedded within them. In one case, an elder explains a seemingly cryptic series of placenames she and others recite to one community member, their recitation giving the woman

> pictures to work on in her mind ... That way she could travel in her mind. She could add to them [the pictures] easily. We gave her clear pictures with placenames. So her mind went to those places, standing in front of them as our ancestors did long ago. That way she could see what happened there long ago. She could hear stories in her mind, perhaps hear our ancestors speaking. She could recall the knowledge of our ancestors.[60]

When the *dindshenchas* poems list placenames, and evoke known characters, episodes and sites from the past, both historical and mythic, they also conjure up and then plant in the mind Ireland's *senchas* and the lessons it encodes. As Keith Basso remarks, rather than being simply referential,

> placenames are arguably among the most highly charged and richly evocative of all linguistic symbols. Because of their inseparable connection to specific localities, placenames may be used to summon forth an enormous range of mental and emotional associations—associations of time and space, of history and events, of persons and social activities, of oneself and stages in one's life. And in their capacity to evoke, in their compact power to muster and consolidate so much of what a landscape may be taken to represent in both

A versified Ireland

personal and cultural terms, placenames acquire a functional value that easily matches their utility as instruments of reference.[61]

Rather than showing a lack of originality and serving only to reference real places, in the *dindshenchas*' allusions to and reworkings of Ireland's places and the events that transpired there we witness clever memory and visualization techniques that accomplish significantly more. In other words, even if a *dindshenchas* place does not reveal any known physical coordinates that allow for its association with an actual site, the poets have presented it in such a way that it does not matter, for through its words we can travel, walk and experience these places. Furthermore, the virtuality of the *dindshenchas* locations, and their role as verbalized, imagined topographies, is germane to historically well-known and highly traveled Irish sites as well. Though Tara or Howth Head can be traversed today, without the words of the poet in one's head or on one's lips that same rich, storied site cannot be encountered. To paraphrase the *Techt Do Róim* poet, if you do not carry the place with you, you will not find it once you get there.

It is of great significance that through the utterance of names, invented or physically real, places are essentially brought into being and claimed. When the poet identified as Macnia mac Oengusa opens successive stanzas by naming landscape features and asking us to envision them, they become real for us:

Fégaid in síd ar bar súil, is fodeirc dúib, is treb ríg ...	Behold the fairy mound before your eyes: it is plain for you to see, it is a king's dwelling ...
Fégaid Imdai nDagdai deirg: forsind leirg, cen galmai ngairg ...	Behold the Bed of the red Dagda: on the slope, without rough rigor ...
Fégaid Dá Cích rígnai ind ríg sund iar síd fri síd-blai síar ...	Behold the two Paps of the king's consort here beyond the mound west of the fairy mansion ...[62]

The poet understands the power of verbally conjuring places through their names, an act which was even more resonant in an oral-literate society like Ireland's in which the spoken word, long after the introduction of literacy, retained significant power. Even when we are not explicitly told, in direct address, to envision the sites, the lists of names are persuasive merely through their articulation, as is witnessed by Cináed úa hArtacáin's litany in *Achall*:

Duma Find, Duma na nDrúad,	The Mound of Finn, the Mound of
Duma Créidne, grúad fri	the Druids,
grúad,	the Mound of Creidne, cheek by cheek;
Duma 'ma ndernad gleicc glé	the Mound about which was fought
Duma nEirc, Duma nAichle. A.	the famous fight,
	the Mound of Erc, the Mound of Achall.⁶³

Written words come to life when verbally articulated, and strings of placenames can have a magical or transformative effect when spoken: as a character in Brian Friel's *Faith Healer* says, 'I'd recite the names to myself just for the mesmerism, the sedation of the incantation.'⁶⁴ Or as Seán Ó Coileáin writes of the many placenames in a *fianaigecht* poem celebrating the sounds of nature, 'as well as designating a place, if it does, each [placename] also forms part of the texture of the poem and the cumulative effect is not so much referential as evocative'.⁶⁵ Placenames are aesthetically satisfying as sounds or musical utterances as well as imagistic strokes that help to paint a certain scene. But the *dindshenchas* poems' long lists of placenames also have the important effect of calling up a more extensive landscape, of annexing or appropriating spaces and territories that can then be populated with ancestral heroes and revered figures that ultimately become part of those imagined local and national Irish communities. Noting the power that uttering a placename confers, Keith Basso has suggested that placenaming should be understood 'as a universal means—and it could well turn out, a universally primary means—for appropriating physical environments'.⁶⁶ The *Dindshenchas Érenn* can be seen as accomplishing this kind of virtual geographic expansion, of mapping out and appropriating an Ireland which was to become threatened in successive years. While this could not have been known to the LL scribes working ca. 1150, before the English invasion and conquest of Ireland began in 1169, the development of a *Dindshenchas Érenn* that claims and preserves a storied landscape encompassing the whole island would become increasingly important as Gaelic control of Irish territory diminished, a scenario which was to increase over subsequent centuries of English colonization.

Dindshenchas Érenn and a changing landscape

To restate the arguments made here, the *Dindshenchas Érenn* thus became the national landscape as created, preserved and performed by the poets of Ireland on multiple fronts. Through its use of a standardized literary language it transcended regional specificity to speak to all of Ireland. Because of the poets' routine border crossings and travel, their ability to both observe and then produce (or reiterate) Ireland's full geography in poetic performances and their role as figures who moved beyond strictly local concerns and ambits, they also became practitioners of a national geography, one which appears to have been disseminated at important provincial fairs, feasts and gatherings, thus making its way through multiple levels of Irish society. The *Dindshenchas Érenn* furthermore gained island-wide relevance and importance from its position on the bardic curriculum where, as a required skill for the highest-grade poets throughout Ireland, it attained prestige, became canonical and came to be recognized as something that the finest poets should be able to deliver to delight high-minded patrons and their followers. When preserved in manuscript form, these national concerns are also manifest in the choice of *dindshenchas* entries pertaining to places throughout all of Ireland, as well as the geographic logic of the organization of *dindshenchas* entries, so that the manuscript user can, with some directional success, undertake a virtual circuit clockwise through all of Ireland. Taken as a whole, the *Dindshenchas Érenn* operates as a unified collection that creates an entire nation in writing—a nation that was at a significant historical and cultural crossroads.

The poets and manuscript compilers of the *Dindshenchas Érenn* were invested in creating a virtual Ireland through their words, an Ireland that, though associated with the actual landscape itself, used words to transmit a sense of belonging to an esteemed and ancient community of Irish predecessors. The *Dindshenchas Érenn*, preserved first in LL but much copied in later manuscripts from the late twelfth century onwards, not to mention the actual oral performance and untracked circulation of the *dindshenchas* poems themselves, must have been deeply important in combating feelings of alienation from the land. Though these texts could be expected to work in multiple historical and political situations, it seems that this national poetry of place would have been especially significant in the twelfth century (and later periods as well) when major swathes of Irish territory were coming under English control and being covered with defensive structures, changing the ownership of the land as well as its appearance.[67] By 1185, for instance, the king of England had seized the cities of Dublin, Waterford and Cork; and Leinster, Meath, eastern Ulster and parts of Cork were controlled by newly arrived English lords, and so a literary topography of Ireland would have provided a culturally important alternative to this newly changed landscape.[68] A verbal topography—the virtual landscape preserved in the tightly woven verses of the *dindshenchas* poems—could remain as an Irish space even though the control, and appearance, of important sites had irrevocably changed. The *Dindshenchas Érenn* could offer an alternate, virtual Ireland, a more welcoming and illustrious space comprising imaginatively habitable lines of poetry. Even if dispossession from the land occurred, even if familiar and revered sites, or access to them, were to become substantially altered, the Ireland of the *Dindshenchas Érenn* was still there. Keith Basso's words aptly describe medieval Ireland's placelore:

> For landscapes are always available to their seasoned inhabitants in more than material terms. Landscapes are available in symbolic terms as well, and so, chiefly through the manifold agencies of speech, they can be 'detached' from their fixed spatial moorings and transformed intro instruments of thought and vehicles of purposive behavior. Thus transformed, landscapes and the places that fill them become tools for the imagination, expressive means for accomplishing verbal deeds, and also, of course eminently portable possessions to which individuals can maintain deep and abiding attachments, regardless of where they travel.[69]

Once laid down in writing, in speech or indeed in memory, these narrative and poetic topographies become portable and always accessible. The narrative topographies and virtual geographies of the *Dindshenchas Érenn*, which evoke a rich, noble, heroic past, are also bulwarks, sites of resistance, fortified places from which to affirm an identity and subjectivity rooted in place.

The *dindshenchas* poems in LL in many ways release Irish places from the physical landscape, and their composers (as well as later manuscript compilers) can be seen as creating poetic resources and defensive tools that anticipated a loss of power over the land resulting from political and cultural changes, most explicitly the English invasion and conquest. In this respect we should understand the topographic poems produced by Seán Mór Ó Dubhagháin (d. 1372) and Giolla na Naomh Ó hUidhrín (d. 1420), which posit an

Ireland in which the English invasion never occurred, as the logical extension of the *Dindshenchas Érenn*. Ó Dubhagháin's poem of 916 lines of *deibide* verse describes the territories of the northern half of Ireland, and Ó hUidhrín later contributes 792 lines (also *deibide*) covering the southern half of Ireland. Though they write almost 200 years after the English invasion of Ireland, both poets completely erase all evidence of English presence, colonial conquest and the dispossession of Gaelic Irish families from ancestral lands—their verbalized topographies depict Irish families in control of territories that were by then the possessions of English lordships. As James Carney wrote in introducing the poems, this might be expected, 'For these poets were above all the custodians of ancient tradition, and contemporary and perhaps unpleasant facts which were common knowledge, would hardly have seemed to them worthy of professional attention.'[70] Conversely, we might argue that these poets deemed the matter supremely worthy of their professional attention. Namely, in response to how 'Gaelic lore, history and traditions had been menaced, and the continuity of national life broken, by the Norman Invasion',[71] they extended the project of the *Dindshenchas Érenn*, and turned to Irish topographical poetry to realize an alternate landscape that could restore, in their verses, a nation's life, its sustaining lore, history and traditions. Even while physically moving through a geography that registered a different and darker contemporary colonial reality, in a small act of rebellion one could nonetheless internalize the map of a revalorized Ireland that placelore poetry makes possible.

We might see the *dindshenchas* as, first, the creation of a valorized Ireland rich with history and noble ancestors and endowed with *senchas*: this is an Irish topography built out of words. Secondly, recourse to these *dindshenchas* texts became an important way for the Irish to engage with, remember and ultimately re-attach themselves at times of extreme change to a recuperated, more traditional Ireland that was deeply rooted in visions of the past. The *Dindshenchas Érenn* was thus a powerful way to appropriate, preserve and create a virtual 'Ireland of the mind',[72] and to allow for a valorizing engagement with a storied Ireland. This reading can help us understand the significance and popularity of the *Dindshenchas Érenn* in the late twelfth century and beyond. Earlier modern commentators have famously thought very little of the *dindshenchas*, dismissing it as derivative, tedious and parasitic, and valuing it only insofar as it preserves otherwise lost bits of legend and story. We should, however, appreciate how it operates as an imaginative and well-executed enterprise, the construction of a virtual Ireland not subject to the constraints of time, nor made inaccessible as its sites and territories underwent physical changes and transfer of ownership. The creation and compilation of the *Dindshenchas Érenn* is a major literary and cultural achievement, and one for which, as the *dindshenchas* poet cited earlier, Cináed úa hArtacán, put it, a seat in the celestial landscape would have been a fitting reward:

> That there may be a place in high heaven
> for Cináed úa hArtacán:
> he knows the rule of rhyme for every verse;
> it is he that goes to and fro in Achall.[73]

Notes

1 Basso, *Wisdom*, p. 70.
2 This count is given in Charles Bowen, 'Historical Inventory of the *Dindshenchas*', *Studia Celtica* 10 (1975), 119. A recent discussion of the *dindshenchas* and its scholarship is Kevin Murray, 'Genre Construction: The Creation of the *Dinnshenchas*', *Journal of Literary Onomastics* 6 (2017), 11–21. A full list of the dated manuscripts, with links to digitized versions, is found at: www.vanhamel.nl/codecs/Dinnshenchas_Érenn.
3 Different scenarios have been posited, yet 'the traditional understanding of the development of this corpus, however, is that the metrical *dinnshenchas* (assembled perhaps in the mid-eleventh century) preserved in the Book of Leinster has priority, that the prose version was partially based on this poetry (perhaps compiled in the early twelfth century), and that the full prosimetric *dinnshenchas* represents the final stage of compilation (dating perhaps to the late twelfth/early thirteenth century)'. Murray, 'Genre Construction', p. 15. Ó Concheanainn has argued that the earliest recension of the *Dindshenchas Érenn* featured both poetic and prose entries (C), and that this was the source for separate metrical (A) and prose versions (B), both represented in LL. See Tomás Ó Concheanainn, 'The Three Forms of *Dinnshenchas Érenn*', *Journal of Celtic Studies* 3 (1981–83), 88–101.
4 Elizabeth Duncan, 'A Reassessment of the Script and Make-up of *Lebor na Nuachongbála*', *Zeitschrift für Celtische Philologie* 59 (2012), 58–9.
5 Regarding characteristics of the LL *dindshenchas* and arguments for codicologically oriented analysis, see Dagmar Schlüter, *History or Fable? The Book of Leinster as a Document of Cultural Memory in Twelfth-Century Ireland* (Münster: Nodus, 2010), pp. 145–90.

6 *MD* I.2–3.
7 *eDIL* s.v. bruig.
8 *MD* I.57.
9 There is little question that the Irish conceived of themselves as a nation—this is attested in numerous ways, with cultural production, including early establishment of an island-wide literary vernacular, being one important indicator. As Dumville has recently shown, while Ireland might not have taken nation-state form, it is clear that 'Ireland and an Irish nation did exist in (and had indeed existed for a long time by) the later twelfth century'. David Dumville, 'Did Ireland Exist in the Twelfth Century?', in Emer Purcell *et al.* (ed.), *Clerics, Kings and Vikings: Essays on Medieval Ireland in Honour of Donnchadh Ó Corráin* (Dublin: Four Courts Press, 2015), p. 126. For further discussion and relevant bibliography, see Thomas Charles-Edwards, 'Nations and Kingdoms: A View from Above', in T. M. Charles-Edwards (ed.), *After Rome* (Oxford: Oxford University Press, 2003), pp. 23–58; Marie Therese Flanagan, 'Strategies of Distinction: Defining Nations in Medieval Ireland', in Hirokazu Tsurushima (ed.), *Nations in Medieval Britain* (Donington: Shaun Tyas, 2010), pp. 104–20; Amy Mulligan, 'Introduction: Ideas of the Irish Nation', *Eolas: Journal of the American Society of Irish Medieval Studies* 8 (2015), 12–19; and Patrick Wadden, 'Theories of National Identity in Early Medieval Ireland' (DPhil. diss., University of Oxford, 2010).
10 Ruairí Ó hUiginn, 'The Background and Development of *Táin Bó Cúailnge*', in J. P. Mallory (ed.), *Aspects of the Táin* (Belfast: December Publications, 1992), pp. 41–9.
11 *MD* III.110–11.
12 Diarmuid Ó Murchada, 'Is the O'Neill-Mac Carthy Letter of 1317 a Forgery?', *Irish Historical Studies* 23 (1982), 61–7.
13 Thomas O'Sullevane in the *Memoirs of the Marquis of Clanricarde*, 1722; quoted in Osborn Bergin, *Irish Bardic Poetry* (Dublin: DIAS, 1970), pp. 5–6.
14 Thurneysen, *Irische Helden- und Konigsage*, p. 66.
15 *MD* II.46–7.
16 *eDIL* s.v. -dan-.
17 *MD* II.46–7.
18 *eDIL* s.v. fégaid, féc(h)aid.
19 *MD* II.48–9.
20 *eDIL* s.v. 2 derbaid.
21 Gwynn, *MD* I, 1.7, pp. 46, 47.
22 *MD* I.81, note 7. See also *eDIL* s.v. 1 rann.
23 *MD* I.50–1.
24 *MD* III.226–7. The emended translation of the third stanza supplied by Gwynn on p. 518 is given here.
25 *eDIL* s.v. fo-gaib, fo-geib.

26 *eDIL* s.v. airfitiud.
27 *MD* III.330–1.
28 *Trebthas* (*trebad*) as source of the poet's knowledge also occurs in the poem (LL) on Mag Luirg, *MD* III.396–7.
29 See, however, the argument that LL scribes had a more encompassing conception of the *dindshenchas* than typically assumed, in Dagmar Schlüter, 'Boring and Elusive? The *Dindshenchas* as a Medieval Irish Genre', *Journal of Literary Onomastics* 6 (2017), 26–9.
30 Murray, 'Genre Construction', pp. 11–12.
31 Schlüter, *History or Fable?*, p. 162.
32 This conservative vocabulary hardly changed over 500 years, making it extremely difficult to determine when, or where, in Ireland or Scotland, poems were composed. Bergin, *Irish Bardic Poetry*, p. 13.
33 Eleanor Knott, *An Introduction to Irish Syllabic Poetry of the Period 1200–1600* (Dublin: DIAS, 1957), pp. 18–19. See also Gerard Murphy, *Early Irish Metrics* (Dublin: Royal Irish Academy, 1961).
34 *MD* III.54–5.
35 Gregory Toner, 'Landscape and Cosmology in the *Dindshenchas*', in Jacqueline Borsje et al. (eds.), *Celtic Cosmology: Perspectives from Ireland and Scotland* (Toronto: Pontifical Institute of Mediaeval Studies, 2014), p. 268.
36 Bowen, 'Historical Inventory', p. 117. See also Rolf Baumgarten, 'Etymological Aetiology in Irish Tradition', *Ériu* 41 (1990), 115–22; and Gregory Toner, 'Authority, Verse and the Transmission of Senchas', *Ériu* 55 (2005), 73–4.
37 In some cases, placenames, such as that of Srúb Brain, were completely manufactured and originated in word-play rather than geography, as shown by Petra Hellmuth, 'The *Dindshenchas* and Irish Literary Tradition', in John Carey et al. (eds.), *Cín Chille Cúile: Essays in Honour of Pádraig Ó Riain* (Aberystwyth: Celtic Studies Publications, 2004), pp. 116–26.
38 Murray, 'Genre Construction', p. 14.
39 *MD* I.75, v. 95.
40 *MD* III.382–3.
41 See *eDIL* s.v. 1 dúnad and 2 dúnad.
42 Rudolf Thurneysen (ed.), 'Mittelirische Verlehren', in Whitley Stokes and Ernst Windisch (eds.), *Irische Texte*, vol. 3, Part 1 (Leipzig: S. Hirzel), pp. 49–51. Translation from Joseph Nagy, 'Orality in Medieval Irish Narrative: An Overview', *Oral Tradition* 1/2 (1986), 273. See also Donncha Ó hAodha, 'The First Irish Metrical Tract', in Hildegard Tristram (ed.), *Metrik und Medienwechsel / Metrics and Media* (Tübingen: Narr, 1991), pp. 207–14.
43 The phrase is that of Proinsias Mac Cana, 'Placenames and Mythology in Irish Tradition: Places, Pilgrimages and Things', in Gordon MacLennan (ed.), *Proceedings of the First North American Congress of*

Celtic Studies (Ottawa: Chair of Celtic Studies, University of Ottawa, 1988), p. 333.
44 This is detailed in the eighth-century *Uraicecht na Ríar: The Poetic Grades of Early Irish Law*, ed. and trans. Liam Breatnach (Dublin: DIAS, 1987).
45 See for instance, *MD* III.6–20, at lines 60, 68, 91, 118, 121, 129, 165–6, 183, 220, 248, and 250.
46 *MD* III.20–1.
47 *MD* III.20–1.
48 See *eDIL* s.v. dub.
49 *MD* III.20–1.
50 Schlüter, *History or Fable?*, p. 164.
51 Elements of the *Dindshenchas Érenn* cohere with what Mary Carruthers has identified as medieval memory techniques such as cognitive route-making, as discussed in Morgan Davies, 'Dindshenchas, Memory and Invention', in Cathinka Hambro and Lars Widerøe (eds.), *Lochlann: Festschrift for Jan Erik Rekdal* (Oslo: Hermes Academic Publishing, 2013), pp. 89–93.
52 Bowen, 'Historical Inventory', pp. 124–5.
53 *MD* III.20–1.
54 *MD* V.20.
55 *MD* I.75, v.126.
56 Michelle O'Riordan, *Irish Bardic Poetry and Rhetorical Reality* (Cork: Cork University Press, 2007), p. xvii.
57 See note 36.
58 Toner, 'Landscape and Cosmology', p. 269.
59 See place-names arising from socially taboo acts, such as *fingal*, or kin-slaying, in Toner, 'Landscape and Cosmology', p. 274.
60 Basso, *Wisdom*, p. 83.
61 Basso, *Wisdom*, pp. 76–7.
62 *MD* II.18–19.
63 *MD* I.46–7.
64 Cited in Piotr Stalmaszczyk, 'Geographical Names in Gaelic Poetry: Function and Problems with Translation', *Ainm* 5 (1991), 72.
65 Séan Ó Coileáin, 'Place and Placename in *Fianaigheacht*', *Studia Hibernica* 27 (1993), 55.
66 Basso, *Wisdom*, p. 76.
67 Excavations of sites such as Castle Skreen suggest that in the late twelfth and early thirteenth centuries, Norman defenses 'were less likely to have been raised on virgin ground than on extant earthworks'. In other words, mottes or motte and bailey castles were sometimes built on existing mounds and over Gaelic structures, as discussed in Tadhg O'Keeffe, 'Rural Settlement and Cultural Identity in Gaelic Ireland, 100–1500', *Ruralia* 1 (1996), 146. See also Paul MacCotter's discussion of landscape continuity over the period in *Medieval*

Ireland: Territorial, Political and Economic Divisions (Dublin: Four Courts Press, 2008).
68 Robin Frame, *Colonial Ireland* (Dublin: Helicon, 1981), pp. 23–4.
69 Basso, *Wisdom*, p. 75.
70 James Carney (ed.), *Topographical Poems by Seaán Mór Ó Dubhagáin and Giolla-na-naomh Ó hUidhrín* (Dublin: DIAS, 1943), p. x.
71 Carney (ed.), *Topographical Poems*, p. x.
72 'Our imaginations assent to the stimulus of the names, our sense of the place is enhanced, our sense of ourselves as inhabitants not just of a geographical country but of a country of the mind is cemented.' Heaney, 'The Sense of Place', p. 132.
73 *MD* I.50–1.

4
National pilgrims: traveling a sanctified landscape with Saint Patrick

... knowledge is grown along the myriad paths we take as we make our ways through the world in the course of everyday activities, rather than assembled from information obtained from numerous fixed locations. Thus it is by *walking along* from place to place, and not by building up from local particulars, that we come to know what we do.[1]

In the travel-tale *Acallam na Senórach* (the 'Conversation' or 'Dialogue' of the 'Ancients' or 'Experts'), Échna, proclaimed as the wisest and fairest woman in the world, welcomes the hero Caílte when his journey across Ireland brings him to her. She states that 'God be your life, oh my soul, oh Caílte ... for it is your own path that you have come on' (*ocus Dia do betha, a m'anum, a Cailti ... 7 issí do chonair féin tángais*, 7433–4).[2] We might understand Échna's allusive words in light of Ingold's statement cited at the opening of this chapter, as suggesting that we come to learn about ourselves and our world, 'we come to know what we do', by forging a path, by moving through the landscape and conducting circuits of Ireland. As we will see, Caílte, a pagan warrior displaced at the *Acallam*'s opening, finds and then travels along his own paths: those of the Christian faith that result in Saint Patrick's promise of heaven, but also the routes of Ireland's heroic past, which the *Acallam* reestablishes as important ways through the newly Christianized landscape of Ireland. For wayfaring pilgrims, both religious and secular, choosing, tracing and moving along such paths were keys to transformation.

Composed in the late twelfth or early thirteenth century, and preserved in four manuscripts from the fifteenth and sixteenth centuries,[3] *Acallam na Senórach* is a Middle Irish prosimetrum more than 8,000 lines long (almost twice the length of the *Táin*).[4] It brings together a great deal of *fianaigecht*, namely the stories, poems and feats celebrating the third-century pre-Christian hero

Finn mac Cumaill and his warrior band (*fían*), as well as the kings and nobles with whom they interact. But it is not simply a reflection on Ireland's heroic past: the *Acallam* is also a text about Saint Patrick's fifth-century evangelizing movement throughout Ireland and, in that respect, develops from Patrician tradition. The larger body of writings associated with Patrick, including his own self-authored *Confessio* and letters, as well the many *Lives* and other important documents associated with him, all feature Patrick's proselytizing movements and give the impression that Patrick, both the historic figure as well as the saintly persona developed by his biographers, never sat down.[5] It is, however, Tírechán, writing in the late seventh century, who is recognized as developing the *topos* of Patrick's great circuit (*circulus*) around the northern half of Ireland, though the *Notulae* also show 'that there already existed by 808 a much more detailed conception of Patrick's circuit round the southern half of Ireland than the brief mention made by Tírechán'.[6] These elements are developed in striking ways in the *Acallam*. Namely, the storytelling journey begins when Saint Patrick encounters Caílte, the ancient pagan warrior and a surviving member of Finn mac Cumaill's *fían* band. The two unlikely companions journey together through Ireland, and when Patrick voraciously calls for stories and historical accounts, Caílte regales him with narratives prompted by the sites they visit and his emotional reactions to the wondrous and tragic events that took place there. Patrick, at the behest of two angels, tells his scribe to write these accounts down, and a narrative topography of Ireland is mapped out as collaborating pagan and Christian heroes walk and talk their way across the country. In the *Acallam*, Ireland's conversion is fused with an ambitious national Irish literary initiative.

Set in Patrick's time, the *Acallam* frequently returns us to the earlier pagan period; the text's imagined past downplays temporal distinctions, with sophisticated results. Adding another historical dimension, it is important to remember that the *Acallam* was composed not long after watershed twelfth- and thirteenth-century changes to Ireland's political, ecclesiastical and literary culture that resulted from religious reform and the English invasion and conquest. This complex, transhistorical text therefore draws on all of these time periods simultaneously to create a new, even subtly forward-looking mode of Irishness rooted in the experience of landscape and narrative, with the Briton Patrick as an important model. Spatial movement constitutes both the framing device and logic of the text in a series of storytelling journeys around Ireland

National pilgrims

and is a useful formal structure for a long, episodic text. Yet journeying and movement are more than just organizational devices. They constitute a resolutely promoted, even mandated behavior, and the composer of the *Acallam* explores dynamic, connective travel between living spaces in its pages. In so doing, the *Acallam* foregrounds the power of movement through and across Irish space to transform ways of being, thinking and acting, and gives us a new kind of pilgrimage text.

Indeed, the *Acallam*'s placement in relation to the nexus of actual pilgrimage is highly relevant to the present analysis. None of the manuscripts identify an author for the *Acallam*, but several details point to its composition in the early thirteenth century in the west of Ireland, a suggestion also borne out by the western provenance of three of the four manuscript witnesses. As Ann Dooley and Anne Connon have demonstrated, the narrative was likely produced under the patronage of the Mac Oireachtaigh/Ua Raduibh (or Muinter Roduib) family, for whom a major source of income was travel by large numbers to Ireland's most popular pilgrimage site, Crúachán Aigle (Croagh Patrick, or in contemporary usage, the 'Reek') on the Mayo coast.[7] With the *Acallam*'s composition convincingly tied to the families and monasteries that controlled Ireland's western Patrician sites, it is fruitful to hypothesize an audience for the *Acallam* acquainted with the images, practices and psychology of pilgrimage. We might not be far off in thinking about the *Acallam* as a kind of guide book seeking to entice people to the places featured (we might even say advertised) in the tale.

Yet the text also defies the easy mapping that a guide book would supply. The *Acallam* does not show an interest in linear trajectories, or in charting the quickest route between any two places. Rather, meandering treks and looping circles around Ireland prevail. The text provides no distances, durations or directions: the journey, or perhaps simply the act of journeying, *is* the point. A productive walking of Ireland involves unfixed, meditative or conversational pacing, not unlike that of Joyce's Dubliners or de Certeau's heroic pedestrians, who are practitioners of everyday space.[8] Caílte's footsteps 'weave places together'[9] into a series of utterances that stimulate an Irish topographical dialogue or conversation, an Irish *acallam* in which multiple speakers and wanderers partake. Caílte eventually finds and follows his own path, and allows the stories generated by his wayfaring to issue from him. By the end of the text, other pathmakers and pilgrims are encouraged to follow, literally and figuratively, in his footsteps.

This chapter explores the *Acallam*'s textual constructions of landscape and its characters' human relationships to environmental phenomena to demonstrate how various figures, including saints, warriors, kings and otherworldly beings, practice Irish space with increasing skill over the course of the narrative. Saint Patrick is the chief example: under Caílte's tutelage, Patrick solicits information about the places visited or glimpsed from afar and learns to practice Irish space himself, thereby transforming the native Briton into a fitting patron saint of Ireland. Patrick becomes an adept verbal performer of Irish place, which, materialized in poetry and actual pilgrimage sites, he leaves for the people to visit and mentally contemplate. Caílte also exemplifies a storied spatial practice as he undergoes his own transformational journey. The *Acallam* thus envisions its audience as a community of pilgrims, both real and readerly, whose ultimate object of devotion is the sanctified, heroic nation of Ireland. In describing how to generate, preserve and circulate a national Irish literature of place, the *Acallam* provides spatial methodologies for the embodied experience of an Ireland simultaneously virtual and real.

Starting an *Acallam* ('Conversation')

The *Acallam*'s opening words take us back to a dark triad of third-century battles in which three mythic kings of Ireland perished and the *fían* bands were almost totally destroyed. We then find ourselves in the company of a few *fíana* survivors, now exceedingly ancient; we have teleported forward 200 years to the narrative's fifth-century Patrician present. Fittingly, in a text in which landscape tells the most important stories, the *fíana*'s near annihilation is environmentally reflected: it is sunset, and the evening clouds of the ninth canonical hour of Nones (*fuinedh néll nóna*, 10) fall on the spatially dislocated wanderers as their two remaining leaders, Oisín and Caílte, wonder where they might seek shelter for the night. Their act of itinerant wandering or wayfaring through Irish space is rewarded with hospitality, and they come to a figure who once guarded over Finn from youth to death: 'the sovereign lady and custodian' (*in bhanflaith 7 in banchoimétaidh*, 15–6), Cáma, who is also one of the three living elders (*senaibh*, 14). Cáma does more than provide food and shelter; the wise woman initiates what becomes half of the *Acallam*'s mission. Cáma speaks with them about the *fían* band; its members, including their leader, Finn mac Cumaill; its battles and so on, and 'these reminiscences caused a great silence to fall on them' (p. 3) (*ro mhuidh tocht mór orro-sumh uime sin*, 34). And as they remember and mourn the loss of their noble fellowship, 'though they were manly warriors, they, together with Lady Cáma, wept deeply and disconsolately' (p. 4) (*gérsat calma na feróglaigh ro cháisetar co dubach do brónach domhenmnach maraon risin mbanflaith .i. re Cámha*, 39–41). Cáma recognizes the need to tell stories about the past, and understands the recuperative effects of moving through places and continuing to talk about them. She creates a situation in which both storytelling and emotions begin to flow, which will later be fostered by Patrick's own encouragement of the ancient heroes.

After three days and nights with Cáma, the last survivors of the *fían* band move into a green, outdoor space—envisioned throughout the text as a locus of meditation and clear judgment—to think. They determine that they must leave each other, and 'their parting was as the parting of the soul from its body' (p. 4) (*ba scaradh cuirp re hanmain a scarad*, 49–50). The dramatic language of the soul severed from the body stresses the broken nature of the surviving *fíana*, and immediately puts Christian concerns about the soul onto the narrative's agenda. Though the text mourns the passing of an earlier heroic age, these lines' placement at the very beginning of the saga also suggests the need for a new leader who can re-unite body and soul in an enduring bond that surpasses the promises of the triad of mythic kings, the sovereign lady Cáma or even Finn himself.

Once painfully severed from his companions, Caílte first travels to *Indber Bicc Loingsig* ('Estuary of Bec the Exile'), which, the text tells us, is now *Mainistir Droichit Átha* (the 'Monastery of Drogheda', or Mellifont Abbey, 52–4). Pointedly, the story attached to this site describes the text's first foreigner, Bec the Exile, son of Airist, King of the Romans, who provides a warning lesson to ambitious invaders. Though he initially wanted 'to conquer Ireland' (*do ghabháil Érenn*), his attack was halted when a *tonn tuile* ('flooding wave', 55) drowned him. The landscape and natural features of Ireland both police its borders and repel unsuitable colonizers, while at the same time they are imaginatively reclaimed for native narration. Caílte quickly walks past the recontextualized site and encounters Patrick; Patrick is also a foreigner, but is, importantly, more interested in conversion than conquest. This provides an important message. When the *Acallam* represents Patick as a cleric willing to preserve Irish narratives and lore, it distinguishes him from the twelfth- and thirteenth-century reformers whose policies resulted in the Mellifont Conspiracy (1216–28). As Ó Néill argues,

> foundations like Mellifont were utterly Anglo-Norman in language and personnel; clearly they were intended as another front in the Norman conquest of Ireland ... The uncompromising attitude of these Norman foundations (especially Cistercian) towards Gaelic culture becomes evident in the early thirteenth century, culminating in the Conspiracy of Mellifont and the imposition of French (and Latin) as the sole language of the Cistercian houses of Ireland.[10]

By referencing the fraught locus of clerical Anglicization while nonetheless rejecting that trajectory, the *Acallam* composer prepares a contemporary audience to see Patrick as a model for another way for both the Church and newly arrived foreigners in Ireland to engage with native, vernacular literary culture: not by attacking and denigrating it, but by offering respect and support.

Caílte's charged encounter with Patrick also marks the text's first positive conjunction of the pagan and the Christian. On a *ráth* or earthen rampart, Caílte finds a prayerful Saint Patrick singing scripture, praising the Creator and blessing Finn's old home, *Ráith Droma Deirc* ('Fort of the Red Ridge'.) The text conjoins a pre-Christian place—the pagan chieftain Finn's fortress—with Patrick's sanctifying actions in the real time of the story. The *Acallam* correspondingly celebrates Patrick with traditional bardic encomiastic epithets alongside more conventional Christian praises—he is both salmon and angel—so that when Caílte appears with his followers,

> Is and sin do éirigh in t-éo flaithemhnais 7 in t-uaithne airechais 7 in t-aingil talmaide .i. Pátraic mac Alprainn .i. apstal na nGaoidhel, 7 gabhus in t-esríat do chrothad uisci choisrictha ar na feraibh móra, uair ro bhúi míle léighionn do dheamhnaibh uas a ceannaibh conuic in lá sin, 7 dochuatar na demhna i cnocaibh 7 i scalpaibh 7 i n-imlibh na críche 7 ind orba uatha ar cach leath. (64–70)

> (Then Patrick, the son of Calpurn, the salmon of Heaven, the pillar of dignity and the angel on earth, he who was apostle to the Irish, arose and sprinkled holy water on these great men, for, until that day, a thousand legions of demons had been above their heads. The demons fled from them in all directions, into the hills and rockclefts and off to the far reaches of the country.) (p. 5)

Throughout the text this act is repeated with variations—Patrick, proclaimed as *apstal na nGaoidhel* ('apostle to the Irish'), blesses the land itself as well as the Irish people, clearing them both of demons and plagues. Demons and otherworldly beings are sent to the geographic periphery or imprisoned below ground, in rocks and beneath hills. This act 'organizes' the environment into good and bad regions and shows Patrick reifying a traditional, native Irish understanding of the Otherworld, the *síd*, as situated beneath hills and mounds.[11] Simultaneously, by driving pagan beings to the hills and rocks, Patrick infuses the land with its heroic, pre-Christian stories that are elements of a past not lost, but remembered and hauntingly embodied in the beauty of the land. In this early *Acallam* scene, Patrick's act, not coincidentally, also sanctifies the space, or clears the stage, for the first of Caílte's poetic placelore performances celebrating an ancient landscape feature.

While his priests are terrified of Caílte and his massive warriors, nearly four times their size, Patrick himself calmly greets Caílte as 'friend' and proceeds to make the first of several inquiries about the land and its natural features. Not surprisingly, there is an emphasis on water, which occupies a prominent, metaphorically rich position in the poetics of Irish space: 'Could you find us a well of pure water close by, so that we might baptize the people of Brega, Meath and Usnagh?' Caílte assents to the request and, joining hands with Patrick, leads him to the pool of a pleasant, pure spring (*lochtobar grinn glaindi*, 87). Caílte then recites a praise poem—he uses the vocative case and several second-person singular forms to address the spring directly, thus turning the landscape into a living character:

A thopuir Trága Dá Ban,	O spring of *Tráig Dá Ban*,
álainn do bilar barrglan:	lovely your bright cress sprigs;
ó ro tréiced do chnuas ort	since your pruning was neglected,
nír léiced fás dot fochlocht.	your brooklime has multiplied.

Do bricc ód bruachaib immach,	Trout off your banks,
do mucca allta it fásach,	wild swine in your wood recesses;
daim do chreca, caín selca,	deer on the rocks for hunting,
do laíg brecca broinnderca.	and dappled, red-breasted fawns.

> Do mes ós barraib do chrann,   Mast on your trees' branches,
> t'iasc i n-inberaib th'abhann: fish in your river estuary,
> álainn lí do gas ngegair,   lovely your stalks of arum,
> a glas uaine foithremail.¹²   O green-wooded stream. (p. 5)

Caílte's verses generate a vividly detailed picture as he draws us into a landscape built out of his words. Landscapes are frequent subjects of poetic laudation, signaling that Irish topography matters deeply, as Patrick learns across the course of the text. As elsewhere in the *Acallam*, however, the place is celebrated not only as beautiful and fruitful, but as a site—a well-spring—of human story. The poem turns from the spring itself to the people who traveled from it:

> Is uait do-chuatar in Fiann   From you the *Fían* set out,
> dár marbad Coinchenn coimfhial,   when generous Coinchenn was slain,
> dár cuired ár Féinne Finn   When Finn's *Fían* was slaughtered,
> isin matain ós Maelglinn ...   in the morning above *Maelglenn* ...

> ... Ar marbad con 7 fer,   ... After the slaughter of dogs and men,
> ar n-athchumma laech lángel,   after the wounding of shining warriors,
> co cuala glaed Garaid glain   bright Garad's cry was heard
> adaig re taeb in topair.¹³   at night beside the spring. (p. 6)

At once celebrating nature and recalling human history as enacted in and from place, this poem exemplifies the *Acallam*'s preoccupation with the relation between narrative and environmental sites. To allay doubts that such conflations and layerings—of place and tale, pagan and Christian, past and present—are unsanctioned, here and throughout the *Acallam* Patrick responds to Caílte's performance with 'May victory and blessing be yours, Caílte ... for you have lightened both our spirits and our minds' (p. 8) (*Adrae buaidh 7 bennacht, a Cháilti! ... as urgairdiugud menman 7 aicenta dhúin sin*, 163–4). The cooperation between indigenous and newly arrived Christian wisdom-bearers confers spiritual and intellectual improvement on all who listen.

The following sequence is routinely repeated over the course of the *Acallam*: a visit to a new place; brief directions that situate us geographically; and an expository question and answer session establishing the place's natural features and history, frequently concluded with a poem on the place along with an appreciative blessing from Patrick (or another, often regal, listener). The text also repeatedly celebrates Patrick's freeing of the land from demonic beings. Indeed, while much of this story is about the places where pre-Christian heroic acts unfolded, the *Acallam* also recounts Christian sanctifying and over-writing of the Irish landscape as part of Patrick's evangelizing mission.[14]

Thus it is that the knowledge-hungry Patrick asks the questions that initiate long conversations about the land and its practitioners; yet he also admits guilt for listening to Caílte's stories about his lord Finn, their adventures, the places they traversed and the people they encountered. At one point, having uttered the formulaic expression thankfully proclaiming blessings on and victory for Caílte, Patrick continues: 'you have lightened our spirits and our mind, even though our religious life is being disrupted and our prayers neglected' (p. 11) (*as gairdiugud menman 7 aicenta dúin sin acht min bhudh coll crábaid, 7 min bhudh maidnechtnaighi urnaigthi dhúin é,* 286–9).[15] Anxious that paying attention to Caílte's storytelling is irresponsible and irreligious, Patrick receives divine confirmation of his mission, which now becomes both evangelical and literary. Aibelán and Solusbrethach, his two guardian angels, appear, and enthusiastically reassure him that he is right to pay attention to native lore. But they also order him to help preserve it: not only should he *listen*, he should *record*, becoming part of the preservation and transmission process of the material himself. The angels tell him in unison that the aged warriors' memories are beginning to fail, to the extent that they can only tell a third of their tales; and the angels urgently command Patrick to

> scríbhthar na scéla sin letsa i támlorguibh filed 7 i mbriathraibh ollaman, ór budh gairdiugudh do dronguibh 7 do degdáinibh deridh aimsire éisdecht frisna scéluib sin. (299–302)

> (have these stories written down on poets' tablets in refined language [literally 'in the words of the highest-grade poets'], so that the hearing of them will provide entertainment for the lords and commons of later times.) (p. 12)

This crucial scene provides an ambitious origin myth for the writing of Irish literature. Patrick's concerns about merging the sacred and secular by spending time learning about Ireland's sites and their histories are allayed by divine approval, which merges the Christian evangelical project with a vernacular national Irish literary project. That project foregrounds itself as national in multiple, overlapping ways. The journey and survey of places takes in all of Ireland; as further discussed next, on two key occasions Caílte's audience for his collected stories consists of all the nobles and learned men of Ireland, convened a year apart at two national assembly sites: the Hill of Uisnech, mythic heart of Ireland, and the Hill of Tara, ritual seat of the legendary High King of Ireland. Furthermore, regarding vernacular literature Patrick's conversation with the angels is exceedingly important. Though Patrick and his scribes would normally have expected to work in Latin, the angels command these tales be written down 'in the words of the *ollamh*s', the highest grade of native Irish poets, who wrote in the elaborate artificial language of bardic poetry that had been codified by the twelfth century. The added clarification that both lords and commoners should be able to enjoy them further confirms that this must be an Irish-language writing project. Self-consciously presented as Ireland's very first vernacular literary text, through Caílte, Patrick, angels and scribes, the *Acallam* installs itself as a foundational literary monument that unifies an entire country, Christian and pagan, past and present.

Following the heavenly authorization of his involvement in native learning, once Patrick has committed to recording the stories of heroic Ireland he immediately asks that Caílte and his companions in turn take on Patrick's own tales and lore: that is, the Christian sacred narrative. Patrick calls on them to do so, 'so that you might submit to the Gospel of the King of Heaven and Earth, the true and glorious God' (p. 12) (*ar dáigh cu ro slechtadh sibh do soiscéla rígh nime 7 talman .i. in fírDia forórda*, 315–17), and baptizes them with waters from the spring Caílte had poetically praised and located for Patrick. The text thus marks the beginning of a divinely approved collaborative project that merges the worlds of a Christian saint and a warrior-hero. Most importantly, the project is framed and organized by a decision to travel jointly through Ireland and pause at sites whose history demands reflection, with Patrick's scribe Broccán keeping an account: 'Write it down', Patrick repeatedly orders.[16] This storytelling journey generates a new Irish landscape whose transcript, of course, is the *Acallam* itself.

Patrick naturalized: a Briton's kinship with the land

Unusual among major Irish saints, Patrick was himself not actually Irish. Born in Roman Britain, this fifth-century figure first came to Ireland as a sixteen-year-old slave, and later returned as a missionary. Being foreign-born is not generally depicted in a positive light in the *Acallam*, however. Heroic defense of Ireland against foreigners is a theme articulated frequently in this text, which celebrates the ways both the *fían*-warriors and the land itself protect the realm from invasion. Previously, we saw the Irish environment rise up in the form of a massive wave drowning Bec the Exile, son of the King of the Romans, as he tries to conquer Ireland. Other figures who come to Ireland include an Artúir (Arthur), son of Benne Brit, elsewhere a king in Britain, portrayed as poorly behaved because he steals Finn's hounds. (Artúir, however, is a 'teachable' Briton who ultimately offers restitution to Finn—he also contributes a new type of horse to Ireland, and serves Finn until his death).[17] Another example is Mílid, the son of the King of the World. When Mílid arrives and attempts to seize the kingdom of Ireland, Finn refuses to submit, and Caílte slays the would-be conqueror in single combat. This high-ranking invader's death at Caílte's hand is thought by the Irish to be so impressive that

> co tucad ní de cacha tulcha aireghda, 7 ro facad da chaelesna ar in tulaig-seo de. Conid uad ata in t-ainm sin [i.e., Caelesna] ... Ocus is e sin, a anum, a rí Laigen...dindšenchas na cnocc 7 na tulach ro fiarfaigis dim (4782–9).
>
> (a part of him was brought to each important mound [providing names for all the hills and the fortified heights]. Two of his slender ribs were placed in this hill. Whence its name Slender-Rib. And that, my dear king of Leinster ... is the topography [literally *dindshenchas*] of the hills and of the mounds you asked of me.) (p. 134)[18]

But, while Caílte is the protector, here the Irish topography also plays a role in repelling the ambitious expansionist from abroad. The most visible parts of the landscape, the hills and mounds, preserve both the foreigner Mílid's fragmented body and the memory of his defeat, becoming the national reliquaries of Ireland's fight against incorporation into someone else's empire. In this example we see how Ireland's topographic features also become narrativized spaces and *dindshenchas* texts containing lessons about Ireland's defense on behalf of the king of Leinster and others.

Patrick himself is in Ireland as a religious missionary rather than a foreign king's son seeking to conquer the country, yet for a late twelfth- or early thirteenth-century Irish audience, an evangelizing Briton's presence in Ireland is complex, for, as discussed in Chapter 5, religious reform, conquest and colonization often go hand in hand. The question of Patrick's own nationality thus required some careful negotiation. While the *Acallam* potentially alludes to Patrick's foreignness by mentioning the details of his enslavement,[19] Patrick's foreign birth is never stated. Were his origins being intentionally occluded to lead an audience to respond to Patrick as fully Irish? Or, was his British birth so commonly accepted as to require no emphasis? Given the number of Welsh colonists participating in the twelfth-century English invasion and conquest of Ireland, if we think of Patrick as a Briton or proto-Welsh speaker, his origins and their parallels with those invaders become quite suggestive. If we accept that Patrick was remembered as British in origin—and this seems the likeliest possibility—he should perhaps be recognized as modeling the integration and absorption of foreigners in a productive, culturally pro-Irish way, through study and promotion of vernacular spatial poetics. Indeed, the *Acallam* itself argues in a profoundly radical manner that Irish spatial knowledge (and practice) trumps ancestry: that is, by using the vernacular, orienting oneself in the Irish environment, learning and embracing native Irish geographic discourse and topographic histories, one can become 'Irish'. As a foreigner without the all-important, and, in the usual Irish terms, legitimating, hereditary attachment to a region of Ireland, Patrick presents both a unique challenge and opportunity.

Lacking an ancestral clan to legitimate and legally empower him, Patrick instead gains kinship with the land itself. His actions and pre-eminence are empowered by the physical geography of the whole of Ireland, investing him with an environmental authority to go with his official and spiritual authority. At significant stages of the journey around Ireland, Patrick sanctifies natural sites, recognizing and maximizing their choicest features, with nature cooperatively thriving in response—the landscape's positive performance for Patrick attests to his fitness as Ireland's most important saint. This happy symbiosis also reflects native Irish sovereignty traditions in which the fitting and rightful leader elicits environmental fecundity and well-being, while the wrong leader provokes droughts, fires, famine and other cataclysmic environmental events.

For instance, towards the end of the *Acallam* Patrick demonstrates an impressive knowledge of Irish place, local and universal, and an ability to prevent the repeated destruction of the land and its harvest when the attacks of a supernatural bird flock leave the people with few options beyond deserting their territory. Caílte asks Patrick, the 'lord of knowledge and computistics' (*tigerna ind eolais 7 na ríme*, 6292–3) for his insights, which Patrick gives, 'for often I have asked questions of you' (p. 176) (*uair minic liumsa fiarfaige do denam dítsu* (6294–5). Patrick provides an esoteric explanation of time, both millennial and immediate, and of the movements of the heavens, which provides the solution for defeating this avian plague while also reminding us of Ireland's place on a larger, cosmic level. In an exchange that further emphasizes Patrick's increasing success as an Irish spatial wisdom-bearer, Caílte assumes the role more frequently taken up by Patrick, that of the appreciative recipient of crucial environmental knowledge: 'May you have victory and blessing, holy Patrick ... and happy were the men of Ireland born the day you came to meet them' (p. 177) (*Adráe buaid 7 bendachtain, a naem Patraic ... 7 mo chin tainic a ngeinemain fer nEirenn in la tangais da n-indsaigid* (6305–7). Caílte develops a vivid image of a transformed Ireland in his praise of Patrick: 'For there was a demon on the bottom of every single blade of grass in Ireland before you, and there is today in Ireland an angel on the bottom of each single blade of grass' (p. 177) (*uair ro bói deman a mbun cach énfeornin inti reomut, 7 atá aingel a mbun cach énféoirnin aniu inti* (6307–8). The land is freed from attacking birds, and individual blades of grass have been sanctified—this saint has been embraced by a now thriving Ireland in a hagiographic reworking of the sovereignty legend. The scene further emphasizes this by staging Caílte's performative articulation of Ireland as being Patrick's, the fusion of Ireland to Patrick and Patrick to Ireland. Caílte admonishes the evil birds:

> nach fetabair in t-apstal fíren fírbrethach indsi Gáeidel .i. naém Patraic mac Alpraind, cenn crabaid 7 irsi Gaeidel. Ocus imthigid-si ar in sleib fiadnusi, 7 fácbaid Eirinn dó sin, uair ní cubhaid duibsi beith re aghaidh sium inti. (6341–4)

> (Do you not know the righteous, true-judging Apostle of the Island of the Gaels, holy Patrick, son of Calpurn, the head of piety and of faith of the Irish? Go on the mountain before us and leave Ireland to him, for it is not fitting for you to be here before his face.) (p. 178)

The birds flee and exterminate each other. Patrick blesses the region and decrees that it shall be free of terrors, witches and destruction from then on, an act that is celebrated by a week of feasting and banqueting. The saint is 'naturalized', attached to and synchronized with Ireland's environment, dedicated to its preservation and restoration, but also, importantly, empowered to protect and improve it. By 'naturalizing' Patrick through earned kinship with a warmly responsive Irish landscape and people, the text gives Patrick place-based roots, making him the fitting patron saint and champion of Ireland.

Environmental education and saintly mastery of Ireland's spatial vernacular

In this tale of a Briton embraced by the Irish land, the *Acallam* traces Patrick's development as a knowledgeable wayfarer who learns, to borrow the poetic lines delivered by Finn, to 'be a listener in the forest, a watcher on the plain' (p. 20) (*bidh co heistechtach cailli, bid co féchsanach muighi*, 600). A wise figure is always expectantly scanning the landscape to grasp the information it contains, but, as illustrated by that first spring-finding scene at the *Acallam*'s opening, Patrick initially lacks the essential environmental knowledge and is unable to access the landscape. Although he cannot find a spring, Patrick does find a teacher and guide who can transfer that knowledge to him: Caílte. In an emphatic demonstration of Caílte's unparalleled topographic fluency and its national reach, in pitch darkness the warrior locates a source of water, 'for there is no place where one might get a cupful of water, whether from a cliff, a river, or an estuary, in the five great provinces of Ireland that I am not familiar with, by day or by night' (p. 48) (*uair ni fuil inad asa tabar lán énchuaich a haill na a habhuinn a cúic ollcoigeduibh Eirenn nacham eolach itir lá 7 oidhchi*, 1549–51). Regarding the kind of knowledge that moving through the landscape produces, which Caílte possesses in abundance and Patrick gains as they travel the country together, Tim Ingold reminds us that 'For the wayfarer, movement is not ancillary to knowing—not merely a means of getting from point to point in order to collect the raw data of sensation for subsequent modelling in the mind. Rather, moving *is* knowing. *The wayfarer knows as he goes along.*'[20] It is important to the logic of the *Acallam* that Caílte does not just pass information on to Patrick, but that Patrick also traverses Ireland himself, that he engages in a spatial practice that is also knowing

National pilgrims

and absorbing Ireland's lessons and wisdom through movement. Just as later pilgrims retrace Patrick's pathways through Ireland, a reverential Patrick initially makes his own pilgrimages to Ireland's important, storied sites as he becomes Ireland's saintly hero and begins to leave his own marks on the country.

Numerous scenes testify to Patrick's increasing environmental knowledge and showcase his respect for the land and its physical and narrative features. Caílte leads Patrick by the hand to that first spring, but midway through the *Acallam* another search for a source of water shows Caílte and an increasingly environmentally savvy Patrick combining forces. At the hospitaller Eógan's *ráth* or earthen rampart, the people suffer from a lack of water, for though there is rumored to be a spring, much searching has turned up no trace of it. Caílte, of course, knows its location, but when ordered by Patrick to find it, he baulks, and states that he is terrified to find the torrent, which he fears will cause a great flood, as nine heroes were required to lift and replace its cover. Patrick intervenes and assures him that God will control the water, and Caílte is convinced to remove the massive stone covering the hidden well, at which point wonderful, clear water gushes from the rock in the flood Caílte had warned against. Yet

> Ann sin tócbus Pátraic an láimh caeimh creadhail ro fóired gach n-airc 7 gach n-ainces frisi tabard hí, 7 sluicter in t-uisqi ar cúl doridisi isin sliabh 7 isin charraic cédna, cu nach raibhi acht lán baisi Pátraic ac snighe aisdi amach don uisgi. (3630–4)
>
> (Patrick then raised his fair, devout hand, that relieved every difficulty and trouble to which it was applied, and the water was swallowed back again into the mountain and into the same rock, so that there was no more water than the contents of Patrick's palm issuing from it.) (p. 110)

In a *dindshenchas*-creating performative act, Patrick's disciple Benén then declares that the well is now to be known as *Bas Pátraic*, 'the Palm of Patrick'. In this case, Patrick and Caílte play largely equal roles, so that, with Caílte's strength and Patrick's miracle-working power, the waters issue forth at a productive, moderate rate. We see Patrick beginning to prove himself as the saint of Ireland, developing a cooperative relationship with nature and the land. When the spring is renamed 'Patrick's Palm', Patrick himself becomes a part of the landscape, with 'Patrick's Palm' turned into a material Patrician relic that subsequent pilgrims can visit. As layers are added, a new placelore is inscribed into Ireland's landscape.

By the later stages of their mutually instructive journey through Ireland, Patrick has become a fully-fledged source of knowledge and a kind of tutelary saint who frees the land from plague, disaster and hardship. Patrick, Caílte, the king of Connaught and their attendant retinues travel to *Muine na n-ammaite* ('Thicket of Witches'), where nine witches have been destroying the territory and its inhabitants for twenty years, and the king pleads with Patrick to deliver them from the witches and their devastation of the countryside. When Patrick asks for water, but none is found, in a Mosaic miracle 'Patrick then raised his arm and thrust his crozier into the earth, and a crystalline spring leaped from the earth' (p. 190) (*Is ann sin tócbais Pátraic in laim, 7 sáidhis in trostan fa chomair in talman, gur moidh in lochtopur glainide asin talmain*, 6771–3). Blessing the water, Patrick also recites a poem in which he makes himself a character:

In t-uisci acaind abus   now we have found water,
ar Patraic gan imarbus,   said Patrick without sin,
bid ordraic íc cách ule   Famous will be to all,
in topur án ainglide. (6775–6)   the brilliant, angelic spring. (p. 190)

Patrick further declares that three days and three nights of protection will come to all who drink from this now holy spring—a land that was cursed has now become a powerful locus of sanctity. When the fearsome witches return, Patrick casts the holy spring's water on them, causing them to flee, weeping, after which Patrick and his companions all seat themselves upon a great tumulus. Patrick releases the land from despoiling demons and creates a sacred well that confers protection on those who travel to this place and use its water. By revisiting this sanctified place, later pilgrims can relive the miracle by remembering the stories, drinking from the same spring and gaining deliverance from trouble, just like the deliverance Patrick offered those who initially sat with him on that grass-covered mound. Patrick is increasingly 'naturalized' and in sync with Ireland's environment: dedicated to its preservation and restoration, but also empowered to protect and improve it.

Most importantly, however, the scene also foregrounds a significant development in Patrick's skill-set: his composition of Irish-language poetry that marks his ability (and desire) to work in a complex literary vernacular. At Muine na n-ammaite Patrick

National pilgrims

composes a quatrain; slightly earlier in the story, at Cashel (an important ecclesiastical site and seat of the kings of Munster), Patrick delivers a twelve-line landscape poem on the *Cloch na Cét*, the 'Stone' or 'Rock of Hundreds', after expelling its 11,000 demons and endowing it with the 'gift of bestowing good counsel' (p. 151) (*buaid comairli do denam dí*, 5406).[21] Practicing an Irish poetics and employing the device of *dúnad*, Patrick begins and ends his composition with *in cloch* ('the stone'). In yet another example of how a poetics and practice of Irish space are fused, we also learn that the stone's blessed nature is the result of repeated spatial practice, namely an angel's daily movement across its surface: *bennachtain urri, 7 aingel dé cacha tratha nóna ic a tairimthecht* (5407–8) ('he put this blessing on it, that an angel of the Lord would traverse it at each time of Nones', p. 151). Though a subtle detail, in it we find a divine model of repeated spatial practice: movement, or wayfaring, to use Tim Ingold's term, is an act of knowing as well as hallowing. Finally, the national political significance of Patrick's movements and poetic acts are emphasized when the king of the province (who has just granted Patrick Cashel and its surrounds) blesses Patrick for his oral performance:

'Adrae buaid 7 bennachtain, 7 a m'anum, a naemPatraic', ar rí Muman, 'is mór d'fis 7 d'ḟireolus ro indsebair duind imaraen'. (5439–40)

('May you have victory and blessing, my dear, holy Patrick', said the King of Munster. 'Great is the knowledge and true lore you have told to all of us.') (p. 152)

The scenes of composition at Cashel and Muine na nAmmaite attest to Patrick's developing skill in vernacular placelore poetry.

After a year of traveling Ireland on his own without Caílte, Patrick becomes a fully-fledged composer and performer of *dindshenchas* poetry for his former teacher.[22] When reunited, Caílte asks Patrick to give an account of his own movements and adventures while they were apart, and Patrick responds with place-making poetry:

In tipra d'áccus as tír | A well I have left in the land,
's ma dá bratan cen imṡnim | and two salmon without care,
is merdait ann co brath ṁbán | Till white Doom they remain there.
adér riut a Chailtican. (7766–7) | Believe me, Caílte mine. (p. 216)

Patrick details his expulsion of three evil brothers and 300,000 demons from Croagh Patrick, and recites further lines:

M'én 7 m'uisci 7 m'ilar	My bird, my water, and my host,
is mo Chruach álaind idhan,	and my Crúach fair,
is siat sin bus chomarchi	They will give protection
do cach uaim a n-añdliged. (7774–5)	to all who suffer wrong. (p. 216)

These deeds, and the story of the sanctification of Ireland, are preserved in vernacular poetry—a newly Christianized landscape of words is created by Patrick.

Paralleling the pacing of the angels on the Cloch na Cét at Cashel, here too spatial practice is given the saint's approval. Benén asks what benefits will accrue to 'each one who will walk about the expanse of the Crúach' (p. 216) (*cach aen imthechus fonn na Cruiache*, 7778) and drink from the spring; Patrick responds that those who honor it will receive sanctuary and protection, while those who do evil there will be cursed. Repeating Patrick's own formula of thanks granting blessing and victory, Caílte also adds that 'great is the benefit that you have left to the Gaels in that place' (p. 216) (*is mor in sochur sin ro facais do Gaédelaib issinn inudh sin*, 7785–6). Patrick's gift to the Gaels is also about a wider enrichment of the landscape that will then go on to be inscribed and reinscribed for generations to come in cultural acts of pathmaking and pilgrimage.

This massive and bleak mountain, Croagh Patrick, by the twelfth century had become a major destination for pilgrims. It unites the people of Ireland, here referred to collectively as *Gaéidelaib* ('Irish', 'Gaels') as a national community in their 'walks about the expanse' of this redemptive Patrician pilgrimage site through which they can access Patrick—these places become his relics, and Patrick has carved out paths to reach them. Movement changes the ground journeyed across, and the topography of Ireland becomes a legible text that invites subsequent spatial practitioners—pilgrims and otherwise—to trace its storylines. In much of Ireland, footprints and tracks are easily glimpsed, grasses are flattened and paths visibly muddied by wayfarers to create a network of spatial trajectories. These inscriptions are particularly visible from the heights of Ireland and the routes to them, such as the path from Ballintubber to Crúachán Aigle, where a pilgrim cannot help but look both backward and forward to trace the route so as to track the

National pilgrims

indentations in the landscape marking centuries of footsteps up to Patrick's fair Crúach.

While we might, like Caílte, come upon our own paths, we also appropriate and share the trails established by the feet of earlier wayfarers, heroes, saints, kings and common pilgrims. Following these paths collapses temporality by connecting the walker to all those who trod the path before him or her, and the wanderer, at least for a while, inhabits a communal space shared with those past beings and practices. The essayist Rebecca Solnit explains in her cultural history of walking that

> To walk the same way is to reiterate something deep, to move through the same space the same way is a means of becoming the same person, thinking the same thoughts. It's a form of spatial theater, but also spiritual theater, since one is emulating saints and gods in the hope of coming closer to them oneself, not just impersonating them for others. It's this that makes pilgrimage, with its emphasis on repetition and imitation, distinct amid all the modes of walking. If in no other way one can resemble a god, one can at least walk like one.[23]

Solnit articulates many of the same insights that inform the *Acallam* and the pathmaking it describes. Caílte and Patrick jointly create a map of Ireland's holy and famed places: sites which repay meditative visits, and which can heal and transform those who journey to them. The *Acallam* composers were well aware of the power of leading its practitioners to walk in those storied footsteps and follow the early circuits delineated and celebrated in its pages.

The view from Ireland's heights:
a verbalized map for the Irish nation

Though not immediately apparent when reading the *Acallam*, if we were to create a relief map of the text we would see that the most important, dramatic and nationally unifying storytelling moments tend to be situated at the highest altitudes. For figures looking down on the ground below, be it from a steep hill in Ireland or a skyscraper in Manhattan, as de Certeau writes, elevation puts the being gazing from a height 'at a distance. It transforms the bewitching world by which one was "possessed" into a text that lies before one's eyes. It allows one to read it, to be a solar Eye, looking down like a god.'[24] An important end-goal of the *Acallam* is to lay Ireland's storytelling landscape out as a text, to enable the viewer to use a god's-eye perspective to read it; appropriately enough, that unified, storied map of the nation unfolds from hills like Tara and Uisnech. Patrick and the King of Ireland take up the organizational role of mobilizing people, storytellers and scribes, leading them to high altitudes where the collected stories will be delivered, orally broadcast and written down so that all present can take some of Ireland's storied geography back to their diverse home territories. Movement up mountains coheres with a more widely encompassing project, with a national—as opposed to a local, site-specific—production, and the spatial mechanics make this clear.[25]

The two major performances take place at notable sites, the Hill of Uisnech and, one year later, the Hill of Tara. In terms of Ireland's sacred places, few sites can rival the Hill of Uisnech, the ceremonial or mythic center of Ireland, which provides a 360-degree view of the nation. With a fame extending beyond Ireland to play a role in England's national myths, according to Geoffrey of Monmouth's *Historia Regum Britanniae* Merlin acquired the pillars for the 'Giant's Ring' from Uisnech and had them erected in England at Stonehenge.[26] Described by Gerald of Wales as the *umbilicus Hiberniae* and Geoffrey Keating as the *Ail na Míreann* ('stone of the divisions'),[27] a fifteen-foot stone at the Hill of Uisnech marks the point at which the borders of Ireland's provinces meet. This hill embodies Mircea Eliade's concept of the *axis mundi* or *omphalos* where the sacred can 'come to earth' and 'the transcendent might enter the immanent'.[28] This Irish *omphalos* brings together Saint Patrick (the 'angel on earth'), a historically anachronistic, not-yet-born King of Ireland, and the impossibly old *fían* warriors, to create the *Acallam*, not to mention the characters generated by the storytelling itself. As discussed in Chapter 3, the Irish sources convey a deep-seated belief that 'wisdom sits in places'—that learning is a spatially embodied practice, often catalyzed by physically inhabiting locations earlier populated by ancestors, real and imagined. In this kind of 'historical theater', in which the past becomes immediate and 'long-elapsed events are made to unfold as if before one's eyes', the place-making narrator is able 'to speak the past into being, to summon it with words and give it dramatic form, to *produce* experience by forging ancestral worlds in which others can participate and readily lose themselves'.[29] The actors in Caílte and Oisín's tales may have perished, but through the stories that are to unfold at Uisnech a connection is

National pilgrims

established and an experience shared by their common occupation, across time, of the same spaces: physical, as well as those conjured in narrative. Site is important:

> Corub hí Accallaim na Senorach ac in chartha a mullach Uisnig sin 7 cachar' chansat d'fis 7 d'eolus d'feraib Eirenn uile ó sin amach. (2702–3)

> (This was 'The Converse of the Elders' by the pillar on the Hill of Uisnech, in which they transmitted all their knowledge and learning to the later men of Ireland.) (p. 82)

The theaters or spaces of utterance appropriate for a text like the *Acallam* are envisioned as sacred and of heightened national significance.

That the country's most important religious and political figures—Patrick, the King of Ireland, and the provincial kings of Ulster, Munster, Connaught and Leinster, as well as the remaining *fían* warriors—convene on the hill where Ireland's provincial boundaries meet to listen to Caílte and Oisín's tales, marks the project as a national undertaking, sealed with both saintly and secular approval. The King of Ireland tells the 'wise men and historians of Ireland' (p. 79) (*filet sin 7 senchaide Eirenn*, 2589) that

> Scribthar i tamlorgaib filed 7 a slechtaib suad 7 a mbriathraib ollaman co mbere cach a chuid lais da crich 7 da ferann bodein da cach ní dar' indis Cailti 7 Oissin da morgnimarthaib gaile 7 gaiscid, 7 do dindṡenchus Eirenn. (2589–93)

> (Whatever Caílte and Oisín have told us of their great deeds of valor and of prowess, as well as all the knowledge, learning, and the placename lore of Ireland, let it all be preserved on the staffs of poets, in the texts of scholars, and in the tales of sages, so that each might carry his share with him to his own native land.) (p. 79)

While the provincial kings all appreciatively collect placelore stories from Caílte, Oisín and Patrick throughout the tale, here at Uisnech it is the King of Ireland who addresses the national importance of preserving this material and recirculating it among the discrete regions of Ireland. As Uisnech's elevation provides a fully panoramic view of Ireland, it is entirely fitting that a verbalized, storied map of all of Ireland is performed here. After all, this is the place, more than any in Ireland, from which one can imaginatively 'be a solar Eye, looking down like a god' to read the 'text' of the Irish nation that visually and verbally unfolds outwards from this sacred center. This performance is, however, also followed up with a second one at the end of the text.

A recap of some important scenes shows how the Caílte who speaks a year later at Tara has been transformed over the course of the looping, storytelling circuit around what is now also Patrick's Ireland. Caílte is certainly dislocated at the *Acallam*'s opening, but his year-long pilgrimage renews him and reveals new paths that he, and the audience with him, might travel. After Patrick exorcises Caílte of his hovering demons and baptizes him, 'for the good of my soul, and the soul of the chief of the Fían' (p. 12) (*do raith mh'anmasa 7 do raith anma in rígh-feinneda duitsi*, 323–4), Caílte bequeaths to Patrick an arm-sized block of gold, Finn's final gift to him, which is turned into Patrick's canonical bells and also decorates psalters and missals.[30] Caílte's transference of loyalties from old lord to new is highlighted in an offering that also marks Patrick out as a rightful inheritor of Finn's wealth, honor and respect—this is emphasized materially by the conversion of pagan gold to Christian liturgical accoutrements. As the story continues, Caílte's cathartic visits to famed Irish sites elicit highly emotional reactions in the manner of a pilgrim's affective engagement with places of religious importance. As he meditates on these places and remembers the people associated with them,

> ro cháiestar déra troma fírthruaga ann, cor'bo fliuch blai 7 bruinde dó 7 adar leis cech cnoc 7 cech céiti 7 cech dingna tar a rachad co teicémad dias no triur nó cethrar nó cuiciur no cuiri don Féind dó, 7 ní bitis acht 'na tulchaib folma 7 'na muighib mínreidi, cen coin, cen gilla, cen oclach d'faicsin orra. (3378–9)[31]

> (he wept heavy, truly sorrowful tears, so that his shirt and breast were drenched. Every hill and mound and fort he would wander by, it seemed to him that two or three or four or five of a band of the *Fían* would appear, but they were only empty hills and smooth, level plains with no hound or warrior or youth on them.) (p. 102)

Caílte weeps for earlier times and the now emptied landscape, but the questions posed by Patrick and Ireland's kings lead Caílte to repopulate these place-worlds with ancient beings and open them for all of his audience through story—like Finn's gold, which ultimately gilds psalters and rings out in canonical bells, here elements of the heroic pagan past become reshaped for and celebrated by a keen Christian audience. We recognize how Caílte, and Ireland

National pilgrims

itself, have been transformed by Patrick's presence and now move towards a new future when Caílte refuses the *síd* folk's offer of a reinvigorated body freed from human aging and death. By rejecting the druidic form (*deilbe druidechta*, 7039–40), Caílte reaffirms his conversion to Christianity and Patrick:

> Ní géb acht in delb tuc mo Déntaid 7 mo Dúilem 7 in fírDia dororda dam, 7 iris chreidme 7 crabaid in Táilgind intí tarrus a nEirinn. (7040–2)
>
> (I shall not have any shape but that which my Maker and my Creator and the glorious True God gave to me, with the faith of belief and piety of the Adze-Head [Patrick], he who has come into Ireland.) (p. 197)

Even more remarkably, the Túatha Dé Danann respond with lines that implicitly support Caílte's conversion by proclaiming that his is the voice of a true warrior (*guth fírlaich*, 7043). In this newly configured Ireland, when Caílte joins the Christian host he even earns the approbation of the Túatha Dé Danann. This otherworldly folk also contribute to the success of Caílte and Patrick's joint placelore project and its performance at Tara a year on, when they provide Caílte with

> deoch cuimnigthi céille d'indlucud duinde duit co Temraig connach tecma duit es nó abhann nó indber nó a cath nó a comlann nach bia a cuimne accut. (7259–61)
>
> (a drink that we give to you to take to Tara for the remembrance of lore, so that any cataract or river or estuary that you encounter, you will remember it, together with its attendant battles and combats.) (p. 203)

Because Caílte understands how important it is to remember these sites, share their stories and give the heroic past a role in a newly Christianized Ireland, he does accept this drink from the Túatha Dé Danann.[32] Caílte—as a result of his travels and conversations about the land with Patrick, and by witnessing Patrick's demonstrations of his sanctity at different natural sites—is reborn, transformed from a pagan warrior into a devout Christian. His pilgrimage has been successful, and he has followed a new path to Tara for the final performance.

It is important to remember that, well before the time the *Acallam* was written, a journey of pilgrimage was a clearly recognized form of penance.³³ Caílte's travels with Patrick function simultaneously as educative for Patrick and as a penitential, cleansing expiation of earlier sins for Caílte himself. Like the angels' daily pacing across the Cloch na Cét and the pilgrims' walk across the Crúach, Caílte's wandering through an Ireland increasingly Christianized by Patrick is a hallowing spatial practice. Though the text is incomplete, by its end Caílte emerges as spiritually and physically ready both to speak at Tara and to take the place in heaven that Patrick promises him. Importantly, we also learn that when the time comes, Caílte will be buried at Tara, his physical form to be enfolded within Ireland's most nationally iconic place.³⁴ Caílte's pilgrimage with Patrick around Ireland has saved his soul as well as Ireland's spatial histories, and the storytelling hero will ultimately become part of the storied landscape itself.

We are, I think, meant to identify with Caílte, to see him in some ways as a model for our own pilgrimage through this text and through an Irish landscape whose secular history has now also been established as sacred. We become virtual or imaginative pilgrims as we wend our way through the *Acallam*'s landscape. We witness the same miracles and wonders, topographical, historical and religious. We hear the stories that frequently reduce Caílte to weeping, his shirt soaked with tears,³⁵ and we can follow his examples of affective piety and reverential remembering. Caílte is like the performer of an Irish lament whose outpourings of poetry, grief and tears allow the audience to participate in the grieving process: Ireland's heroic past is mourned, yet those ancestral histories are also now anchored to a newly sanctified Patrician landscape. By the end of this journey, Caílte, Patrick and the *Acallam*'s many audiences understand that wisdom and lore (*senchas*) sit in places and heights (*dind*), and the importance of traveling to those venerable sites has become undeniable.³⁶ These transformations enable Caílte, and the audience that has followed him on his journey, to return to Tara at the end of the year and participate in the second great storytelling performance that brings all of these narratives, gathered over the year's circuit, together at Tara, Ireland's most regal, mythic site.

Uisnech might be the geographic center of Ireland, but Tara, the mythic seat of Ireland's legendary high kingship, is Ireland's political *omphalos*, and it is significant that this is where the *Acallam* finally takes us. As Caílte reports, it is at the command of Patrick that the nobles of Ireland all gather at Tara, together in one place, to hear Caílte tell mod 7 morgnim gaili 7 gaiscid na Feinde 7 Find meic Cumaill 7 fer nEirenn archena, 7 do lesugud údar 7 olloman dona scelaib indes-mait-ne ann co dered aimsire. (7255–8)

(of the exploits and the great deeds of valour and prowess of the *Fían* and of Finn mac Cumaill. And of the men of Ireland as well, so that the scholars and the sages may preserve the tales that we tell them until the end of time.) (p. 203)

In this joint sacred-secular venture, while Caílte credits Patrick with the summons, it is the King of Ireland who actually oversees this important national event of storytelling and textual preservation at Tara. Celebration of kingly and ecclesiastic cooperative support for Irish literature also offers an approving twelfth- or thirteenth-century nod to western Irish groups like the Muinter Roduib and the Augustinian Canons Regular for producing texts like the *Acallam* itself. The *Acallam* maps out small-scale, often unidentifiable places throughout its 8,000 lines, but ultimately highlights the iconic sites of known national importance that the *Acallam*'s main players move through.

Successful spatial storytelling depends not only on that cohesive utterance from the nation's heights, but also on continued movement, on radiating out to unify the rest of the country. The details of the accounts delivered by the ancient warriors at Uisnech and Tara are to be written down so that 'each might carry his share with him to his own native land' and repeat them 'until the end of time', highlighting an investment in ensuring that Ireland's lore can be absorbed in multiple ways. While holy sites like Patrick's Crúach repay physical contact, a good storyteller can create, through words, a series of inhabitable place-worlds as real and powerful as material sites, and more conveniently accessed. Indeed, the verbal journey through a storied Ireland that takes place at Uisnech and Tara, and which draws together the most important figures in the land, attests to the appeal and power of virtual travel or mental pilgrimage through landscapes made of words. Together at Tara they collectively move through all of Ireland's storied sites and participate in a shared virtual pilgrimage across Ireland led by Caílte and Oisín. These performances are not pale replacements of physical journeys, but alternate and equally valid ways of engaging with Irish place; and by ensuring that a written record is made and carried out to Ireland's diverse regions and inhabitants, a full map of a storied Ireland can be experienced at any corner of the nation.

Never-ending circuits

In a dramatic scene close to the *Acallam*'s end, when the twenty-seven remaining *fíana* traveling with Caílte and Oisín move onto the hill on the western side of Tara, they

> tucsat da n-úidh 7 da n-aire beith a n-ingnais a luith 7 a lánchoib-lidh, 7 gan a beith do rath orro nech ac comrad ríu, 7 tucsat a mbel re lár talman issin tulaig sin, 7 fuaradur bás ann, 7 ro cuired fo thalmain iat, conid Cnoc na nonbur ainm in chnuic sin dia n-eis. (7898–902)
>
> (became aware of their lack of activity and of full vigor, and the fact that they did not have the good fortune that people would talk with them. They put their mouths to the ground of the earth on that hill and perished there. They were placed under the earth there and it is called the Hill of the Nines after them.) (p. 220)

By the end of the text, the landscape has become a chief relic, and in this strange scene these Irish warriors seek contact with the land, placing their mouths on it as if to kiss it and become one with the hill.[37] Though the text leaves much unarticulated, the scene suggests that an obstructed circuit of storytelling exchange—where mouths are blocked from uttering the words they have to say—is fatal. The figures die because there are no speech options open to them—no one will talk to them. The preemptive act of moving around Irish places, mentally and physically, and speaking to people about them and the events which took place there, becomes a matter of life and death. Significantly, as the scene proceeds we see that it is only talking about place that saves the last two surviving *fían* warriors, Caílte and Oisín, and the men of Ireland, from their own crippling grief at this tragedy:

> Ocus ro badur na senoire co toirrsech truag ... Ocus ro badur fir Eirenn uile ina tast gan fer do labra re cheile díb ara mét ro chuir orro a ndernnsat na senóraig do thoirrsi tar éis a Féine 7 a muintire. Ocus adubairt Oissin:
>
> In fuil sunn nech ro feissed . gémad fann, gemad eissel,
>
> in fail ar fácad cuach Find . 'na aenuran a Cromglind.
>
> (7905–12)
>
> (The elders were sad and sorrowful ... All the men of Ireland were silent without a man of them speaking to his fellow, so much were

National pilgrims

they moved by the extent of the grief of the elders for their *Fían* and their people. Oisín recited these lines:

'Can anyone tell us, though humble he be,
Where Finn's cup lies, alone in *Crommglenn?*') (p. 220)

Caílte at first refuses to respond, even though, he points out, never before this moment has there been a day when he would not immediately reply to Oisín. Yet, as if he cannot resist the recuperative call of placelore poetry, Caílte then goes on to recite these answering poetic lines:

Atá sunn nech ro feissed. mar ar' impo for deissel,
in fail ata 'sin glind flais. ní folaig acht feth fithnais. (7915–6)

(One here knows where Finn turned south,
To the deep green valley shrouded in mist.) (p. 221)

And the place-based, memorializing storytelling continues from here. Though reluctant at first, Caílte (with Oisín) continues speaking, sharing his stories of local landscape features with the men of Ireland. Affective connection to Irish places is important, but contact must also be accompanied by verbal performance of these pasts and a shared appreciation of the stories embedded in these Irish sites. Storytelling and speaking Irish place and past are essential to survival, the *Acallam* demonstrates.

Though the *Acallam* is incomplete in all manuscripts, most storylines have been tied up, and scholars generally agree there could not have been much more to follow.[38] Though it is not possible to determine whether several lines have been lost, or if the text has simply been ended *in medias res*, perhaps this Irish storytelling pilgrimage *does not* in fact end. In the penultimate scene, the King of Ireland says to his wife Bé Binn that 'I desire to go on the noble circuit of Ireland' (p. 222) (*Is áil lemsa ... dul ar saerchuaird Eirenn*, 7959), after which arrangements are made for the elders and their retinue to be richly hosted at Tara while the king and queen conduct their circuit. Though we do not walk with them—the story ends less than forty lines later—the narrative 'concludes' with the beginning of another journey across Ireland. This might well be the only appropriate closure to this long saga: the royal couple setting off on their circuit of Ireland to honor and learn from these places by physically visiting them, and retreading what has become a never-ending circuit of Ireland. Their footsteps re-inscribe a circuit around Ireland and reinforce their connection to, and the idea of, a national community unified by movement and story. Before that journey around Ireland takes place, however, Oisín leads the group on a verbal pilgrimage of the wonders of Tara. Regarding a dwarf at Tara whose hand can cure all disease and make peace between battling factions if it is only placed upon them, Oisín describes the stone in Tara that was his bed:

> 'Ocus ba hingnad dala a leaptha', ar Oisin, '.i. in fer ba mhó d'feruibh Eirenn do bídh a choimsi i leapaid in abhuic, 7 in náidhe ba lugha dogheibhthea ní bidh acht a coimsi innti.' (7989–92)

> ('There was a wonderful thing about his bed', said Oisín, 'for the biggest man of the men of Ireland would fit in the bed of the dwarf, and the smallest infant that could be found would also just fit in it.') (p. 223)

This is a space that shifts, like these texts and their narrative trails, to accommodate all. When Oisín goes on to describe the other marvel of Tara, the *Lía Fáil*, the text closes by giving a voice to Ireland's landscape. Oisín declares that

> Ocus intan ticedh rí Eirenn fuirre do ghéised in lecc fái co freacraitís prímthonna Eirenn hí .i. tonn Clídhna 7 tonn Tuaidhe 7 tonn Rudhraigi. Ocus intan ticced rí cóicid fuirre ro bhúiredh in lecc fái. (7998–8001)

> (When the King of Ireland came onto it the stone shrieked under him and the chief waves of Ireland answered it, the Wave of Clidna, the Wave of Tuaide, and the Wave of Rudraige. Whenever the king of a province came onto the stone it roared under him.) (p. 223)

National relics, stones invested with powerful diction, waves endowed with the capacity to respond vocally, and the men and women of Ireland's engagement with them, close the narrative. While the heroes of the past might have expired, their bodies and stories now interred in Ireland's landscape, the end of the *Acallam* models the beginnings of its proper usage. Its conclusion suggests to the audience the different ways they might perform the *Acallam*'s pilgrimage themselves, and move through Ireland's discursive spaces. What is perhaps most exciting about the *Acallam* is that it ends with the possibility of each person conducting his or her own circuit of Ireland, of appropriating and developing the story of Irish place and culture composed here. And through a text like the *Acallam* these circuits can be just as fruitfully conducted in reality, or in virtual, narrative space.

The *Acallam* gives us a large-scale, complex recoding of the vast territories of Ireland, a narrative map for physically engaging with Ireland's landscape. The text tells us what to appreciate, remember and meditate on when physically moving through Ireland and its forest glades, mountains and open plains, past its cliffs and rivers, and when visiting sites infused with Patrician power and sanctity. While the *Acallam*'s advertisements of sacred places presumably increased traffic to established, known pilgrimage sites (like those in the Mayo sequence),[39] other features suggest it was conceived as a description of a virtual or imagined topography. Routes followed are never linear or charted in terms of distance or journey time. The amount of material in the *Acallam* is unwieldy—the sheer number of sites named, visited and described over the course of its 8,000 lines is overwhelming. As a succinct and pragmatic itinerary for physical pilgrimage around Ireland, the *Acallam* is a glorious failure.

Multiple circuits include known religious and national sites, yet unidentifiable locations and places that may have been invented for the *Acallam*'s Ireland also abound. Detailed lists of visited locations are provided, yet editorial attempts to identify most of the placenames or to generate conclusive maps have largely been foiled, leading to the modern scholarly conclusion 'that most of the placenames, both old name and "new" Fenian appellation, are probably themselves part of the literary fiction'.[40] Though Dooley and Roe successfully provide some schematic maps of major sites on the different interprovincial circuits taken by Caílte and Patrick, they also hesitate to confirm the authenticity of the places and their names, asking, 'Are these people and places real? The answer is mainly no for the people, partly yes for some form of the placenames.'[41] The lists of connective placenames do more to perform places, to provide a seductive litany of sites and to evoke an extensive virtual landscape, than to give a real itinerary that can be followed. So many of the *Acallam*'s Irish places could be absolutely anywhere, located in any local landscape; their frequent aesthetic universality means that one can imagine them, and thus imagine visiting them.

Like the *Dindshenchas Érenn* discussed in Chapter 3, the *Acallam* does orient itself with references to known sites and locations at frequent intervals, so that one is never without a general sense of the geographic plan: we are certainly in Ireland, but, as the cast of characters—third-century warriors and wise women, fifth-century holy men, atemporal angels and *síd* folk—also makes clear, we are not in an Ireland physically accessible to any historic audience. It bears pointing out that the *Acallam*'s Ireland, with its layering of time, was never even accessible to Caílte or to Patrick— it is always a constructed, invented, simulated world that exists in words and story, as the composer hints at with the clearly fictionalized time frame. That, I think, is one of the text's main points, and its real success is the development of an Irish poetics of space. To rephrase, the *Acallam* never identifies itself as a guide for pilgrims; but, critically, it temporally and spatially maps out a virtual, constructed Ireland made real in narrative and text. It might defy successful mapping onto an actual landscape, but it does provide a rich and rewarding mental pilgrimage. We become virtual or imaginative pilgrims as we wander through the *Acallam*'s landscape; we witness and meditate on the same miracles and wonders, topographical, historical and religious; we hear the stories that frequently reduce Caílte to weeping, his shirt soaked with tears; and we are perhaps urged to follow his examples of affective piety and reverential remembering, as well as those of other characters who seek, and on grateful receipt treasure the stories of the places they encounter.

The *Acallam* composer, then, in the *textual rendering* of the geography, provides a contoured Irish landscape of words: one made real, enticing and resilient enough to bring audience members into its spaces to experience a specific construction of Ireland. The *Acallam* provides a revalorized heroic and hallowed Ireland for readerly pilgrims to inhabit, move through and be transformed by. This was essential for the vernacular Irish imagination to thrive—perhaps even to merely survive, as mechanisms for Irish literary and cultural production were, with important exceptions, being increasingly eroded, from the twelfth century of the English invasion through to the fifteenth and sixteenth centuries when the extant manuscripts of the *Acallam* were made.

Remarkably, however, the *Acallam*'s respect for and practice of Irish spatial traditions and poetics actually enlarge concepts of Irishness and encourage the participation of new practitioners: a primary model is a foreigner, a Briton recently come to Ireland on an evangelical mission. In the *Acallam*'s Patrick we find a figure who consults Irish tradition-bearers and uses his powers and technologies to support Irish literature and culture. Describing his evangelizing movements around Ireland, Patrick fittingly employs a familiar planting metaphor, that *ni cóir ar an Eclais gan a siled* (1006–7) ('it is not fitting that the Church be without spreading its seed').[42] The result is that as Patrick makes his circuit of the country he hallows the Irish landscape so that it transmits blessing to the Irish people; he simultaneously composes poems that celebrate and materialize these sites in an elaborate, native poetic vernacular. Patrick plants the Irish soil, and empowers and enriches the Irish landscape, through peripateticism and poetry. This Briton exemplifies alternative ways for how foreigners, clerical and lay, might behave in Ireland; how they can, per Patrick's own metaphor, sow seeds in Irish soil and become productive members of a changing Irish nation. As will be seen in Chapter 5, this contrasts sharply with Gerald of Wales, himself a latter-day Briton, who develops a very different poetics of Irish space. In Gerald's *Topographia* there is no Caílte, no slow engagement with native letters, but rather an argument about how Irish misuse of the environment, their bankrupt spatial practices and their lack of culture justify native dispossession and silencing by their English conquerors. *Acallam na Senórach*, written a century after the *Topographia*, might thus be broadly contemplated as a corrective guide, one which is not reactionary or xenophobic, but which carves out complementary positions for both newcomers and native Irish figures to recuperate and rebuild Ireland through indigenous spatial and poetic practices.

Notes

1 Tim Ingold, 'Footprints through the Weather-world: Walking, Breathing, Knowing', *Journal of the Royal Anthropological Institute* 16 (2010), S121–2.
2 Whitley Stokes (ed.), *Acallamh na Senórach*, in *Irische Texte*, vol. IV (Leipzig: S. Hirzel, 1900), lines 7433–4 (henceforth *Acallam*, all references to line numbers). For longer passages the English translations are from Ann Dooley and Harry Roe (trans.), *Tales of the Elders of Ireland* (Oxford: Oxford University Press, 2008) (henceforth *Tales*, all references to page numbers). In some cases, as here, I provide my own translations to clarify certain aspects of the original vocabulary choice.
3 The *Acallam* has four manuscript witnesses: MS Laud 610, Bodleian Library, Oxford, written between 1410 and 1452; The Book of Lismore, Library of the Duke of Devonshire, the most complete text, compiled ca. 1450; MS Rawlinson B 487, Bodleian Library, Oxford, written for a high-status Sligo woman, Sadhbh O'Malley, in the fifteenth century;

and Dublin, University College, MS OFM-A4, sixteenth century. For further detail, see *Tales*, p. xxxi; Petra Hellmuth, 'Laud 610', in *Celtic Culture*, pp. 1108–9; Caoimhín Breatnach, 'Lismore, Book of', in Séan Duffy (ed.), *Medieval Ireland: An Encyclopedia* (New York and London: Routledge, 2005), pp. 270–80; and R. A. S. Macalister, *The Book of Mac Carthaigh Riabhach, Otherwise Called the Book of Lismore* (Dublin: Stationery Office, 1950).

4 On its prosimetric structure, see Geraldine Parsons, '*Acallam na Senórach* as Prosimetrum', *Proceedings of the Harvard Celtic Colloquium* 24/25 (2004/5), 86–100.

5 The scholarship on Patrick is massive, but an excellent account of the Patrician sources and scholarship on Patrick is Pádraig Ó Riain, *A Dictionary of Irish Saints* (Dublin: Four Courts Press, 2011), pp. 526–31.

6 Thomas Charles-Edwards, *Saint Patrick and the Landscape of Early Christian Ireland*, Kathleen Hughes Memorial Lectures 10 (Cambridge: Hughes Hall and Department of Anglo-Saxon, Norse and Celtic, University of Cambridge, 2012), p. 7.

7 Ann Dooley, 'Date and Purpose of the *Acallam*', *Éigse* 34 (2004), 120–2 and 'Pagan Beliefs and Christian Redress', in Jacqueline Borsje et al., *Celtic Cosmology* (Toronto: Pontifical Institute of Mediaeval Studies, 2014), p. 260; and Anne Connon, 'Plotting *Acallam na Senórach*: The Physical Context of the "Mayo" Sequence', in Joanne Findon et al., *Gablánach in Scélaigecht: Celtic Studies in Honour of Ann Dooley* (Dublin: Four Courts Press, 2013), pp. 69–102.

8 See de Certeau, *Practice of Everyday Life*, pp. 91–110.

9 de Certeau, *Practice of Everyday Life*, p. 97.

10 Pádraig Ó Néill, 'The Impact of the Norman Invasion on Irish Literature', *Anglo-Norman Studies* 20 (1998), 179.

11 See Aisling Byrne, *Otherworlds: Fantasy and History in Medieval Literature* (Oxford: Oxford University Press, 2016), especially pp. 9–20; and William Sayers, 'Netherworld and Otherworld in Early Irish Literature', *Zeitschrift für celtische Philologie* 59 (2012), 201–30.

12 The text cited here and following is from Myles Dillon (ed.), *Stories from the Acallam* (Dublin: DIAS, 1970), lines 86–113, pp. 3–4. Translation is from *Tales*, pp. 5–6. The poem employs the device of *dúnad*—it opens and closes with *topair* ('spring, well').

13 Dillon (ed.), *Stories from the Acallam*, lines 98–113, p. 4.

14 As land and buildings had to be sanctified prior to their use by a saint, these are also territorial claims. Cf. the Old English *Guthlac A*, in which the saint exorcises the demons from the Anglian fens to create a space for himself and Christian practice. See Fabienne Michelet, *Creation, Migration, and Conquest: Imaginary Geography and Sense of Space in Old English Literature* (Oxford: Oxford University Press, 2006), pp. 163–97.

15 Repeated at *Acallam*, lines 127–9.
16 *Acallam*, lines 607–10, 870–1, 1061–4; *Tales*, pp. 20, 28, 34, etc.
17 *Acallam*, lines 170–260; *Tales*, pp. 8–10. It is unclear if Artúir should be identified with the legendary British King Arthur—see Ann Dooley, 'Arthur in Ireland: The Earliest Citation in Irish Literature', *Arthurian Literature* 12 (1993), note 3, pp. 165–6. However, if King Arthur is referenced, it is significant that the *Acallam* departs from various English texts from the twelfth century onwards (beginning with Geoffrey of Monmouth's *Historia Regum Britanniae*), which use Arthur's travels to Ireland as historicist justification for subjection of Ireland to England's rule, on which see Rambo, *Colonial Ireland in Medieval English Literature*, pp. 30–2.
18 The last sentence (which does appear in Stokes's edition) is supplied by Fr. 54b, as is bracketed clause. See Stokes (ed.), *Acallam*, p. 314.
19 *Acallam*, lines 3689–91; *Tales*, p. 112.
20 Ingold, 'Footprints', S134.
21 This is also a territorial claim, as the king of Munster grants Patrick all he can see.
22 As Dooley points out, 'by the end of the text Patrick and Caílte have almost changed places and function as co-authors of the work'. Dooley, 'Pagan Beliefs', p. 261.
23 Rebecca Solnit, *Wanderlust: A History of Walking* (London: Granta Books, 2014), p. 68.
24 de Certeau, *Practice of Everyday Life*, p. 92.
25 This also participates in Welsh concepts of 'mound-sitting' as generative of vision or knowledge, famously articulated by Pwyll in the First Branch of the *Mabinogi*. See Sims-Williams, *Irish Influence on Medieval Welsh Literature*, pp. 53–78.
26 Book 8, Chapter 10–12 of *Historia Regum Britanniae of Geoffrey of Monmouth*, ed. Acton Griscom (London: Longmans, Green and Co., 1929), pp. 409–14; and Geoffrey of Monmouth, *The History of the Kings of Britain*, ed. and trans. Lewis Thorpe (London: Penguin, 1996), pp. 195–8.
27 See Roseanne Schot, 'Uisnech Midi a medón Érenn', *Journal of Archaeology* 15 (2006), 41, with references to Giraldus Cambrensis, *Topographia Hiberniae*, ed. John O'Meara, *Proceedings of the Royal Society of Antiquaries of Ireland* 52C (1949), 159 and Geoffrey Keating, *Foras Feasa ar Éirinn*, vol. 3, ed. Patrick Dineen (London: Irish Texts Society, 1908–14), p. 386.
28 Mircea Eliade, *Patterns in Comparative Religion* (New York: World Publishing Co., 1963), p. 231.
29 Basso, *Wisdom*, pp. 32–3.
30 Donations to the Church, here and elsewhere, hint at the *Acallam*'s ecclesiastical sponsorship.
31 The text following *dó* is from page 44b of the Franciscan manuscript.

32 See Dooley's discussion in 'Pagan Beliefs', pp. 266–7.
33 Molly Robinson Kelly, *The Hero's Place: Medieval Literary Traditions of Space and Belonging* (Washington, DC: Catholic University of America Press, 2009), p. 37.
34 *Acallam*, lines 7021–2; *Tales*, p. 197. See also the poem attributed to Caílte in which he names his burial site at Tara: Moira Power, 'Cnucha Cnoc', *Zeitschrift für celtische Philologie* 11 (1917), 44, 51.
35 *Acallam*, lines 3988–94 and 4589–99. See discussion of Caílte's tears in Kristen Mills, 'Sorrow and Conversion in *Acallam na Senórach*', *Éigse* 38 (2013), 1–19.
36 As Parsons points out, the narrative is imbued with the idea that '*dindshenchas* is the gateway to all *senchas*'. Geraldine Parsons, 'The Narrative Voice in *Acallam na Senórach*', in Aidan Doyle and Kevin Murray (eds.), *In Dialogue with the Agallamh* (Dublin: Four Courts Press, 2014), p. 119.
37 For a reading of the scene as the pagan warriors' rejection of Patrick's Ireland, or perhaps the Christian afterlife, see Mills, 'Sorrow and Conversion', p. 4.
38 *Acallam*, p. xiii; *Tales*, p. viii.
39 See Connon, 'Mayo Sequence'.
40 *Tales*, p. xxii.
41 *Tales*, p. xxxiii.
42 It is translated more eloquently as 'The Church must spread its seed', in *Tales*, p. 32.

5
English topographies of Ireland's conquest and conversion

A remarkable depiction of Ireland (Figure 1) is found in a manuscript (Dublin, National Library of Ireland MS 700, henceforth N.L.I. 700) from ca. 1200 sandwiched between the *Topographia Hibernica* ('Topography of Ireland') and *Expugnatio Hibernica* ('Conquest of Ireland').[1] The map was likely made or commissioned by the author of these texts, Gerald of Wales (ca. 1146–1223),[2] a prominent Welsh-born cleric and later bishop whose family members, the Geraldines, were instrumental in the English conquest and colonization of Ireland, which began in 1169.[3] The map thus provides a contemporary, politically invested view of Ireland from what is best described as an elite English perspective, a perspective held by natives of Wales, England, Scotland, France and even Ireland, who participated in and benefited from England's imposition of power over Ireland.[4]

Most surviving maps of the period, both English and continental, place Britain and Ireland at the margins of the world, with Britain almost as distant as Ireland from the religious, intellectual and cultural centers of civilized European life. However, as Kathy Lavezzo argues, N.L.I. 700 has the specific purpose of transforming Britain, which here occupies the middle position on the map, from 'from world margin to regional center'.[5] Emphasizing Ireland's consignment to the role of most distantly located land, Lavezzo makes the point that, as the map successfully 'plays up the problem of Irish geographic marginality as much as possible, it represses the way that problem could extend to Ireland's English neighbor'.[6] In the representation of Europe in N.L.I. 700, Britain—and especially its English cities—is enclosed in mainland Europe's embrace, while Ireland—and, more particularly, the parts of Ireland most resistant to English conquest—sits just outside those community-defining European boundaries in the watery beyond.

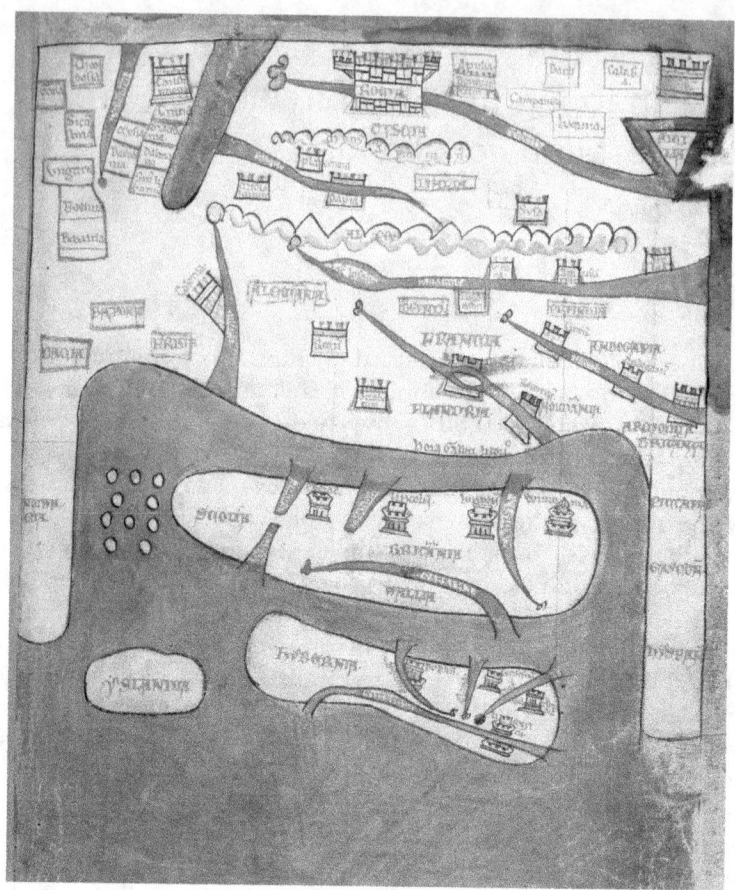

1   Map of Europe attributed to Gerald of Wales, ca. 1200. Dublin, National Library of Ireland (N.L.I.), MS. 700, fol. 48r. Courtesy of the National Library of Ireland.

At the same time, N.L.I. 700 also creates a unified, cohesive whole linking Ireland to Britain. The map downplays formal geographical differences so that Ireland is visually likened to Britain and depicted as a kind of miniature satellite in Britain's orbit; it gives Ireland, like Britain, four major rivers and four marked religious centers. The Ireland of N.L.I. 700 furthermore becomes a fitting part and logical extension of continental Europe, with which it also shares an iconography marking names, rivers and political and ecclesiastical centers. As Thomas O'Loughlin has argued, 'It would seem that the chief interests of its creator lay in the prominently drawn British Isles on the one hand, and the connection between those islands and Rome on the other'.[7] In Gerald's map, centers of power are linked visually through repetition of colors, images and symbols, suggesting easily connected pan-European networks leading back to Rome; Ireland, demarcated as marginal, is nonetheless graphically anchored to Britain and poised to be absorbed into the European Christian community. Though they use verbal rather than visual, cartographic arguments, the texts to be discussed in this chapter, Gerald's *Topographia* and *Expugnatio*, as well as the *Tractatus de Purgatorio Sancti Patricii*, similarly highlight the need for Ireland's conformity to continental Christian practice: reform of a morally and theologically corrupt Irish Church, we will see, provides a major justification for the English invasion and conquest of Ireland.

Examination of these three key texts reveals the extent of that imperialist impulse. And in Gerald's case we see that that, in the words of Jane Jacobs, imaginative—in our case literary or textual—and material historical acts of territorial conquest 'are not incommensurate, nor is one simply the product, a disempowered surplus, of the other'.[8] Instead, they are 'mutually constitutive', for

> the social construction of space is part of the very machinery of imperialism. In the name of the imperial project, space is evaluated and overlain with desire: creating homely landscapes out of 'alien' territories, drawing distant lands into the maps of empire, establishing ordered grids of occupation. These spatial events ... [take it] from the visioned to the embodied, from the global reach of desire to the local technologies of occupation.[9]

This chapter examines this territorial logic—how the sources stylize or create the impression of a natural, inevitable and positive mapping of English identity onto Ireland: specifically, how the 'alien territory' of Ireland is made into a 'homely landscape' for the English; how Irish spaces are constructed through textual culture for the benefit of colonizing clerics, conquerors and settlers; and how the complex interplay between words, images, acts and deeds is performed as Ireland is drawn into medieval England's 'map of empire'. As I will show, the *Topographia*, *Expugnatio* and *Tractatus* strongly emphasize place by verbally detailing, imaging and imagining the topography. This poses a question: how might capturing and disciplining the land through words and imagined spatial practices have contributed to historical and physical acts of colonization and reform? I suggest that, as discussed with reference to vernacular *dindshenchas* poetry (Chapter 3), writing the land is another way of appropriating, controlling and benefiting from a territory, and that by experiencing the text readers and listeners also participated in conquering and colonizing Ireland, an event repeated with each hearing, reading or remembering of the texts. This imaginative process was particularly significant in the case of Ireland, whose conquest never became a full political or historical reality because of ongoing resistance.

Specifically, the literary mappings of Ireland's topography and tales of successful movement through its environments do the work of conquest that neither martial acts nor administrative force alone could accomplish. To shed further light on the way that the land is conquered, described and tamed within textual renderings of Ireland and Irish sites composed just after the time of the English invasion of Ireland, I turn first to Gerald of Wales's *Topographia Hibernica*, which describes Ireland's landscape, creatures and history, and the *Expugnatio Hibernica*, his contemporary account of England's invasion and conquest of Ireland. Both texts, written 1185–89, portray Ireland as having physically rejected the unworthy Irish from the landscape before embracing the new settlers from England and Wales, who are exhorted to plant themselves in the needy Irish soil. The chapter then moves to H. of Saltrey's *Tractatus de Purgatorio Sancti Patricii*, an account of otherworldly travel through a purgatorial pilgrimage site located in the north of Ireland. Here I build on the identification of a twelfth-century English poetics of Irish space—namely, the persuasively crafted verbal renderings of Irish territory used in England's accounts of Ireland—represented by Gerald's more overtly propagandistic writings. I highlight the discursive themes and topographic imagery that the *Tractatus*, which became exceedingly popular throughout medieval Europe, shares with Gerald's work: the *Tractatus* similarly markets a crusading conquest of Ireland's dangerous peripheries where both penitent knights and reforming English clerics become textual heroes welcomed into Irish space. These verbal renderings of Irish landscapes were not produced for a vernacular Irish-Gaelic readership, but offer the colonial inverse of a native poetics of place—they differ radically from the model proposed by the *Acallam* discussed in Chapter 4. Despite an erasure of indigenous voices, these Anglo-Latin accounts also participated in a long tradition of Irish spatial poetics and played a significant role in the colonization of Ireland. Both Gerald's works and the *Tractatus* accomplished the export of an English poetics of

Irish space (and an accompanying imperialist political agenda) that became highly influential throughout Britain and Europe.

Planting the seeds for England's Ireland: the *Topographia Hibernica*

According to Gerald's account given in the *Expugnatio*, in 1155 the English pope Adrian IV issued the papal bull *Laudabiliter* granting Ireland to King Henry II of England and his descendants.[10] *Laudabiliter* gives papal support for the English king's entry into Ireland 'to enlarge the boundaries of the Church, to reveal the truth of the Christian faith to peoples still untaught and barbarous, and to root out the weeds of vice from the Lord's field' (*ad dilatandos ecclesie terminos, ad declarandam indoctis et rudibus populis Christiane fidei veritatem, et viciorum plantaria de agro Dominico exstirpanda*) (*Expugnatio* II.5.29–31, p. 145). *Laudabiliter* shows that Ireland needs saving from the Irish, and it repeatedly expresses this in the imperial terms of expanding boundaries and the topographical language of sowing virtue (*virtutibus inserendis*, II.5.51), planting the Christian faith and weeding out undesirable pests. The rhetoric and imagery of responsible Christian planters who encourage the land to flourish and produce bountiful crops of virtue, strategically employed in English writing about Ireland, rests on a conviction in the superiority of England's agrarian society and economy over Ireland's pastoral economy. Yet in the literature this difference does not remain economic but becomes ethical and moral: the Irish are degenerate and sinful because of their passivity and lack of careful stewardship of the land, thus forsaking any entitlement to the territory. The incoming settlers from Britain, on the other hand, offer an actively engaged and effective mode of overseeing the land, and their organized stewardship will, the rhetoric suggests, result in Irish territories finally being able to come to full fruition as God intended. As Laura Ashe puts it, 'the accepted clerical view of Irish barbarity coalesced with the English sense of the supreme value of land, in a manner which directly challenged the natives' right to hold their own land'.[11]

Agricultural metaphors and underlying logic are also central to Gerald's textual imagining of an Ireland that welcomes its new settlers, stewards and rulers from abroad. While its title varies in different manuscripts, Gerald of Wales himself refers to his account of Ireland's history and mythic prehistory, its people, places and creatures, as the *Topographia*, or 'Topography', a fitting designation in that Gerald does, as its etymology suggests, 'write place'. That is, he verbalizes a specific Ireland into being—and his version of this country is one that endures. Key episodes examined below reveal Gerald's potent topographical strategies, and what the resulting verbalized landscape of Ireland brings into being.

Gerald begins his *Topographia* with a striking valorization of words over material objects. In his dedication to Henry II, Gerald states that he could have sent the king material things, such as Ireland's gold, her sought-after falcons or her hawks. Instead, he gives the highly discerning monarch something more permanent and valuable. Having carefully collected and considered Ireland's marvels, natural features and traditions, Gerald preserves the worthiest of them in his written account for Henry II: 'By them I shall, through you, instruct posterity. For no age can destroy them' (p. 32) (*illis posteritatem per vos instruere, quæ nulla valeat ætas destruere*, Preface, p. 21). A textual rendering of Ireland, Gerald maintains, is of greater value than any physical treasure quarried from the land itself. Gerald ties his literary enterprise to the political enterprise of English expansion at the outset by invoking the king as the head of the body politic, and then verbally mapping his realm. Gerald addresses Henry II as 'invincible king of the English, duke of Normandy, count of Anjou and Aquitaine' (p. 31) (*invictissime Anglorum rex, Normanniæ dux et Aquitanniæ, et comes Andegaviæ*, Preface, p. 20). To recall Jane Jacobs's insight, the *Topographia*'s spaces are in this way 'overlain with desire': Gerald whets the royal appetite by cataloguing the riches and wonders Ireland has to offer, and his *Topographia* participates in Henry II's imperial project by mapping out potential English involvement and 'establishing ordered grids of occupation'.[12]

In the Preface, Gerald introduces his project by claiming that he has examined everything carefully, turning his attention to the country's position and nature, to the origins and customs of the Irish and, most tellingly, to 'how often, and by whom, and how, it was conquered and subjugated' (p. 32) (*quoties, a quibus, et qualiter subacta sit et expugnata*, Preface, p. 20). He begins the main text by mapping his subject: 'Ireland, the largest island beyond Britain, is situated in the western ocean about one short day's sailing from Wales' (p. 33) (*Hibernia, post Britanniam insularum maxima, unius contractioris diei navigatione ultra Britannicas Wallias in occidentali oceano sita est*, I.1). Britain is described as twice the size of Ireland (800 miles long and 200 miles across), and Ireland's size is reckoned in terms of travel time (number of days at forty miles per day): from the west's 'Brendacian mountains [Mount Brandon] to the island of Columba that is called Torach [Tory Island]' (*a Brendanicis montibus usque ad Columbinam quæ Thorach dicitur*, I.2) in Donegal, and 'from Dublin to the hills of Patrick' (pp. 33–4) (*a Dublinia usque ad Patricii colles*, I.2). The places through which Gerald routes the reader, showing the country's size, are not just at its geographic extremes, however. They include Dublin, the English administrative center, as well as sites associated with the early saintly *peregrini*, famed for their movement in and settlement of the larger Irish Sea region: the navigator Brendan (who was enjoying a resurgence of literary popularity); Columba, abbot of Iona; and the Briton, Patrick. Both Columba and Patrick underwent self-imposed exile from their homelands to serve as Christian evangelists, a similarity that would not have been lost on audiences familiar with the rhetoric that Ireland's dire need for Christian reform justified English invasion. Gerald demonstrates control over the land for his audience by first fixing Ireland in relation to Britain and then charting an imagined journey along routes linked by the holy men who earlier colonized the Irish Sea region to advance Christianity—the fame and spatial practices of Ireland's early evangelists and explorers provide templates for the twelfth-century English interventions in Ireland. Importantly, however, the vision of Ireland as a land of saints and scholars, a view promoted by Bede, as discussed in the Introduction, is reversed by Gerald, and religious reform now comes from England to Ireland: the *insula sanctorum* has become an *insula barbarorum* requiring England's intervention.[13]

As in the Preface, throughout the body of the text Gerald stresses his role as an impartial, dispassionately scientific observer, and in his thorough and totalizing view of the island of Ireland seeks to convince us of his account's incontrovertible factuality. For instance, Gerald questions Bede's and Solinus's claims that Ireland lacks bees but has vineyards, explaining that in doing so they relied upon the false reports of others: 'for it is only when he who reports a thing is also one that witnessed it that anything is established on the sound basis of truth' (p. 35) (*tunc enim res quælibet certissimo nititur de veritate subsidio, cum eodem utitur relatore quo teste*, I.6). Analogous to the *Dindshenchas Érenn* and the *Acallam* composers' citation of places both well known and otherwise unattested (and in some cases perhaps invented), Gerald's own combination of uncontroversial geographic, historical and 'scientifically' accurate elements paves the way for the subtle and strategic inclusion of more fictionalized elements. This means that, despite his self-conscious claims about its eyewitness factuality, Gerald's *Topographia* is highly inventive. The *Topographia*'s questionable truth-value was evident to its earliest audiences, who were highly skeptical, as Gerald states explicitly in the *Expugnatio* (discussed in the next section).

While most criticisms of Gerald's xenophobic portrayals of Ireland have focused on the bestializing depictions of the Irish people, Gerald's subtler development of the land itself as an actor in the drama of English conquest emerges, on examination, as even more dangerously persuasive. In contrast to his ethnographic profiles of the Irish people, Gerald's descriptions of the land may come across as neutral, yet his sophisticated narratives of Irish topography successfully create Ireland as a place *meant for* English and Welsh colonists. Gerald crafts a poetics of Irish space that 'naturalizes' the myth of English superiority and conquest of Ireland long before that conquest was actually achieved. While Gerald did visit Ireland on two occasions before composing the *Topographia*, he probably did not travel extensively.[14] His Ireland is, accordingly, in many ways invented. The *Topographia* constitutes a highly rhetorical argument about Ireland's need for discipline, reform and tending at the hands of the English. For instance, Gerald writes of a people in the north of Ireland highly prone to vice (*vitiossisima*), and especially bestiality (*et præcipue vitio coeundi cum bestiis*, II.9), even more than the rest of the Irish. One story tells of a well that, if left uncovered, threatens to overflow. A woman eventually neglects to replace its lid, and all of the people and livestock of the province are immediately drowned in the ensuing flood; this act then leaves its mark on the landscape in the form of a lake thirty miles long and fifteen miles wide. Gerald provides a reading of this environmental event: 'It looked as if the author of nature [God] had judged that a land which had known such filthy crimes against nature was unworthy not only of its first inhabitants but of any others in the future' (p. 65) (*tanquam terram, tam turpium contra naturam facinorum consciam, non tantum primis, sed et cunctis imposterum habitatoribus indignam auctor naturæ judicasset*, II.9). Gerald historicizes and localizes what is in essence the account of the flood in Genesis to show Irish vice punished by an actively disciplining Irish environment that enforces moral precepts and God's own will on a sinful Irish population, while also providing lessons in morality for English audiences.

Other exempla point directly to improper stewardship and ongoing mishandling of the land itself, suggesting that the Irish deserve neither Ireland nor its rich resources. Gerald declares that the Irish, a wild people (*gens silvestris*, III.10) who reject the civilizing agricultural work of planting fields and orchards,[15] 'live on beasts only, and live like beasts. They have not progressed at all from the primitive habits of pastoral people' (p. 101) (*ex bestiis solum et bestialiter vivens; gens a primo pastoralis vitæ vivendi modo non recedens*, III.10). Furthermore, Ireland's soil is rich, but its bounty is lost because the Irish 'despise work on the land' (pp. 102) (*agriculturæ labores aspernans*, III.10] and neglect to plant the exotic, foreign species of trees (*peregrinas ... arborum species*, III.10) that would thrive there. Gerald presents the need for new stewardship and cultivation of Ireland's resources, and shows the land as primed to receive settlers from Britain with their worthy agricultural technologies—the human equivalent of those foreign trees that would grow well in Irish soil.

In some passages, Gerald shows the Irish landscape itself accepting the English, despite the voiced dismay of the native Irish people (and Gerald's infrequent citations of Irish speech typically ventriloquize colonialist desires). In one instance, as if to dispel criticism that the English who come to Ireland are anathema to it, Gerald describes how Ireland does not contain or tolerate poisons, such that, even if imported into Ireland, any poisonous thing is immediately neutralized (I.28–9) because the Irish landscape is powerfully endowed. This poison motif plays out strategically in Gerald's description of contemporary events. When a frog, an animal considered poisonous in the Middle Ages, is found near Waterford, both the English and the Irish wonder at it. A famously wise Irish king of Ossory explains that the frog portends bad tidings for Ireland, for it is a sign (*signum*) 'of the coming of the English, and the imminent conquest and defeat of his people' (p. 52) (*adventus Anglorum, imminentisque conquistionis et expugnationis gentis suæ*, I.32). The presence of this poisonous frog—which Ireland was previously empowered to reject or neutralize, and which here is read by the seemingly fatalistic Irish themselves to represent the English and their coming conquest—implies that the Irish landscape now accepts these English newcomers and their power over the native Irish. Gerald's accounts of the land's reaction to both the native Irish and the newly arrived English are complex, but through representations of the land and its attributes,

Gerald's *Topographia* depicts an Ireland primed for the successful and inevitable establishment of the English.

Textual conquest of Ireland: *Expugnatio Hibernica*

Many of the elements of a colonialist English poetics of Irish space evidenced in the *Topographia* (ca. 1187), which describe Ireland's nature, history and culture from the beginnings of time to Gerald's present, also inform the *Expugnatio* (ca. 1189), a focused political account of Ireland's conquest in which Gerald's own family feature as major players. In the Preface to the *Expugnatio*, Gerald theorizes the role of language and literary craft, which bears upon his textualization of a conquered Ireland. As in the *Topographia*, Gerald justifies his writing by arguing that knowledge of the events described in his account will be valuable to posterity; he also employs agricultural metaphors in the *Expugnatio* to align his literary production with the political conquest of Ireland. His writing and the scribal planting of ideas reap, like English agricultural practices, an essential harvest from the Irish landscape: 'just as granaries which have not been kept full by the constant addition of new stocks are quickly emptied' (p. 21) (*sicut ergo cito expediuntur horrea que assidua non fuerint adieccione referta,* Preface, 313–14), he says, so too must knowledge and historical accounts be continually cultivated and replenished. His own project of writing the English conquest of Ireland is thus framed in terms of land improvement and bringing a neglected territory to fruition; he declares: 'I have decided that my Muse, as yet untrained, should exercise itself by way of practice in this field which, though it is confined and arid, rough and untilled, may yet be cultivated with the aid of my pen' (p. 25) (*Hac igitur in area, arta licet et arida, hispida quoque et inculta, sed stili beneficio forsan excolenda, musam adhuc rudem se tanquam preludio quodam exercere constitui,* Preface, 358–60). In the Preface to the *Topographia*, Gerald promotes the concept that a well-crafted verbal construction of Ireland possesses more power than mere reports or material evidence of the land. The *Expugnatio* records his aim as keeping the noble deeds (and figures) of the English conquest of Ireland from being forgotten or lost to posterity by preserving them in a carefully cultivated style, for while spoken words quickly vanish, he states hopefully that 'written works, once they have been published, do not pass away' (p. 11) (*scripta vero, quoniam edita semel et publicata non pretereunt,* Preface, 123–4). Gerald confidently asserts that with this textual act he creates a substantial, verbal world; his words remain in circulation when events, speeches and memories have dissipated, so that it is his version of Ireland that endures, and we might see the potential for his words to replace a darker and less satisfying historical reality. Gerald thus theorizes his own poetics of Irish place and justifies the importance of his Irish landscape of words, promoting both his personal authorial achievements as well as the larger project of the English conquest.

The text radiates both the entitlement of settlers from Britain to establish themselves in Ireland, as well as their especial suitedness to it, with particular emphasis given to Gerald's noble family, the Geraldines, dispossessed from their own native lands in Wales. In a speech attributed to Robert FitzStephen, Gerald's half-uncle and one of the leaders of the invasion of Ireland, Robert declares that 'the broad acres of our inheritance and our native soil are lost to us through treachery at home and malice among our own people' (p. 49) (*dolo domestico intestinaque malicia natali cum solo ampla perdidimus patrimonia*, I.9.12–13). They are enticed to Ireland not by monetary greed but by promise of a new homeland, a 'gift of lands and cities in perpetuity to us and to our children' (p. 49) (*terrarum et urbium nobis et nostris perpetua largicio*, I.9.15), for the Irish king Diarmait Mac Murchada (further discussed later in the chapter) loves Robert's people, encourages their migration and, in phrasing rich with planting imagery, 'has decided to settle them in this island and give them permanent roots there' (p. 49) (*in insula plantare et immobiliter radicare proposuit*, I.9.20–1). In Gerald's telling, the desired outcome of the Geraldine migration and establishment on Irish soil is that Ireland's five provinces will be united, and that 'sovereignty over the whole kingdom will devolve upon our race for the future' (p. 49) (*ad nostrates in posterum totius regni dominium devolvetur*, I.9.22–3). Their presence, grafted onto Irish land, sought by an Irish king, will generate politically unifying growth. In Gerald's accounts, even Irish leaders use an agricultural logic and language to envision and accomplish a conquered, improved Ireland.

Throughout the *Expugnatio* Gerald highlights specific historical figures, from both Wales and England, who have properly mastered the poetics of Irish place: they correctly read Ireland and understand what the landscape requires, or what the land itself teaches through production of wonders. This is exemplified by the episode of the ox-man, a remarkable Irish figure born with a human body but bovine extremities, whom Gerald writes about in the two works (he is introduced at *Topographia*, II.21 and mentioned in the *Expugnatio*, II.15). After one of the most prominent invaders of Ireland, Maurice FitzGerald, and his followers take possession of Wicklow and its castle in 1174, they marvel at the cow-man, and allow this extraordinary being a place at court, where he dines with them, using his hooves; in contrast, the Irish unjustly (Gerald tells us) persecute and kill this prodigy (*Topographia*, II.21). The native Irish are flummoxed by such wonders produced in Ireland, and respond with violence against things they do not understand, Gerald shows us, whereas the new conquerors accept and accommodate God's wonders in the Ireland they govern and control. In the *Expugnatio* Gerald reinforces the appropriate reading of Ireland's marvels with emphatic moralizing: 'None of His [the 'Lord of Nature,' i.e. God's] creatures ought to criticize these things, but rather wonder at them and stand in awe of the works of the Creator' (p. 7) (*Nec detestari debet sed admirari, sed venerari Creatoris opera quevis creatura*, Preface, 68–9). While the Irish fail to comprehend and appropriately handle Ireland's prodigies (they murder this being), the English revere and correctly respond to the wonders God produces in Ireland.

Several Irish figures in the *Expugnatio* are governed by the land, even merged with and overcome by it, rather than able to demonstrate mastery over it. This is seen in Gerald's portrait of one of Ireland's most important and powerful political figures, Diarmait Mac Murchada, the exiled king of Leinster who invites England's lords to Ireland and implores them to bring great numbers of their own race and people (*genus et gentem*, I.12.8–9). This Irish king provides a foil to the newcomers who skillfully take Ireland and its governance in hand. As exemplified by his depiction of Diarmait, Gerald is not exposing Irish lack of interest in the land itself; his strategy, we will see, is rather to show that the Irish are more like the beasts dependent on and subject to the land, incapable of the human reason necessary to effectively read, rule and cultivate it. When Diarmait is abroad in Britain and Normandy, seeking support so that he might reclaim the kingship of Leinster, Gerald characterizes him as consumed by the desire to see his native soil (*natale solum*, I.2.17–18) to such an extent that Diarmait races to the shores of Wales, where Ireland remains just visible and

> aëris Hibernici salubritatem zephyr beneficio propinquius hauriens, et quasi desiderate nidorem patrie naribus trahens ... terre sue prospectu lum na pascit. (I.2.24–8)

English topographies of Ireland's conquest and conversion

(drinking in at closer quarters, with the aid of the west wind, the wholesome Irish air, and, as it were, inhaling with his nostrils the sweet savor of the homeland he was longing for, he fed his gaze on the prospect of his native land.) (p. 29)

The depiction of Diarmait's homesickness is humanizing, yet the problem of his overwhelming attachment is made clear in successive lines. In exchange for significant land grants and power in Ireland, Diarmait obtains the promise of support from Robert FitzStephen and Maurice FitzGerald; yet he is unable to wait for the winds to change so that they can all cross with their troops in safety the following spring, when west winds and swallows mark the season for propitious travel. With a break in the weather in August, an impatient Diarmait, unable to further bear 'the deprivations of an exile' (p. 31) (*exulantis ultra damna*, I.2.46), sets off, despite the dangers posed by the unseasonal journey and by his return to a hostile Ireland where, without reinforcements, he is vulnerable to several enemies. In contrast, Diarmait's allies in Wales circumspectly delay travel until the more favorable month of May. These passages paint Diarmait as rash and driven by emotion (overwhelming homesickness) and bodily desires (his nostrils flare to take in the Irish air) rather than rationality and strategy. Consequently, his excessive attachment to the land compels him to follow an imprudent course of action rather than a tactically motivated one. Here and elsewhere Gerald constructs a binary between the subject—the impassioned Irishman enslaved to and overwhelmed by the land—and his opposite, the agent—actively strategic English and Welsh barons ruled by logic who know how to enforce order and discipline, and so obtain the most from the land.

Elsewhere, Diarmait and other Irish leaders are portrayed as savage and animalistic, negating the civility or nobility that would ordinarily be indicated by their regal status. For instance, following a victory, 200 heads of the defeated are brought to Diarmait.[16] Examining and recognizing the heads of each of the slain, he leaps with joy and delightedly thanks God for victory. But, in stark contrast with the image of a Christian leader's expected behavior, when he finds a particularly hated victim's head 'he lifted up to his mouth the head ... and taking it by the ears and hair, gnawed at the nose and cheeks—a cruel and most inhuman act' (p. 37) (*capite per aures et comas ad os erecto, crudeli morsu et valde inhumano nares et labra dente corrosit*, I.4.21–3). Other Irish rulers receive similarly dehumanizing treatment: an ignoble raid by the Irish prince of Bréifne, Tigernán Ua Ruairc, is presaged by a nightmare had by one Welsh hero, Griffin, in which the important leaders in the conquest of Ireland, Hugh de Lacy and Maurice FitzGerald, are attacked by a herd of wild swine with one huge, fearsomely tusked boar at the forefront. Accordingly, following this dreaming representation of the Irish as swine (their invading opponents retain human form), at the actual encounter Ua Ruairc is slain by Griffin and the Irish prince's head is sent off as a prize to Henry II, dehumanized as a trophy from this Irish hunt (I.41). Representatives of the English conquest repeatedly figure as the humans in the landscape while the Irish are its beasts, and examples in the *Expugnatio* reiterate, with historic specificity, the *Topographia*'s claim, discussed previously, that the Irish are a wild people who live like beasts.

Finally, as the narrative turns to address the later stages of the conquest of Ireland, one of the king's retainers, John de Courcy, is sent to Ireland and begins making forays into the 'wild North', where, in Ireland as in other nations, 'the people of the North are always more warlike and savage' (p. 175) (*gens borealis semper bellicosa magis et truculenta reperitur*, II.17.29). When his forces advance to Downpatrick and make a surprise attack, various figures intervene to try and arrange a truce whereby the Irish will retain their lands yet pay a tribute to the English, but to no avail, and with pointed rhetorical phrasing the Irish king, 'Mac Duinn Shléibe saw that words would get him nowhere' (p. 175) (*videns autem Dunlevus se verbis minime profecturum*, II.17.26), and so battle breaks out. Fulfilling Saint Columba's prophecy that their enemies will wade in their blood, an outnumbered de Courcy nonetheless seizes victory and kills the Irish, taking refuge on the seashore:

> Pre glisis namque mollicie, dum ad ima penetraret humana ponderositas, terre lubrice sanguis profluus superficiem tenens genua cruraque de facili pertingebat. (II.17.56–9)
>
> (For because the surface of the shore was soft and yielding, the weight of their bodies caused men to sink deep into it, and the blood pouring from their wounds remained on the surface of the slippery ground and easily came up to the knees and legs of their pursuers.) (p. 177)

Irish blood merges with the landscape and becomes sought-after territory, rather than inhering in the individuals who might themselves rule over it. Irish people become silent, environmental elements in a conquered landscape, as foreshadowed in Mac Duinn Shléibe's realization that the words of the Irish will be unheard and native voices rendered mute in this changed Ireland. Importantly, the words (referred to rather than actually spoken) of the Irish speaker that *do* have binding power in this episode are those articulating the predestined Irish defeat. As in the case of the wise Irish king of Ossory, discussed previously, here too Gerald shows that Irish defeat is preordained by citing a prophecy, not attested elsewhere, by the sixth-century Saint Columba.[17] As in *Laudabiliter*, conquest of Ireland is a divinely sanctioned and, ultimately, inevitable act.

In Gerald's account, the Irish people become indistinguishable from the land that needs governance. Irish bodies are shown to be forms dependent on or inherent in the land: part of the environment rather than capable, reasoning human actors. They are represented as animals, or become landscape features without distinct voices or powers of agency. The Irish, Gerald's spatial poetics show, are the fruits of conquest rather than competitors for governance of Ireland, and, like the land, in the *Expugnatio* they find themselves subdued by English forces.

Performing a poetics of Irish space in England

To read closely as we have been doing is to suggest that the text alone was the sole engine of Gerald's imaginary Ireland, but its circulation among diverse audiences far from Ireland was just as important, as Gerald himself realized. An active self-promoter who did not want to hide 'the candle which he had lit under a bushel but to lift it aloft on a candlestick that it might shine forth' (p. 97) (*lucernum accensam non sub modio ponere, sed super candelabrum ut luceret erigere cupiens*, XVI, p. 72), in 1188 Gerald staged an elaborate performance of the *Topographia* in Oxford, 'where of all places in England the clergy were most strong and pre-eminent in learning' (p. 97) (*ubi clerus in Anglia magis vigebat et clericatu præcellebat*, XVI, p. 72).[18] Not content with seeking elite approval merely from the king to whom his account was dedicated, in Oxford Gerald pursues an expanded audience for his tripartite *Topographia* by entertaining three different groups over the three-day reading. Gerald details how he first hosted all of Oxford's poor (*pauperes*), moving the next day to entertaining the doctors of diverse subjects (*doctores diversarum facultatem*) and their finest disciples (*discipulos*) and finally, on the third day, the remaining scholars, soldiers (*militibus*), and citizens (*burgensibus*) of Oxford (XVI, p. 73). This sumptuous (*sumptuosa*) and noble (*nobilis*) occasion, in which 'the ancient and authentic times of the poets were in some manner revived' (p. 97) (*renovata sunt quodammodo authentica et antiqua in hoc facto poetarum tempora*, XVI, p. 73), Gerald records, was unparalleled by anything seen in his day or before.

Gerald accomplished a great deal both in the actual performance and in his textual account of it. First, by framing it as a twelfth-century recovery of the estimable tradition of classical rhetoric and recital, of 'the ancient and authentic times of the poets', Gerald gave prestige and venerability to his delivery (and its subject, the text he composed)—he picks up where the rhetors and poets of antiquity left off, and introduces conceptions of his *Topographia Hibernica*, his Ireland, as timeless, rather than contemporary apologist propaganda for England's invasion and annexation of Ireland. Here Gerald privileges classical models and references, it is worth noting, over Irish ones, despite the well-attested richness of Ireland's own venerable and ancient poetic culture. This is of course not at all surprising, but it is essential to observe the many ways in which indigenous Irish voices are absent from Gerald's Ireland project. Secondly, in important ways, Gerald's convening of the diverse members of the body politic in Oxford for this recital highlights many of the same issues (discussed in Chapter 4) raised by the descriptions of Saint Patrick and the King of Ireland summoning kings, leaders, the men of Ireland and the country's sages and scholars to the Hill of Tara to participate in the group event of Caílte and Oisín's delivery of their own narrative topography of Ireland in the later text, the *Acallam na Senórach*. As elaborated in Chapter 4, consumption of virtual Irelands as part of a group brought together at a particular site of marked national significance was transformative and community-building. Oxford, which Gerald identifies as the home of England's most powerful clergy and finest scholars, parallels Tara, Ireland's cultural capital through association with the legendary high kingship, as a chief cultural and intellectual center—in Oxford, as in Tara, communities were created and reinforced through collective experience and consumption of storied Irish landscapes. Thirdly, and finally, Gerald's reading also accomplished the importation of a specific Ireland back to England: Gerald's oral performance of his virtual Ireland, shaped for his audience as much as the *Acallam*'s Ireland was created for its own audience, presented a far more comfortable, confidence-inspiring version of an Ireland open to and indeed welcoming of the English at a time when that recently invaded island resisted full conquest and submission to English rule. Gerald's Ireland was certainly not performed at Tara, nor even in Dublin, England's administrative capital—far from it. Gerald's *Topographia* is fully detached from the Irish landmass, fittingly exported from Ireland to become, through performance in Oxford, part and product of England's geography.

The Oxford oral performance provided a virtual Ireland that was traveled, conquered and imaginatively inhabited by the diverse members of English society, there to hear Gerald's account of the land and its wonders. While I have focused on this particular staging of the *Topographia* in England, Gerald's Ireland—as represented by the *Topographia* as well as the *Expugnatio*—could also be mentally visited and imaginatively occupied at each individual reading, private or public. For, as Gerald often noted, the virtue of words over material elements, and the merit of a written topography in particular, is that, once composed and preserved in manuscript form, words remain accessible and traversable for posterity. Furthermore, a well-crafted topography, a place built from language and conjured through story, can possess more potency and convincingly real contours than material artifacts or physical landscapes. Gerald's Ireland is an imagined land that points to England's superiority in religion, in land use and stewardship, and in political and social customs; and Gerald maps it out in words. His version of Ireland is fantastic, heavily crafted and manipulated, yet it nonetheless becomes very real, and for many people in England, Gerald's *was* the version of Ireland that obtained.[19] As the varied practitioners of the poetics of Irish space, Irish and English, demonstrate, landscapes and topographies made of words can be detached from their original sites and transformed into persuasive instruments of thought and power. Effectively used by the vernacular poets who sought to preserve an Ireland for the Irish, this poetics of Irish space was also employed by a Welsh-born cleric whose texts participated in England's conquest of Ireland to create an Ireland for England. The *Tractatus*, we will see, evidences similar patterns.

Saint Patrick's Purgatory: an Irish testing ground

The *Tractatus de Purgatorio Sancti Patricii*, which details a knight's visit to Saint Patrick's Purgatory, a remote pilgrimage site at Lough Derg in Ireland's northwest (contemporary County

Donegal), is a text that is intertwined with Gerald of Wales's own writings about Ireland. In the *Topographia* Gerald describes a remarkable island situated in an Ulster lake. One part of the island, featuring a church, is quite pleasant and is visibly frequented by angels and saints, while the other part is rough and horrible, and 'it is nearly always the scene of gatherings and processions of evil spirits, plain to be seen by all' (p. 61) (*quæ et visibilibus cacodaemonum turbis et pompis fere semper manet exposita*, II.5). Here, Gerald explains, there are nine pits, and anyone who dares spend the night in them is attacked by evil spirits who torment and crucify to the point of death; yet the person who suffers these torments can avoid the pains of hell. A microcosm of many English representations of Ireland, this island space is dichotomously holy and hellish. Unnamed in the first recension (written just before 1185) of Gerald's obsessively revised *Topographia*, it is only in the second recension (written before July 1189) that the site is explicitly identified as Patrick's Purgatory,[20] an expansion probably resulting from Gerald's encounter with the newly composed *Tractatus de Purgatorio Sancti Patricii* (henceforth *Tractatus*).

Written in England ca. 1180–84 by a Cistercian monk of the abbey of Saltrey, Huntingdonshire, identified only as 'H.', an expanded version of the *Tractatus* was likely composed between 1186 and 1188, and is preserved with Gerald's *Topographia Hiberniae* (third recension) in the British Library, Royal 13 B viii, written in the 1190s.[21] The *Tractatus* became 'one of the best sellers of the Middle Ages',[22] repeatedly copied, circulated and translated over the next 500 years. One hundred and fifty manuscripts of the Latin text survive, and translations into almost every European vernacular (Irish versions are conspicuously absent) fill at least a further 150 extant manuscripts; this is a narrative that brought Irish geospatial discourses into the full range of European medieval literatures. Accounts of the Purgatory in Latin include those by Peter of Cornwall (d. 1200) and Roger of Wendover (d. 1236), a monk working at St Albans, whose *Flores Historiarum* ('Flowers of History'), completed before 1231, features the knight of H.'s *Tractatus*, but which explicitly makes the knight a native of Ireland—Wendover's text appears to be the first extant version to do so.[23] When Matthew Paris later reproduced Wendover's version in his influential *Chronica Majora*, the popularity of Paris's text appears to have helped canonize a belief in the knight's Irish identity.

The first vernacular accounts were Anglo-Norman verse translations—Marie de France's *Espurgatoire* is the earliest vernacular translation (her Owein is not explicitly Irish).[24] The *Tractatus* makes its way into English in the *South English Legendary* (second half of the thirteenth century) in a verse legend on Patrick along with two further Middle English verse translations, the most famous of these preserved in the Auchinleck manuscript (early fourteenth century). The Auchinleck text is noteworthy for explicitly making the protagonist English: as a native of Northumberland, Auchinleck's knight carves out an additional role for the English in this narrative of Irish space.[25] The text moves beyond Britain across Europe, and Patrick's Purgatory (though not necessarily the pilgrim knight Owein) is described by several writers, including Vincent of Beauvais (*Speculum Historiale*), Jacobus de Voraigne (*Legenda Aurea*), Caesarius of Heisterbach (*Dialogus Miraculorum*) and Ranulf Higden (*Polychronicon*). The Purgatory is even depicted in the fourteenth-century northern Italian Todi Fresco, with some scholars claiming that the Irish Purgatory influenced Dante's own otherworldly renderings.[26] Patrick's Purgatory is a verbal landscape of Ireland well traveled by those who moved through the text as audience members, scribes and translators.

While the *Tractatus*, a text on transformative journeys to purgatory and the earthly paradise within Irish space, must be recognized as a terrestrial development of the *Navigatio Sancti Brendani* and *immrama* that opened this book, it also exemplifies a distinctly English poetics of Irish place. Chapter 4 analyzed how Patrick's circuit of Ireland (led by ancient warriors) was developed in Irish vernacular literature, with major emphases being placed on Patrick's spatially undertaken study of the storied Irish environment, in particular his embrace (and eventual practice) of Irish vernacular poetic culture in the manner of *dindshenchas* or placelore poetry. The English similarly made extensive use of Saint Patrick in their appropriation of Irish territories both physical and textual, but which were in some ways remarkably different from the Irish vernacular sources. As one might expect, the *Tractatus*'s depictions of Irish space as a challenge-filled testing ground, which ultimately provides bountiful rewards for the hero who can successfully negotiate it, cohere in important ways with Gerald's accounts of an Ireland in need of England's stewardship, discipline and reform.

Chapter 1 examined voyage texts in which monks like Brendan and secular sinners like Máel Dúin travel to island outposts to test themselves and their spiritual rigor, but also to locate Western holy spaces and Edens within the Great Ocean. The island site of Patrick's Purgatory in Lough Derg, and its geographic placement in the wild northwestern periphery of Ireland, itself on the farthest borders of the Western world, locally embody links to those earlier travelers who abandon the material, known world and its trappings to sail into the western ocean in search of spiritual testing sites. The journeys undertaken are also structurally similar: to get to the terrestrial *insula repromissionis* at Lough Derg, the medieval traveler first negotiates the hostile, wild spaces of Ireland, then moves across waters with a monstrous past—legends attribute the lake's eponymous red (*derg*) to the blood of a demonic monster slain by Saint Patrick[27]—before accessing the purgatorial cave where demons first torment sinners but the blessed ultimately witness heavenly joys. The North Atlantic and its islands became Ireland's wild, untrafficked deserts of penance and prayer, a scheme reproduced on the Irish landmass itself: *dísert* ('solitary place', translating Latin *dēsertus*) is a common placename element (Hogan writes of ca. 500 examples) for solitary sites associated with Christian foundations in particular,[28] and provides onomastic proof that the concept of holy desert spaces was successfully overlain onto the Irish landscape. Like Saint Anthony, Mary of Egypt, Brendan or Máel Dúin, the intrepid visitor to an Irish desert island witnesses marvelous visions, is tested by demons and, if emerging alive from the trials, is reaffirmed as a Christian with the promise of heaven. The Anglo-Latin *Tractatus*, which has the Lord take Patrick *in locum desertum* (l. 127), 'to a desert place' where the Purgatory is situated, thus belongs to the long-standing yet still vigorous genre of otherworldly travel and vision literature in which Ireland (and Irish figures) plays a prominent role. Additionally, accounts of the famed voyager Brendan enjoyed increasing popularity in the twelfth century, the most relevant witness here being its Anglo-Norman translation and reworking into *Le Voyage de Saint Brendan* by Benedeit ca. 1118–21.[29] Much of the spatial logic associated with Patrick's Purgatory in Lough Derg has roots in earlier voyage tales and accounts of travel to holy sites, yet it was also meaningfully reinvigorated and repurposed for H.'s twelfth-century audience. Ireland provided a testing landscape: hellish and a source of death for some, but rich in sanctity and rewards for the resilient. England's texts about Ireland and its deserted, otherworldly spaces advertise this.

In contrast to Christian otherworldly spaces typically accessed through visions, Patrick's Purgatory is characterized as a physically real place: it is frequently depicted on maps of Ireland, and numerous travel accounts of actual pilgrims from the Middle Ages to today (the Lough Derg pilgrimage is still active) map the route to be taken. Yet simultaneously it is rhetorically figured as being at the very edge of the known world, and participates in the long-developed trope of Ireland's geographic marginality. Lough Derg sits at Ireland's northwestern fringes and beyond its civilized 'Pale'; a certificate of pilgrimage given to George Grissaphan in 1353 records its location 'at the ends of the earth'.[30] As the accounts emphasize, only the bravest and most heroic should venture into the Purgatory: Irish pilgrimage sites, situated on the borders of the mappable world and in the wilds of remote Donegal, are dangerous, and more sanctifying in proportion to their geographic peripherality.

While the larger Lough Derg area was a place of religious significance from the pre-Christian period onwards, and seems particularly associated with a Saint Dabeoc (Dobheóg), Lough Derg itself is not connected with Patrick in the early Patrician hagiographic material.[31] Lough Derg is not mentioned by Tírechán or in the *Tripartite Life*, and lack of early references indicates that Patrick's association with the site may have been part of twelfth-century ecclesio-political strategy.[32] It has been suggested that pilgrimage to Patrick's Purgatory at Lough Derg was only fully developed in the mid-twelfth century, when, as part of archdiocesan reform and restructuring at the synod of Kells in 1152, the Archbishopric of Armagh lost jurisdiction over (and financial benefits from) Croagh Patrick to the newly created archdiocese of Tuam; Armagh thus promoted Patrick's Purgatory at Lough Derg instead.[33] It was, however, the English-authored *Tractatus* that succeeded in circulating the fame of Patrick's Purgatory beyond Ireland.

The way the *Tractatus* renders this otherworldly Irish space as representing both perdition and paradise, and illustrates to whom and how it is granted, is most relevant to an understanding of the English poetics of Irish space. Parallel framing, telling scenes and powerful asides instruct the audience how to engage with Irish spaces and Irish people from an English perspective, as subtly advanced in the opening and closing sections in particular. A central mechanism, exhibited in Gerald's works as well, situates key places *in* Ireland, but ensures that the Gaelic Irish themselves have no agency, cannot maintain control and are unable to manage the landscape; rather, Ireland and Irish purgatorial spaces are offered to those who are aligned with and act on behalf of Christian Europe, especially England, in its many forms.

Here these lessons are worked out in terms of the Church and reform rather than in the more explicit terms of military conquest (as in Gerald). However, as much scholarship has shown, it is also true that 'the pacification and legal transformation of occupied Ireland was unthinkable without the ecclesiastical reform that occurred in Ireland even before the conquest', as 'the Cistercian colonization and ecclesiastical reform of Ireland represented the spiritual arm of invasion'.[34] It is telling that the major Irish proponent of reform based on continental models, Saint Malachy (1095–1148), Archbishop of Armagh, is depicted in the *Vita Malachi*, written ca. 1148–53 by the French Cistercian Bernard of Clairvaux in the same positive terms as Gerald was to depict his agriculturally adept English colonists who clear the wild, savage landscape of Ireland, replacing so many Irish weeds with more fruitful imported stock. In his *Vita Malachi* Bernard characterizes Malachy as violently purging the Irish landscape and environment of evil and superstition in order to plant continental practices and virtues:

> Diceres ignem urentem in consumendo criminum vepres. Diceres securim vel asciam in dejiciendo plantationes malas, exstirpare barbaricos ritus, plantare ecclesiasticos (III.6).[35]
>
> (You might say he was a fire burning the briars of crime. You might say he was an axe or a mattock hacking down bad sprouts in uprooting barbarous rites, supplanting them with the Church's.)[36]

This zealous rhetoric exemplifies the ways in which native Irish reformers might be appropriated and depicted in European-authored texts as some of the country's most brutal topographical practitioners, planting continental reforms—but only after native religious growth has been uprooted, slashed and burned. The Irish clergy featured in the *Tractatus*, including the reformist Augustinian Canons Regular, an order brought to Ireland (along with the Cistercians and others) through work led by Malachy, are similarly difficult to identify as characters representative of native Gaelic agency in the *Tractatus*. In the text they play little part aside from helping generate access to the Purgatory: they welcome pilgrims, but also provide the testimony and proof that the Anglo-Cistercian community could use to convert the Purgatory's traditions into the verbal landscape authorized by the *Tractatus*.

Testing, reward and the heroes of Patrick's Purgatory

The Irish are introduced in the *Tractatus* as a savage, backward and un-Christian people saved by the Briton Patrick. In H. of Saltrey's first mention of Patrick, the evangelizing newcomer is contrasted with the sinful Irish: Patrick preaches God's word, shines in performing 'glorious miracles' and works tirelessly to discourage 'from evil the savage souls of the men of this land' (p. 46) (*bestiales hominum illlius patrie animos*, 80–1). Instead of proceeding to describe Patrick and the Purgatory, however, the text pauses to emphasize the barbarity of the Irish. A statement by the cleric Gilbert records that 'I myself have a true expert knowledge of how savage they are' (p. 123) (*Eos uero ... bestiales esse, ueraciter et ipse comperi*, 82–4), followed by the story of an old man who requests Holy Communion, but who casually admits to killing five men or perhaps more—he has not even, the text alarmingly tells us, bothered to keep count or noted that homicide is a sin. Gilbert stresses that

> Habent enim hoc quasi naturaliter homines illius patrie ut, sicut sunt alterius gentis hominibus per ignorantiam proniores ad malum, ita, dum se errasse cognouerint, promptiores et stabiliores sunt ad penitendum. (103–7)
>
> (The men of this country have the kind of natural disposition that, while they are more prone to do evil through ignorance than the people of another country, they are also swifter and more steadfast in repentance once they learn their error.) (pp. 46–7).

Though he admits that the Irish are teachable and only require proper guidance and monitoring, the cleric's overarching point is clear: 'I have put forward this story in order to show their savagery' (p. 47) (*Hec ideo proposui ut eorum ostenderem bestialitatem*, 107–8). Like the early Irish commentators who questioned the truth of Gerald's assertions about Irish barbarity, one editor of the *Tractatus*, J. M. Picard, comments that 'the story of the pagan Irishman who did not know that killing was a sin seems to be an Anglo-Norman invention', as the early Irish penitential literature condemning murder clearly shows.[37] As in other texts describing the Irish and Ireland disseminated from the twelfth century onwards (Gerald provides the most well-known examples), emphasis on Irish ignorance of Christian codes, the erasure of their long history of Christian piety and accusations of their savagery paint the picture of a barbaric, backward Irish people in need of saving by clerics properly versed in the tenets of Christianity.

After introducing the Irish in such stereotypical terms—their savagery, sinfulness and ignorance of Christian principles—the *Tractatus* records that the Briton Patrick was unable to deliver the Irish from error despite his performance of miracles and preaching about heaven and hell. The Irish tell him they will not be converted until one of them witnesses the torments and joys he speaks about because they 'have more confidence in things seen than in promises' (p. 47) (*quatinus rebus uisis certiores fierent quam promissis*, 115–16). The Irish need to have a physical experience and visible evidence of a place, of a purgatory, to believe; 'the Word' is not enough for them, and, the narrative suggests, neither theological nor intellectual arguments suffice for a people characterized by their savagery. God, however, grants Patrick, who prays, fasts and undertakes vigils and good deeds for this people's salvation, the concrete means to convince the skeptical Irish: Jesus appears to Patrick and first gives him a copy of the Gospels and a staff, which become valuable relics; then

> Sanctum uero Patricium Dominus in locum desertum eduxit, et unam fossam rotundam et intrinsecus obscuram ibidem ei ostendit, dicens, quia quisquis ueraciter penitens uera fide armatus fossam eandem ingressus unius diei ac noctis spacio moram in ea facerat, ab omnibus purgaretur tocius uite sue peccatis, sed et per illam transiens non solum uisurus esset tormenta malorum uerum etiam, si in fide constanter egisset, gaudia beatorum. (127–34)

> (the Lord took saint Patrick to a deserted place. There he showed him a round pit, dark inside, and said to him that whoever, being truly repentant and armed with true faith, would enter this pit and remain for the duration of one day and one night, would be purged of all the sins of his life. Moreover, while going through it, he would see not only the torments of the wicked, but also, if he acted constantly according to the faith, the joys of the blessed.) (pp. 47–8).

Patrick immediately has a church built there and, to keep impetuous and imprudent visitors out, he encloses the pit with a wall, doors and locks. Control of the site is then given by Patrick to the Augustinian Canons Regular.

The *Tractatus* opens with God's gift of Irish land to a Briton, the Christian evangelist Patrick, to save the savage Irish from their errant ways. This divinely willed transfer of land to a foreign-born religious reformer is significant in an account written during the period of English conquest of Ireland. Though Patrick is a fifth-century saint, the Augustinian Canons Regular he establishes at Lough Derg is an order which, following its increasing popularity on the Continent and spread in England, only appeared in Ireland in the twelfth century.[38] While few extant sources detail how these reformed orders came to be established in Ireland—the *Tractatus* itself actually provides the first references to the Augustinian Canons at Lough Derg—we can nonetheless say that this order was relatively new and associated with pan-European reforms and political interests in France, England and Ireland. Legitimized by being set in a remote fifth-century past and authorized by Patrick himself, the scenes in which the Purgatory is revealed and its administration assigned to the Augustinian Canons Regular are crafted to speak to a twelfth-century audience.

The theme of an important Irish holy space being granted to a Briton to expedite the conversion of the Irish, with its access monitored by a religious order newly introduced to Ireland, thus anticipates and proleptically endorses the concluding scenes that privilege English control of Irish holy lands. At the close of the *Tractatus*, Gervase, identified as abbot of Louth in the diocese of Lincoln, having been granted land by a king to build a monastery, sends the monk Gilbert 'to the [same] king in Ireland so that he might receive the land and found a monastery' (p. 71) (*ad eundem regem in Hyberniam misit, ut et locum susciperet et monasterium fundaret*, 1075–6). In this narrative, Irish land passes into English ecclesiastical hands with as little resistance as when Patrick is granted land by God. The unnamed 'king in Ireland' probably references the Leinster king Diarmait Mac Murchada, based on the location of the property granted and the likely date range, though later sources like Wendover identify him as the king of England, Stephen (or Etienne) of Blois (r. 1135–54). Harnessing a common founding narrative for colonial purposes, the text further emphasizes the divinely ordained nature of Anglo-Cistercian establishment in Ireland when the knight reveals that, in the Purgatory, he witnessed the Cistercians being specially honored by God, and thus the king should certainly welcome them to his kingdom. The *Tractatus* maps out multiple Cistercian colonizations in Ireland and Wales: the story of the Purgatory is also the story of Gilbert's journey from England to establish a Cistercian monastery at Baltinglass in Ireland (contemporary County Wicklow) and his subsequent movement to Wales, where he becomes abbot at Basingwerk. The *Tractatus* is framed by and celebrates the importation of English clerics and significant Irish land grants to new, reforming orders associated with major political changes in twelfth-century Ireland.

Navigating the Purgatory

The *Tractatus* provides the audience with a guide through whose eyes, ears and other senses we come to know this place, 'a knight called Owein, who is the subject of this narrative' (p. 50) (*militem quemdam nomine Owein, de quo presens est narratio*, 207–8). Following his confession to the local bishop, the knight agrees to undertake a testing, transformative experience in Ireland's Purgatory (which lies in the bishop's diocese) as an act of expiation. Described as 'a true penitent and a true soldier' (p. 52) (*uere penitentis et uere militis*, 221), the knight figures as both a bold adventurer and a humble pilgrim. The protagonist's duality, along with this genre-bending text's fusion of some of the most popular elements of spiritual and secular narrative, adventure stories and apocalyptic visions, could only have increased its wide appeal. When he enters the pit of Purgatory, for instance, this knight, 'thus instructed for a new kind of chivalry' (p. 54) (*ad noui generis militiam instructus*, 295–6), is armed with faith, and the rhetoric throughout the text celebrates the heroic and militant nature with which this 'true soldier of Christ' (p. 56) (*uerus miles Christi*, 335) battles the Purgatory's demons. We are positioned to relate to the knight as an idealized chivalric hero, yet this pilgrim also provides an aspirational model for the audience by exhorting everyone to become a metaphoric soldier for Christ, fighting for goodness in the ongoing and extremely familiar human battle against sin. The *Tractatus* works in other ways to bring the audience into its virtual purgatory. As with Arculf in *De locis sanctis*, we encounter the holy space through this protagonist, with his bodily, sensory details helping us to mentally traverse the paths through Patrick's Purgatory.

The *Tractatus*'s detailed and image-rich topographic descriptions also lead us to envision the Purgatory with great precision. We enter the Purgatory through a cavernous mouth that suggests the low, narrow opening passageways of caves and souterrains found throughout Ireland, yet it also resembles the caves serving as otherworld entry points throughout the wider world's myths and literature.[39] That is, it is both a local Irish environmental feature and a universal otherworldly trope. The knight bravely proceeds for a long time, alone but armed with faith in God, and 'as the

English topographies of Ireland's conquest and conversion

darkness grew more and more dense he soon lost sight of any light. At last, as he went along the cavern a tiny glimmer began to shine weakly from the opposite direction' (p. 53) (*Ingrauescentibus magis magisque tenebris, lucem amisit in breui tocius claritatis. Tandem ex aduerso lux paruula cepit eunti per foueam tenuiter lucere*, 258–60). The dramatic prose moves us into the Purgatory, and the darkness impels us to clear our minds and senses, so that when we come into the light with the knight, our mind's eye is focused on the marvels and visions that we soon behold. As the knight looks around, 'casting his eyes here and there and greatly admiring its magnificence and beauty' (p. 53) (*oculos huc illucque iactans, eius apparatum et pulcritudinem satis ammirans*, 268–9), our own eyes sympathetically dart about as the visions simultaneously unfold before us on the page, and even more vividly in the imagination.

The *Tractatus*'s engagement of our senses to permit an embodied reading continues throughout the text. We wince, for instance, when the horrific growling demons build an enormous fiery pyre where they 'pushed the knight bound hand and foot into the blaze and, howling, they dragged him with iron hooks backwards and forwards through the flames' (p. 56) (*ligatisque manibus ac pedibus militem in ignem proiecerunt uncisque ferreis huc illucque per incendium clamantes traxerunt*, 341–3). We feel his deep torments (*graue tormentum*, 344), and, if we have given ourselves over to the drama of moving through this inferno, our nostrils might even twitch when the knight experiences 'a horrible flame stinking of foul sulphur' (p. 63) (*flammam teterrimam et sulphureo fetore*, 509–10) shooting up. Though it is technically the knight the demons address, the *Tractatus*'s frequent use of direct speech means that the demons also speak directly to us: 'You will suffer what these suffer unless you are willing to turn back. But first you will see what they endure' (p. 60) (*Hoc quod isti patiuntur patieris, nisi reuerti uolueris. Que tamen tolerant, prius uidebis*, 455–7). Finally, having successfully extracted himself (and, by extension, us) from the diverse tortures inflicted across the ten torments by calling out Christ's name, the knight brings us, shaken, to the earthly paradise where the tortured screams, scorching flames, freezing waters and burning sulfurous stinks are thankfully replaced by a sweetly harmonious chorus of the saints, a temperate air neither hot nor cold and an intensely sweet fragrance giving strength and protection from any torture. As the *Tractatus*'s calming refrain convinces us, 'There everything was peaceful, everything was calm, everything was pleasant' (pp. 67–8) (*Omnia ibi placata, omnia placita, omnia grata*, 827–8). Following our dramatic and emotionally heightened imaginative experience of the initial pains and ultimate pleasures of the Purgatory, when told by the archbishops in this paradise that 'you must now return the same way you came' (p. 70) (*redeas per eandem uiam qua uenisti*, 903–4), we, like the knight, sorrowfully resist leaving the blissful space. Like the knight, though, we can take comfort in the instructions that leading a holy life will secure peace and the heavenly mansion (*celorum mansione*, 905).

As I have tried to demonstrate, the *Tractatus* functions as a highly successful spatial narrative that brings the audience on its journey. The Purgatory's fame depended on it being a real, concrete place geographically situated in Ireland, yet the *Tractatus*'s structure promotes a productive *mental* pilgrimage rather than advertising *actual* travel through an Irish landscape. While isolated elements of the Purgatory, such as its cavernous entrance, might resonate with Irish landscape features (though not exclusively so), this English-authored verbal landscape is built of words and images rooted in other vision narratives and biblical traditions. As has been pointed out, the majority of the torments and their accompanying sounds and smells—the slippery, narrow bridge the knight must cross; the attributes of the paradise he finally encounters; and even the *Tractatus*'s unusual, four-fold, otherworldly structure consisting of hell, purgatory and the celestial and earthly paradise—are also found in other popular biblical and vision accounts.[40] As Zaleski observes, there is 'little that is characteristically Irish' about the descriptive accounts of Patrick's Purgatory, and 'the most we can say is that once St. Patrick inherited the patronage over Lough Derg, it proved admirably suited to English and Continental views of how a pilgrim's gate to the other world should look'.[41] It is no surprise that this Irish space is textually developed to map out the goals and worldview of its author(s), and a thorough consideration of one architectural feature exposes the mechanics at play.

When the knight emerges from the dark passageway into a large field he finds a hall that 'did not have solid walls but was built on all sides with columns and arches like a monk's cloister' (p. 53) (*non habebat parietem inetgrum, sed columpnis et archiolis erat undique constructa in modum claustri monachorum*, 263–4). Cloisters came to Ireland with the Augustinian and Cistercian communities and are unrepresented in Irish architecture before 1157, when Mellifont Abbey ('An Mainistir Mór' or 'The Great Monastery'), Ireland's first Cistercian foundation, was officially consecrated, though its cloisters might date to the late twelfth century.[42] Mellifont's buildings helped 'to introduce to the country European concepts of planning and design'[43] and stood in stark contrast to native Irish oratories in both structure and scale. It marked such an architectural break that its construction was overseen by French clerics whom Malachy had brought to Ireland from Clairvaux. Since internal historical references in the *Tractatus* establish the date of the knight's visit to the Purgatory as no later than ca. 1146–47,[44] with the text itself having been written 1185–90, the cloistered structure described in the *Tractatus* would have been, like the Augustinian Canons Regular or the Cistercians praised by the knight, a feature with non-Irish origins and associations, perhaps not even found in Irish architecture at that point. The *Tractatus*'s cloistered hall is thus likely an element from the world of the Cistercian narrator and composer, reflecting their views of what a holy space should look like rather than anything drawn from the built Irish landscape. Furthermore, given that twelfth-century Cistercian literary practices identified cloisters in monasteries as purgatorial spaces wherein one might witness otherworldly visions,[45] the cloistered space encountered by the knight appears to be an even more clearly troped spatial detail of Cistercian provenance. Both the literary purgatorial landscapes and the localization of a purgatory within the monastic space constitute two intertwined ways that the Cistercians allowed for imaginative pilgrimage and transformation while maintaining adherence to the ideal of *stabilitas loci*. The *Tractatus*'s emphasis on the cloisters in Patrick's Purgatory therefore appears to have significantly more to do with an English, Cistercian-authored poetics and practice of Irish space, and is thus detached from the Irish landscape in some important ways.

Cultivating a textual Purgatory

The *Tractatus* returns again and again to questions of the imaginative, virtual nature of the purgatorial landscape and the role of words, spoken and written, in constituting it. When Christ appears to Patrick, his very first act is to bestow on Patrick 'the text of the Gospels and a staff' (p. 47) (*textum ewangeliorum et baculum unum*, 120–1). These precious relics, symbols of the archbishop's office venerated throughout Ireland, give divine status and pride of place to writing and verbal testimony—indeed, the Purgatory is only necessary because the Irish, doubting Patrick's preaching, are shown to be suspicious of words. A few lines later we learn that written accounts of pilgrim experiences are made on site: when pilgrims emerge after witnessing the Purgatory's torments and joys, 'blessed Patrick ordered that their accounts be recorded in the same church' (p. 48) (*quorum relationes iussit beatus Patricius in eadem ecclesia notari*, 147–8). Their testimony is immediately converted into reliable (and relatable) text; through these proofs others accept Patrick's teachings and become converted. While spoken accounts are crucial, written accounts have the highest status and most lasting value.

Accordingly, H. draws attention to his own authorship and role in the process of cultivating a purgatory that, now textualized, can be visited by all readers and listeners. This is emphasized in the Prologue and Epilogue particularly. The Prologue explicitly states the goal of H. of Saltrey and Gilbert before him: to use words and testimony to convince and (morally) improve the story's audience. Whenever the knight is asked by Gilbert to speak of his experience, 'he would relate all these things most scrupulously for the sake of edification' (p. 73) (*ob edificationem hec omnia dilegentissime narrare consueuerat*, 1093–4), and Gilbert later repeats the story in Britain for other listeners' benefit. H. of Saltrey records that he has committed to writing (*scriptum*, 6) Gilbert's account at the command of his own abbot, H. of Sartris, so that 'many may find improvement through me' (p. 43) (*utilitatem multorum per me*, 9–10). Reading and hearing the Purgatory's narrative is powerful; as H. advertises before continuing to tell the account, 'I have never read nor heard anything from which I have grown more in fear and love of God' (p. 43) (*me numquam legisse quicquam uel audisse, unde in timore et amore Dei tantum proficerem*, 12–13). The importance of reading and hearing bookends the narrative and is again addressed in the Epilogue: H. has written this account or book (*litteris*, 1253) for those who want to grow 'in love and fear of God' *(in amorem et timorem Dei*, 1252), for reading and listening to this text, traveling and experiencing the Purgatory as mapped out in H.'s narrative, are all transformative.

H. also makes a subtle argument validating place-writing as a form of spatial practice. When he asks to receive the same reward for his task that the knight (and other pilgrims) received for penitential journeys through the Purgatory, he assumes his audience's shared investment in the belief that writing (and reading or hearing) a place confers some of the same sanctity as traveling it. Describing himself as a sinner who has 'divided this modest work into chapters' (*interserens opusculum istud per capitula distinxi*, 1256–7) and added further proverbs, he calls upon

qui illud legitis uel auditis, Deum exorare, quatinus me, a peccatis omnibus in presenti purgatum et a supradictis, et si que sunt alie, penis extorrem, una uobiscum / post huius mortis horrorem transferat in prefatam beatorum requiem Ihesus Christus, dux et dominus noster, cuius nomen gloriosum permanet et benedictum in secula [seculorum]. Amen. (1258–64)

(those of you who read it as well as those who listen to it—to pray to Almighty God so that I may be purified of all my present sins and be free from the punishments described here and whatever others there may be and that I may be conveyed together with you to the place of rest of the blessed, as described above, by Jesus Christ, our leader and our Lord, whose name remains glorious and blessed for ever and ever. Amen.) (p. 78).

Using second person direct address, H. asks his fellow believers to pray to God that his work writing this Purgatory, and organizing its verbal landscape into chapters filled with convincing torments, otherworldly delights and the wisdom of the Holy Fathers, will grant him expiation. Expiation, however, is for everyone: H. requests it for himself 'together with you', the entire reading and listening community. The emphasis on salvation for all involved magnifies both the writer's virtuous deed but also the significance of belonging to the community newly established through a shared experience of his spatial text. Finally, he uses the appropriate divine formula to make sure this textual pilgrimage through Patrick's Purgatory is successful. Just as the knight continually vanquishes demons by uttering the name of Christ, H. invokes Jesus's name when praying that he and his audience will all escape the torments and gain the paradise described in his text. Thus, H. performs the knight's acts verbally in the closing lines of his text to ensure that he and his audience are similarly delivered from the pains of purgatory to the joys of heaven. The claims H. makes for his purgatorial Irish landscape of words are substantial, and his performance is elegantly actualized.

The *Tractatus* did motivate real travel to Lough Derg, as subsequent pilgrims' accounts attest. However, it had its greatest impact as a virtual pilgrimage text written for audiences with no intention of traveling to Ireland. It is appropriate, then, that the *Tractatus* advances the idea that reading and hearing are powerful ways to experience this Irish purgatorial landscape: that the imaginative, armchair pilgrim can strengthen his or her relationship to God and receive immense spiritual benefits in this life and the next.

The Cistercian reformer Bernard of Clairvaux (d. 1153) preached the Second Crusade but simultaneously dissuaded his monks from actual travel, arguing that 'Jerusalem is your cell', a popular sentiment articulated earlier on by the Irish author of *Techt do Róim* (discussed in the Introduction). The benefit of virtual, imaginative travel over physical journeying with its worldly temptations continued to be articulated centuries later: when consoling a monk denied permission to visit Patrick's Purgatory, Catherine of Siena (d. 1380) 'urged him to seek its finer analogue in spiritual exercises'.[46] H. of Saltrey, and those who commissioned and circulated his text, understood the value of converting this purgatory, far away in Irish territory, into a landscape of words over which they could exert control, and through which they could change behavior. The Cistercians did not run the pilgrimage at Lough Derg, but in some ways this did not matter, as it was through H.'s *Tractatus* (and its adaptations) that Europe really visited Patrick's Purgatory.

Irish presence and erasure

In conclusion, it is clear that the *Tractatus*'s Cistercian-authored purgatorial landscape of Ireland exemplifies the goals of a spiritually enriching imaginative literature of mental pilgrimage. But it also articulates political strategy and replicates colonialist structures, though far more subtly than Gerald's texts do. As R. Howard Bloch observes,

> Stated bluntly, the legend of Saint Patrick represents a significant ideological weapon in the conquest and colonizing of Ireland in the last two decades of the reign of Henry II. In the specific historical context of the colonial expansion of the Angevin monarchy, the legend of Saint Patrick's Purgatory is linked to the attempt—aided by Irish ecclesiastical reform—to bring Ireland into the Anglo-Norman orbit.[47]

Though God gives the Purgatory to Patrick ostensibly for the good of the Irish, they are nonetheless quickly written out of it, with the early comments on the savagery of the race serving as some of the most memorably explicit Irish identifiers in the *Tractatus*. There are not, perhaps surprisingly, as many explicitly Irish characters in the text as has been assumed: the knight is the chief example of this lack of identification. Though many follow Easting's statement that 'the *Tractatus* leaves no doubt that Owein was Irish',[48] the *Tractatus* actually remains silent on this point. The *Tractatus* includes details that certainly make the knight's status as an Irish native possible: the knight is said to be in the service of a lord in Ireland, and his virtue is speaking the languages of both the Irish and the Cistercian newcomers from England (again, not specified, though Latin, Irish and English, or perhaps French, are feasible). While Irish birth is historically viable, the knight could also be a native of Britain who entered service in Ireland rather than an Irishman whose career took him in the other direction: as Marie Therese Flanagan has shown, following 1066, several political exiles in Britain relocated to the Hiberno-Norse towns, and mercenaries routinely moved through the larger Irish Sea region.[49] The knight is identified in the *Tractatus* as 'Owein', which, as Picard suggests, 'could be the Welsh form of a like-sounding Irish name',[50] with the use of that Welsh (or English) linguistic form obscuring the knight's national identity. Indeed, his everyman nature and anonymity seem to be intentionally promoted: the narrative primarily refers to him as 'the knight', only once employs his proper name and uses neither surname nor patronymic, neither kin-based nor geographic affiliation. This lack of detail allows all readers and listeners (few of whom were Irish, as the manuscript record shows) to see themselves in this courageous, generalized everyman through the literary goal of inclusivity. Some later versions of the story do fill out the *Tractatus*'s silences on the knight's identity, some making him Irish, some English and some even Italian, as mentioned already. But an explicit identification of the knight's nationality is not provided by the *Tractatus* itself.

It would be interesting if the most celebrated visitor to the Purgatory, and the first pilgrim whose experience was written and circulated (there are no extant traces of those accounts mandated by Patrick from early visitors to the cave described at the beginning of the *Tractatus*), might have been another foreigner who, like Patrick and Gilbert, came to tame this wild Irish space. This would have intriguing implications both for the English poetics of Irish space and the circulated ideas about who used and who conquered Ireland's challenging landscapes. As the manuscript histories and their overwhelming non-Irish provenance show, the audiences who experienced the Purgatory and overcame its hellish challenges to reap paradisiacal bounty with the knight did so from without—from the position of their own non-Irish nativity. The audience was already a non-native readership, conquering Ireland's purgatorial spaces alongside the knight. Ultimately, the

Tractatus does not permit us to determine with certainty whether or not the knight should be identified as Irish. The implication is that there is very little explicit native Gaelic-Irish presence in the *Tractatus*'s representations of Saint Patrick's Purgatory and those who move through it.

One figure who is identified as Irish in the *Tractatus* deserves final mention: the unnamed king who grants land to the Anglo-Cistercian clerics to build a monastery. As mentioned previously, historical details identify the *Tractatus*'s anonymous king as Diarmait Mac Murchada, one of twelfth-century Ireland's most powerful figures. This king of Leinster sponsored significant Irish church reforms and was patron of several religious establishments and structures built in the new Romanesque style.[51] He is perhaps the most well-known Irish figure in contemporary accounts of the English conquest of Ireland, including the early thirteenth-century French *Chanson de Dermot et du comte* ('The Song of Dermot and the Earl'), composed in Ireland, as well as Gerald's *Expugnatio* (as discussed earlier).[52] The *Tractatus*, however, anonymizes him as a 'king in Ireland' (*regem in Hyberniam*, 1075). H.'s text, it bears pointing out, would tell a radically different story if the controversial Diarmait Mac Murchada were legitimized in the narrative as a powerful, named Irish political leader, proponent of monastic reform and generous donor of ecclesiastical lands who sought to improve the Irish Church and bring it into a continental European network. As the *Tractatus* gives no detail on this Irish king, we witness, just as we did in Gerald's texts, a kind of erasure of native voices and presence. This may not have been an intentional suppression of detail or misrepresentation, and was likely in part due to the fact that the *Tractatus* was written (and later copied) outside of Ireland by Cistercian clerics with little knowledge of (or interest in) native Gaelic structures and figures. H. was clearly not writing for Irish audiences or patrons who might desire a greater role for the Irish in the tale or would have contested the depiction of the Irish as savage and sinful; yet, given the care accorded to the various names of English clerics in the text, many of them comparatively minor figures, the name of a powerful royal patron seems a curiously significant detail to omit. Indeed, perhaps the important point is that it was possible, and even preferable, for an Anglo-Cistercian cleric to write about and capitalize on an Irish holy site by detaching it from Ireland and the Irish as completely as possible.

The instances of negative portrayals, and the minimizing or even erasure of Irish identity, might seem to amount to little when taken individually. However, taken collectively we find a forceful English poetics of Irish place that devalorizes, disempowers and disappears Irish people, and the few Irish figures presented are employed to facilitate English accession of Irish lands and holy places. The Purgatory and its holy, hellish landscape was given to Patrick by Jesus so that the Irish could see proof of God and the afterlife and be convinced to join the Christian community. Yet, the extant accounts largely erase the native Irish population from the Purgatory and its narratives. It is remarkable that no medieval Irish accounts of the Purgatory survive,[53] and that the first account of the Purgatory actually written in Ireland is one by James Yonge, an Anglo-Irish Dublin notary, and even he was employed by Laurence Rathold of Pászthó to record the Hungarian nobleman's own 1411 visit to the site.[54] In the accounts of this sacred Irish place, the Gaelic-Irish are curiously absent, and the holy island is presented as an open territory inviting new and fitting inhabitants, stewards and adventurers. Like the Holy Land in European accounts, the sanctified landscape of Ireland's Purgatory is presented as largely cleared of contemporary native inhabitants who might complicate the text's invitation to its visitors to partake of it and to benefit from the Purgatory's spiritual riches and blessings.

In their different ways, these Latin landscapes of words— Gerald's *Topographia* and *Expugnatio* as well as H. of Saltrey's *Tractatus*—had a significant impact on the ideas and understandings of Ireland and Irish space, and how Irish territories might be profitably used. Their own treatments certainly eclipsed vernacular renderings of the Irish landscape, which, despite a richness and development across a range of Irish-language sources, never made it into foreign manuscripts or translation into other vernaculars. As discussed in this book's Conclusion, England's narratives about Ireland were circulated widely to establish a highly resilient poetics of Irish space that has maintained its influence throughout the succeeding centuries.

Notes

1 References to the *Topographia Hibernica* (henceforth *Topographia*) are from *Giraldi Cambrensis Opera*, Rolls Series, vol. 5, ed. James. F. Dimock (London: Longman, 1867). Citations refer to book and section number of the Latin text. English translations are from Gerald

of Wales, *The History and Topography of Ireland*, ed. and trans. John O'Meara (New York: Penguin, 1982), and citations refer to page numbers. References to the *Expugnatio Hibernica* (henceforth *Expugnatio*) are from Giraldus Cambrensis, *Expugnatio Hibernica: The Conquest of Ireland*, ed. and trans. A. B. Scott and F. X. Martin (Dublin: Royal Irish Academy, 1978). Citations are to book, section, and line numbers of the Latin text; page numbers refer to the facing English translation. Parts of this chapter previously appeared in Amy Mulligan, 'Norman Topographies of Conquest: Mapping Anglo-Norman Identities onto Ireland', in Stefan Burkhardt and Thomas Foerster (eds.), *Norman Tradition and Transcultural Heritage* (Burlington, VT: Ashgate, 2013), pp. 253–78.

2 Welsh on his maternal side, English on the paternal side, Gerald's complex identity has been widely discussed. See, for instance, Robert Bartlett, *Gerald of Wales: A Voice of the Middle Ages* (Stroud, Gloucestershire: Tempus, 1982, repr. 2006), pp. 16–30; Jeffrey Jerome Cohen, *Hybridity, Identity and Monstrosity in Medieval Britain: On Difficult Middles* (New York: Palgrave Macmillan, 2006), pp. 77–108; and Huw Pryce, 'Giraldus and the Geraldines', in Peter Crooks and Seán Duffy (eds.) *The Geraldines and Medieval Ireland: The Making of a Myth* (Dublin: Four Courts Press, 2016), pp. 53–68.

3 For overviews of English conquest and colonization of Ireland, see Thomas Bartlett, *Ireland: A History* (Cambridge: Cambridge University Press, 2010), pp. 34–78, and Seán Duffy, *Ireland in the Middle Ages* (New York: St. Martin's Press, 1997).

4 Following current scholarly convention I use 'English' rather than 'Norman' to describe the invasion and partial conquest of Ireland, and the full range of peoples (primarily Welsh and English though also Scottish and French natives) who participated in it. On the term 'Norman' and a history of its usage in Ireland, see Flanagan, 'Defining Nations in Medieval Ireland', pp. 104–20; and Bartlett, *Ireland*, p. 34.

5 Lavezzo, *Angels*, p. 68.

6 Lavezzo, *Angels*, p. 68.

7 Thomas O'Loughlin, 'An Early Thirteenth-Century Map in Dublin: A Window into the World of Gerald of Wales', *Imago Mundi* 51 (1999), 28.

8 Jane Jacobs, *Edge of Empire: Postcolonialism and the City* (London and New York: Routledge, 1996), pp. 158–9.

9 Jacobs, *Edge of Empire*, pp. 158–9.

10 Found only in Gerald's *Expugnatio*, *Laudabiliter*'s authenticity has long been questioned (see Goddard Henry Orpen, *Ireland under the Normans 1169–1333*, [Dublin: Four Courts Press, 2005], pp. 107–19). As Duggan shows, 'It was Giraldus Cambrensis, writing in the late 1180s as a propagandist defender of the deeds of his own close relatives (the Geraldines), who constructed the myth of a papally-approved

Cambro-Norman-Angevin conquest of the Irish, by associating *Laudabiliter* with Henry II's triumphant assumption of authority in 1171–3 in such a way that readers would assume the king's actions were somehow based on, or at least legitimized by, the English pope's "privilege."' Anne Duggan, '*Totius Christianitatis caput*', in Brenda Bolton and Anne Duggan (eds.), *Adrian IV, the English Pope, 1154–1159* (Aldershot: Ashgate, 2003), p. 139.

11 Laura Ashe, *Fiction and History in England, 1066–1200* (Cambridge: Cambridge University Press, 2007), pp. 176–7.
12 Jacobs, *Edge of Empire*, pp. 158–9.
13 See also Lavezzo, *Angels*, pp. 54–8.
14 Though Gerald visited Dublin, Cork and Waterford, 'the rest of the country was probably unvisited by him, as most of it was, up to that time, by his fellow Normans'. O'Meara, *History and Topography of Ireland*, p. 14.
15 On the motif's later development see Joep Leerssen, 'Wildness, Wilderness, and Ireland: Medieval and Early-Modern Patterns in the Demarcation of Civility', *Journal of the History of Ideas* 56.1 (1995), 25–39.
16 On decapitation in an Irish context, see Patricia Palmer, *The Severed Head and the Grafted Tongue: Literature, Translation and Violence in Early Modern Ireland* (New York: Cambridge University Press, 2014), especially pp. 15–17.
17 Gerald of Wales, *Expugnatio*, note 307, p. 333.
18 *De rebus a se gestis*, in *Giraldi Cambrensis Opera*, Rolls Series, vol. 1, ed. J. S. Brewer (London: Longman, 1861–91), pp. 72–3. References are to *De Rebus* section numbers, followed by page number of the edition. The English translation is from Harold Edgeworth Butler, *The Autobiography of Gerald of Wales* (Woodbridge: Boydell Press, 2005). References are to page numbers.
19 See Sarah McKibben, 'In their "owne countre": Deriding and Defending the Early Modern Irish Nation after Gerald of Wales', *Eolas* 8 (2015), 39–70 on Gerald's subsequent impact.
20 In Chapter 126 of the *Vita Patricii* (written 1185–86), Jocelin of Furness also details Patrick's Purgatory, though he places it in the west at Croagh Patrick. See Helen Birkett, *The Saints' Lives of Jocelin of Furness* (York: York Medieval Press, 2010), pp. 7–8.
21 The Latin edition of the *Tractatus* cited here is the expanded version, in Robert Easting (ed.), *St Patrick's Purgatory: Two Versions of Owayne Miles and the Vision of William Stranton Together with the Tractatus de Purgatorio Sancti Patricii* (Oxford: Oxford University Press for the Early English Text Society, 1991). References are to line numbers. The English translation is from Jean-Michel Picard (trans.), *Saint Patrick's Purgatory: A Twelfth Century Tale of a Journey to the*

Otherworld (Dublin: Four Courts Press, 1985). References are to page numbers.
22 Shane Leslie, *Saint Patrick's Purgatory: A Record from History and Literature* (London: Burns, Oats and Washbourne, 1932), p. xvii.
23 A knight named Owein *profectus est in Hiberniam ad natale solum, ut parentes visitaret* ('went to Ireland to his native country to visit his parents'.) Roger of Wendover, *Chronica, sive Flores Historiarum*, vol. 2, ed. H. O. Coxe (London: English Historical Society Publications), pp. 256–7.
24 See Hugh Shields, 'The French Accounts', in Michael Haren and Yolande de Pontfarcy (eds.), *The Medieval Pilgrimage to St Patrick's Purgatory. Lough Derg and the European Tradition* (Enniskillen: Clogher Historical Society, 1988), pp. 83–98, and R. Howard Bloch, *The Anonymous Marie de France* (Chicago, IL: University of Chicago Press, 2003), pp. 206–310.
25 See Robert Easting, 'The English Tradition', in Haren and Pontfarcy (eds.), *Medieval Pilgrimage*, pp. 62–6.
26 See Alison Morgan, *Dante and the Medieval Otherworld* (Cambridge: Cambridge University Press, 2008), pp. 154–5, 162; and Jean-Michel Picard, 'The Italian Pilgrims', in Haren and Pontfarcy (eds.), *Medieval Pilgrimage*, pp. 169–89.
27 See Máire MacNeill, *The Festival of Lughnasa* (Oxford: Oxford University Press, 1962), pp. 503–8, 524.
28 *eDIL* s.v. dísert. See Edmund Hogan, *Onomasticon Goedelicum locorum et tribuum Hiberniae et Scotiae* (Dublin: 1910), 347 ff. for a list of place-names containing *dísert*.
29 Ian Short and Brian Merrilees (eds.), *The Anglo-Norman Voyage of St Brendan* (Manchester: Manchester University Press, 1979).
30 St John Seymour, *St. Patrick's Purgatory: A Medieval Pilgrimage in Ireland* (Dundalk: W. Tempest, 1918), p. 33.
31 Ó Riain, *A Dictionary of Irish Saints*, pp. 268 and 529–31.
32 Yolande de Pontfarcy, 'The Historical Background to the Pilgrimage to Lough Derg', in Haren and Pontfarcy (eds.), *Medieval Pilgrimage*, pp. 21–34.
33 Yolande de Pontfarcy, 'Introduction,' in Jean-Michel Picard (trans.), *Saint Patrick's Purgatory*, pp. 23–6.
34 Bloch, *Anonymous Marie*, pp. 281, 284. Important accounts of reform and conquest include Orpen, *Ireland under the Normans 1169–1333*; A. J. Otway-Ruthven, *A History of Medieval Ireland* (London: Ernest Benn, 1968); and Marie Therese Flanagan, *Irish Society, Anglo-Norman Settlers, Angevin Kingship: Interactions in Ireland in the Late Twelfth Century* (Oxford: Clarendon Press, 1989) and *The Transformation of the Irish Church in the Twelfth Century* (Woodbridge: Boydell Press, 2010).

35 Bernard of Clairvaux, *Vita sancti Malachiae* in J.-P. Migne (ed.), *Patrologiae cursus completes. Series Latina*, 221 vols (Paris, 1844–64), vol. 182, columns 1078D–1079A.
36 Bernard of Clairvaux, *The Life and Death of Saint Malachy the Irishman*, trans. Robert Meyer (Kalamazoo: Cistercian Publications, 1977), p. 22.
37 Picard (trans.), *Purgatory*, p. 47.
38 The visit of Malachy, Archbishop of Armagh, to the monastery of Arrouaise (Picardy, France) in 1139/1140 resulted in the Augustinian rule's introduction into Ireland. See Flanagan, *Transformation of the Irish Church*, p. 14.
39 See Byrne, *Otherworlds*, p. 76.
40 Cf. the third-century *Vision of Saint Paul* (*Visio Sancti Pauli*), the *Vision of Dryhthelm* preserved in Bede's *Historia Ecclesiastica* (ca. 731), the *Vision of Tnugdal* (*Visio Tnugdali*, ca. 1149) and the *Vision of Adomnán* (*Fís Adomnáin*, tenth–eleventh century), the latter two describing visions experienced by Irishmen. See Ad Putter, 'The Influence of Visions of the Otherworld on Some Medieval Romances', in Carolyn Muessig and Ad Putter (eds.), *Envisaging Heaven in the Middle Ages* (New York: Routledge, 2006), pp. 237–51; Morgan, *Dante and the Medieval Otherworld*, pp. 156–62; and Yolande de Pontfarcy, 'Accounts and Tales of Lough Derg or of the Pilgrimage', in *Medieval Pilgrimage*, ed. Haren and Pontfarcy, pp. 51–6.
41 Carol Zaleski, 'St. Patrick's Purgatory: Pilgrimage Motifs in a Medieval Otherworld Vision', *Journal of the History of Ideas* 46.4 (1985), 469.
42 R. A. Stalley, 'Mellifont Abbey: A Study of its Architectural History', *Proceedings of the Royal Irish Academy*, lxxx (1980), 312.
43 Colum P. Hourihane (ed.), *The Grove Encyclopedia of Medieval Art and Architecture*, 2 vols (Oxford and New York, 2012), 2.262–3, pp. 263–354.
44 See Easting, 'Owein at Patrick's Purgatory', p. 166 and Katharine Walsh, '... *in finibus mundi*: The Late Medieval Pilgrims to Saint Patrick's Purgatory, Loch Derg, and the European Dimensions of the Diocese of Clogher', in Henry Jefferies (ed.), *History of the Diocese of Clogher* (Dublin: Four Courts Press, 2005), p. 42.
45 See B. P. McGuire, 'Purgatory, the Communion of Saints, and Medieval Change', *Viator* 20 (1989), 61–84.
46 Zaleski, 'Pilgrimage Motifs', p. 483.
47 Bloch, *Anonymous Marie*, p. 266.
48 Easting, 'Owein at Patrick's Purgatory', p. 160. Zaleski, writing only about H.'s *Tractatus*, similarly states that 'The Knight Owen, a crusader under King Stephen (1134–54), returns to his native Ireland after a successful campaign', Zaleski, 'Pilgrimage Motifs', p. 473.
49 Flanagan, *Irish Society*, pp. 57–8.

50 Pontfarcy, 'Introduction', p. 16.
51 Marie Therese Flanagan, 'Mac Murchada, Diarmait (*ca.* 1110–1171)', *Oxford Dictionary of National Biography* (Oxford: Oxford University Press, 2004), [www.oxforddnb.com/view/article/17697, accessed June 24, 2017].
52 A recent discussion of the *Song*'s downplay of Irish and English differences is Ashe, *Fiction and History*, pp. 159–204.
53 There is an uncorroborated reference that David Scottus ('of Ireland') wrote a text in Würzburg entitled *De Purgatorio Patricii*, ca. 1120. Easting, 'The English Tradition', p. 59, n. 4.
54 For an edition and discussion of Yonge's account, see Teresa O'Byrne, 'Dublin's Hoccleve: James Yonge, Scribe, Author, and Bureaucrat, and the Literary World of Late Medieval Dublin' (Unpublished PhD diss., University of Notre Dame, 2012).

Conclusion

Dúnad, act or method of closing up, barring, fastening; close of a poem. (*Dineen's Dictionary*)

At the pilgrimage site of Station Island in Lough Derg, as Saint Patrick's Purgatory in Donegal is now known, a circling devotional practice is the norm—pilgrims loop the basilica clockwise while saying the rosary. Often on their bare knees, they trace the spirals of the penitential stone prayer beds that are the likely remains of early anchoritic beehive cells associated with saints Brendan, Brigit, Columba and Patrick. Over and over as they walk, the pilgrims recite prayers that are themselves cyclical liturgical forms, repeating refrains as their feet orbit the island's holy sites. Irish spatial practice, as we have seen, is often also verbal and poetical, and it involves a surprising amount of circling, looping: in a word, *dúnad*. This important Irish structuring principle of repetitive, circular movement allows one to return, illuminated, to a point of origin that also becomes a destination: *dúnad* is the poetical reflex of the circuits exemplified throughout Irish media and practice. At Ireland's Purgatory some pilgrims recite the *Lorica* ('breastplate'), an encompassing prayer attributed to Saint Patrick. Its incantatory power lies in the repetition of its words again and again, a verbal ringing-around that poetically embodies the request that Christ's protection also encompass the supplicant as he or she moves through creation: Christ above me, Christ below me, Christ before me, Christ behind me, Christ beside me, the prayer goes. Emphasizing the divinity of circular patterns, and forming one part of a triskele—a kind of triple spiral, triangular in shape, prominent in Celtic metalwork and manuscript illumination—along with the basilica and the prayer beds, in 2004 a labyrinth was added to the pilgrimage site at Lough Derg. As explained in the visitors' guide,

Just as labyrinths have puzzled people for thousands of years, Lough Derg has always been a bit of an enigma—a place where people fast and walk barefoot and walk in circles repeatedly does not make much sense to those on the outside—but to the pilgrim the experience is profound. A labyrinth, then, with its seemingly endless twists and turns is therefore a good fit for this ancient site of pilgrimage. As we begin to understand the importance of integrating mind, body and spirit to achieve true wellbeing, the labyrinth can act as a tool. Unlike mazes you cannot get lost in a labyrinth—they have just one path—they are about guidance, trust and reflection—it acts as a metaphor for the journey of life.[1]

Conducting circuits and moving thoughtfully in spiraling, labyrinthine circles—spatial, poetic and prayerful—permeates Irish practices at Patrick's Purgatory, but also extends well beyond physical sites in Irish tradition. The discussion throughout *A landscape of words* has evidenced the primacy of circuits in the poetics of Irish space. Additionally, these circling patterns had *visual* prominence and expressive power in medieval Irish textual culture. Famed insular gospel manuscripts, as well as the lesser-known drawings in Adomnán's *De locis sanctis* and the Book of Ballymote's ogam 'wheels' or alphabetical schemes, all concretize verbal, spatial circularity and conceive of it as a key, a means to achieving enlightenment.

The illuminated version of the gospels known as the Book of Kells, and many other insular manuscripts such as the Book of Durrow and the Book of Lindisfarne, employ circling and wandering designs: in each, an illuminated path winds through intervening lines and conceptual iconography on the surface of the manuscript page before depositing us at the intended endpoint, oftentimes situated in the structure's very center. Gazing on a carpet page, with the eye swirling around the magnificent interlace, becomes a kind of meditative, prayerful practice. Similarly, for the oarless voyagers we saw circling a mystery-filled ocean for several years, drifting where the winds willed them, the destination was often uncertain, but the participants had faith in the benefits that following these winding and initially unknown paths might confer. As Ben Tilghman writes, 'insular calligraphers may have sought to remind their readers that the path to spiritual knowledge is fraught with twists and turns, and marked only by obscured and fragmentary signs'.[2] Often ending up at the center or back at the beginning of the spatial (or visual or verbal) journey, movement through—sometimes even outside—the frame allows one to glimpse the logic of the whole and gain knowledge through it, like those drifting travelers who undertook epiphanic voyages with Brendan or Máel Dúin.

Conclusion

Penelope Reed Doob describes how these complex winding forms work on us, and her observations are as germane to manuscript pages and verbal texts as they are to architectural labyrinths made of tiles or turf slightly raised above the ground. As Doob writes, one's gaze might initially dart around the structure's circuits and turns in a hesitant manner. Yet these medieval labyrinths and manuscript images are unicursal—that is, there is a single, path to be followed—and

> one's eye eventually finds rest and stability at the center: confusion leads to certainty, for a unicursal labyrinth's structure and process are fixed. And because the maze is diagrammatic, it offers us a privileged God's- or artist's-eye view of the whole. Eventually our eye can take it all in, seeing where, how, and why confusion is converted to order.[3]

She continues to discuss their formal specifics, of relevance here in terms of circling spatial and poetic practices:

> Most medieval (and many ancient) labyrinths are not merely diagrammatic and unicursal; they are also round, constructed—usually by compass—on the basis of a series of concentric circles ... Typical medieval mazes thus consist of a perfect form, the circle—the shape of the world, the universe, eternity. They are stamped with the cross, perhaps suggesting the impact of Christ on the world or, less favorably, indicating a disruption of perfect order. They combine two important principles: the path defines linear progress (the march of time, of Christian history, of human life); the whole pattern illustrates circular perfection (the cosmos, eternity, liturgical and seasonal repetition and renewal).[4]

It is easy to see why many of the popular medieval mazes that decorated church floors were called *chemins à Jerusalem* ('paths to Jerusalem'), though the phrase only enjoys post-Renaissance attestation. There is very little medieval evidence on how these widespread labyrinths were used, yet an enduring conjecture is 'that the feeble, the sick, and stay-at-homes during the crusades performed token pilgrimages on their feet or knees in these church labyrinths in lieu of undertaking a real voyage to Jerusalem'.[5] Lough Derg provides apt illustration. An Irish site of pilgrimage featuring Irish saints and other uniquely Irish elements, the pilgrimage to Patrick's Purgatory at Lough Derg was (and is) very much about finding a path to Jerusalem, experiencing the Holy Land within the boundaries of an Irish holy island. Liturgical practice performed locally, but focused in large part on Christological sacred events located in Jerusalem, animate Irish *chemins à Jerusalem*. For instance, the Stations of the Cross, which are still prominent features of the Lough Derg pilgrimage (and the architecture of the basilica itself), enact Jesus's movements through Jerusalem in such a way. The development of an actual labyrinth at Lough Derg is a fitting addition that reminds us of the other circling practices already operative at this Irish pilgrimage site.

Some remarkable images—spatial plans of Jerusalem sites—provided by Adomnán in *De locis sanctis* (*DLS*) intriguingly resemble circular medieval labyrinths and invite the eye to mentally travel these spaces (see Figure 2). Adomnán's works, which began this book, provided a critical foundation for the Irish poetics of space that developed over the subsequent centuries. He subtly led his audiences to appreciate the links between repeated spatial practice—our guide in *DLS* visits sites multiple times—and the importance of meditating on these spatial circuits at home. That this was Adomnán's clear intention is attested by the inclusion in *DLS* of architectural drawings—some of the earliest we have—of important holy places in Jerusalem. Adomnán's integration of the illustrations into his textual discussion means that the reader might inhabit these Jerusalem spaces and mentally move through them from afar.

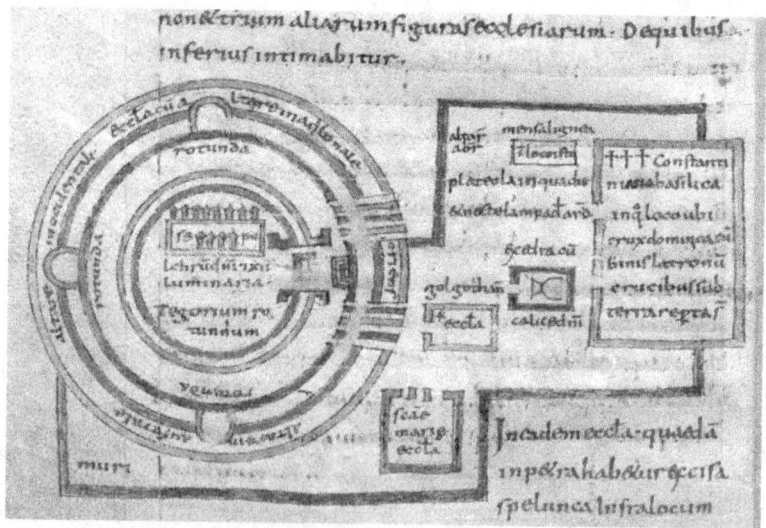

2 Plan of the Church of the Holy Sepulchre, from Adomnán's *De locis sanctis*. Vienna, Österreichisches Nationalbibliothek MS 458, fol. 4v (ninth century). Courtesy of the Österreichisches Nationalbibliothek.

Conclusion

As Michael Gorman has pointed out, they are an integral part of the text itself, as well as its many copies, and show their popularity and value to medieval scribes, who continued to reproduce them.[6] As Bede tells us when he praises Adomnán and King Aldfrith, who made *DLS* available throughout his realm, Adomnán's text on the holy places is to be admired and valued as it allows those in the world's farthest corners to come to know the Holy Land.[7]

Adomnán's schematic representations of the Holy Sepulchre and the Church of the Holy Ascension were based, he tells us, on what the pilgrim Arculf drew on wax tablets for him. They are noteworthy in particular for their concentric design: while they are architectural plans, they are also manuscript forms that draw the eye to wander through and inhabit the elaborate images as in the Book of Kells, which they structurally resemble, and whose origins are also tied to Adomnán's island of Iona. Adomnán's images, as well as the interlacing structures in insular illuminated gospel manuscripts, are a metaphorical way for manuscript viewers to get to Jerusalem, to visit the holy places from far away. The images themselves are *chemins à Jerusalem*.

When a pair of English architects (Clutton and Burges) entered a contest to design the cathedral of Notre-Dame-de-la-Treille at Lille, as a *hommage* to medieval cathedral mazes, their ambitious, prize-winning plan featured a maze to be laid out on the church floor (though work began in 1855, their design was never completed).[8] Their maze, or *chemin à Jerusalem*, was based on the images provided in Bede's *Historia Ecclesiastica*, which Bede in turn drew from Adomnán's *DLS*.[9] Following the paths planned for this cathedral floor we find ourselves returned to an origin point, the initial form now nuanced and interlaced with other images, notions, beliefs and types of spatial practice, both imaginative and physical. Ranging from an Irishman's manuscript drawings of Jerusalem monuments to a maze planned for a French cathedral floor as a *chemin à Jerusalem*, Irish concepts and schemes of spatial practice have a wide ambit and sphere of influence.

Turning to another illustration, and one that fuses word and image, some of the schemes for the 'secret' or cryptic ogam alphabets featured in the fourteenth-century Book of Ballymote also resemble Adomnán's architectural illustrations and labyrinthine structures (Figure 3):

Two of these ogam schemes are strikingly organized in spherical shapes, which also resemble depictions of the world, universe or cosmos as described and illustrated in several cosmological

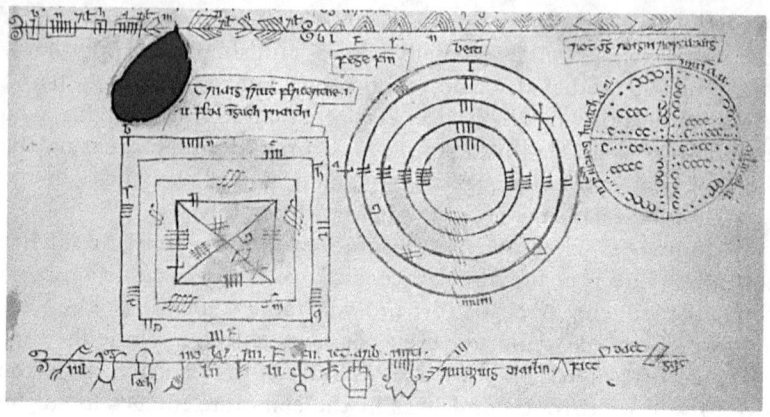

3   Three ogam schemes. Book of Ballymote (fourteenth century),
Royal Irish Academy MS 23 P12. By permission of
the Royal Irish Academy © RIA.

treatises in circulation in the Irish Sea region throughout the Middle Ages—one late twelfth-century example maps the earth surrounded by concentric celestial circles (Figure 4). We hear echoes of the biblical refrain linking creation and speech (*in principio erat verbum*), and the Irish embrace of the Judeo-Christian concept that words, language and the physical world are connected in some important ways, harmonious, unified, perhaps even mutually constitutive. In these ogam schemes, notched letters are organized or mapped spatially, in maze-like, concentric structures that follow the same patterns as Adomnán's Jerusalem church diagrams, representations of the cosmos and later mazes or labyrinths described as 'ways to Jerusalem'. Though it would be unwise to make strong assertions regarding these fourteenth-century drawings about which we know very little, it is perhaps not overreaching ourselves to see in them links between verbal and spatial practices, as well as a belief that there are mysteries, secrets—these are cryptic ogams—that are best contemplated and only revealed through thoughtful, circling, spatially imaginative meditation.

I want to return now to words. The fourteenth-century Book of Ballymote, which features the concentric designs of ogam alphabets, also gives us more explicit considerations of the device of *dúnad*, the poetical reflex of many types of circuits and circles that populate Irish media. As P. L. Henry describes it, this feature 'depends on the principle—or at worst the pious hope—that a work of art is whole and complete and its full potentialities realized, that

Conclusion

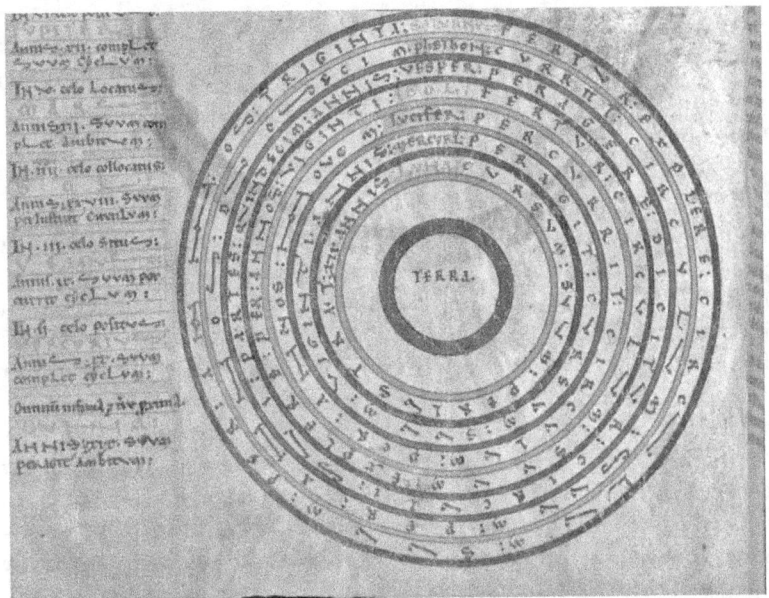

4 Twelfth-century English depiction of the cosmos showing the earth ringed by celestial circles. Walters Art Museum, Baltimore, MS W.73, fol. 2v. Courtesy of the Walters Art Museum.

the circle has been fully traversed, when end-point and beginning have been made to coincide'.[10] Preserved with the *Auraicept na nÉces* ('Primer of the Poets', the popular medieval poetic and bardic treatise) in the Book of Ballymote are the following verses:

Dunta for nduan decid lib,	Look at the closings of your poems,
A æs in dana dlighthig,	You people of the lawful art.
Cest, nocho caingen falaigh	Query—it is no secret matter—
In daingen ros-dunsabair.	Have you closed them firmly?
[...]	
Saighith, ascnam, uaim do rind,	*Full approach, approach, alliteration at end,*
Dunait curpu duan, derb lind;	Close bodies of poems, it is plain to us;
Cach iarcomarc is gloir glan,	Every concluding word is a pure glory,
Comindsma is coir dia ndunad.	*Riveting* is proper for closing them.
Dunta.	Closed.

A æs dana in domain tiar tair	You poets of the world, West and East,
Eter Erinn is Albain,	Both in Ireland and in Scotland,
Ni dleghait seoto sona	They deserve no lucky treasures
Cach duaine na ba dunta.	For every poem that will not be closed.
d. d. d. Dunta.	Closed.[11]

Dúnad is such a canonical feature that, as Gerard Murphy sums it up, 'absence of *dúnad* in a verse text, unless it be a short epigram, may be taken as a sign that the poem has not been preserved in its entirety'.[12] So integral is *dúnad* to conceptions of proper poetic form that a poem is suspected of being fragmented or partial if it does not provide this encircling metrical feature.

Dúnad is one of the medieval poetical devices that endures throughout Irish literature, from the earliest texts to the most recent, and shows the ways in which a medieval Irish poetics of space has become deeply entrenched in Irish literature more globally. Take, for example, the lines that locate divine majesty in the spaces of this world in Psalm 8, attributed to the warrior-poet King David, which both opens and closes with these words: *Domine, Domine noster, quam admirabile est nomen tuum in universa terra* ('Oh Lord, Our Lord, how miraculous is your name in all the earth.') The ninth-century Irish scribe glossing this passage in the Codex Ambrosianus C manuscript writes that *Amal as hō molad ocus adamrugud in Choimded in-tinscana in salmsa, is samlaid for-centar dano, amal dund-gniat ind filid linni cid in sin* ('As this psalm begins with praise and admiration of the Lord, it is thus moreover that it is concluded, even as the poets do with us.')[13] The Irish commentator approvingly identifies here a biblical example of *dúnad*, which was to become a definitive Irish spatial poetical device and marker of poetic excellence in vernacular Irish literature.[14] According to this scribe, like the Irish poets King David practices a type of *dúnad*, and improves upon one of its most exquisite forms, *saigid* ('attainment'), by repeating not only the first word but the whole first line, to close the psalm. As ever, Irish authors draw our attention to the ways that vernacular Irish literature and poetic practice, while geographically located in a marginal space, nonetheless connect with Judeo-Christian traditions. *Dúnad*, this Irish structuring principle of a circular yet illuminating return to the point of origin, is also one with a biblical exemplar. The Irish scribe glossing the psalms in the Codex Ambrosianus C commentary, in attending to the aesthetic, and perhaps even sanctifying, practice of circling back to repeat the opening, was working in many ways within the same tradition as the Columban monks who produced the Book of Kells.

Moving forward one thousand years, Seamus Heaney's 'Digging', which describes his poetic excavations of the Irish landscape, also features *dúnad*. The poem opens 'Between my finger and my thumb/The squat pen rests.' Just as his father dug the literal earth, the peat, with a spade, Heaney, like so many Irish poets before him, opens up the layers of the Irish landscape with the tools of writing. By the end of the poem, the opening lines are repeated and meaningfully extended to form the poem's conclusion, and Heaney declares that

> Between my finger and my thumb
> The squat pen rests.
> I'll dig with it.[15]

The poetry of this Nobel Prize-winning author (and his extensive oeuvre of placelore poetry and retellings of medieval narratives) attests to how the medieval Irish spatial turn has changed the landscape of literature. In Chapter 5, I pointed out how the *Tractatus de Purgatorio Sancti Patricii* erases native Irish people in some telling ways. It becomes interesting that Seamus Heaney might finally be the most famous Irish person to have visited Patrick's Purgatory and written about it, with the account of his transformative visions at Lough Derg expressed in the *Station Island* poems. Heaney describes his own movements, the 'granite airy space/I was staring into, on my knees, at the hard mouth of St Brigid's Bed', a purgatorial specter appearing to him there 'at the bed's stone hub'.[16] Heaney begins at Ireland's Purgatory at Lough Derg, follows this foundational purgatorial account's influence throughout medieval Europe via a meditation on Dante's *Purgatorio*, and ultimately circles back to Station Island, now a multi-temporal, connective site interlaced with broader European concepts, narratives, practice, and belief systems. Heaney's verbal landscape of Patrick's Purgatory models a medieval Irish poetics of space, as does the use of *dúnad* in Heaney's conceptualization of writing in 'Digging'.

Heaney's use of English, a language with global reach in the modern world, made his poetry accessible to a wider audience inside and outside of Ireland. Similarly, Adomnán's choice of Latin, medieval Christendom's culturally prestigious and unifying *lingua franca*, ensured that King Aldfrith could circulate *DLS* among the English, bringing it into Bede's extensive and influential orbit. Similarly, the choice of Latin by the author of the *Navigatio Sancti Brendani* also ensured a substantial European readership. As a consequence, Brendan's voyage became well known, embraced and recopied in both Latin and vernacular European translation throughout the Middle Ages, while Máel Dúin's *immram* (literally, 'rowing about'), an equally rich and edifying North Atlantic adventure, remains relatively unknown. Even in the eleventh and twelfth centuries, it was the more universal accessibility of Latin that propelled the *Tractatus de Purgatorio Sancti Patricii* into wide readership, with its version of Irish otherworldly spaces translated into virtually every European vernacular as well—this was one way the poetics of Irish space permeated European literature and imagination. In this period, these Latin texts (and their translation into Europe's other languages and cultures) had far more influence than the Irish-language compositions and spatial discourses described in Chapters 2, 3 and 4. Despite their genius and impressive development of a poetics of space, they did not, it must be conceded, attract much interest or have direct impact outside of Ireland during the Middle Ages or Early Modern period. Ireland's development of a national literature and valorization of the vernacular from the ninth century on meant that while the land itself continued to be translated, and thus maintained its global relevance, the speech and literary discourses of the Irish themselves, in their uniquely peripheral island landscape, remained local to Ireland. Though some of the vernacular Irish sources must have been known and used—for instance, the third part of Gerald of Wales's *Topographia* is based largely on the Irish pseudo-historical text *Lebor Gabála Érenn*—very little of these Irish-language developments of a poetics of Irish space seem to have traveled outside of Ireland.[17] This may appear to suggest that a medieval vernacular literature and language like Irish, a product localized at the world's edge, was doomed to marginalization and might have been expected to disappear from the world stage. However, when we take a long view, we realize that, as Heaney's poetry and the health of Irish placelore and spatial writing produced by so many Irish authors show, the tradition endured and continues to maintain an important position in Irish literature.

As discussed throughout this book, the appropriate way to conclude a poetic text is to return to the beginning and provide *dúnad*, closure, fastening: that literary device whose homograph, *dúnad*, is also an enclosure, an encampment, a fort or chief's residence, and thus a home, sanctuary and place of protection.[18] Those pilgrim

Conclusion

voyagers featured early in the book, 'rowing about' (*immram*) in the otherworldly North Atlantic, were not just going around in circles. Their spatial movements changed them, just as the opening words of a poetic text have been transformed by the time we revisit and repeat them at the close of the poem, hearing them resonate with the echoes of the intervening meaning-making verses. While literature of and about Ireland innovatively developed to address varied cultural contexts and worldviews over the 600 years considered in this study, the constant touchstones to which the texts consistently return are place and the poetics of space. Arculf, Brendan, Cú Chulainn, the great bulls of the *Táin*, the *dindshenchas* poets who map Ireland in their verses, Patrick and Caílte, the nobles of Ireland and the knight who goes through Patrick's Purgatory, glimpsing paradise but finally returning, like Brendan, Máel Dúin and the others, to resume a life in Ireland itself—they also accomplish *dúnad*, circling closure, in their journeys. They ring the literary landscapes with their *imm*s and varieties of *cuairt*. They model how one might be transformed by these loops around and through Irish landscapes. Most importantly, they show us how we might visit Ireland's sloping 'soft gradient[s] of consonant' and 'vowel-meadows',[19] to travel and imaginatively dwell within a landscape of words.

Notes

1. www.loughderg.org/heritage/the-labyrinth-of-lough-derg/, accessed August 9, 2017.
2. Ben Tilghman, 'The Shape of the Word: Extralinguistic Meaning in Insular Display Lettering', *Word & Image* 27.3 (2011), 304.
3. Penelope Reed Doob, *The Idea of the Labyrinth from Classical Antiquity through the Middle Ages* (Ithaca, NY: Cornell University Press, 1990), p. 102.
4. Doob, *Labyrinth*, p. 103.
5. Doob, *Labyrinth*, p. 119.
6. Gorman, 'Diagrams', pp. 11–12, 36–7.
7. Bede, *Historia*, v. 15, pp. 506–7. Quoted in Chapter 1.
8. Colum Hourihane (ed.), *The Grove Encyclopedia of Medieval Art and Architecture*, vol. 1 (Oxford: Oxford University Press, 2012), p. 68.
9. W. H. Matthews, *Mazes and Labyrinths* (London and New York: Longmans, Green and Co., 1922), p. 66; and Gorman, 'Diagrams', pp. 11–12.
10. P. L. Henry, 'A Celtic-English Prosodic Feature', *Zeitschrift für celtische Philologie* 29 (1962/64), 98.

11 Text and translation (with some updating of the language) is from Henry, 'A Celtic-English Prosodic Feature', 92–4. The text is also edited in Thurneysen, 'Mitterlirische Verslehren', *Irische Texte*, vol. III, p. 121.
12 Murphy, *Irish Metrics*, p. 45.
13 Gloss and psalm are quoted in Murphy, *Irish Metrics*, p. 44.
14 See discussion of the device in Murphy, *Irish Metrics*, pp. 43–5, and Henry, 'A Celtic-English Prosodic Feature', 93–4.
15 Seamus Heaney, 'Digging,' (1966), from *Death of a Naturalist* (London: Faber & Faber, 1991), reprinted in Seamus Heaney, *Opened Ground: Poems 1966–1996* (London: Faber & Faber, 2001), p. 4.
16 Seamus Heaney, *Station Island* (London: Faber & Faber, 1984), p. 81.
17 For instance, apart from brief mentions of Fergus and Conchobar, medieval English literature preserves no clear references to Irish literary characters. Rambo, *Colonial Ireland in Medieval English Literature*, pp. 35–40.
18 *eDIL* s.v. 1 dúnad.
19 Seamus Heaney, 'Anahorish', *Wintering Out* (London: Faber & Faber, 1972), p. 16.

Bibliography

Primary Sources

Adomnán, *De locis sanctis*, ed. and trans. Denis Meehan (Dublin: DIAS, 1958).

Adomnán, *Life of St Columba*, trans. Richard Sharpe (London: Penguin, 1995).

Adomnán, *Vita Sancti Columbae* [*Adomnán's Life of Columba*], ed. and trans. Alan Orr Anderson and Marjorie Ogilvie Anderson (London: Thomas Nelson and Sons, 1961).

Ahlqvist, Anders, ed., *The Early Irish Linguist: An Edition of the Canonical Part of the Auraicept na nÉces*, Commentationes Humanarum Litterarum 73 (Helsinki: Societas Scientiarum Fennica, 1983).

Augustine of Hippo, *De civitate dei*, ed. Bernard Dombart and Alfonso Kalb (Turnhout: Brepols, 1955).

Bede, *Historia ecclesiastica*, in *Bede's Ecclesiastical History of the English People*, ed. and trans. Bertram Colgrave and R. A. B. Mynors (Oxford: Clarendon Press, 1969).

Bernard of Clairvaux, *Vita sancti Malachiae*, in *Patrologiae cursus completus. Series Latina*, ed. J.-P. Migne, 221 vols (Paris: Apud Garnieri Fratres, 1844–64), CLXXXII.

Bernard of Clairvaux, *The Life and Death of Saint Malachy the Irishman*, trans. Robert T. Meyer (Kalamazoo: Cistercian Publications, 1977).

Best, R. I. and Osborn Bergin, eds., *Lebor na Huidre: Book of the Dun Cow* (Dublin: Hodges Figgis, 1929).

Breatnach, Liam, ed. and trans., *Uraicecht na Ríar: The Poetic Grades of Early Irish Law* (Dublin: DIAS, 1987).

Carmody, F. J., ed., *Physiologus latinus* (Paris: E. Droz, 1939).

Carson, Ciaran, trans., 'The Scribe in the Woods', in *The Finest Music: Early Irish Lyrics*, ed. Maurice Riordan (London: Faber & Faber, 2014), p. 4.

Columbanus, *Epistolae*, in *Sancti Columbani Opera*, ed. and trans. G. S. M. Walker (Dublin: DIAS, 1957), pp. 2–59.

Cook, Albert, ed., *The Old English Physiologus* (New Haven, CT: Yale University Press, 1921).

Cummian, *De Controversia Paschali*, in *Cummian's Letter De Controversia Paschali*, ed. and trans. Moira Walsh and Dáibhí Ó Cróinín (Toronto: Pontifical Institute for Mediaeval Studies, 1988).

Dillon, Myles, ed., *Stories from the Acallam* (Dublin: DIAS, 1970).

Dooley, Ann and Harry Roe, trans., *Tales of the Elders of Ireland* (Oxford: Oxford University Press, 2008).

Easting, Robert, 'The English Tradition', in Michael Haren and Yolande de Pontfarcy (eds.), *The Medieval Pilgrimage to St Patrick's Purgatory. Lough Derg and the European Tradition* (Enniskillen: Clogher Historical Society, 1988), pp. 58–82.

Easting, Robert, ed., *Tractatus de Purgatorio Sancti Patricii* in *St Patrick's Purgatory: Two Versions of Owayne Miles and the Vision of William Stranton Together with the Tractatus de Purgatorio Sancti Patricii* (Oxford: Oxford University Press, 1991), pp. 121–54.

Gantz, Jeffrey, trans., *Early Irish Myths and Sagas* (New York: Viking Penguin, 1981).

Geoffrey of Monmouth, *Historia Regum Britanniae of Geoffrey of Monmouth*, ed. Acton Griscom (London: Longmans, Green and Co., 1929).

Geoffrey of Monmouth, *The History of the Kings of Britain*, ed. and trans. Lewis Thorpe (London: Penguin, 1996).

Gerald of Wales, *De rebus a se gestis*, in *Giraldi Cambrensis Opera I*, ed. J. S. Brewer (London: Longman, 1861), pp. 1–122.

Gerald of Wales, *De rebus a se gestis*, in *The Autobiography of Gerald of Wales*, trans. Harold Edgeworth Butler (Woodbridge: Boydell Press, 2005).

Gerald of Wales, *Expugnatio Hibernica: The Conquest of Ireland*, ed. and trans. A. B. Scott and F. X. Martin (Dublin: Royal Irish Academy, 1978).

Gerald of Wales, *The History and Topography of Ireland*, ed. and trans. John O'Meara (New York: Penguin, 1982).

Gerald of Wales, *Topographia Hibernica*, in *Giraldi Cambrensis Opera V*, ed. James F. Dimock (London: Longman, 1867), pp. 5–204.

Gwynn, Edward, ed. and trans., *The Metrical Dindshenchas*, 5 vols (Dublin: Royal Irish Academy, 1903–35).

Hamel, A. G. van, ed., *Immrama* (Dublin: DIAS, 1941).

Hamel, A. G. van, ed., *Aided Óenfir Aífe* ('Death of Aife's One Son') in *Compert Con Culainn and Other Stories* (Dublin: DIAS, 1978a), pp. 9–15.

Hamel, A. G. van, ed., *Compert Con Culainn*, in *Compert Con Culainn and Other Stories* (Dublin: DIAS, 1978b), pp. 1–8.

Heaney, Seamus, 'Anahorish', in *Wintering Out* (London: Faber & Faber, 1972), p. 16.

Heaney, Seamus, 'Digging', in *Death of a Naturalist* (London: Faber & Faber, 1991), pp. 1–2.

Heaney, Seamus, *Opened Ground: Poems 1966 – 1996* (London: Faber & Faber, 2001).
Heaney, Seamus, *Station Island* (London: Faber & Faber, 1984).
Hennessey, William M., ed., *The Mesca Ulad, or, The Intoxication of the Ultonians* (Dublin: Royal Irish Academy, 1889).
Isidore of Seville, *Etymologiae*, ed. W. M. Lindsay (Oxford: Clarendon Press, 1911).
Isidore of Seville, *The Etymologies*, trans. Stephen Barney *et al.* (Cambridge: Cambridge University Press, 2006).
Keating, Geoffrey, *Foras Feasa ar Éirinn*, ed. Patrick Dineen (London: Irish Texts Society, 1908–14).
Kinsella, Thomas, trans., 'Death of Aife's One Son', in *The Táin* (London: Oxford University Press, 1969), pp. 39–45.
Knott, Eleanor, ed., *Togail Bruidne Da Derga* (Dublin: DIAS, 1936).
Lehman, Ruth, ed. and trans., *Dom-farcai fidbaide fál* ('The Scribe in the Woods'), in *Early Irish Verse* (Austin, TX: University of Texas Press, 1982), p. 25.
Macalister, R. A. S., ed., *Book of Mac Carthaigh Riabhach, Otherwise Called the Book of Lismore* (Dublin: Stationery Office, 1950).
Meyer, Kuno, ed., 'Die Wiederauffindung der Táin Bó Cúalnge [Egerton 1782, fo. 87 b]', *Archiv für celtische Lexikographie* 3 (1905), 2–4.
Meyer, Kuno, ed., *Triads of Ireland* (Dublin: Hodges Figgis, 1908).
Murray, Kevin, ed., 'The Finding of the *Táin*', *Cambrian Medieval Celtic Studies* 41 (Summer 2001), 17–23.
O'Meara, John, trans., *The Voyage of Saint Brendan* (Gerrards Cross: Colin Smythe, 1961).
O'Rahilly, Cecile, ed. and trans., *Táin Bó Cúalnge from the Book of Leinster* (Dublin: DIAS, 1967).
O'Rahilly, Cecile, ed. and trans., *Táin Bó Cúailnge: Recension I* (Dublin: DIAS, 1976).
Orlandi, Giovanni, ed., *Navigatio Sancti Brendani* (Milan: Istituto Editorial Cisalpino, 1968).
Oskamp, H. P. A., ed. and trans., *The Voyage of Máel Dúin: A Study in Early Irish Voyage Literature* (Groningen: Wolters-Noordhof, 1970).
Patrick, *Confessio*, in *Libri Epistolarum Sancti Patricii Episcopi*, ed. Ludwig Bieler (Dublin: Royal Irish Academy, 1993), pp. 56–91.
Picard, Jean-Michel, trans., *Saint Patrick's Purgatory: A Twelfth Century Tale of a Journey to the Otherworld* (Dublin: Four Courts Press, 1985).
Roger of Wendover, *Chronica, sive Flores Historiarum*, ed. H. O. Coxe, 4 vols (London: Sumptibus Societatis, 1841–42).
Saxo Grammaticus, *Gesta Danorum: The History of the Danes, Volume I*, ed. Karsten Friis-Jensen and trans. Peter Fisher (Oxford: Clarendon Press, 2015).
Selmer, Carl, ed. *Navigatio Sancti Brendani Abbatis from Early Latin Manuscripts* (Notre Dame, IN: University of Notre Dame Press, 1959).

Short, Ian and Brian Merrilees, eds., *The Anglo-Norman Voyage of St Brendan* (Manchester: Manchester University Press, 1979).
Stokes, Whitley, ed. and trans., 'Cuchulainn's Death', *Revue Celtique* 3 (1876–78), 175–85.
Stokes, Whitley, ed., *Acallamh na Senórach*, in Whitley Stokes and Ernst Windisch, eds., *Irische Texte*, 5 vols (Leipzig: Hirzel, 1880–1909), IV.
Stokes, Whitley and Ernst Windisch, eds., *Irische Texte*, 5 vols (Leipzig: Hirzel, 1880–1909).
Thurneysen, Rudolf, ed., 'Mittelirische Verlehren', in Whitley Stokes and Ernst Windisch, eds., *Irische Texte*, 5 vols (Leipzig: Hirzel, 1880–1909), III.
Thurneysen, Rudolf, ed., *Teicht do Róim* ('Going to Rome'), in *Old Irish Reader* (Dublin: DIAS, 1981), p. 41.
Watson, J. Carmichael, ed. *Mesca Ulad* (Dublin: DIAS, 1941, rept. 1983).

Secondary Sources

Ashe, Laura, *Fiction and History in England, 1066–1200* (Cambridge: Cambridge University Press, 2007).
Bachelard, Gaston, *The Poetics of Space*, trans. Maria Jolas (Boston, MA: Beacon Press, 1994).
Bartlett, Robert, *Gerald of Wales: A Voice of the Middle Ages* (Stroud: Tempus, 1982).
Bartlett, Thomas, *Ireland: A History* (Cambridge: Cambridge University Press, 2010).
Basso, Keith, *Wisdom Sits in Places* (Albuquerque, NM: University of New Mexico Press, 1996).
Baumgarten, Rolf, 'Etymological Aetiology in Irish Tradition', *Ériu* 41 (1990), 115–22.
Baumgarten, Rolf, 'Geographical Orientation of Ireland in Isidore and Orosius', *Peritia* 3 (1984), 189–203.
Benozzo, Francesco, *Landscape Perception in Early Celtic Literature* (Aberystwyth: Celtic Studies Publications, 2004).
Bergin, Osborn, *Irish Bardic Poetry* (Dublin: DIAS, 1970).
Bergin, Osborn, 'Varia. I', *Ériu* 12 (1938), 215–35.
Birkett, Helen, *The Saints' Lives of Jocelin of Furness* (York: York Medieval Press, 2010).
Bitel, Lisa, *Landscape with Two Saints: How Genovefa of Paris and Brigit of Kildare Built Christianity in Barbarian Europe* (Oxford: Oxford University Press, 2009).
Bloch, R. Howard, *The Anonymous Marie de France* (Chicago, IL: University of Chicago Press, 2003).
Borsje, Jacqueline, *From Chaos to Enemy: Encounters with Monsters in Early Irish Texts* (Turnhout: Brepols, 1996).

Bowen, Charles, 'Historical Inventory of the *Dindshenchas*', *Studia Celtica* 10 (1975), 113–37.
Breatnach, Caoimhín, 'Lismore, Book of', in Séan Duffy (ed.), *Medieval Ireland: An Encyclopedia*, (New York and London: Routledge, 2005), pp. 270–80.
Byrne, Aisling, *Otherworlds: Fantasy and History in Medieval Literature* (Oxford: Oxford University Press, 2016).
Campbell, Mary, *The Witness and the Otherworld: Exotic European Travel Writing, 400–1600* (Ithaca, NY: Cornell University Press, 2001).
Carey, John, 'The Valley of the Changing Sheep', *Bulletin of the Board of Celtic Studies* 30 (1983), 277–80.
Carey, John, 'Varia II: The Address to Fergus's Stone', *Ériu* 51 (2000), 183–7.
Carney, James, *Studies in Irish Literature and History* (Dublin: DIAS, 1955).
Carney, James, 'Review of Carl Selmer, ed., *Navigatio Sancti Brendani Abbatis from Early Latin Manuscripts*', *Medium Aevum* 32 (1963), 37–44.
Carruthers, Mary, *The Craft of Thought: Meditation, Rhetoric, and the Making of Images, 400–1200* (New York: Cambridge University Press, 1998).
Certeau, Michel de, *The Practice of Everyday Life*, trans. Stephen F. Rendall (Berkeley and Los Angeles, CA: University of California Press, 1984).
Chareyron, Nicole, *Pilgrims to Jerusalem in the Middle Ages* (New York: Columbia University Press, 2005).
Charles-Edwards, Thomas, *Early Christian Ireland* (Cambridge: Cambridge University Press, 2000).
Charles-Edwards, Thomas, 'Nations and Kingdoms: A View from Above', in T. M. Charles-Edwards, ed., *After Rome* (Oxford: Oxford University Press, 2003), pp. 23–58.
Charles-Edwards, Thomas, 'The Social Background of Irish *peregrinatio*', *Celtica* 11 (1976): 43–59.
Chatillon, François, 'Arculfe a-t-il réellement existé?', *Revue du Moyen Âge latin* 23 (1967), 134–8.
Clancy, Thomas Owen, 'Subversion at Sea: Structure, Style and Intent in the *Immrama*', in Jonathan Wooding, ed., *The Otherworld Voyage in Early Irish Literature: An Anthology of Criticism* (Dublin: Four Courts Press, 2000), pp. 194–225.
Cohen, Jeffrey Jerome, *Hybridity, Identity and Monstrosity in Medieval Britain: On Difficult Middles* (New York: Palgrave Macmillan, 2006).
Connon, Anne, 'Plotting *Acallam na Senórach:* The Physical Context of the "Mayo" Sequence', in Joanne Findon, Sarah Sheehan and Westley Follett, eds., *Gablánach in Scélaigecht: Celtic Studies in Honour of Ann Dooley* (Dublin: Four Courts Press, 2013), pp. 69–102.

Davies, Morgan, 'Dindshenchas, Memory and Invention', in Cathinka Hambro and Lars Widerøe, eds., *Lochlann: Festschrift for Jan Erik Rekdal* (Oslo: Hermes Academic Publishing, 2013), pp. 86–104.

Doob, Penelope Reed, *The Idea of the Labyrinth from Classical Antiquity through the Middle Ages* (Ithaca, NY: Cornell University Press, 1990).

Dooley, Ann, 'Arthur in Ireland: The Earliest Citation in Irish Literature', *Arthurian Literature* 12 (1993), pp. 165–72.

Dooley, Ann, 'Date and Purpose of the *Acallam*', *Éigse* 34 (2004), 97–126.

Dooley, Ann, 'Pagan Beliefs and Christian Redress', in Jacqueline Borsje *et al.*, eds., *Celtic Cosmology* (Toronto: Pontifical Institute of Mediaeval Studies, 2014), pp. 249–67.

Dooley, Ann, *Playing the Hero: Reading the Irish Saga Táin Bó Cúailnge* (Toronto: University of Toronto Press, 2006).

Dooley, Ann, 'Speaking with Forked Tongues', in Sarah Sheehan and Ann Dooley, eds., *Constructing Gender* (New York: Palgrave Macmillan, 2013), pp. 171–90.

Duffy, Seán, *Ireland in the Middle Ages* (New York: St. Martin's Press, 1997).

Duggan, Anne, '"Totius Christianitatis caput". The Pope and the Princes', in Brenda Bolton and Anne Duggan, eds., *Adrian IV, the English Pope, 1154–1159* (Aldershot: Ashgate, 2003), pp. 105–55.

Dumville, David, 'Did Ireland Exist in the Twelfth Century?', in Emer Purcell *et al.*, eds., *Clerics, Kings and Vikings: Essays on Medieval Ireland in Honour of Donnchadh Ó Corráin* (Dublin: Four Courts Press, 2015), pp. 115–26.

Dumville, David, 'Two Approaches to the Dating of *Navigatio Sancti Brendani*', *Studi Medievali* 29 (1988), 87–102.

Duncan, Elizabeth, 'A Reassessment of the Script and Make-up of *Lebor na Nuachongbála*', *Zeitschrift für celtische Philologie* 59 (2012), 27–66.

Edel, Doris, *Inside the* Táin*: Exploring Cú Chulainn, Fergus, Ailill, and Medb* (Berlin: Curach Bhán, 2015).

Eliade, Mircea, *Patterns in Comparative Religion* (New York: World Publishing, 1963).

Esposito, Mario, 'L'édition de la "Nauigatio S. Brendani"', *Scriptorium* 15 (1961), 286–92.

Findon, Joanne, *A Woman's Words: Emer and Female Speech in the Ulster Cycle* (Toronto: University of Toronto Press, 1997).

Flanagan, Marie Therese, *Irish Society, Anglo-Norman Settlers, Angevin Kingship: Interactions in Ireland in the Late Twelfth Century* (Oxford: Clarendon Press, 1989).

Flanagan, Marie Therese, 'Mac Murchada, Diarmait (*ca.* 1110–1171)', *Oxford Dictionary of National Biography* (Oxford: Oxford University Press, 2004). [www.oxforddnb.com/view/article/17697, accessed June 24, 2017].

Flanagan, Marie Therese, 'Strategies of Distinction: Defining Nations in Medieval Ireland', in Hirokazu Tsurushima, ed., *Nations in Medieval Britain* (Donington: Shaun Tyas, 2010), pp. 104–20.

Flanagan, Marie Therese, *The Transformation of the Irish Church in the Twelfth Century* (Woodbridge: Boydell Press, 2010).

Follett, Westley, 'Allegorical Interpretation in Adomnán's *Vita Columbae*', *Eolas* 2 (2007), 4–27.

Frame, Robin, *Colonial Ireland* (Dublin: Helicon, 1981).

Gorman, Michael, 'Adomnán's *De locis sanctis*: The Diagrams and the Sources', *Revue Bénédictine* 116 (2006), 5–41.

Heaney, Seamus, *Preoccupations* (London: Faber & Faber, 1980).

Hellmuth, Petra 'The *Dindshenchas* and Irish Literary Tradition', in John Carey *et al.*, eds., *Cín Chille Cúile: Essays in Honour of Pádraig Ó Riain* (Aberystwyth: Celtic Studies Publications, 2004), 116–26.

Hellmuth, Petra, 'Laud 610', in John T. Koch, ed., *Celtic Culture: A Historical Encyclopedia*, (Santa Barbara, CA: ABC-CLIO, 2006), pp. 1108–9.

Henry, P. L., 'A Celtic-English Prosodic Feature', *Zeitschrift für celtische Philologie* 29 (1962–64), 91–9.

Henry, P. L., '*Furor Heroicus*', *Zeitschrift für celtische Philologie* 39 (1982), 235–42.

Hogan, Edmund, *Onomasticon Goedelicum locorum et tribuum Hiberniae et Scotiae* (Dublin: Hodges Figgis, 1910).

Hourihane, Colum P., ed., *The Grove Encyclopedia of Medieval Art and Architecture*, 2 vols (New York: Grove, 2012).

Hull, Vernam, 'The Middle Irish Version of Bede's *De Locis Sanctis*', *Zeitschrift für celtische Philologie* 17 (1928), 225–40.

Ireland, Colin, 'Where Was King Aldfrith of Northumbria Educated? An Investigation of Seventh-Century Insular Learning', *Traditio* 70 (2015), 29–73.

Jacobs, Jane M., *Edge of Empire: Postcolonialism and the City* (New York: Routledge, 1996).

Johnston, Elva, *Literacy and Identity in Early Medieval Ireland* (Woodbridge: Boydell Press, 2013).

Johnston, Elva, 'A Sailor on the Seas of Faith: The Individual and the Church in *The Voyage of Máel Dúin*', in Judith Devlin and Howard Clarke, eds., *European Encounters: Essays in Memory of Albert Lovett* (Dublin: University College Dublin Press, 2003), pp. 239–52.

Johnston, Elva, 'The Salvation of the Individual and the Salvation of Society in *Siaburcharpat Con Culaind*', in Joseph Falaky Nagy, ed., *The Individual in Celtic Literatures* (Dublin: Four Courts Press, 2001), pp. 109–25.

Jones, Valerie, 'The Phoenix and the Resurrection', in Debra Hassig, ed., *The Mark of the Beast: The Medieval Bestiary in Art, Life, and Literature* (New York: Garland, 1999), pp. 99–115.

Kelly, Molly Robinson, *The Hero's Place: Medieval Literary Traditions of Space and Belonging* (Washington, DC: Catholic University of America Press, 2009).

Kelly, Patricia, 'The *Táin* as Literature', in J. P. Mallory, ed., *Aspects of the* Táin (Belfast: December Publications, 1992), pp. 69–102.

Knott, Eleanor, *An Introduction to Irish Syllabic Poetry of the Period 1200–1600* (Dublin: DIAS, 1957).

Koch, John T., ed., *Celtic Culture: A Historical Encyclopedia* (Santa Barbara, CA: ABC-CLIO, 2006).

Künzler, Sarah, *Flesh and Word: Reading Bodies in Old Norse-Icelandic and Early Irish Literature* (Berlin: De Gruyter, 2016).

Lavezzo, Kathy, *Angels on the Edge of the World* (Ithaca, NY: Cornell University Press, 2006).

Layzer, Varese, *Signs of Weakness: Juxtaposing Irish Tales and the Bible* (Sheffield: Sheffield Academic Press, 2001).

Leerssen, Joep, 'Wildness, Wilderness, and Ireland: Medieval and Early-Modern Patterns in the Demarcation of Civility', *Journal of the History of Ideas* 56 (1995), 25–39.

Leslie, Shane, *Saint Patrick's Purgatory: A Record from History and Literature* (London: Burns, Oats and Washbourne, 1932).

Lowe, Jeremy, 'Contagious Violence and the Spectacle of Death', in Maria Tymoczko and Colin Ireland, eds., *Language and Tradition in Ireland: Continuities and Displacements* (Amherst and Boston, MA: University of Massachusetts Press, 2003), pp. 84–100.

Lowe, Jeremy, 'Kicking over the Traces: The Instability of Cú Chulainn', *Studia Celtica* 34 (2000), 119–29.

Mac Cana, Proinsias, 'Placenames and Mythology in Irish Tradition: Places, Pilgrimages and Things', in Gordon MacLennan, ed., *Proceedings of the First North American Congress of Celtic Studies* (Ottawa: University of Ottawa, 1988), pp. 319–41.

MacCotter, Paul, *Medieval Ireland: Territorial, Political and Economic Divisions* (Dublin: Four Courts Press, 2008).

Mac Eoin, Gearóid, 'The Provenance of the Book of Leinster', *Zeitschrift für celtische Philologie* 57 (2009–10): 79–96.

Mac Gerailt, Uáitéar, 'The Edinburgh Text of *Mesca Ulad*', *Ériu* 37 (1986), 133–80.

Mac Neill, Eoin, 'Varia. I', *Ériu* 11 (1932), 130–5.

MacNeill, Máire, *The Festival of Lughnasa* (Oxford: Oxford University Press, 1962).

Matthews, W. H., *Mazes and Labyrinths* (New York: Longmans, Green and Co., 1922).

McGuire, B. P., '*Purgatory*, the Communion of Saints, and Medieval Change', *Viator* 20 (1989), 61–84.

McKibben, Sarah E., '"In Their 'owne countre"': Deriding and Defending the Early Modern Irish Nation after Gerald of Wales', *Eolas* 8 (2015), 39–70.

McManus, Damian, *A Guide to Ogam* (Maynooth: An Sagart, 1991).
McManus, Damian, 'A Chronology of the Latin Loan-Words in Early Irish', *Ériu* 34 (1983), 21–71.
McMullen, A. Joseph and Kristen Carella, 'Locating Place and Landscape in Early Insular Literature', *Journal of Literary Onomastics* 6 (2017), 1–10.
McNamara, Martin, *The Psalms in the Early Irish Church* (Sheffield: Sheffield Academic Press, 2000).
Mathis, Kate, 'Review: Edel, Doris, *Inside the* Táin', *Zeitschrift für celtische Philologie* 64 (2018), 459–68.
Melia, Daniel, 'A Poetic Klein Bottle', in A. T. E. Matonis and Daniel Melia, eds., *Celtic Language, Celtic Culture: A Festschrift for Eric P. Hamp* (Van Nuys, LA: Ford and Bailie, 1990), pp. 187–96.
Michelet, Fabienne, *Creation, Migration, and Conquest: Imaginary Geography and Sense of Space in Old English Literature* (Oxford: Oxford University Press, 2006).
Mills, Kristen, 'Sorrow and Conversion in *Acallam na Senórach*', *Éigse* 38 (2013), 1–19.
Morgan, Alison, *Dante and the Medieval Otherworld* (Cambridge: Cambridge University Press, 1990).
Muhr, Kay, 'Water Imagery in Early Irish', *Celtica* 23 (1999), 193–210.
Mulligan, Amy, 'The Anatomy of Power and the Miracle of Kingship: The Female Body of Sovereignty in a Medieval Irish Kingship Tale', *Speculum* 81 (2006), 1014–54.
Mulligan, Amy, 'Cú Chulainn, Isidore of Seville and the Erasure of a Warrior's Body: Heroic Crisis and Irish Independence', in James Buickerood, ed., *From Enlightenment to Rebellion* (Lewisburg, PA: Bucknell University Press, 2018), pp. 33–46.
Mulligan, Amy, 'Form and Function of the Grotesque Body in Medieval Irish and Norse Literature', D.Phil. diss., University of Oxford, 2003.
Mulligan, Amy, 'Introduction: Ideas of the Irish Nation', *Eolas: Journal of the American Society of Irish Medieval Studies* 8 (2015), 12–19.
Mulligan, Amy, 'Norman Topographies of Conquest: Mapping Anglo-Norman Identities onto Ireland', in Stefan Burkhardt and Thomas Foerster, eds., *Norman Tradition and Transcultural Heritage* (Burlington: Ashgate, 2013), pp. 253–78.
Mulligan, Amy, '"The Satire of the Poet Is a Pregnancy": Pregnant Poets, Body Metaphors and Cultural Production in Medieval Ireland', *Journal of English and Germanic Philology* 108 (2009), 481–505.
Murphy, Gerard, *Early Irish Metrics* (Dublin: Royal Irish Academy, 1961).
Murphy, Gerard, *Ossianic Lore and Romantic Tales of Early Ireland* (Dublin: Colm O Lochlainn, 1955).
Murray, Kevin, 'The Finding of the *Táin*', *Cambrian Medieval Celtic Studies* 41 (Summer 2001), 17–23.

Murray, Kevin, 'Genre Construction: The Creation of the *Dinnshenchas*', *Journal of Literary Onomastics* 6 (2017), 11–21.

Nagy, Joseph Falaky, *Conversing with Angels and Ancients* (Ithaca, NY: Cornell University Press, 1997).

Nagy, Joseph Falaky, 'How the *Táin* Was Lost', *Zeitschrift für celtische Philologie* 49/50 (1997), 603–9.

Nagy, Joseph Falaky, 'Orality in Medieval Irish Narrative: An Overview', *Oral Tradition* 1/2 (1986), 272–301.

Nagy, Joseph Falaky, 'The Rising of the River Cronn in *Táin Bó Cúailnge*', in Anders Ahlqvist, ed., *Celtica Helsingiensa* (Helsinki: Societas Scientiarium Fennica, 1996), pp. 129–48.

Neville, Jennifer, *Representations of the Natural World in Old English Poetry* (Cambridge: Cambridge University Press, 1999).

Ní Chatháin, Próinséas, 'Bede's Ecclesiastical History in Irish', *Peritia* 3 (1984), 115–30.

Ní Mhaonaigh, Máire, 'Of Bede's "Five Languages and Four Nations": The Earliest Writing from Ireland, Scotland and Wales', in Clare Lees, ed., *The Cambridge History of Early Medieval English Literature* (Cambridge: Cambridge University Press, 2012), pp. 99–119.

O'Byrne, Teresa, 'Dublin's Hoccleve: James Yonge, Scribe, Author, and Bureaucrat, and the Literary World of Late Medieval Dublin', Ph.D. diss., University of Notre Dame, 2012.

Ó Carragáin, Tomás, *Churches in Early Medieval Ireland: Architecture, Ritual and Memory* (New Haven, CT: Yale University Press, 2010).

Ó Cathasaigh, Tomás, 'The Body in *Táin bó Cúailnge*', in Sarah Sheehan, Joanne Findon and Westley Follett, eds., *Gablánach in Scélaigecht* (Dublin: Four Courts Press, 2013), pp. 131–42.

Ó Coileáin, Seán, 'Place and Placename in *Fianaigheacht*', *Studia Hibernica* 27 (1993), 45–60.

Ó Concheanainn, Tomás, 'The Manuscript Tradition of *Mesca Ulad*', *Celtica* 19 (1987), 13–30.

Ó Concheanainn, Tomás, 'The Three Forms of *Dinnshenchas Érenn*', *Journal of Celtic Studies* 3 (1981–3), 88–101.

O'Connor, Ralph, *The Destruction of Da Derga's Hostel* (Oxford: Oxford University Press, 2013).

Ó hAodha, Donncha, 'The First Irish Metrical Tract', in Hildegard Tristram, ed., *Metrik und Medienwechsel / Metrics and Media* (Tübingen: Narr, 1991), pp. 207–44.

Ó hUiginn, Ruairí, 'The Background and Development of *Táin Bó Cúailnge*', in J. P. Mallory, ed., *Aspects of the Táin* (Belfast: December Publications, 1992), pp. 29–67.

O'Keeffe, Tadhg, 'Rural Settlement and Cultural Identity in Gaelic Ireland, 1000–1500', *Ruralia* 1 (1996), 142–53.

O'Loughlin, Thomas, *Adomnán and the Holy Places: The Perceptions of an Insular Monk on the Locations of the Biblical Drama* (London and New York: T & T Clark 2007).

O'Loughlin, Thomas, 'An Early Thirteenth-Century Map in Dublin: A Window into the World of Gerald of Wales', *Imago Mundi*, 51 (1999), 24–39.

O'Loughlin, Thomas, 'Patrick on the Margins of Space and Time', in K. McGroarty, ed., *Eklogai: Studies in Honour of Thomas Finan and Gerard Watson* (Maynooth: National University of Ireland, Maynooth, 2001), pp. 44–58.

Ó Murchada, Diarmuid, 'Is the O'Neill-Mac Carthy Letter of 1317 a Forgery?', *Irish Historical Studies* 23 (1982), 61–7.

Ó Néill, Pádraig, 'The Impact of the Norman Invasion on Irish Literature', *Anglo-Norman Studies* 20 (1998), 171–85.

O'Reilly, Jennifer, 'Reading Scriptures in the Life of Columba', in Cormac Bourke, ed., *Studies in the Cult of Saint Columba* (Dublin: Four Courts Press, 1997), pp. 80–106.

Ó Riain, Pádraig, 'Boundary Association in Early Irish Society', *Studia Celtica* 7 (1972), 12–29.

Ó Riain, Pádraig, *A Dictionary of Irish Saints* (Dublin: Four Courts Press, 2011).

O'Riordan, Michelle, *Irish Bardic Poetry and Rhetorical Reality* (Cork: Cork University Press, 2007).

O'Sullivan, William, 'Notes on the Scripts and Make-up of the Book of Leinster', *Celtica* 7 (1966), 1–31.

Oliver, Lisi, 'Forced and Unforced Rape in Early Irish Law', *Proceedings of the Harvard Celtic Colloquium* 13 (1993), 93–106.

Orpen, Goddard Henry, *Ireland under the Normans 1169–1333* (Dublin: Four Courts Press, 2005).

Otway-Ruthven, A. J., *A History of Medieval Ireland* (London: Ernest Benn, 1968).

Overbey, Karen, *Sacral Geographies: Saints, Shrines and Territory in Medieval Ireland* (Turnhout: Brepols, 2012).

Palmer, Patricia, *The Severed Head and the Grafted Tongue: Literature, Translation and Violence in Early Modern Ireland* (New York: Cambridge University Press, 2014).

Parsons, Geraldine, '*Acallam na Senórach* as Prosimetrum', *Proceedings of the Harvard Celtic Colloquium* 24–25 (2004–5), 86–100.

Parsons, Geraldine, 'The Narrative Voice in *Acallam na Senórach*', in Aidan Doyle and Kevin Murray, eds., *In Dialogue with the Agallamh* (Dublin: Four Courts Press, 2014), pp. 109–24.

Parsons, Geraldine, 'The Structure of *Acallam na Senórach*', *Cambrian Medieval Celtic Studies* 55 (2008), 11–39.

Picard, Jean-Michel, 'The Italian Pilgrims', in Michael Haren and Yolande de Pontfarcy, eds., *The Medieval Pilgrimage to St Patrick's*

Purgatory. Lough Derg and the European Tradition (Enniskillen: Clogher Historical Society, 1988), pp. 169–89.

Picard, Jean-Michel, 'The Purpose of Adomnán's *Vita Columbae*', *Peritia* 1 (1982), 160–77.

Pontfarcy, Yolande de, 'Accounts and Tales of Lough Derg or of the Pilgrimage', in Michael Haren and Yolande de Pontfarcy, eds., *The Medieval Pilgrimage to St Patrick's Purgatory. Lough Derg and the European Tradition* (Enniskillen: Clogher Historical Society, 1988), pp. 35–57.

Pontfarcy, Yolande de, 'The Historical Background to the Pilgrimage to Lough Derg', in Michael Haren and Yolande de Pontfarcy (eds.), *The Medieval Pilgrimage to St Patrick's Purgatory. Lough Derg and the European Tradition* (Enniskillen: Clogher Historical Society, 1988), pp. 7–34.

Pontfarcy, Yolande de, 'Introduction', in Jean-Michel Picard, trans., *Saint Patrick's Purgatory: A Twelfth Century Tale of a Journey to the Otherworld* (Dublin: Four Courts Press, 1985), pp. 9–33.

Power, Moira, 'Cnucha Cnoc os cionn Life', *Zeitschrift für celtische Philologie* 11 (1917), 39–55.

Pryce, Huw, 'Giraldus and the Geraldines', in Peter Crooks and Seán Duffy, eds., *The Geraldines and Medieval Ireland: The Making of a Myth* (Dublin: Four Courts Press, 2016), pp. 53–68.

Putter, Ad, 'The Influence of Visions of the Otherworld on some Medieval Romances', in Carolyn Muessig and Ad Putter, eds., *Envisaging Heaven in the Middle Ages* (New York: Routledge, 2006), pp. 237–51.

Quin, E. G., ed., *Dictionary of the Irish Language Based Mainly on Old and Middle Irish Materials: Compact Edition* (Dublin: Royal Irish Academy, 1983), available in updated, electronic form *(eDIL)* online at www.dil.ie.

Rambo, Elizabeth, *Colonial Ireland in Medieval English Literature* (Selingrove, PA: Susquehanna University Press, 1994).

Ritari, Katja, *Pilgrimage to Heaven: Eschatology and Monastic Spirituality in Early Medieval Ireland* (Turnhout: Brepols, 2016).

Sayers, William, 'Concepts of Eloquence in *Tochmarc Emire*', *Studia Celtica* 26–27 (1991–2), 125–54.

Sayers, William, 'Netherworld and Otherworld in Early Irish Literature', *Zeitschrift für celtische Philologie* 59 (2012), 201–30.

Sayers, William, 'The Smith and the Hero: Culann and Cú Chulainn', *Mankind Quarterly* 25 (1985), 227–60.

Sayers, William, '*Airdrech, Sirite* and Other Early Irish Battlefield Spirits', *Éigse* 25 (1991), 45–55.

Schlüter, Dagmar, 'Boring and Elusive? The *Dindshenchas* as a Medieval Irish Genre', *Journal of Literary Onomastics* 6 (2017), 22–31.

Schlüter, Dagmar, *History or Fable? The Book of Leinster as a Document of Cultural Memory in Twelfth-Century Ireland* (Münster: Nodus, 2010).

Schot, Roseanne, 'Uisneach Midi a medón Érenn: A Prehistoric "Cult" Centre and "Royal Site" in Co. Westmeath', *Journal of Irish Archaeology* 15 (2006), 39–71.

Selmer, Carl, 'The Vernacular Translations of the *Navigatio Sancti Brendani*: A Bibliographical Study', *Medieval Studies* 18 (1956), 145–57.

Severin, Timothy, *The Brendan Voyage* (London: Abacus, 1978).

Seymour, St. John D., *St. Patrick's Purgatory: A Medieval Pilgrimage in Ireland* (Dundalk: W. Tempest, 1918).

Shields, Hugh, 'The French Accounts', in Michael Haren and Yolande de Pontfarcy, eds., *The Medieval Pilgrimage to St Patrick's Purgatory. Lough Derg and the European Tradition* (Enniskillen: Clogher Historical Society, 1988), pp. 83–98.

Siewers, Alfred, 'Orthodoxy and Ecopoetics: The Green World in the Desert Sea', in John Chryssavgis and Bruce Foltz, eds., *Towards an Ecology of Transfiguration: Orthodox Christian Perspectives on Environment, Nature and Creation* (New York: Fordham University Press, 2014), pp. 243–62.

Siewers, Alfred, 'The *Periphyseon*, the Irish "Otherworld", and Early Medieval Nature', in Willemien Otten and Michael Allen, eds., *Eriugena and Creation* (Turnhout: Brepols, 2014), pp. 321–47.

Siewers, Alfred, *Strange Beauty: Ecocritical Approaches to Early Medieval Landscape* (New York: Palgrave Macmillan, 2009).

Sims-Williams, Patrick, *Irish Influence on Medieval Welsh Literature* (Oxford: Oxford University Press, 2010).

Smyth, Marina, 'The Word of God and Early Irish Cosmology', in Ann Dooley *et al.*, eds., *Early Irish Cosmology* (Toronto: Pontifical Institute of Mediaeval Studies, 2014), pp. 112–43.

Solnit, Rebecca, *Wanderlust: A History of Walking* (London: Granta Books, 2014).

Stalley, R. A., 'Mellifont Abbey: A Study of Its Architectural History', *Proceedings of the Royal Irish Academy* 80 (1980), 263–354.

Stalmaszczyk, Piotr, 'Geographical Names in Gaelic Poetry: Function and Problems with Translation', *Ainm* 5 (1991), 71–81.

Thurneysen, Rudolf, *Die irische Helden- und Königsage* (Halle: M. Niemeyer, 1921).

Tilghman, Ben, 'The Shape of the Word: Extralinguistic Meaning in Insular Display Lettering', *Word & Image* 27 (2011), 292–308.

Tipp, Dan and Jonathan Wooding, 'Adomnán's Voyaging Saint: The Cult of Cormac ua Liatháin', in Jonathan Wooding *et al.*, eds., *Adomnán of Iona: Theologian, Lawmaker, Peacemaker* (Dublin: Four Courts Press, 2010), pp. 237–52.

Toner, Gregory, 'Authority, Verse and the Transmission of Senchas', *Ériu* 55 (2005), 59–84.

Toner, Gregory, 'Landscape and Cosmology in the *Dindshenchas*', in Jacqueline Borsje *et al.*, eds., *Celtic Cosmology: Perspectives from Ireland*

and Scotland (Toronto: Pontifical Institute of Mediaeval Studies, 2014), pp. 268–83.

Toner, Gregory, 'The Transmission of *Tochmarc Emire*', *Ériu* 49 (1998), 71–88.

Tuffrau, Paul, *Le merveilleux voyage de Saint Brandan à la recherche du Paradis* (Paris: L'artisan du livre, 1925).

Turner, Victor and Edith Turner, *Image and Pilgrimage in Christian Culture* (New York: Columbia University Press, 1996).

Wadden, Patrick, 'Theories of National Identity in Early Medieval Ireland', DPhil. diss., University of Oxford, 2010.

Walsh, Katharine, '... *in finibus mundi*: The Late Medieval Pilgrims to Saint Patrick's Purgatory, Loch Derg, and the European Dimensions of the Diocese of Clogher', in Henry Jefferies, ed., *History of the Diocese of Clogher* (Dublin: Four Courts Press, 2005), pp. 41–69.

Warner, Richard, 'Láeg's Line: A Route for the Gods?', in Martin Huld *et al.* eds., *Archaeology and Language: Studies Presented to James P. Mallory* (Washington, DC: Institute for the Study of Man, 2012), pp. 55–72.

Williams, Mark, *Ireland's Immortals: A History of the Gods of Irish Myth* (Princeton, NJ: Princeton University Press, 2016).

Wilkinson, John, *Jerusalem Pilgrims Before the Crusades* (Warminster: Aris & Phillips, 2002).

Wooding, Jonathan, 'St Brendan's Boat: Dead Hides and the Living Sea in Columban and Related Hagiography', in John Carey, Máire Herbert and Pádraig Ó Riain, eds., *Studies in Irish Hagiography: Saints and Scholars* (Dublin: Four Courts Press, 2000), pp. 77–92.

Wooding, Jonathan and Dan Tipp, 'Adomnán's Voyaging Saint: The Cult of Cormac ua Liatháin', in Jonathan Wooding *et al.*, eds., *Adomnán of Iona: Theologian, Lawmaker, Peacemaker* (Dublin: Four Courts Press, 2010), pp. 237–52.

Woods, David, 'Adomnán, Arculf and the True Cross', *Aram* 18–19 (2006–7), 403–13.

Woodward, David, 'Medieval Mappaemundi', in J. B. Harley and David Woodward, eds., *The History of Cartography, Volume 1: Cartography in Prehistoric, Ancient, and Medieval Europe and the Mediterranean* (Chicago, IL: University of Chicago Press, 1987), pp. 286–368.

Yeager, Suzanne, *Jerusalem in Medieval Narrative* (New York: Cambridge University Press, 2008).

Yorke, Barbara, 'Adomnán at the Court of King Aldfrith', in Jonathan Wooding, ed., *Adomnán of Iona: Theologian, Lawmaker, Peacemaker* (Dublin: Four Courts Press, 2010), pp. 36–50.

Zaleski, Carol, 'St. Patrick's Purgatory: Pilgrimage Motifs in a Medieval Otherworld Vision', *Journal of the History of Ideas* 46 (1985), 467–85.

Index

Acallam na Senórach 5, 12, 18–19, 92, 102, 111, 141–71, 178, 181, 190
   Christianized landscape of Ireland in 141, 150, 152–4, 158, 163
   as guide for pilgrims 141, 143, 158–9, 169–70
   interactions between humans and environment in 144, 146–8, 155–6
   manuscripts of 141, 167, 171–2n.3
   as response to English colonialism in Ireland 19, 142–3, 145–6
   Saint Patrick in 18, 92, 102, 141–65, 169–71
   as travel literature 143–4
   twelfth- and thirteenth-century audiences of 145–6, 152
   virtual topography of 159, 169–70
Achall (poem by Cináed úa hArtacáin) 115–16, 132, 136
Achall (toponym) 115–16, 136
Achall, daughter of Cairpre 115–16
Adam 6–7
Adomnán, abbot of Iona 9, 13, 16, 24–38, 41–3, 66, 79, 128, 216, 218–20, 223

De locis sanctis 5, 16, 24–34, 42–3, 46–7, 66, 79, 128, 200, 216, 218
Vita Sancti Columbae 16, 25, 32–7, 42–3, 47
Aibelán (angel) 149
Ailill, consort of Medb 79–81, 85, 89, 92–3, 97
Ailill Ochir Ága 49
Aldfrith (Anglo-Saxon king of Northumbria) 24, 58n.2, 219, 223
Amairgen, son of Míl 94
Amairgen (Ulster poet) 68
Áne Chlíach (Cnóc Áine or Knockainy) 96
angels 142, 146, 149–50, 153, 157–8, 160, 164, 170, 192
Anthony, Saint 47, 194
Apache, Western 23n.38, 108, 130
Arculf (bishop) 26–32, 34, 38, 41, 56, 200, 225
   as invented persona 32
   as source for Adomnán's *De locis sanctis* 26, 219
Ard Cuillen 80
Armagh 51, 56–7, 195–6
Artúir, son of Benne Brit (British king) 151, 173n.17
Ashe, Laura 179
Athanasius, *Life of Saint Anthony* 47

Áth Clíath *see* Dublin
Áth Fir Diad 85
Áth Luain 91, 94
Áth na Foraire 72, 125
Áth nGrena 81
Áth nImfúait 77
Áth Tamuin 85
Áth Troim 94
Augustine, Saint 25
Augustinian Canons Regular 165, 196–9, 203
Auraicept na n-Éces 5–6, 12, 221

Bacca 90
Bachelard, Gaston 12
Baitán (monk) 37
Baithéne (monk) 34–5
Ballintubber 158
Ballymote, Book of 219–21
Banba (patron goddess of Ireland) 87–8
baptism 27, 30–1, 33, 55, 58, 147, 150, 162
Barinthus (monk) 39–41, 47
Basingwerk 199
Basso, Keith 66, 109, 130, 132, 134
Bé Binn (queen of Ireland) 167
Bec, son of Airist 145, 151
Bede 1–2, 16, 20, 24, 26, 32, 181, 219
 Historia ecclesiastica gentis Anglorum 1–2, 16, 20
Bend Etair II 112–13
Benén (scribe of Saint Patrick) 100–2, 155, 158
Berach (monk) 34
Bergin, Osborn 68–9, 104n.14
Bernard of Clairvaux 196, 206
Bethlehem 27
Bible 1–2, 25, 30, 33–4, 45, 47, 113, 202, 222
 Acts 1:8 1
 Acts 13:47 1
 Genesis 30:31–43 53
 Job 12:8–9 53
 John 1:1 113
 Luke 24:27 1
 Psalm 8 222
 Psalm 47:12–14 30
 Psalm 64 46–7
 Psalm 102:5 56
birds 2, 10–12, 28, 43, 46, 55–7, 68, 73, 87, 89–91, 100, 153–4, 158, 180
Bitel, Lisa 9
Bloch, R. Howard 206
Boand *see* rivers
Boand I and *II* (topographic poems) 6–8
Bodb (Morrígan, war deity) 76, 84, 95, 97–8
Boniface IV, Pope 1, 3
Borsje, Jacqueline 45
Bowen, Charles 127
Brega 147
Bréifne 188
Brendan, Saint 5, 16, 25, 37–48, 50–1, 63n.113, 89, 193–4, 215–16, 224–5
Bricriu 96
Brigit, Saint 9, 125, 215
Britain 2, 4, 15–16, 18, 24–5, 28, 31, 58, 151, 175–7, 179–81, 183, 185–6, 193, 204, 207
Bruig Meic in Óc 73
Brú na Bóinne (Newgrange) 68, 99

Caesarius of Heisterbach 193
Caílte (legendary hero of Finn Cycle) 13, 18, 92, 141–51, 153–71, 190, 225
 conversion and baptism of 162–3
 as performer of placelore 143–4, 147–9, 154, 161
 travels with Saint Patrick in *Acallam na Senórach* 142–51, 153–9, 164, 169
Calpurn, father of Saint Patrick 146, 153

Index

Cáma 144–5
Carmun (poem) 125–6, 128
Carmun (toponym) 125
Carney, James 38, 135
Carson, Ciaran 10
Cashel 157–8
Cassian 37
Cathbad (druid) 71
Catherine of Siena, Saint 206
cattle 17, 65–7, 71, 78–9, 90–4, 96, 103n.10, 125, 186, 225
Ceilbe 119–20
Cend Febrat (poem) 116–17
Cend Febrat (site in Limerick) 116–17
Cennáit Ferchon 85
Certeau, Michel de 72, 143, 159
Chanson de Dermot et du comte 208
chariots 17, 66, 68–75, 78, 80–2, 84–6, 89, 92–3, 95–7, 99–100, 125
Ciarán, Saint 66
Cináed úa hArtacáin (poet) 115, 132, 136
circuits (type of spatial practice) 7, 17, 29, 32, 47, 52–3, 64n.120, 68–9, 71, 74, 79, 83–4, 87, 93–5, 98–9, 101, 123, 125, 127–8, 133, 141–2, 159, 162, 164, 166–9, 171, 193, 215–18, 220
Cistercians 146, 192, 196, 202–3, 206–8
Clairvaux 203
Clancy, Thomas 55, 57–8
Cleitech 73
Cloch na Cét 157–8, 164
Clonmacnoise 66
Cnogba 73
Cogitosus (hagiographer of Brigit) 9
Columba, Saint 33–9, 125, 181, 189, 215
  meaning of name of 34
  as possible author of *Navigatio Sancti Brendani* 37–8

Columbanus, Saint 1, 3, 9, 61n.48
Compert Con Culainn 67–8, 104n.12
Conaille Muirthemne 88
Conaire (king) 69
Conchobar (king) 69–71, 73, 76, 90, 95–8
Conchobar (river) *see* rivers
Connacht 90, 93, 127
Connla, son of Cú Chulainn 70
Connon, Anne 143
conversion to Christianity 121, 142, 145, 163, 199
Corco M'rúad 90
Cork 134, 211n.14
Cormac, Saint 35–7
Cormac Cond Longas, son of Conchobar 70, 93
Courcy, John de 188
creation 113, 115, 215, 220
Croagh Patrick *see* Crúachan Aigle
Crommglenn 167
Crúachán Aigle (Croagh Patrick) 143, 158–9, 195
  as pilgrimage site 158–9
Crúachna Áe 93–4
Crúachu 93
Crúfóit 77
Cú Chulainn (hero of Ulster Cycle) 13, 16–17, 66–78, 80–91, 93, 95–102, 105n.25, 105n.30, 111, 121, 124–5, 225
  called Sétanta 17, 68–71
  claims kinship with Ireland's rivers 76, 83
  environmental damage caused by 96
  parentage and circumstances of birth of 68–9
  ríastrad (bodily distortions) of 71, 83–4
  'Sétanta' connected etymologically with 'way-finding' 68–9

spatial practices of 71–7
woos Emer 74–7, 85–6
Culand (smith) 70–1
Cummian, Irish bishop 1
currachs 13, 39, 41–2, 48, 50
Cú Ruí (king of Munster) 95

Dante 193
David (biblical king) 29, 222
Dead Sea 16, 27, 58
Deichtine (Deichtire, charioteer, mother of Cú Chulainn) 68–9, 76, 82
  as spatial practitioner 69
De locis sanctis see Adomnán
Desert Fathers 52
Devil 45, 47
Diarmait Mac Murchada (Irish king) 185–6, 199, 208
dindshenchas 13, 17–18, 31, 76–8, 100, 103n.10, 108–36, 136n.3, 151, 155, 157, 177, 193, 225
  as part of bardic curriculum 119, 124
  as placelore 111–14
  Saint Patrick as creator of 155, 157–8
  standardized vocabulary of 119
  in *Tochmarc Emire* 111
  verbalized landscapes in 118
Dindshenchas Érenn 17–18, 103n.10, 108–36, 136n.3, 169, 181
  create a national topography of Ireland 110, 133–5
  as link to the past 129–30, 135
  manuscripts of 108–9, 126–7
  as response to colonization of Ireland 133–5
Diurán Leccerd 51, 56
Dobheóg (Dabeoc), Saint 195
Do Foillsigud na Tána Bó Cúailnge 65–6
dogs 70–1, 81, 83, 93, 99, 148, 151, 169

Donegal (county in Ireland) 181, 192, 195, 215
Doob, Penelope Reed 217
Dooley, Ann 67, 79–80, 92, 118, 143, 169
Downpatrick 188
Druim nDairbrech 113–15
Dublin (Áth Clíath) 94, 134, 181, 191, 209
  as English administrative center 181, 191
dúnad 7, 22n.17, 81, 115, 123, 157, 215, 220–5
Duncan, Elizabeth 109
Dún Dá Bend 95–6, 99, 106n.46
Dún Delga 96
Durrow, Book of 216

Easter 1, 43–6
Échna 141
ecocriticism 14–15, 38
ecopoetics 14
Eden, Garden of 2, 6–7, 39, 52, 121
education 124–5, 154–7
  environmental 154–7
  of Irish bardic poets 18, 124–5
Eliade, Mircea 160
Emain Macha 68–71, 73, 76, 95, 99, 125–6
Emer 17, 67, 74–7, 85–6
England 4, 19–20, 58n.2, 109, 134, 160, 175, 178–9, 181, 185, 189–92, 196, 199, 207
English conquest and colonization of Ireland 3–4, 18–19, 30, 132, 134–5, 142, 145–66, 152, 175, 177–8, 181–5, 188–9, 191, 196, 199, 206, 208, 210n.4
environmental destruction 90–1, 95–9, 100, 152–4, 182
  in *Mesca Ulad* 100
  as punishment from God 182
  in *Táin Bó Cualnge* 90–1, 95–9

Index

Eógan (hospitaller in the *Acallam*) 155

Fer Diad (foster-brother of Cú Chulainn) 85–8, 93, 96
Fergus mac Róich (warrior in the *Táin*) 65–6, 68–70, 79–82, 89–93, 100
Findcharn 73
Finn mac Cumaill 121, 142, 144, 165
Fintan, son of Níall Níamglonnach 95
FitzGerald, Maurice 186–8
FitzStephen, Robert 185, 187
Flanagan, Marie Therese 207
Flann Fína *see* Aldfrith
Follett, Westley 37
Forgaill, father of Emer 77
Fox, Cyril 75
France, Marie de 193
Friel, Brian 132
Fúal Medba 91
Fuil Iairn 85
Furbaide, foster-son of Conchobar 95, 99

Galway (county in Ireland) 118
Gantz, Jeffrey 68–9
Geoffrey of Monmouth, *Historia Regum Britanniae* 160, 173n.17
Geraldines 185, 210n.10
Gerald of Wales 2, 5, 18–19, 31, 160, 171, 175–6, 178–92, 196–7, 208–9, 224
  description of Ireland by 180–4
  Expugnatio Hibernica 5, 19, 175, 177–9, 182, 184–9, 191, 208–9
  influence of work on English attitudes towards Ireland 191
  map of Europe attributed to 175–6
  as propagandist 178, 190
  as topographer 180
  Topographia Hiberniae 2, 5, 19, 31, 171, 175, 177–84, 186, 189–92, 209, 224
  performance of 189–91
  xenophobic attitude towards Irish 182
Gervase, abbot of Louth (England) 199
Gilbert (English monk) 197, 199, 204, 207
Gildas 37
Giraldus Cambriensis *see* Gerald of Wales
Glondáth 77
Gregory I, Pope 37
Griffin (Welsh warrior in *Expugnatio*) 188
Grissaphan, George 195
Gwynn, Edward 17, 110, 115, 130

Heaney, Seamus 5, 21n.12, 135, 140n.72, 223
heaven 28, 65–6, 89, 100–1, 115–16, 136, 141, 146, 150, 164, 194, 198, 205
hell 45, 100, 192, 198, 202
Hennessy, William 96–7
Henry, P. L. 220–1
Henry II, king of England 179–80, 188, 206
hermits 37, 47, 52, 55
Higden, Ranulph 2, 193
H. of Saltrey *see Tractatus de Purgatorio Sancti Patricii*
Holy Land 7–9, 13, 16, 24–33, 121, 128, 209, 217, 219
horses 70, 74, 77, 80–1, 87, 89, 91–2, 95–7, 100–1, 151
Howth Head 112, 131

Ibar mac Riangabra (charioteer) 71–3, 75
Iceland 54
immrama 5, 16, 25, 48–9, 58, 88, 193, 224–5

Immram Curaig Maíle Dúin 5, 42, 49–58, 88
Immram Snédgusa 7 Mac Riagla 64n.133
imperialism 177
Indber Bicc Loingsig 145
Ingold, Timothy 141, 154, 157
Iona 9, 24–5, 29–31, 33–8, 181, 219
Irish Sea 9, 16, 58, 181, 207, 220
Isidore of Seville 3, 45, 54, 65, 122
islands 1–3, 20, 33, 35, 37–40, 42–5, 47, 52–8, 127, 132, 153, 180–1, 185, 192–4, 209, 215, 217, 219, 223–4
  in *Immram Curaig Maíle Dúin* 52–8
  Ireland as *insula barbarorum* and *insula sanctorum* 181
  Island of Delights, in *Navigatio Sancti Brendani* 39
  island revealed to be sea-beast Jasconius, in *Navagatio Sancti Brendani* 43–5, 89
  island smelling of pomegranates, in *Navigatio Sancti Brendani* 47
  Paul the Hermit's island, in *Navigatio Sancti Brendani* 47
  Torach (Tory) 57, 181

Jacobs, Jane 177
Jasconius (sea-monster) 44–5, 55, 89
  etymology of name of 44–5
Jerusalem 3, 9, 16, 24, 26, 29–34, 46–7, 56, 206, 217–20
Jesus Christ 8, 25–8, 32–6, 40, 56, 198, 200, 205, 209, 215, 217
  appears to Saint Patrick 198, 203
  Harrowing of Hell by 45
Jews 28
John Scotus Eriugena 10

Johnston, Elva 47, 49, 102
Jonah (prophet) 45, 61n.48
Joyce, James 123, 143
Judas Iscariot 43, 55

Keating, Geoffrey 160
Kells, Book of 31, 216, 219, 223
Kells, synod of 195
Kerry (county in Ireland) 95
Kevin, Saint 125
Knott, Eleanor 119

labyrinths 215–20
Lacy, Hugh de 188
Láeg (charioteer) 86–7, 95
Lavezzo, Kathy 175
Lebor Gabála Érenn 121, 224
Lebor na hUidre 49, 68, 94, 98 103n.10, 104n.12, 105n.24, 107n.51
Lehmann, Ruth 10
Leinster 125, 127, 134, 151, 161, 186, 199, 208
Leinster, Book of 17, 65, 67, 74, 78, 88, 91–2, 94, 98, 102, 103n.10, 109, 113, 116, 118, 120–1, 125–7, 132–4, 136n.3
Lía Fáil *see* Tara
Limerick (county in Ireland) 95–6, 116
Lindisfarne, Book of 216
Loegaire (king of Tara) 100–1
Lough Derg *see* Saint Patrick's Purgatory
Lugh (deity) 68

Mac Duinn Shléibe (Irish king) 188–9
Macgnímrada see Táin Bó Cualnge
McNamara, Martin 47
Macnia mac Oengusa (poet) 131
Mac Oireachtaigh/Ua Raduibh dynasty 143
Mac Raith úá Paain (poet) 116

Index

Mac Roth (messenger of Connacht) 89
Máela Mide 90–91
Máel Dúin 49–58, 64n.120, 193–4, 216, 224–5
Mag Aidne 118
Mag mBreg 73
Mag Muirthemne 69, 95
Mag Túaga 90
Mainistir Droichit Átha *see* Mellifont Abbey
Malachy, Saint 196, 203, 213n.38
manuscripts 11, 13–14, 19–20, 24–5, 31–2, 34–5, 38, 41–2, 44, 48–9, 51, 58, 65–6, 68, 78, 82, 94, 98, 102, 108–10, 114–15, 118, 120–1, 126–8, 133–4, 141, 143, 167, 170, 171–2n.3, 175, 179, 191–3, 207, 209, 215–17, 219, 222
   Baltimore, Walters Art Museum, MS W. 73 221
   Derbyshire, Chatsworth House, The Book of Lismore 172n.3
   Dublin, National Library of Ireland, MS 700 175–6
   Dublin, Royal Irish Academy, MS 23 E 25 (Lebor na hUidre) 49
   Dublin, Royal Irish Academy, MS 23 P12 (Book of Ballymote) 216, 220
   Dublin, Trinity College, MS 57 (Book of Durrow) 216
   Dublin, Trinity College, MS 58 (Book of Kells) 31
   Dublin, Trinity College, MS H2.18 (Book of Leinster) 17, 65
   Dublin, Trinity College, MS 1318 (Yellow Book of Lecan) 49
   Dublin, University College, MS OFM-A4 172n.3
   Edinburgh, National Library of Scotland, MS Adv. 19.2.1 (Auchinleck manuscript) 192
   London, British Library, MS Royal 13 B viii 192
   Milan, Biblioteca Ambrosiana, MS C 301 inf 222
   Oxford, Bodleian Library, MS Laud Misc. 610 171n. 3
   Oxford, Bodleian Library MS Rawlinson B 487 171n.3
   Vienna, Österreichisches Nationalbibliothek, MS 458, 218
mappae mundi 2–3, 7, 22n.16, 109, 175
maps 4, 13, 17, 21n.9, 38, 72, 109, 159–61, 165, 169, 175–7, 195
   Gerald of Wales's map of Europe 175–7
   mental 79, 99, 135
   verbal 3, 29, 31, 72, 78, 128, 160–1, 169
Mary of Egypt, Saint 194
Mavias (Muʾāwiyah ibn ʾAbī Ṣufyān, Saracen king) 27
Mayo (county in Ireland) 143, 169
mazes *see* labyrinths
Meath (county in Ireland) 90, 94, 127, 134, 147
Medb (queen of Connacht) 79–80, 82, 85, 89–93, 97, 121
   in *Acallam na Senórach* 92
   misogynist treatment of 91–2
Melia, Daniel 11
Mellifont Abbey 145–6, 202–3
Mellifont conspiracy 145–6
Merlin 160
Mesca Ulad 17, 67, 94–102
meter, poetic 119
Míl (legendary Irish ancestor-figure) 94
Mílid 151

miracles 27–8, 33–4, 47, 58, 155–6, 164, 170, 197–8
Moses 47, 156
Muine na n-ammaite 156–7
Muirches mac Pháidín Uí Máolchonaire (poet) 119–20
Muirgein, son of Senchán Torpéist 65
Munster 49, 127, 157, 161, 173n.21
Murray, Kevin 118, 122

nature 2, 10–11, 20, 50, 67–8, 74, 85, 121, 132, 148, 152, 155
  celebration of in medieval Irish culture 10–11
  God as author of 182, 186
  Saint Patrick's cooperation with 152, 155
Navigatio Sancti Brendani 5, 16, 25, 37–52, 55, 193, 224
  date of composition of 38
  manuscripts containing 38
  vernacular versions of 38, 194
Nechtan, Síd of 7
Nechta Scéne 73
Neville, Jennifer 10
Ní Mhaonaigh, Máire 20
Norman conquest of Ireland *see* English conquest and colonization of Ireland
Normandy 180, 186

Ó Coileáin, Seán 132
O'Donovan, John 96
Ó Dubhagháin, Seán Mór (poet) 134–5
ogam 12, 73, 80–2, 100, 105n.36, 216, 219–20
Ó hUidhrín, Giolla na Naomh (poet) 134–5
Ó hUiginn, Ruairí 111
Oisín 144, 160–1, 165–8, 190
O'Loughlin, Thomas 25, 30, 33, 176–7

O'Meara, John 2
Ó Néill, Pádraig 146
O'Neill-McCarthy letter 112
O'Reilly, Jennifer 33
O'Riordan, Michelle 129
Ossory 183, 189
Oxford 19, 189–91

Paris, Matthew 192
Patrick, Saint 1, 12–13, 17–18, 66, 92, 100–2, 125, 141–71, 181, 190, 193–5, 197–9, 202–7, 209, 215, 225
  in *Acallam na Senórach* 12–13, 18, 92, 141–71
  as apostle to the Irish 1, 142, 145–9, 152
  Confessio 142
  environmental education of 149–50, 154–7, 164
  as performer of placelore 144, 147, 149, 153, 161
  place of origin of 151–2
  as preacher 197–8, 203
  in *Siaburcharpat Con Culaind* 17, 66, 100–2
  as spatial practitioner 153–5, 164
  in *Tractatus de Purgatorio Sancti Patricii* 197–9, 202–5
  Tripartite Life of 195
Patrick's Palm (spring) 155
Paul, Saint 1, 9
Paul the Hermit 47
peregrinatio see pilgrims and pilgrimage
peripherality 1–2, 5–6, 67, 175, 195, 224
Peter, Saint 1, 9
Peter of Cornwall 192
Physiologus 45
Picard, J. M. 197, 207
pilgrims and pilgrimage 3, 7–9, 13, 16, 18, 25–6, 29–31, 33, 47–8, 51, 56, 66, 127–8,

Index

141, 143–4, 155–6, 158–9, 162–5, 167–70, 178, 191, 193, 195–6, 200, 202–7, 215–19, 224–5
  in *Acallam na Senórach* 18, 141, 143–4, 155–6, 158–9, 162–5, 167–70
  to Crúachán Aigle 143, 158–9
  in *De locis sanctis* 25–6, 29–31, 33, 66, 128
  in *Navigatio Sancti Brendani* 47–8, 51
  in *Tractatus de Purgatorio Sancti Patricii* 19, 178, 191, 193, 195–6, 200, 202–7
  virtual 29, 66, 165, 202, 205
place, Irish poetics of 12, 18, 118–19, 178
placelore 4–5, 17, 67, 72, 76–8, 81, 90, 100, 102, 108–11, 115–16, 118, 124, 127–9, 134–5, 147, 155, 157, 161, 163, 167. 193, 223–4
placenames *see* toponyms

Ráe Bán 77
Ráith Droma Deirc 146
relics 26–8, 30, 33, 51, 57, 64n.133, 155, 158, 166, 168, 198, 203
rivers 5–8, 17, 27, 39, 47, 56, 76–8, 83, 87–8, 91, 96, 99–100, 121, 148, 154, 163, 169, 176
  Boyne (Boand) 5–8, 121
  Conchobar 76
  Dofolt 76
  Euphrates 6–7
  Jordan 6–8, 27, 56
  Severn 6
  Shannon 78
  Tiber 6
  Tigris 7
  twenty-one rivers named in *Táin Bó Cualnge* 88
Roe, Harry 169
Roger of Wendover 192

Rome 3, 5, 8–9, 65, 177
  Irish term *róm* referring to a saint's burial site 8–9

Saint Patrick's Purgatory 5, 13, 19, 191–208, 215–17, 223, 225
  in Gerald of Wales's *Topographia* 192
  Lough Derg as location of 191, 194–5, 217
  present-day pilgrimages to 215–17, 223
Saxo Grammaticus (Danish historian) 54
Sayers, William 75
Scenmenn 77
Schlüter, Dagmar 118–19, 126
Segais, spring or well of 6–7
Sencha (sage of Ulster) 68
Senchán Torpéist (chief poet of Ireland) 65
Sétanta *see* Cú Chulainn
Severin, Timothy 38
sheep 40, 53, 64n.121
Siaburcharpat Con Culaind 17, 66–7, 100–2
Siewers, Alfred 10
Slíab Moduirn 73
Slieve Reagh 116
Solinus 181
Solnit, Rebecca 159
Solusbrethach (angel) 149
South English Legendary 193
space, Irish poetics of 5, 13–15, 25, 50–1, 58, 123, 170, 179, 218, 222–3
spatial discourse 4–5, 14, 20, 75, 192, 224
  dindshenchas as 111–12
spatial practice 8, 13, 15, 18, 29, 33, 38, 42, 46, 48, 55, 57, 67, 69, 71–5, 77, 82–3, 91, 94–9, 115, 123, 126–7, 144, 154–5, 157–8, 164, 171, 177, 181, 204, 215, 218–20

in *Acallam na Senórach* 144,
  152, 154–5, 157–8, 164
Cú Chulainn as spatial
  practitioner 67, 71–5, 77,
  99, 204
definition of 13
in *De locis sanctis* 29, 33
immrama as form of 48–9, 55, 57
Medb as spatial practitioner 91
in *Mesca Ulad* 94–9
in *Navigatio Sancti Brendani*
  38, 42, 46
place-writing as form of 115,
  123, 204
Saint Patrick as spatial
  practitioner 101, 144,
  154–5, 157–8, 164
in *Togail Bruidne Da Derga* 69
Stephen of Blois, king of England
  199, 213n.48
Súaldaim mac Róich 68

Tailtiu 73
Táin Bó Cualnge 5, 15–17, 65–74,
  76–100, 111, 121, 125, 141,
  225
  composition and provenance of
    103n.10
  Macgnímrada (boyhood deeds)
    of Cú Chulainn in 69–71
  as placelore 66, 111
Tamon (jester of Medb and Ailill)
  85
Tara (Temair) 73, 75, 100, 109–10,
  113, 120, 126–7, 131, 150,
  160, 162–8, 190–1
  as central place in Irish politics
    150, 164–5
  in *Dindshenchas Érenn* 109–10
  Lía Fáil as marvel of 168
Techt do Róim 9, 131, 206
Temair *see* Tara
Temair Lúachra 95, 97
Tígernán Ua Ruairc (Irish prince)
  188
Tilghman, Ben 216

Tírechán (hagiographer of Patrick)
  142, 195
Tochmarc Emire 17, 67, 74–8, 83,
  100 111, 125
Todi Fresco 193
Togail Bruidne Da Derga 69, 98
Toner, Gregory 121–2, 129
toponyms 8, 14, 17, 74–9, 81, 85,
  91, 95, 97–8, 100, 108,
  120–5, 128–32, 138n.37,
  161, 169, 194
  in *dindshenchas* poems 120–5,
    128–32
  as literary creations 122
  see also entries for individual
    placenames
Torach (Tory Island) 57, 181
Tower of Babel 6, 9
*Tractatus de Purgatorio Sancti
  Patricii* 19, 31, 177–9,
  191–209, 223–4
  as example of English poetics of
    Irish space 178–9, 195–6
  H. of Saltrey's authorship of
    31, 192
  Owein (knight), protagonist of
    193, 200, 206–7, 212n.23
  vernacular translations of 192–3
Trága Dá Ban 147
trees and woodland 10–13, 16–17,
  40–1, 44, 46–7, 55–6, 58,
  76, 80–3, 86–7, 95–6, 100,
  105n.36, 121, 147–8, 154,
  169, 183
Tromdám Gúaire 66
Tuam 195
Túatha Dé Danann (race of
  supernatural beings) 85,
  88, 94–6, 121, 163
Tuffrau, Paul 37–8

Uisliu 70
Uisnech (Usnagh) 127, 147, 150,
  160–2, 164–5
  as central place in Ireland
    160–2, 164

Index

Ulaid 67–8, 73, 90, 96–9
Ulster 17, 68–74, 76–80, 88–90, 93–100, 127, 134, 161, 192
Ulster Cycle 17, 67, 111, 121

Vergil, *Aeneid* 51
Vincent of Beauvais 193
Vita Sancti Columbae see Adomnán
Voraigne, Jacobus de 193
Voyage de Saint Brendan 194

Wales 175, 178, 180, 185–7, 199
Waterford 134, 183
Whale, The (Old English poem) 45
whales 34–5, 44–5
Wicklow (county in Ireland) 186, 199

Yellow Book of Lecan 49, 63n.109

Zaleski, Carol 202

EU authorised representative for GPSR:
Easy Access System Europe, Mustamäe tee 50,
10621 Tallinn, Estonia
gpsr.requests@easproject.com

www.ingramcontent.com/pod-product-compliance
Lightning Source LLC
Chambersburg PA
CBHW071406300426
44114CB00016B/2202